SERIES
IN
HUMAN
RELATIONS
TRAINING

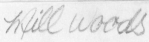

THE
1978 ANNUAL
HANDBOOK
FOR GROUP
FACILITATORS

(The Seventh Annual)

Editors

J. WILLIAM PFEIFFER, Ph.D.
and
JOHN E. JONES, Ph.D.

UNIVERSITY ASSOCIATES, INC.
7596 Eads Avenue
La Jolla, California 92037

PREFACE

This 1978 *Annual* continues a theme we hope is evident in all past and current University Associates publications: a practical, *user* orientation. We define users as group facilitators in educational, governmental, business, and nonprofit organizations: people whose work is to help others learn about human behavior, understand their own behavior better, and develop new behavioral skills to cope more effectively with a complex and changing environment.

The materials in this *Annual*—as in previous volumes—were developed by users for users. Our reproduction policy gives users the freedom to duplicate (and adapt) *Annual* materials *for educational and training purposes*. We ask only that such materials be identified with the credit statement given on the copyright page. (Some materials in this *Annual* are copyrighted by others; in that case, permission to reproduce the materials for any purpose must be obtained from the copyright holder, unless otherwise indicated.)

If University Associates materials are to be reproduced in publications for sale or are intended for large-scale distribution, prior written permission of the editors is required.

In previous *Annuals*, we had some concern over "authorship." Many of the structured experiences we have published have "been around," and it has often been impossible to attribute authorship to any one person (even though several people might feel justified in being called "the" author and might feel upset at not being credited). Such concerns are now rare, for while the first few *Annuals* did much to "codify" and record common practices, this *Annual* (and recent past *Annuals*) consists of newly developed materials that have not yet widely circulated through informal channels.

We want to acknowledge three persons for work not otherwise credited in this 1978 *Annual*. Marion Fusco, University Associates managing editor, has had day-to-day responsibility for supervising the *Annual's* production from manuscript to finished product. Marshall Sashkin, consulting editor, was responsible for section introductions in this volume. Colleen Kelley, consultant, assisted in the preparation of the structured experiences.

The *Annual* does seem to have become, as we intended, a clearing house for and a repository of resource materials. An indicator of our success in producing useful materials is their incorporation into many classroom texts. Another measure is the continued flow of new materials that we receive—structured experiences, instruments, lecturettes, and theory papers. We believe that our efforts have contributed to less frequent "wheel reinventions" and helped strengthen the professional norms of sharing new materials and ideas. We also continue to learn through the experience of editing the *Annual*; we hope some of the excitement of our discoveries comes through to the user.

La Jolla, California   J. William Pfeiffer
December, 1977   John E. Jones

UNIVERSITY ASSOCIATES
Publishers and Consultants

 University Associates is an organization engaged in publishing and consulting in the broad area of human relations. UA consultants are experienced group facilitators who conduct training programs (both public and private), train trainers, work with organizations and communities on developmental problems, and provide editorial direction for the publication of useful training materials.

The organization attempts to maintain a balance among its three major activities— publishing, consulting, and training—to ensure that each is current and that each provides a source and an outlet for practical ideas to improve human relations. As the clients of University Associates are varied, its training and publications are intended to encourage the development of facilitator skills in all types of settings and institutional contexts. The international focus of UA makes it a clearing house for the emerging theory and technology of human relations training, organization development, and community development.

TABLE OF CONTENTS

---

*See Structured Experience Categories, p. 6, for an explanation of numbering.

GENERAL INTRODUCTION TO THE 1978 *ANNUAL*

The basic format of this seventh *Annual Handbook for Group Facilitators* will be familiar to well over 100,000 practitioners in the field of human relations training. For first-time users, however, a basic orientation to the content framework will be useful. Apparently, the pattern developed for the first *Annual* continues to be useful, for the strongest recommendation for change from users in the past few years has been the request for a return to a three-ring binder for the looseleaf version (a suggestion that has been followed). As in all previous *Annuals*, the materials included are new—there is no overlap with prior *Annuals*—and are carefully chosen to provide a variety of practice-relevant resources.

Each *Annual* has five basic divisions: Structured Experiences, Instrumentation, Lecturettes, Theory and Practice, and Resources.

In the *Structured Experiences* section users will find a dozen designs arranged in approximate order of difficulty and classified according to the eleven-category scheme developed to organize the structured experiences contained in the *Annuals* and the six volumes of *A Handbook of Structured Experiences for Human Relations Training*. As in past *Annuals*, the reader will note that some structured experiences are new variations of previously published experiences. As was discussed in the introduction to the Structured Experiences section of the 1977 *Annual*, the facilitator can easily convey his overuse of an excellent structured experience through boredom or inattention and add to the possibility of failure. This risk is a major reason that facilitators should consider designing their own structured experiences. (See the introduction to the Structured Experiences section of this volume for a set of design guidelines.)

One of the structured experiences selected for this issue("Sexual Assessment:Self-Disclosure") deals more directly with the sensitive area of sexual relations than structured experiences we have previously published. Although this experience may require particularly perceptive handling by the facilitator, we feel that it accurately reflects society's changing morality and that it is both a workable and useful experience for facilitators to include in their repertoires.

The *Instrumentation* section presents four structured learning tools—an opinionnaire, a questionnaire, and two inventories. These have been chosen primarily for utility in training (see the discussion in the introduction to the Instrumentation section of the 1975 *Annual*). This *Annual*'s introduction to the Instrumentation section contains a brief discussion of the psychological "depth" probed by instruments and of the facilitator's ethical responsibilities.

Lecturettes are brief, concise discussions of very specific theoretical issues. Facilitators will find some of them most useful when "internalized" and used in the context of their own thinking as the basis for short lecture presentations. Many lecturettes are valuable as handouts following a structured experience. In either case, the intent is to provide brief, clear cognitive inputs that can easily be coordinated with experiential training activities. The introductions to this section in previous *Annuals* focused on the nature and applications of lecturettes. This year, a specific practice is discussed: the use of visual aids in lecturettes.

The fourth major section, *Theory and Practice*, consists of papers that, like lecturettes, can be used as handouts, especially in professional-development training ("training of trainers"), but that are directed primarily toward group facilitators. While papers in this section are intended to be more theoretical, complex, or research based than lecturettes, they are still oriented toward the practitioner rather than the scholar. Topics are selected for current relevance to human relations training. While the study of a paper in this section will not make one an expert on that topic, it *will* provide a sound, basic background, as well as some new ideas.

Finally, the *Resources* section contains professional support and development materials. It is intended to facilitate access to the "tools of the trade": books, research, professional associations, etc. The 1978 *Annual*'s introduction to Resources includes a chronological listing of topics and articles published in this section in prior *Annuals*. The section is highlighted by a directory based on a national survey of graduate programs in applied behavioral science and by a completely revised list of film resources for human relations training facilitators. Also included in this section is a bibliography of resources in humanistic education and a guide to selecting training sites.

At the end of this *Annual* is a list of contributors, with mailing addresses and phone numbers. More information about individual contributors can be found in the brief biographical sketches at the end of each piece in the *Annual*.

As much as possible, we have tried to model the behavioral processes we advocate. The editors are responsible for the selection of items in this *Annual*, but authors are responsible for their own ideas. Selection criteria are practicality, communicability, and current relevance within an overall framework of diversity. One further intent of the *Annuals*—beyond serving as a clearing house for useful training materials—is stimulation. We continue to encourage users of the *Annuals* to submit materials and feedback—including criticism, praise, and, most useful of all, suggestions for change, development, and improvement.

INTRODUCTION TO THE STRUCTURED EXPERIENCES SECTION

In previous *Annuals* a variety of topics have been discussed in introductions to this section. The brief table below provides a useful index for those interested in specific issues.

Year	Pages	Topic
1972	3–4	General discussion of issues about structured experiences
1973	4–5	Considerations in using structured experiences—a list of questions with brief discussions, centered on the group to be involved in the experience
1974	3–4	Considerations in developing a structured experience—a list of issues (with brief discussions) to review when creating structured experiences
1975	3–4	An experiential model—a model of how learning occurs
1976	3–5	Nature of structured experiences—three dimensions defined: objectives, content, structure
	5	Conducting structured experiences—brief guidelines
1977	3–5	"Blow-ups"—how to avoid failures with structured experiences and what to do when failures do occur
	5–9	Forming subgroups—tables for various-sized groups

DESIGNING STRUCTURED EXPERIENCES[1]

Before creating a new structured experience, the facilitator should first ask whether it is necessary to do so or whether some design already exists that could be used or easily adapted. (The index of structured experiences that follows this introduction is useful for identifying those resources published by University Associates.) It may be that an existing design does not quite fit the needs of the group one is working with, does not make the intended learning point, or has simply been used too often by the facilitator. In any of these circumstances, creation of a new structured experience is desirable.

All structured experiences have a set of required elements. First, there should be a specific learning objective. This could be a concept or hypothesis, if the experience is in the cognitive domain; for a structured experience in the affective domain, it could be a feeling state, awareness, or insight about such a state of the experience; or it could be a specific behavior or set of behaviors, if the experience aims at skill building.

Second, the facilitator must create a set of stimulus materials that will evoke the specific learning objective that has been identified. It is here that the greatest creative latitude exists. A truly immense range is available. Typically, the materials developed—a role play, a simulation game, a task activity, etc.—should be tested and modified. Research experiments can often be modified for use in experiential learning—particularly when a specific concept is the learning objective. One useful guideline here is to *avoid* creating materials too close to the everyday world of the participants. The participants can

---

[1]This discussion is based largely on a presentation by Robert J. House to the Fourth Annual Organization Behavior Teaching Conference, held at the University of Toronto, May 16, 1977.

become so involved in the content of the experience that process learnings are severely diminished. Or the participants may criticize the structured experience as a gross over-simplification of the "real" situation, leading them to reject potential learnings.

Third, there should be a structured or semistructured data-collection method built into the structured experience. This could, for example, be a videotape of group activity, a questionnaire, observers' notes. Whatever the method, the data about what happened should be "published"—shared with the full group. This procedure allows the facilitator to lead a discussion around generalizations from the experience. The concept can be defined and supported; the feeling defined and shared; or the skill identified and speci-fied behaviorally. In the last instance, a fourth necessary design element is an opportunity to practice and repractice the skill.

DESIGN EXAMPLES

The "New Truck Dilemma"

A well-known, excellent design example is Maier's "New Truck Dilemma."[2] The learn-ing point—conceptual, with a secondary skill-building focus—can be stated as follows: Problem situations can be categorized in terms of (1) the solution's quality requirements and (2) the importance of acceptance of the solution by those who must carry it out. Situations in which the latter issue is predominant are typically questions of *fairness*. In such cases, the group leader obtains the best results by acting as a facilitator rather than as an active participant and allowing group members to arrive at a mutually acceptable—and fair—solution. In summary, these are the learning objectives of this structured experi-ence:

1. To provide experiential groundwork for understanding the quality/acceptance categorization dimensions;
2. To demonstrate the positive effects of nondirective, facilitative leadership in a problem situation centered on acceptance as the primary issue.

The stimulus materials are brief roles and a description of the situation to induce appropriate role sets. Participants become telephone servicepersons, meeting with their boss. The roles give each person a reason for wanting a new truck that has become available; the supervisor is told to let the workers make the decision. In most groups, the desired behaviors occur as a result of the role-instruction materials. When such behaviors do not occur, the common reason is the supervisor's insistence on making the decision. In this case, however, the results also illustrate the learning point, though in a negative rather than a positive way.

When all groups are finished, supervisors report results, which are tabulated on a simple chart prepared by the facilitator during the last few minutes of the role play. These results are then discussed by the entire group, with the facilitator drawing out the learn-ing points.

The "Kidney Machine"

A second example, oriented toward affective awareness, is the "Kidney Machine."[3] The learning objectives are increased awareness of (1) one's own value system and (2) the fact

---

[2]This role-play structured experience can be found in N. R. F. Maier, A. R. Solem, & A. A. Maier, *The Role-Play Technique: A Handbook for Management and Leadership Practice*. La Jolla, Calif.: University Associates, 1975. A film is available from BNA, Inc., for use along with this structured experience.

[3]This structured experience, 135, appears in the 1974 *Annual*, p. 78.

that different people have—and act upon—different values. Stimulus materials call for small, subgroup discussions to elicit decisions concerning which of a set of kidney-failure patients will receive life-sustaining treatment on a kidney machine (which cannot accommodate all those in need). Information is provided about the various patients. There is no "correct" answer derivable from the information. Each group makes its decision, and, when all groups have finished, decisions are shared, along with rationales. The facilitator then leads the full group in a discussion to draw out the fact that no group has made or can make "the" correct decision. Rather, group members come to recognize explicitly the implicit values they used to arrive at their decisions, and they become aware that members of other subgroups hold different values.

CONCLUSION

It is not possible to design structured experiences that "guarantee" certain, specific learnings. Rarely will a facilitator use the same structured experience in *exactly* the same way twice; it is, in fact, desirable to modify structured experiences to meet the needs of different groups. However, if facilitators follow the design guidelines discussed here and clearly specify the learning goals, outcomes can be made more predictable and participants' learnings can become more clearly focused.

STRUCTURED EXPERIENCE CATEGORIES

Numbers of
Structured Experiences

1–24	Volume I, *Handbook*
25–48	Volume II, *Handbook*
49–74	Volume III, *Handbook*
75–86	1972 *Annual*
87–100	1973 *Annual*
101–124	Volume IV, *Handbook*
125–136	1974 *Annual*
137–148	1975 *Annual*
149–172	Volume V, *Handbook*
173–184	1976 *Annual*
185–196	1977 *Annual*
197–220	Volume VI, *Handbook*
221–232	1978 *Annual*

Ice Breakers

	Vol.-Page
Listening and Inferring (1)	I–3
Two-Four-Eight (2)	I–5
Who Am I? (5)	I–19
Group Conversation (25)	II–3
Jigsaw (27)	II–10
First Names, First Impressions (42)	II–88
"Who Am I?" Variations (49)	III–3
Peter-Paul (87)	'73–7
"Cold" Introductions (88)	'73–9
Participant-Staff Expectations (96)	'73–29
Getting Acquainted (101)	IV–3
Hum-Dinger (125)	'74–7
Energizers (149)	V–3
Limericks (173)	'76–7
Labeling (174)	'76–10
Communication Analysis (191)	'77–32
Best Friend (197)	VI–5
Choose an Object (198)	VI–7

Awareness Expansion

	Vol.-Page
Fantasies (16)	I–75
Awareness Expansion (19)	I–86
Graphics (20)	I–88
Nonverbal Communication (22)	I–101
Nonverbal Communication (44)	II–94
Life Planning (46)	II–101
Microlab (47)	II–113
Feelings and Defenses (56)	III–61
Think-Feel (65)	III–70
Lemons (71)	III–94
Nonverbal Communication (72)	III–97
Personal Journal (74)	III–109
Frustrations and Tensions (75)	'72–5
Psychomat (84)	'72–58
Growth and Name Fantasy (85)	'72–59
Gunnysack (89)	'73–11
Make Your Own Bag (90)	'73–13
Group Exploration (119)	IV–92
Expressing Anger (122)	IV–104
Re-Owning (128)	'74–18
Relaxation and Perceptual Awareness (136)	'74–84
What Do You See? (137)	'75–7
Live Case (142)	'75–40
Ideal Cards (143)	'75–43
Boasting (181)	'76–49
The Other You (182)	'76–51
T'ai Chi Chuan (199)	VI–10
Bread Making (201)	VI–19

Interpersonal Communication

	Vol.-Page
Submission/Aggression/ Assertion (206)	VI–36
Sherlock (213)	VI–92
Roles Impact Feelings (214)	VI–102
Numbers (221)	'78–9
Young/Old Woman (227)	'78–40
Pygmalion (229)	'78–51

Interpersonal Communication

	Vol.-Page
One-Way, Two-Way (4)	1–13
Broken Squares (7)	1–25
Listening Triads (8)	1–31
Rumor Clinic (28)	II–12
Status-Interaction Study (41)	II–85
Behavior Description Triads (50)	III–6
Not-Listening (52)	III–10
Quaker Meeting (76)	'72–11
Symbolic Closing Exercise (86)	'72–61
Perception of Task (91)	'73–15
Building Open and Closed Relationships (93)	'73–20
Ball Game (108)	IV–27
Organization Structures (110)	IV–34
The "T" Test (112)	IV–41
Toothpicks (121)	IV–99
Party Conversations (138)	'75–10
Helping Relationships (152)	V–13
Babel (153)	V–16
Blindfolds (175)	'76–13
Consulting Triads (183)	'76–53
Poems (185)	'77–13
Dominoes (202)	VI–21
Headbands (203)	VI–25
Escalation (219)	VI–127
Sexual Assessment (226)	'78–36

Intergroup Communication

	Vol.-Page
Hollow Square (33)	II–32
Polarization (62)	III–57
Discrimination (63)	III–62
Sex-Role Stereotyping (95)	'73–26
Dimensions of Trust (120)	IV–96
Absentee (158)	V–49
Sex-Role Attributes (184)	'76–63
Who Gets Hired? (215)	VI–106
Negotiating Differences (217)	VI–114

Personal Feedback

	Vol.-Page
Johari Window (13)	I–65
Leveling (17)	I–79
Dependency-Intimacy (18)	I–82
Coins (23)	I–104
Role Nominations (38)	II–72
Verbal Activities Within Groups (43)	II–91
Nominations (57)	III–33
Peer Perceptions (58)	III–41
Puzzlement (97)	'73–38
The Johari Window (99)	'73–38
Motivation (100)	'73–43
The Gift of Happiness (104)	IV–15
Sculpturing (106)	IV–21
The Portrait Game (107)	IV–24
Growth Cards (109)	IV–30
Stretching (123)	IV–107
Forced-Choice Identity (129)	'74–20
Payday (146)	'75–54
Cups (167)	V–111
Adjectives (168)	V–114
Person Perception (170)	V–131
Introspection (209)	VI–57
Affirmation of Trust (216)	VI–110
Golden Awards (222)	'78–12
Cards (225)	'78–34

Dyads

	Vol.-Page
Dyadic Encounter (21)	I–90
Helping Pairs (45)	II–97
Intimacy Program (70)	III–89
Dialog (116)	IV–66
Dyadic Renewal (169)	V–116
Disclosing and Predicting (180)	'76–46
Letter Exchange (190)	'77–28
Dyadic Risk Taking (220)	VI–130

Leadership

	Vol.-Page
T-P Leadership Questionnaire (3)	1–7
Committee Meeting (9)	1–36
Conflict Resolution (14)	1–70
Hampshire In-Basket (34)	II–41
Line-Up and Power Inversion (59)	II–46
Dividing the Loot (60)	III–49
Leadership Characteristics (127)	'74–13
Conflict Fantasy (130)	'74–22
Styles of Leadership (154)	V–19
Fork-Labyrinth (159)	V–53
Pins and Straws (162)	V–78
Pyramids (187)	'77–20
Motivation (204)	VI–28
Staff Meeting (207)	VI–39

University Associates

221. NUMBERS: A PROBLEM-SOLVING ACTIVITY

Goals

I. To demonstrate how new information and assistance can improve performance.

II. To discover how experience facilitates task accomplishment.

Group Size

Unlimited number of participants.

Time Required

One to one and one-half hours.

Materials

I. Five copies of the Numbers Work Sheet and a pencil for each participant.

II. Newsprint, masking tape, and a felt-tipped marker.

Physical Setting

A chair and work surface for each participant.

Process

I. The facilitator gives each participant a Numbers Work Sheet and a pencil. He tells the participants that they will have thirty seconds to draw a line between as many of the numbers as possible in numerical sequence. (He may draw sequential numbers randomly on newsprint and demonstrate the procedure.)

II. The facilitator calls time and distributes a second Numbers Work Sheet. He says that the experience gained in the first round should aid the participants in completing the task the second time.

III. At the end of thirty seconds, the facilitator calls time again, distributes a third Numbers Work Sheet, and tells participants to draw a vertical line down the center of the page. He tells the participants that the line separates the odd numbers (on the left side of the page) from the even numbers (on the right side of the page). He again instructs the participants to connect as many numbers as they can, in numerical sequence, within the same period of time.

IV. A fourth Numbers Work Sheet is distributed; participants are instructed to draw a vertical line down the center of the page *and* a horizontal line across the center of the page. They are informed that the vertical line performs the same function as before and that the horizontal line across the page divides groupings of five numbers: i.e., the numbers one through five are above the line, six through ten are below the line, eleven through fifteen are above, etc., with the exception of the sets fifty-one to fifty-five and fifty-six to sixty, which can be matched diagonally. The facilitator again allots thirty seconds for the sequencing task.

V. A fifth Numbers Work Sheet is distributed and prepared in the same way as the fourth; participants again perform the task in the same amount of time.

VI. Participants are asked to report how many numbers they located in each round, and the facilitator tabulates these figures on newsprint. He points out the value of clear inputs on task accomplishment and makes the following points:

1. During round two, as a result of having gained experience in performing the task, the "typical" participant locates two or three more numbers than he did on the first try.

2. During the third attempt, the typical participant locates approximately 65 percent more numbers than he located on the first sheet. The guidance received from the leader, i.e., the indication of the function of the vertical line, is generally the cause of this improvement.

3. In the fourth round, with the information about the horizontal line, the typical participant increases his score 140 percent over his first attempt.

4. Since the fifth round is a repetition of the fourth, the improvement here is attributed to the value of experience.

The facilitator may also equate the information received by participants as experience gained and passed on by another person.

Variations

I. Participants can report their results to the facilitator after each round.

II. Teams of two or three individuals can work together on the problem.

Similar Structured Experiences: *Vol. II:* Structured Experience 31; *Vol. IV:* **102, 103.**

Lecturette Source: *'78 Annual:* "Configurational Learning: Principles for Facilitating Change and Learning from Experience."

Submitted by Brent D. Ruben and Richard W. Budd. Adapted from "Learning and Change," in Brent D. Ruben and Richard W. Budd, *Human Communication Handbook*, Rochelle Park, N.J.: Hayden, 1975. Used with permission.

Brent D. Ruben, Ph.D., is the assistant chairman of the Department of Human Communication and the director of the Institute for Communication Studies, Rutgers University, New Brunswick, New Jersey. He is the editor of Communication Yearbook, *a co-author and the author of* Human Communication Handbook: Simulations and Games, *Vol. I and II, respectively, and the author of a number of books on communication and experiential learning. Dr. Ruben's background is in communication, experiential learning, and cross-cultural and group training.*

Richard W. Budd, Ph.D., is a Distinguished Professor and the chairman of the Department of Human Communication, Rutgers University, New Brunswick, New Jersey. He is the president of the International Communication Association, a co-author of Introduction to Content Analysis, Content Analysis of Communications, *and* Human Communication Handbook: Simulations and Games, *Vol. I, and a co-editor of* Approaches to Human Communication *and* Mass Communication and Mass Communication Institutions. *Dr. Budd's background is in teaching and research, human relations group work, and educational and organization development and consulting.*

(1)　31　21　32　12　34

25　13　5　22　4　54

35　41　45　42　52　58

11　3　33　56　24　2

23　43　15　14　60　44

17　29　39　8　26　10

49　55　9　40　48　28

19　47　59　36　50　6

51　7　37　20　16　38

27　53　57　46　30　18

222. GOLDEN AWARDS: A CLOSURE ACTIVITY

Goals

I. To provide an opportunity for group and self-appraisal.

II. To allow members a chance to see how others perceive them.

III. To practice giving feedback to others in a constructive and helpful manner.

Group Size

An unlimited number of groups of four to six members, who have worked together previously as a group.

Time Required

Approximately two hours.

Materials

I. A copy of the Golden Awards Instruction Sheet for each group.

II. Blank 3" x 5" cards, felt-tipped markers of various colors, safety pins, masking tape, and a scissors for each group.

Physical Setting

A room large enough to allow groups to meet separately at tables and a separate private space where group members can engage in reflection without being disturbed.

Process

I. The facilitator discusses the goals and design of the activity and presents a lecturette on giving constructive feedback.

II. The facilitator forms groups of four to six participants who have previously worked together, gives each group a Golden Awards Instruction Sheet to read, and distributes 3" x 5" cards, felt-tipped markers, safety pins, masking tape, and a scissors to each group.

III. The first candidate from each group retires to the group's private space to reflect on the kind of award he would give himself and the award he thinks the group will give him, while the group decides on and constructs his award. (Fifteen minutes.)

IV. The group calls the absent member back. The group presents him with a Golden Award and then shares its reasons for the particular form the award has taken. The recipient then shares his own feelings and expectations. (Five minutes.)

V. The activity continues until all members of each group have received their Golden Awards.

VI. All participants are instructed to move around the room wearing their awards in order to show their awards to each other and exchange comments and feelings.

VII. The facilitator leads a wrap-up discussion on the feelings generated by the activity.

Variations

I. Instead of retiring from the group individually, award candidates may meet in pairs or with the facilitator to share feelings and expectations.

II. The entire group decides on the award for each person.

III. Before members receive their awards, they can disclose their expectations and feelings about the process and the expected result.

IV. Individuals can sit outside their groups and listen to the discussion, take notes on their reactions, and share these with the group after the award is given, e.g., "Things that were confirmed for me," "Things I was surprised to hear (pleasantly or not)," "Things I expected to hear but did not."

V. Groups may also give awards to the facilitator(s).

VI. The activity can be used to allow members to change their awards or work toward new awards.

VII. The structured experience can be used as a "medial feedback" activity, to permit participants to plan new behavior for the second half of a training event.

Similar Structured Experiences: *Vol. I:* Structured Experiences 13, 17, 23; *Vol. II:* 38; *Vol. III:* 57, 58; '73 Annual: 99; *Vol. IV:* 104, 107, 109; '75 Annual: 146; '78 Annual: 225.

Lecturette Sources: '72 Annual: "Openness, Collusion, and Feedback"; '73 Annual: "Johari Window"; '75 Annual: "Re-Entry," "Giving Feedback: An Interpersonal Skill."

Submitted by John Elliott-Kemp and Graham Williams.

John Elliott-Kemp is a principal lecturer in education management at Sheffield City Polytechnic, Sheffield, England. He is involved in teaching change-agent courses in education management and educational guidance, facilitating small-group experiences, and doing organization development consulting in education. Mr. Elliott-Kemp's background is in teaching, teacher education, planned change in education, and human relations training.

Graham Williams is a senior lecturer in social psychology in the Department of Education Management, Sheffield City Polytechnic, Sheffield, England. He is currently involved in teaching in the education management program, facilitating small-group experiences, and doing organization development consulting in education. Mr. Williams' background is in personnel management, training management, and adult education, with special interests in experiential learning, group and organization development, and the training of adult educators.

GOLDEN AWARDS INSTRUCTION SHEET

During this activity, you (and, in turn, every other member of your group) will be presented with an award by the rest of the group members.

You will take your turn spending fifteen minutes alone reflecting about what award you think you deserve, based on your personal contributions, and the type of award you expect to receive from the group. While you are away from the group, the other members will prepare an award, designed to appropriately illustrate/symbolize/reflect your personal contributions. The award may incorporate such things as behavioral characteristics, personal qualities, values, social skills, etc.

The group will be given fifteen minutes to design and construct your award, after which you will return to receive the award. The group will share its rationale for the form of the award with you, and you will share your expectations and feelings with the group.

223. ADMISSIONS COMMITTEE: A CONSENSUS-SEEKING ACTIVITY

Goals

I. To compare decisions made by individuals with those made by groups.

II. To teach effective consensus-seeking techniques.

III. To teach the concept of synergy.

Group Size

Any number of groups of five to seven.

Time Required

Approximately one and one-half to two hours.

Materials

I. A pencil, a copy of the Admissions Committee Fact Sheet, a set of Admissions Committee Applicant Profile Sheets I-VIII, and a copy of the Admissions Committee Decision Work Sheet for each participant.

II. Newsprint, masking tape, and a felt-tipped marker for the facilitator.

Physical Setting

A room that will accommodate a table for each group to work at without distraction.

Process

I. The facilitator distributes to each participant a copy of the Admissions Committee Fact Sheet, a set of Admissions Committee Applicant Profile Sheets I-VIII, an Admissions Committee Decision Work Sheet, and a pencil.

II. Participants are asked to read the fact sheet and each applicant profile and to rank order the eight applicants on the work sheet according to their potential for good academic performance in a program of graduate business study. Participants are to enter their ranking in column (1). (Thirty minutes.)

III. The facilitator divides participants into groups of five to seven members, each group constituting an admissions committee, and gives them the following instructions for reaching consensus:

1. Avoid arguing for your individual judgments. Approach the task on the basis of logic.

2. Avoid changing your mind simply to reach agreement and to avoid conflict, but support solutions with which you are able to agree somewhat.

3. Avoid "conflict-reducing" techniques such as majority vote, averaging, or trading in reaching your decision.

4. View differences of opinion as a help rather than a hindrance in decision making.

The facilitator then asks the groups to derive a consensus ranking to be entered in column (2) on the Admissions Committee Decision Work Sheet. (Forty-five minutes.)

IV. The facilitator posts on newsprint the actual performance ranking of each applicant at the completion of his or her graduate program:[1]

1. Sam Dameon
2. Tim Miller
3. Richard Morris
4. Jim Lorain
5. Anne Wa-Wen Chek
6. Larry Hutch
7. Edward Jakes
8. Frank Green

Participants are instructed to enter this ranking in column (3) on the Admissions Committee Decision Work Sheet.

V. Participants complete columns (4) and (5) on the work sheet. Column (4) provides an indication of the individual participant's "correctness," and column (5) provides an equivalent measure of each group's performance.

VI. The facilitator posts total scores for each group, including an average of individual scores and the committee score.

VII. The facilitator leads a discussion of the activity, focusing on:

1. The consensus process within each group: assets and difficulties, whether the rules were followed, and the dynamics behind the posted scores.
2. Ways in which performance could be improved in future consensus-seeking activities.
3. Work situations to which the principles of achieving consensus could be applied.

Variations

I. The facilitator can experiment with various group sizes. Participants can be assigned randomly to groups and the groups given a time limit for consensus seeking. They can be asked to rate their satisfaction with the outcomes before the scoring is begun. Groups' average satisfaction ratings can be compared and discussed in relation to other statistical outcomes.

II. Time limits can be varied. For example, one group can be given twenty minutes, another thirty minutes, and one unlimited time. (A more complex design would be to study the effects of group size and time limit simultaneously, as in the following model requiring nine groups.)

---

[1]Applicant profiles are based on actual case histories. Actual performance rankings were derived from the students' grade-point averages (G.P.A.'s) at the conclusion of their two-year program of study.

Time	Group Size		
	Small	Medium	Large
Brief			
Long			
No Limit			

III. Participants in each group can be asked to rank order each other (independently) in terms of the amount of influence each had on the consensus-seeking outcome. Then each participant computes a score based on the differences between his ranking of the applicants and the consensus ranking. Influence rankings and deviation scores can then be compared, noting the effects of individual influence and "expertise" on the group outcome.

Similar Structured Experiences: *Vol. I:* Structured Experiences 11, 15; *Vol. II:* 30; *Vol. III:* 64; '72 *Annual:* 77; *Vol. IV:* 115; '75 *Annual:* 140; *Vol. V:* 157; '76 *Annual:* 177.

Suggested Instrument: '75 *Annual:* "Decision-Style Inventory."

Lecturette Sources: '73 *Annual:* "Synergy and Consensus-Seeking"; '76 *Annual:* "A Gestalt Approach to Collaboration in Organizations."

Submitted by William J. Heisler.

William J. Heisler, Ph.D., is an associate professor of management at the Babcock Graduate School of Management, Wake Forest University, Winston-Salem, North Carolina. He is currently teaching and doing research on work-life quality, organization development, and personal causation and is a co-editor of A Matter of Dignity: Inquiries into the Humanization of Work. *Dr. Heisler's background is in organizational behavior, organization development, and human resource management and research.*

ADMISSIONS COMMITTEE FACT SHEET

The Situation

You are a faculty member of Southern Business School. In addition to your teaching responsibilities, you are a member of the Admissions Committee, which screens applicants for admission to the M.B.A. (Master of Business Administration) program. It is the committee's function to review each application for admission and decide whether to admit or reject the applicant and whether to extend an offer of financial aid. The committee meets every other Friday to review applications received during the interim two weeks and to rank the applicants on the basis of potential for success in Southern's graduate program. It is your policy to review applicant profiles before each meeting and arrive at your own ranking of applicants.

Applicant profiles, prepared and distributed to each committee member, provide information concerning the applicant's undergraduate grade-point average (A=4.0; B=3.0; C=2.0, D=1.0), Graduate Management Admissions Test (GMAT) scores, records of extracurricular activity, work experience, recommendations, and general personal data.

Southern Business School

Southern Business School, located on the campus of a small Southern university, has a relatively new M.B.A. program. Although its present reputation is regionally based, its long-range goal is to become a nationally prominent business school. Pressures for academic achievement appear to be moderate but can be expected to increase. Approximately 40 percent of all applicants are accepted, with 60 to 70 percent of those accepted ultimately enrolling at Southern. Approximately 75 percent of the faculty has a doctoral degree, most earned at major Eastern and Midwestern universities. The student-faculty ratio is about 12:1. Southern's admissions policy reflects a desire to develop a quality student body with a diversity of interests and backgrounds. Maturity and motivation are judged to be as important as intellectual ability.

Specific Directions

Step 1. During the last two weeks, you have received eight applicant profiles. Tomorrow the Admissions Committee will meet to consider the applications. As is your policy, you wish to make your own decisions before the meeting. You will have a total of thirty minutes to rank these applicants on the basis of their relative potential for success in Southern's graduate program. Make these decisions now. Record your individual decisions in column (1) on the Admissions Committee Decision Work Sheet. When you have finished, wait for the facilitator's instructions to proceed to the next step.

Step 2. It is now Friday. You are to meet with the other members of the Admissions Committee and decide by consensus on a ranking for each applicant. You will have forty-five minutes to reach consensus. Record the committee's decisions in column (2) on the Admissions Committee Decision Work Sheet.

ADMISSIONS COMMITTEE APPLICANT PROFILE SHEET I

Sam Dameon

Sam is a graduate of a small, private, church-affiliated institution in the South, where he majored in psychology and received a B.S. degree two years ago.

Educational
Record:

Cumulative G.P.A.:	2.3
G.P.A. last two years:	2.5
Rank in class:	340/551
GMAT scores:	
total	487 (55 %ile)
verbal	32 (70 %ile)
quantitative	24 (30 %ile)
Best subject:	psychology

Major
Activities:
Social fraternity (social chairman); R.O.T.C.; Interfraternity Council

Work
Experience:
First Lieutenant (U.S. Army); summer work as construction laborer, salesperson; part-time employment as laborer, research assistant, sandwich sales business operator

Recommendations: None provided

Personal Data:
Age: 23
Marital status: married
U.S. citizen: yes
Military service: yes
Father's occupation: certified public accountant
Mother's occupation: newspaper editor
Hobbies: fishing, golf, painting

Additional
Information: None

Frank Green

Frank attended a small, Southern, church-affiliated school for two years before transferring to a large metropolitan university in the North. Frank will receive a B.S. degree this year with a major in accounting.

Educational Record:		
	Cumulative G.P.A.:	2.2
	G.P.A. last two years:	2.4
	Rank in class:	not available
	GMAT scores:	
	total	486 (53 %ile)
	verbal	32 (70 %ile)
	quantitative	22 (23 %ile)
	Best subjects:	banking, finance

Major Activities: Social fraternity (president); Accounting Club (treasurer)

Work Experience: Summer employment at textile plant and as junior auditor

Recommendations: Two excellent; one average

Personal Data: Age: 24
Marital status: single
U.S. citizen: yes
Military service: no
Father's occupation: accountant
Mother's occupation: legal secretary
Hobbies: flying, stamp collecting, soccer, reading

Additional Information: None

ADMISSIONS COMMITTEE APPLICANT PROFILE SHEET III

Larry Hutch

Larry attended a medium-sized, church-affiliated school in the upper Midwest, majored in psychology and biology, and will receive a B.A. degree this year.

Educational
Record:

Cumulative G.P.A.:	2.7	
G.P.A. last two years:	2.7	
Rank in class:	not available	
GMAT scores:		
total	476 (51 %ile)	
verbal	23 (3 %ile)	
quantitative	34 (74 %ile)	
Best subject:	biology	

Major
Activities: Student productions (producer); theater (publicity manager)

Work
Experience: Summer work on a farm, in a hospital, and as a student laborer

Recommendations: One good; one average

Personal Data: Age: 22

Marital status: single

U.S. citizen: yes

Military service: no

Father's occupation: farmer

Mother's occupation: roadside produce business

Hobbies: skiing, canoeing

Additional
Information: None

ADMISSIONS COMMITTEE APPLICANT PROFILE SHEET IV

Edward Jakes

Ed, a graduate of a medium-sized school in the South that serves predominantly minority cultures, majored in political science and received a B.A. degree two years ago.

Educational
Record:

Cumulative G.P.A.:	3.1
G.P.A. last two years:	3.0
Rank in class:	31/437
GMAT scores:	
total	283 (4 %ile)
verbal	14 (7 %ile)
quantitative	13 (2 %ile)
Best subject:	politics

Major
Activities: Student Government Association (attorney general); various student committees; Political Science Club

Work
Experience: Full-time work as an insurance salesperson; part-time employment as a sales clerk, restaurant worker, and legislative assistant for the General Assembly of a Southern state

Recommendations: Two good

Personal Data: Age: 25
Marital status: single
U.S. citizen: yes
Military service: no
Father's occupation: deceased
Mother's occupation: teacher of government
Hobbies: reading

Additional
Information: None

ADMISSIONS COMMITTEE APPLICANT PROFILE SHEET V

Jim Lorain

Jim is a graduate of a very small, private, church-affiliated college in the South, where he majored in economics. He will receive a B.A. degree this year.

Educational Record:	Cumulative G.P.A.:	2.7
	G.P.A. last two years:	3.2
	Rank in class:	not available
	GMAT scores:	
	total	410 (27 %ile)
	verbal	23 (30 %ile)
	quantitative	22 (23 %ile)
	Best subjects:	economics, business

Major Activities: Student Government Association (chairman of a committee); intramural sports

Work Experience: Summer employment for a construction firm and management intern for a large corporation

Recommendations: Two good

Personal Data: Age: 22

Marital status: single

U.S. citizen: yes

Military service: no

Father's occupation: doctor

Mother's occupation: volunteer work, homemaker

Hobbies: sports

Additional Information: None

ADMISSIONS COMMITTEE APPLICANT PROFILE SHEET VI

Tim Miller

Tim is a graduate of a large, land grant college in the South, where he majored in electrical engineering and received a B.S.E.E. one year ago. He is presently in the Army.

Educational Record:	Cumulative G.P.A.:	2.3
	G.P.A. last two years:	2.6
	Rank in class:	1542/2117
	GMAT scores:	
	total	534 (72 %ile)
	verbal	31 (66 %ile)
	quantitative	33 (70 %ile)
	Best subjects:	electronics, physics

Major Activities: R.O.T.C. (adjutant); Student Government Association (senator); Honor Court (associate justice)

Work Experience: Second Lieutenant (U.S. Army); store worker (summer)

Recommendations: One excellent; one good

Personal Data: Age: 22
Marital status: single
U.S. citizen: yes
Military service: yes
Father's occupation: research chemist
Mother's occupation: program director for local TV station
Hobbies: reading; ham radio

Additional Information: Granted full fellowship by U.S. Army

ADMISSIONS COMMITTEE APPLICANT PROFILE SHEET VII

Richard Morris

Richard, a graduate of a very small school in the South that serves predominantly minority cultures, majored in business administration and received a B.A. degree one year ago.

Educational Record:	Cumulative G.P.A.:	3.3
	G.P.A. last two years:	3.2
	Rank in class:	11/244
	GMAT scores:	
	total	398 (21 %ile)
	verbal	20 (17 %ile)
	quantitative	24 (28 %ile)
	Best subjects:	business, economics
Major Activities:		Student Government Association (director of financial affairs); class government (president); Business Club (president)
Work Experience:		Accountant (full time); management intern (summer)
Recommendations:		None provided
Personal Data:		Age: 22
		Marital status: married
		U.S. citizen: yes
		Military service: no
		Father's occupation: auto mechanic
		Mother's occupation: nurse
		Hobbies: reading, listening to jazz
Additional Information:		None

ADMISSIONS COMMITTEE APPLICANT PROFILE SHEET VIII

Anne Wa-Wen Chek

Anne, a graduate of Cheng-Kung University, Republic of China, with a major in mathematics, received a B.A. degree two years ago.

Educational Record:	Cumulative G.P.A.:	B (approximate)
	G.P.A. last two years:	B+ (approximate)
	Rank in class:	not available
	GMAT scores:	
	total	357 (14 %ile)
	verbal	12 (5 %ile)
	quantitative	27 (45 %ile)
	Best subject:	business
	Test of English as a Foreign Language (TOEFL):	578 (national TOEFL average about 500)
Major Activities:	Catholic Student Organization; swimming team; basketball team	
Work Experience:	Assistant to professors (part time)	
Recommendations:	Two good	
Personal Data:	Age: 22	
	Marital status: single	
	U.S. citizen: no	
	Military service: no	
	Father's occupation: school teacher	
	Mother's occupation: homemaker	
	Hobbies: reading, travel, camping, sports	
Additional Information:	None	

ADMISSIONS COMMITTEE DECISION WORK SHEET

Applicant	(1) Personal Ranking	(2) Committee Ranking	(3) Actual Performance Ranking	(4) Difference Between (1) and (3)	(5) Difference Between (2) and (3)
Sam Dameon					
Frank Green					
Larry Hutch					
Edward Jakes					
Jim Lorain					
Tim Miller					
Richard Morris					
Anne Wa-Wen Chek					

	Individual Score	Committee Score
*Total Scores		

*The total score for each column is the sum of the differences between the "correct" rank for each applicant and the rank attributed to each applicant. (All differences are to be considered positive, regardless of their sign.) The lower the score, the better.

224. CONTROVERSIAL ISSUES: CASE STUDIES IN CONFLICT

Goals

    I. To examine the effects of conflict on members of problem-solving groups.

    II. To acquaint members with alternative methods of coping with conflict in groups.

    III. To examine individual styles of handling conflicts and their effects among members of problem-solving groups.

Group Size

    Any number of groups of five to seven members each.

Time Required

    Approximately one and one-half to two hours.

Materials

    I. A copy of the same Controversial Issues Case Study Sheet for each participant in a group.

    II. A copy of the Controversial Issues Discussion Guidelines for each participant.

    III. Newsprint, masking tape, and a felt-tipped marker.

Physical Setting

    A separate room for each group or one large room with space enough for each group to deliberate privately and without distraction.

Process

    I. The facilitator forms groups containing members with differing values and perspectives.

    II. The facilitator introduces the case study as an exercise in decision making; participants are not advised that conflict is being studied. (If participants are aware of the actual purpose of the experience, they tend to behave less naturally and attempt to minimize intragroup conflict, thus defeating the purpose.) The facilitator mentions that group problem solving sometimes involves differences of opinion and that these should not be minimized during the activity. He defines consensus as *substantial agreement*, not unanimity.

    III. A time limit of thirty to forty-five minutes for reaching consensus can be specified, depending on group size. If observers are to be used, they are appointed and briefed on the real nature of the experience.

    IV. The facilitator distributes a copy of the same Controversial Issues Case Study Sheet to each participant within a group and instructs the groups to begin discussing their case studies.

V. When the allotted time has elapsed or when the groups have reached consensus, the facilitator distributes copies of the Controversial Issues Discussion Guidelines and instructs participants to discuss their interaction process within their groups.

VI. After this phase, the facilitator opens the discussion to the entire group. He attempts to draw a distinction between constructive or integrative handling of conflict and disruptive or distributive handling of conflict[1] by using examples from the discussions that just occurred. The observers may participate by offering examples they noted during the discussions. The facilitator focuses on the manner in which participants handled conflict and the effects of different ways of managing disagreement.

Variations

I. Other case studies may be designed around a current and controversial issue that is of interest to the participants.

II. The facilitator may employ a stop-process approach that involves halting discussions when salient (conflict-prone) actions occur. Using this method, the facilitator or observer can give immediate feedback to participants about how personal behaviors contribute to the climate of a discussion.

III. Participants can be encouraged to let conflict emerge and to attempt to deal with it as constructive or integrative conflict.

IV. After the entire group has considered the two ways to deal with conflict and has understood the distinction, the facilitator may wish to repeat the activity using another case study. This allows the participants to experiment with their new skills immediately.

Similar Structured Experiences: *Vol. I:* Structured Experience **14;** *'74 Annual:* **130;** *'77 Annual:* **186.**

Lecturette Sources: *'73 Annual:* "Confrontation: Types, Conditions, and Outcomes"; *'74 Annual:* "Conflict-Resolution Strategies"; *'77 Annual:* "Constructive Conflict in Discussions: Learning to Manage Disagreements Effectively," "Handling Group and Organizational Conflict."

Submitted by Julia T. Wood.

Julia T. Wood, Ph.D., is an assistant professor of speech communication at the University of North Carolina at Chapel Hill. In addition to teaching, she does consulting and meets with informal groups. Dr. Wood is especially interested in small-group problem solving and small-group leadership.

---

[1] See Lecturette Sources above.

CONTROVERSIAL ISSUES CASE STUDY SHEET I

Appropriate for professional people or students who plan to enter law, medicine, or the mass media

In the last few years, a controversy has arisen regarding advertising policies. Some doctors and lawyers want to advertise their services in order to attract patients and clients. These professionals claim that medicine and law are just like any other fields; each doctor or lawyer is a specialist in certain areas and should be allowed to tell the public where his expertise lies. Further, argue the proponents of advertising, free commercial enterprise would encourage healthy competitive prices so that the doctor or lawyer who charges a fee far above the norm would be forced to lower his charge or get out of business. This should benefit the public.

On the other hand, many doctors and lawyers feel that such commercialism would be detrimental to the professional images of their fields. These people claim that law and medicine are *not* like other fields; instead, law and medicine are professions (as distinguished from businesses and industries), and it would be demeaning to have professions engaging in commercial and competitive practices. Moreover, according to the opponents of advertising, commercialism would encourage doctors and lawyers to become more concerned with competitive prices and snappy ads than with proper care of patients and clients. If a doctor or lawyer is competent, he will gain an active and ample following without advertising; if he is not competent, he should not be allowed to attract a following by creating catchy slogans and offering discount prices.

The American Medical Association and your local Bar Association are presently considering their stands on this issue. As they do so, they would like to have the benefit of general public opinion. Consequently, they have asked your group to act as a representative of people in your area. Please discuss this issue and develop your recommendations.

CONTROVERSIAL ISSUES CASE STUDY SHEET II

Appropriate for people in business or in union workshops

Since its beginnings in 1940, Pacific Packaging Company (PPC), like many U.S. firms, has used a policy of "last hired—first fired." This means that when PPC cannot support all its workers, the first people to be fired are those who were the last to be hired. This policy was originally adopted to protect the seniority and to reward the loyalty of long-time personnel at PPC.

During the past four years of economic difficulty, PPC has managed to retain most of its employees, although it has hired only enough new people to meet the minority-quota requirements established by the Department of Labor. Now, however, due to the recession, PPC must fire 5 percent of its employees—forty-two people.

If PPC follows its "last hired—first fired" policy, the following employees would be among those released: eleven black men, six black women, nine Caucasian women, one Chinese man, and two Vietnam veterans. Firing so many minority workers would create major legal problems. PPC is committed to nondiscrimination; however, it feels a moral responsibility to those workers who have been with the company for longer periods of time.

Your group has been asked to consider this problem and to make recommendations to PPC. The president of PPC has indicated that if PPC decides to protect long-standing workers and fire twenty-nine minority people, he is willing to face the legal battles. He simply wants to come up with the fairest policy for all.

Appropriate for general participants—no special backgrounds or career interests necessary

For some time now, this country has had the technological means necessary to detect certain types of genetic defects prior to the birth of infants. A relatively safe procedure, amniocentesis, involves extracting a small amount of the amniotic fluid that surrounds a fetus and running laboratory tests on that fluid. From those tests, over sixty types of genetic defects can be correctly detected. The procedure involves less than a 1 percent risk of harm to the fetus or to the mother.

Until 1970 the use of amniocentesis was entirely voluntary—that is, parents could request it if they wished, but they were not required to do so. If genetic defects were detected, therapeutic abortions were encouraged by doctors. In the past few years, however, a number of states have made amniocentesis a mandatory procedure for all pregnant women. In your state, Atlantia, amniocentesis is required for all pregnant women.

The detection procedure was originally mandated so that prospective parents would have the information necessary to make rational choices regarding the birth of a child. Now, however, certain people are arguing that the state should take action in regard to some types of genetic defects.

The particular genetic defect that you are asked to consider is the case of XYY males, those born with an extra Y chromosome. Several studies of this abnormality have indicated that an apparently higher percentage of XYY males than of normal (XY) males wind up in prisons or mental hospitals. Some scientists have concluded that the XYY chromosomal factor is an indicator of aggressive or criminal tendencies and behavior. The XYY chromosomal combination has also been shown to be related to other characteristics such as above-average height, below-average intelligence, and severe acne.

Prominent public and professional people have proposed that all XYY males be immediately registered at birth in order to keep them under proper scrutiny over the years. These people argue that such action would be a safeguard against crime.

You are asked to recommend action regarding the registration of XYY males at birth.

CONTROVERSIAL ISSUES DISCUSSION GUIDELINES

1. How different were initial opinions within your group?

2. Do you feel the conflicting opinions were handled effectively for the task and the interaction process?

3. Do you feel that each member listened fairly to your ideas?

4. Do you feel that you, in turn, listened fairly and with an open mind to the ideas of the other members?

5. When you presented your ideas, did you feel that having them accepted was the only way you could be satisfied?

6. If your ideas were not accepted by the others, did you feel you had lost?

7. Do you feel that you were *personally* attacked at any point during the discussion?

8. Do you feel that you attacked any of the others *personally* when you disagreed with them?

9. Did you feel like withdrawing from the group at any time?

10. Now that the discussion has ended, how do you feel toward the other members? Do you tend to feel you can or cannot trust them? Do you feel friendly or hostile toward one another?

11. How satisfied are you with the decision that was reached by your group?

225. CARDS: PERSONAL FEEDBACK

Goals

    I. To encourage the exchange of personal feedback.

    II. To provide a means for giving and receiving personal feedback.

Group Size

    An unlimited number of groups of five members each.

Time Required

    Approximately two hours.

Materials

    I. Five blank 3" x 5" cards for each participant.

    II. A pencil for each participant.

Physical Setting

    A room large enough to accommodate several groups working independently.

Process

    I. The facilitator introduces the activity and gives some guidelines to follow and some of the benefits of giving and receiving personal feedback.[1]

    II. He divides the participants into groups of five members each and gives five blank index cards and a pencil to each member.

    III. The facilitator instructs each participant to write a *different* group member's name (including the participant's own name) on each card and then to turn the card over and write a description, characteristic, or impression of that person, based on any of the following topics:

        1. A positive characteristic of this person is . . .

        2. This person is a good leader because . . .

        3. This person could be a more effective leader . . .

        4. What impresses me most about this person is . . .

        5. I think this person should . . .

        6. I would like to know if this person . . .

        7. My first impression of this person was . . .

        8. This person performs the role of . . .

    IV. Each participant completes one card for each member in his group. On the participant's own card, he writes something that he thinks or feels which the other group

---

[1] See Lecturette Sources at the end of this structured experience.

members do not know about him and which he would be willing to share with the group.

V. The cards for each group are collected (names down), shuffled, and placed in a pile. The description on the first card is read aloud, and the group members decide by consensus whom the card describes and place the card—still with the name facing down—in front of that person. This step is repeated until all the cards in the group have been assigned to the group members.

VI. Each member, in turn, briefly gives his reaction to each card he has received.

VII. The cards are then turned over and the names on the cards are compared with the person who received them. The group discusses (1) why cards were given to the right or wrong people and (2) whether the descriptions on the cards are accurate for the people for whom they were intended.

VIII. The entire group is reassembled, and the facilitator elicits comments from the members on their reactions to and feelings about other members' impressions of them. The facilitator then leads a discussion of the things that can be learned from the experience and how they can be applied to other situations.

Variations

I. Feedback can be given through symbols or imagery (an oak, a fawn, etc.) rather than words.

II. Participants can sign their names to the cards.

III. In process step V, before the group decides who is described on each card, participants can be given a chance to nominate themselves for that particular card and say why they feel it belongs to or describes them.

Similar Structured Experiences: *Vol. I:* Structured Experiences 13, 17, 23; *Vol. II:* 38; *Vol. III:* 57, 58; *'73 Annual:* 99; *Vol. IV:* 104, 107, 109; *'75 Annual:* 146; *'78 Annual:* **222.**

Lecturette Sources: *'72 Annual:* "Openness, Collusion, and Feedback"; *'73 Annual:* "Johari Window"; *'75 Annual:* "Re-Entry," "Giving Feedback: An Interpersonal Skill"; *'76 Annual:* "Interpersonal Feedback as Consensual Validation of Constructs."

Submitted by J. Ryck Luthi.

J. Ryck Luthi is the coordinator of student programs at the University of Utah, Salt Lake City, Utah, and is currently teaching in the areas of leadership training and value clarification and doing consulting for a number of community agencies. He has authored several articles in communication and personal development. Mr. Luthi's background is in counseling and student personnel development.

226. SEXUAL ASSESSMENT: SELF-DISCLOSURE

Goals

   I. To share sexual perceptions, feelings, attitudes, values, behaviors, and expectations.

   II. To clarify one's sexuality through self-disclosure.

   III. To gain insight into the sexual dimensions of other persons.

Group Size

Any number of triads.

Time Required

Approximately two and one-half hours.

Materials

A copy of the Sexual Assessment Discussion Sheet for each participant.

Physical Setting

A quiet room where triads can have privacy and sit comfortably.

Process

   I. The facilitator discusses the importance of sexuality and the value of the disclosure of sexual information in interpersonal relationships.

   II. The participants are instructed to form triads with individuals they are least familiar with and to sit facing one another, within touching distance.

   III. The facilitator gives each participant a copy of the Sexual Assessment Discussion Sheet and tells the participants to share their information with the other members of their triad. Each participant will have about thirty seconds per item. (One and one-half hours.)

   IV. The group is reassembled to discuss how the members felt about sharing sexual attitudes and perceptions. Members are not to report what *answers* their partners gave to statements, but rather how their perceptions affected their communication. The facilitator leads a discussion of the implications of this activity. (Thirty minutes.)

Variations

   I. For a total-group activity, the statements can be written on 3" x 5" cards and placed face down. Participants can draw a card one at a time and read the statement aloud; any person who so desires can complete the statement. Any person may choose not to respond to a statement. The cards may be repeated as long as time permits. (This works best with a very open group.)

II. This activity may be used in conjunction with "Dyadic Encounter" (*Vol. I:* Structured Experience 21) or "Dyadic Renewal" (*Vol. V:* Structured Experience 169).

III. Selected items can be posted for discussion by the whole group.

IV. Participants can "brainstorm" their own list of topics at the beginning of the session.

V. The activity can be preceded by a guided group fantasy or group discussion to bring the area of sexuality more closely into focus.

VI. Participants can complete the Sexual Assessment Discussion Sheet before forming triads.

Similar Structured Experiences: *Vol. II:* Structured Experiences **25, 45;** *Vol. III:* **70;** *Vol. IV:* **116, 118;** *Vol. V:* **169;** *Vol. VI:* **220.**

Suggested Instruments: *'72 Annual:* "Interpersonal Relationship Rating Scale"; *'73 Annual:* "Scale of Feelings and Behavior of Love," "The Involvement Inventory"; *'74 Annual:* "Interpersonal Communication Inventory," "Self-Disclosure Questionnaire"; *'75 Annual:* "Scale of Marriage Problems."

Lecturette Sources: *'72 Annual:* "Openness, Collusion and Feedback"; *'73 Annual:* "The Johari Window: A Model for Soliciting and Giving Feedback," "Risk-Taking," "Dependency and Intimacy"; *'75 Annual:* "Giving Feedback: An Interpersonal Skill."

Submitted by Paul S. Weikert.

Paul S. Weikert is a consultant with Human Relations Consultants, Inc., in Williamston, Michigan. He is a co-editor of Readings in Marriage and the Family, *'77-'78 (3rd ed.) and a co-author of* Parents and Teenagers. *His special areas of interest are sexual fantasy, jealousy, and communication about contraception. Mr. Weikert's background is in empathy and value-exploration workshops, group facilitation, and family and sexual therapy.*

SEXUAL ASSESSMENT DISCUSSION SHEET

This discussion sheet consists of a series of open-ended statements that focus on your sexual perceptions and feelings. Self-disclosure of sexual information often helps to form a better basis for understanding in personal relationships.

Note the following guidelines.

- Consider any personal data you hear to be confidential.
- Respond to each statement before continuing to the next statement.
- Take turns being first to complete the statements.
- Complete the statements in the order in which they appear.
- You may decline to complete any statement by saying that you prefer not to answer. You do not have to explain why, and the other members of your triad are not to ask questions.
- You may stop the activity if you become uncomfortable. Try to talk over the source of such feelings, and continue if and when it seems appropriate.
- Be willing to take risks.

1. The best aspect of my personality is . . .
2. The emotion I find most difficult to talk about is . . .
3. I feel that my body is . . .
4. What my parents told me about sex is . . .
5. I started to change my feelings about sex when . . .
6. Now I think sex is . . .
7. It's hard for me to share sexual thoughts because . . .
8. If I were really open and honest right now I'd say . . .
9. The quality I look for most in a sexual partner is . . .
10. To me, sex in a relationship is . . .
11. Maintaining more than one sexual relationship is . . .
12. When talking about sex and personal hygiene, I feel . . .
13. Our sexual attitudes are similar in that . . .
14. Something new I learned about sex recently is . . .
15. I perceived my parents' sexuality to be . . .
16. Our sexual attitudes are different in that . . .
17. To me a meaningful sexual relationship consists of . . .
18. Emotional involvement in a sexual relationship is . . .
19. Sexual satisfaction means . . .
20. When I am in a sexual relationship, my emotions . . .
21. I feel close sexually when . . .
22. My sexual enjoyment is sometimes determined by . . .
23. I feel most affectionate when . . .
24. My most caressable spots are . . .
25. The physical preliminaries to sex that are important to me are . . .

26. Something I really like to do sexually is . . .
27. Something I want from a sexual relationship that I feel lacking now is . . .
28. My sex drives could be described as . . .
29. Something I especially want out of a sexual relationship is . . .
30. I enjoy taking a dominant (submissive) role because . . .
31. My greatest pleasure in sex comes from . . .
32. The first experience I ever had that I would define as sexual was . . .
33. The thought of intercourse brings feelings of . . .
34. I think my sexual experiences have affected me by . . .
35. Sex usually changes relationships for me by . . .
36. When rating my sexual experience, I guess I'd fall somewhere between . . .
37. As far as masturbation is concerned, I . . .
38. I feel really sexually inadequate when . . .
39. Something I'd really like to do sexually that I haven't told anyone is . . .
40. I used to have a problem sexually with . . .
41. Sometimes sexually I have trouble . . .
42. I'm not altogether happy with my sexual functioning when . . .
43. One thing that can keep me from feeling fully satisfied sexually is . . .
44. One of my recurring sexual fantasies is . . .
45. To me the importance of orgasm is . . .
46. If I don't have an orgasm during sex, I . . .
47. After having sex, I sometimes feel . . .
48. In the future, I think my feelings about sex will . . .
49. My feelings toward you right now are . . .
50. What I've learned most about my sexuality from this experience is . . .

(You may expand this list with other open-ended statements.)

227. YOUNG/OLD WOMAN: A PERCEPTION EXPERIMENT

Goals

I. To focus on individual reactions to the same stimulus.

II. To examine the effects of the immediate environment on an individual's perception.

Group Size

Any number of participants divided into an even number of groups of seven or eight members each.

Time Required

Fifty minutes.

Materials

I. Copies of Discussion Guide A for half the participants and copies of Discussion Guide B for the other half.

II. A copy of the Work Sheet for each group.

III. A copy of the Young/Old Woman picture[1] for the facilitator.

IV. A pencil for each participant.

V. Newsprint, masking tape, and a felt-tipped marker for the facilitator.

Physical Setting

A room large enough for separate groups to meet privately.

Process

I. The facilitator divides the participants into an even number of groups and gives each participant in half of the groups a copy of Discussion Guide A and each participant in the other half of the groups a copy of Discussion Guide B to read and discuss. All participants receive pencils.

II. The facilitator goes in turn to each group to answer any questions while the discussions are being conducted. (Ten minutes.)

III. The facilitator stops the discussions, holds up the Young/Old Woman picture, and tells all participants to look at the picture he is holding up and then silently, with no

---

[1] This picture was brought to the attention of psychologists by Edwin G. Boring in 1930. Created by cartoonist W. E. Hill, it was originally published in *Puck*, November 6, 1915, as "My Wife and My Mother-in-law."

discussion among themselves, to write down on their discussion guides a brief description of the subject of the picture. (Five minutes.)

IV. Each group tabulates the responses of its members, according to the subject described. (Five minutes.)

V. The facilitator lists the results on newsprint, using a chart such as the following, and points out any trends. (Five minutes.)

Subject of Picture	"A" Groups	"B" Groups
Young Woman		
Old Woman		
Other		

VI. The facilitator gives each group a copy of the Work Sheet and tells the group members to discuss each question and prepare a short report for the large group. (Ten minutes.)

VII. The facilitator leads a discussion of the experience, hearing reports from each group. (Fifteen minutes.)

Variations

I. Each individual can be given ten seconds to look at the picture and then write down perceptions for discussion.

II. Other pictures may be used, with appropriate changes in the discussion guides.

III. Groups may be formed according to sex or some other appropriate criterion.

IV. A projective object or story may be used, instead of the picture. For example, "She walked with an aristocratic carriage, and under her fox fur she wore a classic suit that would always be in style." Participants can then briefly describe the woman they picture in their minds, estimating her age and general appearance.

Similar Structured Experiences: *Vol. III:* Structured Experience 50; *'72 Annual:* 77; *'75 Annual:* 137, 142; *'76 Annual:* 180.

Lecturette Sources: *'72 Annual:* "Communication Modes: An Experiential Lecture"; *'74 Annual:* "Figure/Ground."

Submitted by William R. Mulford.

William R. Mulford, Ph.D., is a senior lecturer in education administration in the School of Teacher Education, Canberra College of Advanced Education, Canberra City, Australia, and is also doing consulting with schools and inservice personnel. He is a pioneer in the use of organization development in Australian schools, has written extensively in the field, and is the author of Structured Experiences for Use in the Classroom *(1977). Dr. Mulford has held positions in teaching and school administration in Australia, the United Kingdom, Canada, and Papua New Guinea and university positions in Canada and Australia.*

DISCUSSION GUIDE A
Young Women's Fashions

It is often said that today's young woman is not fashion conscious; she prefers dirty blue jeans and scruffy men's shirts to furs and silk scarves. What does your group think about this statement? Discuss the issue quietly among yourselves.

DISCUSSION GUIDE B
Old People's Homes

It is sometimes said that old people's homes are sad places, for all elderly people need the company of their families and grandchildren, not only the company of other elderly people.

Put yourself in the place of an older person. Pretend your group is made up of residents of an old people's home. How do members of your group feel about their lives? Discuss this quietly among yourselves.

WORK SHEET

1. How many participants first saw a young woman? An old woman?

2. Were there any other consistent differences in perception? Did women respond differently from men?

3. Why did individuals react differently to the same stimulus?

4. What influence did the previous group discussions have on what people saw?

5. What comparisons can you draw with real-world situations?

228. HOMESELL: INTERGROUP COMPETITION

Goals

    I. To explore the ways in which members interact in a work group.

    II. To demonstrate different methods of group problem solving.

    III. To relate members' group behavior to back-home situations.

Group Size

    Up to twenty-four participants, divided into groups of five or six members each.

Time Required

    Approximately three hours. (May be conducted in two sessions of one and one-half hours each.)

Physical Setting

    A large room with a table and chairs for each group.

Materials

    I. For each participant: one copy each of the Homesell Background Sheet, Homesell Instruction Sheet, and Homesell Processing Sheet.

    II. For each group: scissors, 150 3″ x 5″ index cards, a roll of cellophane tape, a map of any metropolitan area, pencils, and felt-tipped markers.

Process

    I. Participants are divided into groups, and each group is assigned to a work area in which there are a table and chairs, scissors, index cards, tape, a map, pencils, and felt-tipped markers.

    II. Each member receives a Homesell Background Sheet and a Homesell Instruction Sheet. Members are directed to read their sheets and then to begin the group's task. (One and one-half hours.)

    III. The facilitator announces the time at fifteen-minute intervals for one hour and fifteen minutes; then he announces when ten minutes remain, five minutes, and one minute. When time is called, all materials are collected by the facilitator. (In a two-session format, the remaining steps take place at the second session.)

    IV. The facilitator returns each team's materials in turn, and each team makes its presentation to the other participants. (A maximum of ten minutes for each presentation.)

    V. After all group presentations have been made, each group takes a secret vote on which individual in the group made the greatest contribution to the group's effort. Each person is required to vote for *two* people, one of whom may be himself; he is not allowed to cast both votes for the same person. (The results are not important; the dynamics of the process are.)

VI. The Homesell Processing Sheet is distributed to all participants, and team members complete the sheet and share their responses with each other.

VII. The facilitator leads the entire group in discussing the experience, using team members' reactions to the questions on the Homesell Processing Sheet. The facilitator can point out that people learn and change through experience. Thus, even the *same* group would have different results if the activity were done a second time.

Variations

I. The Homesell Processing Sheet may be used as the basis for a general group discussion.

II. Company representatives can be chosen to serve as process observers and to be the focus of group presentations.

III. Participants with specific hidden agendas can be incorporated into each group.

IV. A prize can be offered for the winning building and the rental contract awarded.

Similar Structured Experiences: *Vol. II:* Structured Experience 32; *Vol. III:* **54**; *'72 Annual:* **82**; *Vol. V:* **160, 161**.

Lecturette Sources: *'73 Annual:* "Win/Lose Situations"; *'76 Annual:* "Role Functions in a Group."

Submitted by Joel Zimmerman.

Joel Zimmerman, Ph.D., is an associate professor of management in the College of Business Administration, Creighton University, Omaha, Nebraska. He is also the research director for Creighton's Institute for Business, Law and Social Research. Dr. Zimmerman's background is in applied social science research in the areas of marketing, management, evaluation, and law.

HOMESELL BACKGROUND SHEET

Homesell is a relatively young company that has grown steadily in the last few years. Its managers are young but generally credited with being imaginative and skillful. People who have dealt with the company say that its attitude toward investing company funds (whether into research, personnel benefits, advertising, or other areas) is best described as "careful, but definitely not cheap."

The Homesell Company sells nonperishable foods (primarily gourmet items), hardwares and housewares (including some small appliances), inexpensive jewelry, and some gift items on a retail basis. About 50 percent of sales are through catalog mail orders; the other 50 percent of sales are through direct personal selling in private homes and small businesses.

The company is now looking in your area for a new location for its headquarters to house its executives and clerical staff. The headquarters also will be the home base for the thirty-five or more salesmen who work in nearby districts. Other employees who will work there include five people who produce the company's yearly catalog; fifteen people who perform advertising, personnel, and other functions; and five buyers. Finally, the headquarters will be the central location for receiving goods, storing them, "picking" merchandise to fill orders, and preparing completed orders for delivery through the mails or by salesmen. These tasks employ about forty more people and a small computer that manages the automated part of the work.

The company is concerned with maintaining and improving its image. It wants to be seen as modern, clean, and efficient, yet friendly and personable. Official company policy is that the public is welcome at any time to come to the warehouse and offices to inspect merchandise or to talk with company management. Homesell is concerned about public relations; it frequently donates merchandise and the time of its personnel to community activities, and it occasionally makes its offices and meeting rooms available to community groups after regular working hours.

HOMESELL INSTRUCTION SHEET

You are a corporate group (give your organization a name) that owns and manages large buildings. You would like the Homesell Company to rent space in one of your buildings, and you must, of course, compete for its business. Your task, fundamentally, is to persuade the Homesell Company to become a tenant in your building.

To do this, your group must accomplish three things: (1) design and construct a three-dimensional model of the building into which you wish the Homesell Company to move its headquarters; (2) "locate" your building somewhere in your area; and (3) prepare and deliver a ten-minute presentation to the Homesell Company to persuade it to move into your building. Homesell Company representatives will be interested in seeing your model and in hearing why features of your building and its location would be advantageous to them. They also would like a recommendation about what kinds of terms they should be looking for in a lease.

At the end of one and one-half hours, your group must be ready to give its presentation to the Homesell Company representatives. At that time, your group will give any presentation notes and materials to the facilitator; these materials will be returned to your group when it is your turn to make your presentation. The presentation will complete your group's task—no question-and-answer period will follow. Each presentation will be limited to ten minutes.

After all groups have made their presentations, each team will vote on the two members of its group who made the greatest contribution to the group's effort.

You may use the following materials: tape, 3″ x 5″ index cards, a map, scissors, pencils, and felt-tipped markers. You may *not* use any other paper, books, or tools (ruler, compass, knife, etc.).

Your group *may:*

- Use index cards and tape to construct models or any other kinds of displays for the presentation. These may be written and drawn on.
- Use index cards for recording notes for the presentation.
- Write on the map and use it in the presentation.
- Use the Homesell Instruction Sheet and Background Sheet for scratch paper and for recording notes for the presentation.

Your group *may not:*

- Use pens or pencils structurally in your model.
- Communicate with anyone on another team, although you are free to "eavesdrop."

HOMESELL PROCESSING SHEET

1. How did you feel while you were participating? What emotions were you experiencing and how did these emotions affect your work?

2. What difference did it make to the members' behavior that there was going to be a vote on who made the greatest contribution to the group?

3. Describe the group's organization.

4. In what ways did the personalities of people in the group help or hinder the completion of the group's task?

5. What made a person "valuable" to your group?

6. Who was the group's leader? What characteristics of this person were critical in his/her emergence as a leader?

7. What motivated your group? Why did your group's members try to do a good job?

8. In what ways were communications important to the accomplishment of the task? What were the major communication difficulties?

9. What would be the advantages of accomplishing this task *by yourself* (in a proportionately longer period of time—about six hours), rather than having a group do it? What would be the disadvantages?

10. If you had this to do over again, what would you do differently (as a group)?

11. Think about the role you usually play in groups such as the family, your work group, or a group of friends. What kinds of behaviors or relationships do you usually assume in such groups? Did these same behaviors or relationships emerge in this activity? How might these behaviors relate to your personal satisfaction or success in this group?

229. PYGMALION: CLARIFYING PERSONAL BIASES

Goals

    I. To discover how preconceived ideas may influence collective and/or individual actions.

    II. To allow participants to assess their current behavior in terms of previous "scripting" and social pressure.

Group Size

    Eight to twenty participants. Several groups may be directed simultaneously in the same room.

Time Required

    Approximately forty-five minutes.

Materials

    I. A copy of Training Evaluation Instruction Sheet A for each member of Team A.

    II. A copy of Training Evaluation Instruction Sheet B for each member of Team B.

    III. A copy of the Training Evaluation Rating Sheet for each participant.

    IV. A pencil for each participant.

    V. Newsprint and a felt-tipped marker.

    VI. A short five- to ten-minute training film, slide show, audio tape, or other presentation.[1] The facilitator should exercise judgment as to what type of presentation is suitable, but it is suggested that the presentation be outside the group's area of expertise. Suggested areas might be safety, communications, study skills, first aid, or other topics of a general and innocuous nature.

Physical Setting

    A room large enough that the group may be divided into two separate and physically distinct teams and that both teams may view the presentation.

Process

    I. The facilitator explains that the purpose of the experience is to evaluate the effectiveness of a training exercise.

    II. He divides the members into two groups, Group A and Group B, and explains that the purpose of the two groups is to facilitate processing the evaluation portion of the activity. The groups are instructed to assemble on opposite sides of the room.

    III. The facilitator distributes a copy of the appropriate Training Evaluation Instruction

---

[1]See "Human Relations Films for Group Facilitators" in the Resources section of this *Annual*.

Sheet, the Training Evaluation Rating Sheet, and a pencil to each individual. He does not divulge the fact that the teams are receiving different instruction sheets.

IV. The facilitator directs the members to read their instruction sheets silently. Then the training presentation is shown for evaluation.

V. Participants are directed to complete the Training Evaluation Rating Sheet. Scoring is done in the following way: individuals (first of one group and then of the other group) give their responses to each question orally, while the facilitator records their scores on newsprint.

VI. The facilitator notes the discrepancy between the two groups' scores and asks a representative of each group to read his team's instruction sheet for the benefit of the other team's members.

VII. The facilitator explains that the purpose of the activity was not to practice the evaluation process or to try to evaluate according to group norms, but rather to demonstrate how two groups could respond very differently to the same stimulus because of the bias or preconceived ideas of individual members.

VIII. The facilitator leads a discussion centered around the following questions:

1. How often are our perceptions influenced by preconceived notions?
2. Did the group members feel "tricked" by the facilitator? If so, do they also feel "tricked" by individuals or events in their past experience that now bias their present perceptions and actions?
3. What effect did "group pressure" or "trying to evaluate in the same manner as other team members" have on individual responses?
4. How do we become aware of our biases, and how do we evaluate and change them?

The discussion may then lead into specific areas such as social prejudice, the "Pygmalion effect," interpersonal relationships, or biases between group members.

Variations

I. The activity may be done with three teams, Team A and Team B and a third team working on an independent, unbiased basis.

II. Instruction sheets and rating sheets may be altered to "evaluate" other experiences, such as lecturers, teaching methods, commercial products, organizations, new systems, etc.

Similar Structured Experiences: *Vol. I:* Structured Experience 9; *Vol. III:* **63;** *'73 Annual:* **95.**

Submitted by Richard L. Bunning.

Richard L. Bunning, Ph.D., *is the director of organization development for Samaritan Health Service, Phoenix, Arizona. He coordinates and facilitates many OD activities within Samaritan Health Service's hospitals and does consulting for various outside organizations. Dr. Bunning's background is in adult education, human relations developmental activities, supervisory training, and organization development.*

TRAINING EVALUATION INSTRUCTION SHEET A

Read the instructions that follow carefully and silently. Do not convey any of your instructions to Team B. You are receiving *different* instructions from those of Team B.

Each member of Team B has been told to view the upcoming presentation "objectively and critically, weighing the presentation's strengths as well as its weaknesses, and make an honest judgment as to its utility." (Actually the presentation is a perfect example of "industrial theft." That is, its content is based almost word-for-word on a similar presentation done twelve years ago by a small firm that designed it specifically for the use of its own employees. A successful advertising campaign has made this latest "rework" a successful financial undertaking, but industrial psychologists have pointed out that merely viewing such a presentation does little to change the attitudes of the viewer.)

Your job, then, as a member of Team A, is *not* to evaluate the presentation "objectively and critically," but rather to evaluate it as you think the *other members of your team* will view it.

After the evaluations are completed, the scores of your team members (who tried to consider the viewpoints of other team members in the evaluation process) will be compared with the scores of Team B members, who were told to do the evaluations as individuals.

Do not converse with your teammates, so that Team B will not be aware of any collusion on your part. Consider only your teammates' probable responses when making your own evaluations.

TRAINING EVALUATION INSTRUCTION SHEET B

Read the instructions that follow carefully and silently. Do not convey any of your instructions to Team A. You are receiving *different* instructions from those of Team A.

Each member of Team A has been told to view the upcoming presentation "objectively and critically, weighing the presentation's strengths as well as its weaknesses, and make an honest judgment as to its utility." (Actually the presentation has been acclaimed by the industrial community for its originality and content, and the producers have sold it on a "break even" basis. In addition, industrial psychologists have measured significant changes in the attitudes of the viewers who have been exposed to this presentation.)

Your job, then, as a member of Team B, is *not* to evaluate the presentation "objectively and critically," but rather to evaluate it as you think the *other members of your team* will view it.

After the evaluations are completed, the scores of your team members (who tried to consider the viewpoints of other team members in the evaluation process) will be compared with the scores of Team A members, who were told to do the evaluations as individuals.

Do not converse with your teammates, so that Team A will not be aware of any collusion on your part. Consider only your teammates' probable responses when making your own evaluations.

TRAINING EVALUATION RATING SHEET

Instructions: The purpose of this instrument is to measure, on five descriptive scales, how you think your teammates will judge an instructional presentation. Circle the number that best corresponds to the way they would rate the presentation. If you think they would rate it near one end of the scale, mark the appropriate number; if you think they would rate a particular criterion in the middle of the scale, choose a number toward the middle. Work quickly and accurately. It is your immediate impression of your teammates' feelings about the items that is important.

I. Originality

0	1	2	3	4	5	6	7	8	9	10

Duplication of Previous Materials · Some Originality · Largely an Original Presentation

II. Effectiveness

0	1	2	3	4	5	6	7	8	9	10

No Significant Effect on Viewer · Some Effect on Viewer · Significant Change in Viewer Probable

III. Scholarship

0	1	2	3	4	5	6	7	8	9	10

No Significant Contribution to Existing Field of Knowledge · Some Contribution to Field of Knowledge · New and Valuable Addition to Field of Knowledge

IV. Organization

0	1	2	3	4	5	6	7	8	9	10

Little or No Organization · Some Organization but Not Always Clear · Well Organized, Parts Clearly Related

V. Value

0	1	2	3	4	5	6	7	8	9	10

Little or No Value in Terms of Time and Money · Some Value · Well Worth the Time and Money Invested

University Associates

230. WILLINGTON: AN INTERVENTION-SKILLS ROLE PLAY

Goals

I. To determine the appropriate intervention strategy for a simulated organization.

II. To implement a strategy for entering, initially diagnosing, and contracting with the simulated organization.

III. To provide feedback on the consulting team members' intervention skills and strategy.

IV. To explore theory, skills, values, and strategies of organization development (OD).

Group Size

From nine to nineteen people (four organization role players and up to three five-person consulting teams). Smaller groups can be accommodated by reducing the team size or number of teams, and simultaneous simulations can be used with larger groups.

Time Required

Two and one-half to three hours.

Materials

I. A copy of the Willington Background Sheet, the Willington Financial Statement, and the Willington Organizational Structure Sheet for each participant.

II. An appropriate Willington Role Sheet for each role player.

III. A copy of the Willington Consulting Agenda Sheet for each member of the consulting teams.

IV. Paper and a pencil for each participant.

V. Name tags to identify each role player and members of the consulting teams.

VI. Newsprint, masking tape, and felt-tipped markers for each consulting team and for the facilitator.

Physical Setting

A room large enough to accommodate the entire group and allow space for the consulting teams to meet in relative privacy at separate tables. Each role player is assigned to a separate room to simulate a private office, or, if extra rooms are not available, role players can be placed in the four corners of the room.

Process

I. The facilitator introduces the role play by discussing the goals of the activity and outlines on newsprint the timing of events in the role play.

II. The facilitator selects four participants to play the Willington roles of Robin Barker, Lee James, Dale Thomas, and Gerry Shurtluff. He gives each role player a pencil, an appropriate name tag and role sheet, and a copy of the Willington Background Sheet, the Willington Financial Statement, and the Willington Organizational Structure Sheet. He assigns each role player to a separate room or area, but before role players depart for their assigned areas, they caucus to discuss their roles.

III. The remaining participants are divided into three consulting teams, Abco, Defco, and Ghico. (Teams can be chosen by the amount of experience individuals have had in OD, or all teams can be mixed.) Each team member receives the appropriate identification tag, a pencil, and copies of the Willington Background Sheet, the Willington Financial Statement, the Willington Organizational Structure Sheet, and the Willington Consulting Agenda Sheet. The facilitator points out that the teams are to follow the agenda on the Willington Consulting Agenda Sheet.

IV. The facilitator assigns each team a place to work and indicates where Robin Barker, Dale Thomas, Gerry Shurtluff, and Lee James can be found. Interviews are not to exceed ten minutes. The teams are told to record their activities and strategy for use in a wrap-up session. The teams have one hour to develop an intervention strategy, conduct interviews, and prepare a presentation for the Willington role players.

V. Each team, in turn, has five minutes to present its strategy, initial diagnosis, and list of action steps to the role players. (Fifteen minutes.)

VI. Willington personnel hold a group-on-group meeting to discuss the three teams' presentations and to record on newsprint their reactions to each. (Twenty minutes.)

VII. The facilitator leads a discussion of the strengths and weaknesses of each proposal from the standpoint of OD, considering the consultants' values versus the company's values, the question of money, project time commitment, and who the client is. (Twenty minutes.)

VIII. The facilitator leads a discussion on what has been learned from the activity. (Twenty minutes.)

Variations

I. If time is limited, the consulting teams can be formed in advance, or they can meet in advance to develop a strategy, in which case the facilitator would have to meet in advance with the role players.

II. The organizational situation and roles can be altered to fit any kind of organizational setting: a public school system, hospital, church, or social service agency.

III. While waiting for teams to prepare a diagnosis and action steps, the facilitator can meet with the company members to develop a list of criteria for evaluating team proposals.

Similar Structured Experiences: *Vol. II:* Structured Experience **40**; *Vol. IV:* **111**; *'74 Annual:* **131**; *'75 Annual:* **144**; *Vol. VI:* **211**.

Lecturette Sources: *'72 Annual:* "An Introduction to Organization Development"; *'73 Annual:* "The Sensing Interview," "An Informal Glossary of Terms and Phrases in Organization Development"; *'78 Annual:* "Strategies for Designing an Intervention," "Types of Process Interventions."

<hr/>

Submitted by W. Alan Randolph, John C. Ferrie, and David D. Palmer.

W. Alan Randolph, Ph.D., is an assistant professor of organization behavior in the College of Business Administration, University of South Carolina, Columbia, South Carolina. He is currently involved in teaching and research in organization development, organization technology, and communications and is writing a book on macro-organization behavior simulation entitled SIMORG: Simulated Organizations. Dr. Randolph's background is in teaching in business schools and consulting and training in private industry and with government agencies.

John C. Ferrie, Ed.D., is a senior consultant with Integrative Systems, West Hartford, Connecticut. He is currently involved in management training and organization development in public and private organizations and is an adjunct faculty member in the School of Business, University of Hartford. Dr. Ferrie's background is in psychological counseling, the teaching of organizational behavior, and organization and community action programs.

David D. Palmer, Ph.D., is an assistant professor in the Department of Management and Administrative Sciences, University of Connecticut, Storrs, Connecticut. He is currently involved in research and teaching in organizational theory and labor relations. Dr. Palmer's background is in motivation research, organizational change efforts, human resources utilization, and research in higher education.

WILLINGTON BACKGROUND SHEET

Willington, Inc., a medium-sized manufacturer (2,000 employees) of material-handling equipment (conveyors, hoists, castors, and related equipment) has experienced a 15 percent decline in profits over the past three years. Two new competitors have entered the field in the last few years and have gained a sizable share of the market. Several of Willington's middle managers have left to join the competitors. Latest sales figures indicate another decline.

Willington was founded fifteen years ago by Robin Barker, the president. Barker has called in three consulting teams to diagnose and suggest solutions to the current difficulties. Other personnel who are available today to meet with the consultants are Lee James, vice president of personnel, who has held that position for the past four years and has an M.B.A.; Dale Thomas, vice president of manufacturing, who has been with the company since the beginning and holds a B.S. in engineering; and Gerry Shurtluff, production manager, who also has a B.S.E. and has been with Willington for ten years.

WILLINGTON FINANCIAL STATEMENT
(000's omitted)

	1978	1976	1974	1972
Net Sales	$28,803	$29,895	$28,521	$25,455
Cost of Goods Sold	19,010	19,690	18,838	16,721
Depreciation	939	991	948	845
Selling and General Expenses	6,183	5,969	5,662	5,076
Interest, Discounts, and Miscellaneous Expenses	291	354	264	255
Net Income After Taxes	1,163	1,406	1,355	1,387

University Associates

WILLINGTON ORGANIZATIONAL STRUCTURE SHEET

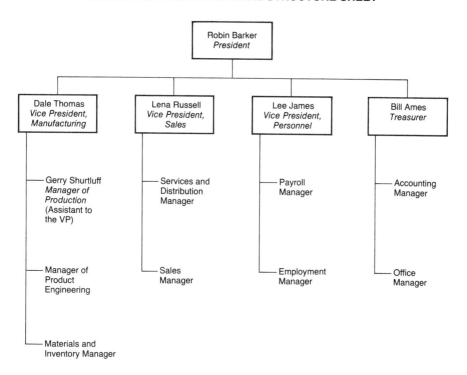

Robin Barker
President

Dale Thomas
*Vice President,
Manufacturing*

Lena Russell
*Vice President,
Sales*

Lee James
*Vice President,
Personnel*

Bill Ames
Treasurer

Gerry Shurtluff
*Manager of
Production*
(Assistant to
the VP)

Services and
Distribution
Manager

Payroll
Manager

Accounting
Manager

Manager of
Product
Engineering

Sales
Manager

Employment
Manager

Office
Manager

Materials and
Inventory Manager

WILLINGTON ROLE SHEET I

Robin Barker: You are the 45-year-old president of Willington, Inc., a small manufacturing firm you founded fifteen years ago. From the beginning, you have been the driving force behind the organization: you raised the money and you worked long and hard in the early years, even taking over many of the key roles in the operations of the company yourself.

You have carefully selected additional employees as the company has grown, and you have recognized the need to delegate some of your former duties to various production and staff departments. You still maintain close contact with day-to-day operations, but you try to let your middle managers do their jobs in their own ways, as long as they get results.

Over the past three years, profits have declined 15 percent, and your return on investment has dropped to 10 percent. The latest figures show sales are down another 1 percent against this month last year, and another middle manager in production has just submitted his resignation to join one of the two new companies that have entered the picture in the last three years. Your competitors are taking their share of the market, but you believe that the decline in profits and sales and the high turnover of your middle managers are connected and are caused by internal problems. You believe that an increase in cooperation between the management staff and the production departments could be the answer to your problems.

Your vice president of personnel, Lee James, has attempted several programs to increase cooperation and coordination among staff and production departments, but all of them have failed. You believe the fault may lie with the production people and not with the programs. Therefore, at the suggestion of James, you have asked several organization development consulting firms to visit your company to interview James; Dale Thomas, vice president of manufacturing; Gerry Shurtluff, production manager; and yourself, and to present their ideas for solving the company's problem.

Unfortunately, your vice president of sales, Lena Russell, is away on business, but you do not believe the problems are in sales anyway, and your treasurer, Bill Ames, does not need to meet with the consultants.

WILLINGTON ROLE SHEET II

Lee James: You are the 35-year-old vice president of personnel for Willington, Inc., a small manufacturing company. You have been with the company for four years, since receiving your M.B.A. from Downtown University. The president of the company, Robin Barker, has a lot of confidence in your ability and has gone along with several unsuccessful programs you designed to alleviate problems caused by lack of cooperation among the departments. You believe the program failures have been due to the attitudes of production people, especially the production manager, Gerry Shurtluff, who seems to do everything possible to make your job difficult.

You have convinced Barker that cooperation and coordination problems between managers and production departments are the key to the declining profits of the company (15 percent decline over the last three years) and the high turnover among middle managers. The increases in outside competition are important considerations, of course, but you believe a united management effort can overcome any competition, especially since Willington has a twelve-year head start.

You are at odds with the vice president of manufacturing, Dale Thomas, who has said that there are too many managers in the company and that Barker should take greater control. On the contrary, you believe that cooperation among departments would be enhanced if Barker decentralized control.

You are strongly in favor of initiating a long-term, comprehensive program of organization development and have asked Barker to invite several consulting firms in to talk with key people. You suggested several firms yourself, and you look forward to meeting with their representatives and starting a program.

WILLINGTON ROLE SHEET III

Dale Thomas: You are the 50-year-old vice president of manufacturing for Willington, Inc., a small manufacturing company. You have been with the company since its beginning fifteen years ago and have worked your way up from production worker to your present position. Along the way you have earned a B.S. in engineering in night school. You know that you are competent and doing a good job.

As the company has grown, you have seen the organization structure become overloaded with managers and have seen the president, Robin Barker, become less decisive and more dependent on the nonproducers. The overload created by these managers has, you believe, resulted in declining profits for the company (15 percent decline over the last three years). The production manager, Gerry Shurtluff, who acts as your assistant, agrees with you and has some good ideas that you believe Barker should hear and act on.

People like Lee James, the vice president of personnel, are always introducing new people-oriented programs that inevitably fail. You are having a hard time convincing Barker that the overload of staff people is the real problem in the company. Sometimes you think, "What I would do if *I* were president!"

Now, to top things off, Barker has invited several organization development consultants to interview key people in the organization and try to identify existing problems. You don't really know anything about OD, but somehow this just sounds like more management types, which is the *last* thing the company needs.

WILLINGTON ROLE SHEET IV

Gerry Shurtluff: You are the 40-year-old production manager of Willington, Inc., a small manufacturing company. You have been with the company for ten years and hold a B.S. in engineering.

In the last three years, company profits have declined about 10 to 15 percent, and yet you feel sure the production departments have actually reduced their costs during this time, although it is hard to document this. You wish the president, Robin Barker, would ask you about the declining profits because you have some good ideas, but Barker seems to want to keep all control at the top.

You know that some of the high turnover among middle managers in the production area has been caused by the "bright kids" on the management staff. Lee James, the vice president of personnel, has Barker's ear and keeps introducing ridiculous personnel programs that are doomed to failure before they begin. James is an O.K. sort of person but needs to talk to people who are closer to the problems before designing programs.

If Barker would only ask your opinion, you could show how the competition could be beaten by making a few minor product changes and by getting rid of some of the management staff. The production people can provide as many good ideas as the management, and the ideas will be more relevant.

You know that Dale Thomas, vice president of manufacturing, who hired you ten years ago as chief production assistant, backs your position, but Barker does not ask advice of either of you. Now Barker has asked you to talk with some outside organization development people, who, you are sure, will want to institute some human relations training. What a waste of time!

WILLINGTON CONSULTING AGENDA SHEET

1. Develop and record a strategy for entry, initial diagnosis, and contracting with Willington, Inc.
2. Implement the strategy.
   - Interviews limited to ten minutes each
   - Only one consulting team present at an interview
3. Develop and record diagnosis and suggested action steps.

(One hour for items 1, 2, and 3.)

4. Present strategy, diagnosis, and action steps to Willington role players. (Presentations limited to five minutes each.)
5. Company discusses presentations and records reactions. (Twenty minutes.)

231. BALANCE OF POWER:
A COOPERATION/COMPETITION ACTIVITY

Goals

I. To explore the effects of collaboration and competition strategies in group problem solving.

II. To study how task-relevant information is shared between groups.

III. To increase awareness of the influence that leaders (or political systems) have on decision making in groups.

Group Size

Three groups of ten members each. Several three-group sections may be directed simultaneously.

Time Required

Approximately two and one-half hours.

Materials

I. A copy of the Balance of Power Instruction Sheet for each participant.

II. A copy of one of the following for each participant, according to group: Balance of Power Alpha Information Sheet, Balance of Power Gamma Information Sheet, or Balance of Power Omega Information Sheet.

III. A copy of the Balance of Power Computation Table for the facilitator.

IV. The following 3" x 5" file cards:

35 cards with the word "food";

20 cards with the word "uranium";

20 cards with the word "lead";

80 cards with the words "atomic weapon."

V. Blank paper and a pencil for each participant.

VI. Newsprint, masking tape, and a felt-tipped marker.

Physical Setting

A room large enough for the three groups to meet comfortably and independently.

Process

I. The facilitator divides participants into three groups of ten each: Alpha, Gamma, and Omega.

II. The facilitator distributes a copy of the Balance of Power Instruction Sheet to each group member, answering any questions.

III. The facilitator gives a copy of the appropriate information sheet to each group member, according to group.

IV. Each group has thirty minutes to:

A. Choose a leader (or establish a political system).

B. Assign workers to different jobs according to each group's list of resources and goals and the joint decision of the group.

C. Record all worker assignments and compute the number of unit cards needed.

D. Send a representative to the facilitator (only one group's representative may be with the facilitator at a time) to have unit card computations verified, to give the facilitator a list of worker assignments, and to receive unit cards. (The facilitator computes unit cards according to the Balance of Power Computation Table, which is not to be shown to the teams because it contains information that is not shared by all groups.)

E. Decide as a group what to trade with other groups and appoint a representative to meet with representatives of the other two groups to engage in international discussion and trade.

V. Representatives negotiate a distribution of food and atomic power, using a group-on-group design, in three fifteen-minute rounds (or until a stalemate or acceptable solution has been reached). After the first two rounds, representatives check back with their groups for approximately five minutes of strategy planning. A qualified physicist can present unit cards for uranium and lead to the facilitator during this time and receive an atomic weapon. (Fifty-five minutes.)

VI. Each team meets separately to discuss how it worked together as a team, how well its actual needs were met, and its feelings about the activity, taking notes for a large-group discussion. (Ten minutes.)

VII. The three teams meet to share what their actual needs were, how well these were met, and their strategies with each other. (Ten minutes.)

VIII. The facilitator reassembles the large group and leads a discussion of the activity. Any or all of the following questions may be helpful.

1. How did you select a leader for your nation? On what did you base your decision?

2. How did your nation decide to divide your resources? How much influence did the leader have on that decision?

3. If you thought your nation was successful/unsuccessful, how did it succeed in achieving its needs or fail to achieve them?

4. If you were unsuccessful, what would you do differently now?

5. Do nations and people in similar situations use competitive or cooperative models to solve intergroup problems?

6. What are the good and bad points of competitive models?

7. Was it possible to agree on more than one way to solve the problem presented in this activity?

8. What communication and decision-making techniques were revealed?

9. Can we come to consensus on a solution that will help each of us deal with a similar situation in real life?

Variations

I. Group-on-group negotiation sessions may be replaced by rotating representatives conferring with their teams about the negotiation and returning continually to relieve one another.

II. Cooperation and competition may be increased or decreased by varying the number of atomic weapons needed to maintain the balance of power.

Similar Structured Experiences: *Vol. II:* Structured Experience **36;** *Vol. III:* **61;** *'72 Annual:* **78, 83;** *'75 Annual:* **147;** *Vol. V:* **164;** *'76 Annual:* **179;** *'77 Annual:* **189.**

Lecturette Sources: *'72 Annual:* "Assumptions About the Nature of Man"; *'73 Annual:* Win/Lose Situations"; *'74 Annual:* "Conflict-Resolution Strategies"; *'76 Annual:* "Power."

Submitted by Lucian Parshall.

Lucian Parshall, Ed.D., is a co-director of the Human Relations Training Institute of Michigan and a special education consultant for the Michigan Department of Education, Compliance Unit. Dr. Parshall's background is in special education compliance and program development and sociotherapy.

BALANCE OF POWER INSTRUCTION SHEET

Your group represents a separate nation, which to survive must organize and work together. Your nation seeks to gain atomic capabilities while satisfying the basic food requirements of its population, as listed on your information sheet. You are to work as a group, to assign members to do certain jobs and to make trade agreements with other nations. In this situation, of course, the most successful nation is the one that can both feed and protect itself. Within each nation, the manpower used to develop atomic weapons cannot be used to grow food, but with these weapons a nation can maintain a balance of power. The goals of each nation are to feed all citizens successfully and to protect the nation successfully.

When assigning jobs to the individual members of your nation, try to produce the maximum of your nation's needs with the minimum of workers. You can then trade for things that would take more of your nation's workers to produce and that you could not get otherwise. Workers who have been assigned to one job may not be assigned to another during any period. After your nation decides what it wants and assigns tasks, workers send one representative to the facilitator and submit a list of worker assignments. You will receive the appropriate number of unit cards. After you have your unit cards, you must decide what you are going to trade with other nations to fulfill your national needs. Each time your nation obtains one unit card of uranium and one unit card of lead, send your physicist to the facilitator to exchange the cards for four atomic weapon unit cards.

University Associates

BALANCE OF POWER ALPHA INFORMATION SHEET

Procedure

1. Choose a leader (or establish a political system).
2. Assign workers to different jobs according to your list of resources and goals and your joint decision on how best to obtain your goals.
3. Each member writes down worker assignments and computes the number of unit cards received from the facilitator.
4. After obtaining your cards, you are to decide, as a group, what to trade with other groups. Appoint a representative to meet with representatives of the other two groups for up to three fifteen-minute negotiation sessions which other group members are to observe silently. The representatives are to check back with the group after each of the first two negotiation sessions for approximately five minutes of strategy planning before continuing.
5. After the final session, your group is to discuss the activity and how well its actual needs were met and how you worked together as a team, taking notes for a large-group discussion.

Resources and Goals

Natural Resources: There is a lead mine in your nation. Each worker assigned to mining can produce two units of lead.

Food: Your nation needs ten units of food to prevent starvation. One worker (doing nothing else) can produce one unit.

Workers: You may assign as many people to be miners or farmers as you wish; they cannot be both. No one in your nation knows how to produce an atomic weapon. You must find a physicist in another nation who is willing to make the atomic weapons for you.

Goals: (a) You must feed all the citizens of your nation.

(b) You need at least ten atomic weapons to maintain a "balance of power." To produce four atomic weapons, you need one unit of uranium, one unit of lead, and the expertise of a physicist.

BALANCE OF POWER GAMMA INFORMATION SHEET

Procedure

1. Choose a leader (or establish a political system).
2. Assign workers to different jobs according to your list of resources and goals and your joint decision on how best to obtain your goals.
3. Each member writes down worker assignments and computes the number of unit cards received from the facilitator.
4. After obtaining your cards, you are to decide, as a group, what to trade with other groups. Appoint a representative to meet with representatives of the other two groups for up to three fifteen-minute negotiation sessions which other group members are to observe silently. The representatives are to check back with the group after each of the first two negotiation sessions for approximately five minutes of strategy planning before continuing.
5. After the final session, your group is to discuss the activity and how well its actual needs were met and how you worked together as a team, taking notes for a large-group discussion.

Resources and Goals

Natural Resources: There is a uranium mine in your nation. One worker can mine two units of uranium.

Food: Your nation needs nine units of food to prevent starvation. Two workers (doing nothing else) can produce one unit.

Workers: You may assign as many people to be miners or farmers as you wish; they cannot be both. Only one person in your nation knows how to make an atomic weapon; he is a nuclear physicist. He is able to make as many weapons as you have materials for, but he can do nothing else. You do not have to assign this expert to making weapons if you do not wish to do so.

Goals: (a) You must feed all the citizens of your nation.
       (b) You need at least ten atomic weapons to maintain a "balance of power." To produce four atomic weapons, you need one unit of uranium, one unit of lead, and the expertise of a physicist.

BALANCE OF POWER OMEGA INFORMATION SHEET

Procedure

1. Choose a leader (or establish a political system).
2. Assign workers to different jobs according to your list of resources and goals and your joint decision on how best to obtain your goals.
3. Each member writes down worker assignments and computes the number of unit cards received from the facilitator.
4. After obtaining your cards, you are to decide, as a group, what to trade with other groups. Appoint a representative to meet with representatives of the other two groups for up to three fifteen-minute negotiation sessions which other group members are to observe silently. The representatives are to check back with the group after each of the first two negotiation sessions for approximately five minutes of strategy planning before continuing.
5. After the final session, your group is to discuss the activity and how well its actual needs were met and how you worked together as a team, taking notes for a large-group discussion.

Resources and Goals

Natural Resources: You have enough good farm land to produce food for all three nations, but no uranium or lead.

Food: Your nation needs six units of food to prevent starvation. One worker (doing nothing else) can produce two units.

Workers: There are three physicists in your nation who know how to make an atomic weapon. Any physicist can make as many weapons as you have materials for, but he can do nothing else. You do not have to assign these experts to making weapons if you do not wish to do so.

Goals: (a) You must feed all the citizens of your nation.
      (b) You need at least ten atomic weapons to maintain a "balance of power." To produce four atomic weapons, you need one unit of uranium, one unit of lead, and the expertise of a physicist.

BALANCE OF POWER COMPUTATION TABLE

Group Alpha: 10 Members

Receives:

1 *food* unit card per person assigned
2 *lead* unit cards per person assigned
May *not* qualify a physicist

Survival Needs

10 food unit cards
10 atomic weapon unit cards

Group Gamma: 10 Members

Receives:

.5 *food* unit cards per person assigned
2.0 *uranium* unit cards per person assigned
May qualify 1 physicist

Survival Needs

9 food unit cards
10 atomic weapon unit cards

Group Omega: 10 Members

Receives:

2 *food* unit cards per person assigned

May qualify up to 3 physicists

Survival Needs

6 food unit cards
10 atomic weapon unit cards

- No physicist may be qualified to do any other work, if that person is assigned to be a physicist.
- No worker may be assigned to more than one type of work.
- Atomic weapons are awarded only to qualified physicists, who are given four atomic weapons for one unit of uranium plus one unit of lead.

SAMPLE OPTION

Group Alpha:	6 people produce 6 food	*Group Omega:*	9 people produce 18 food
	4 people produce 8 lead		1 physicist
	10 people		10 people
Group Gamma:	5 people produce 2.5 food		
	4 people produce 8 uranium		
	1 physicist		
	10 people		

TOTAL AVAILABLE

$$\left.\begin{array}{l}\text{8 lead}\\\text{8 uranium}\\\text{physicist}\end{array}\right\} = \text{32 atomic weapons} \qquad \left.\begin{array}{l}\text{6 food}\\\text{2.5 food}\\\text{18 food}\end{array}\right\} = \text{26.5 food}$$

TOTAL NEEDS

$$\left.\begin{array}{l}\text{Alpha: 10 food, 10 weapons}\\\text{Gamma: 9 food, 10 weapons}\\\text{Omega: 6 food, 10 weapons}\end{array}\right\} \begin{array}{l}= \text{30 atomic weapons}\\\text{25 food}\end{array}$$

232. MANDOERS: ORGANIZATIONAL CLARIFICATION

Goals

  I. To enable groups undergoing team-building efforts within the same organization to examine management and employee development, organizational effectiveness, and reward systems in the work organization.

 II. To explore the diversity of views among participants regarding complex social and behavioral phenomena.

III. To examine feelings resulting from organizational problems and to identify corrective actions that can be taken to deal with them.

Group Size

Fifteen to thirty-five participants.

Time Required

Two to two and one-half hours.

Materials

  I. A copy of the MANDOERS Precepts for Employee Development, the MANDOERS Precepts for Organizational Effectiveness, and the MANDOERS Precepts for Reward Systems for each participant.

 II. Paper and a pencil for each participant.

III. Newsprint, masking tape, and felt-tipped markers.

Physical Setting

A room large enough for all teams to meet privately.

Process

  I. The facilitator tells the participants that they will be given three sets of "precepts" to read and then work on. He explains that "MANDOERS" (pronounced MAN-DO-ERS) is an acronym for

(1) *MAN*agement and employee *D*evelopment,

(2) *O*rganizational *E*ffectiveness, and

(3) *R*eward *S*ystems in the work organization (both financial and nonfinancial).

He tells the participants that the domain of "precepts"—that is, practical guides to action—lies somewhere between universally applicable personnel principles and highly theoretical concepts. Alleged principles of personnel administration and employee relations often fall flat when diagnosed concretely because so little in the field of personnel management can be accepted unconditionally. Likewise, many concepts, even the most popular and those well grounded in research, seem over-generalized or too vague. Precepts are useful and can be communicated to the practitioner (or manager) who accepts them for what they are: rough judgments about what works in management. These precepts, however, are subject to modification as more experience is reported.

II. The facilitator subdivides the group into teams of four to five members each, either on the basis of expressed interest in management and employee development, organizational effectiveness, or reward systems or on some other basis (such as similarity in organizational employment or previous team assignment).

III. The facilitator assigns each group to work on one of the sets of precepts: employee development, organizational effectiveness, or reward systems. (Each of the three sets of precepts should be assigned to at least one of the groups, depending on the apparent needs and interests of the teams.)

IV. Each team is given forty minutes to reach a consensus and prepare a report on the following questions, using the appropriate set of precepts as a guide:

1. What are the main problems in organizational effectiveness (or employee development or the reward systems) in your present organization?

2. How do you propose to deal with these problems *personally* in your organizational role during the next twelve months?

3. What levels of success do you predict, and how will you measure them?

The facilitator explains that participants are not to blame the proverbial "they" for MANDOERS problems (i.e., top management or some higher echelon of the work organization not present) but are to use the precepts as a stimulus to focus attention and energy on a problem.

V. The facilitator calls the teams together and posts the team reports on newsprint.

VI. The facilitator leads a discussion of what was learned in the groups, new information generated during the activity, generalizations that could be made, and possible applications to the work situation. (This is often a heady experience for an organization and may lead to an open airing of suppressed feelings about "how rewards are given out around here," secret pay policies, "phony" promotions, folklore about particular classifications and jobs, and status symbols.)

Variations

I. The activity may be conducted separately for top management and middle management teams, followed by a confrontation meeting conducted by the facilitator in the action-planning mode.

II. All levels of management can share the perceptions and work through various proposals for change at the same time.

III. The activity may be used with individuals who have no work or employment bond. A task can be created for the teams that would lead to a discussion of the MANDOERS precepts.

IV. A wage and salary specialist knowledgeable about the employer's compensation policies and practices can be present to answer technical questions. This specialist may be able to recommend changes in the pay system or policies of the organization at a later date based on what has been learned during the session.

Similar Structured Experience: *Vol. III:* Structured Experience **66.**

Lecturette Sources: *'74 Annual:* "Team-Building"; *'77 Annual:* "Team Development: A Training Approach," "Intervening in Organizations Through Reward Systems"; *'78 Annual:* "Strategies for Designing an Intervention."

Submitted by Thomas H. Patten, Jr.

Thomas H. Patten, Jr., Ph.D., is a professor of organizational behavior and personnel management in the School of Labor and Industrial Relations, Michigan State University, East Lansing, Michigan. He is the author of fifty articles and five books, his latest being Pay: Employee Compensation and Incentive Plans. *Dr. Patten's background is in personnel management, human resource planning and development, employee compensation systems, and organization development (with an emphasis on team building and management by objectives).*

MANDOERS PRECEPTS FOR EMPLOYEE DEVELOPMENT

Every executive or manager should:

1. Treat each employee as an individual.
   - Recognize individual differences.
   - Vary developmental methods to suit each employee.
2. Recognize that every person's development is ultimately self-development.
   - Understand that development is not something you "do" to a person.
   - Avoid trying to live the other person's life; encourage employees to get in touch with themselves and to work toward personal goals.
3. Allow employees to express themselves at work by not forcing them to conform to a mold.
   - Recognize that there are many successful and organizationally acceptable ways to accomplish the same task.
   - Build upon employees' personal strengths.
4. Use the present job and day-to-day work assignments to develop employees.
   - Plan to "stretch" people by exhausting their learning opportunities in their present jobs.
   - Do not emphasize promotions as the sole goal of development.
5. Provide an atmosphere of equal opportunity for development.
   - Allow everyone to grow.
   - Avoid artificial barriers of sexism, racism, and ageism.
   - Recognize that moral values beyond the work place have an effect on development.
6. Recognize the distinction between "person" as the individual contributor and "manager" as the supervisor of the work of others.
   - Provide opportunities for the growth of individuals who appear to lack interest or skill in supervising others.
   - Allow managers wide discretion in problem solving and decision making.
   - Take risks and tolerate some errors until subordinates have learned their jobs well.
7. Hold subordinate managers responsible for the development of employees reporting to them.
   - Do not abdicate developmental responsibilities to the personnel office.
   - Inquire about developmental activities carried out by subordinates.
8. Provide open, honest feedback on job performance.
   - Level with employees.
   - Accept feedback from subordinates.
   - Formalize the feedback process in writing when possible.

MANDOERS PRECEPTS FOR ORGANIZATIONAL EFFECTIVENESS

Every executive or manager should:

1. Establish and communicate organizational objectives.
   - Develop organizational objectives that are consistent with those of the organization.
   - Communicate objectives to subordinates.
   - Adjust objectives to meet changing needs.
   - Establish criteria for determining the progress of subordinates in meeting these objectives.

2. Establish an organization that is simple in concept and responsive to new requirements and that defines individual responsibilities clearly.

3. Develop a competent staff.
   - Staff the organization with capable people, develop replacements for all positions, and initiate action to replace employees not adequately discharging their responsibilities.
   - Provide opportunities for all employees to realize their full potential through regular review of achievements and shortcomings and guidance to improve performance.

4. Ensure organizational effectiveness.
   - Perform completed staff work and develop and recommend solutions for problems.
   - Understand line and staff relationships and use staff members effectively.
   - Encourage innovation by developing an atmosphere in which employees will freely contribute ideas.
   - Hold administrative procedures and controls to a minimum.
   - Seek changes in policies and procedures when improved efficiency will result.
   - Communicate employee attitudes to organizational superiors and resolve employee complaints quickly.

5. Represent the employing organization to the public.
   - Show enthusiasm for the employing organization, its products, and/or its services.
   - Use discretion in making public statements about the organization.
   - Make no commitments that cannot be fulfilled.
   - See that outside inquiries or complaints are handled promptly and well.

MANDOERS PRECEPTS FOR REWARD SYSTEMS

Every executive or manager should:

1. Reward employees according to job performance.
   - Use pay as an incentive.
   - Recommend pay changes, status changes, and other formal recognition for high performance.
   - Reward subordinates in accordance with their contributions and performance.
2. Communicate performance results formally and informally to all employees.
3. Assure that every employee is properly classified and compensated.
   - Take the initiative in seeking changes in classification and pay where warranted.
   - Keep job descriptions up-to-date and properly applied.
4. Determine if financial rewards beyond base salary are justified.
   - Attach an incentive bonus to key managerial and professional jobs.
   - Restrict the remuneration of those in lower echelon positions to base compensation and fringe benefits.
5. Insist upon and fairly administer an "exceptional" pay policy.
   - Seek exceptions to policies and rules if equity and/or outstanding performance are involved.
   - Do not overextend an exceptional policy.
6. Help weak performers improve and take corrective action as needed.
   - Remove weak performers if coaching and counseling do not help them improve.
   - Use the power to demote and discharge with care, considering such alternatives as attrition, outplacement, early retirement, medical retirements, etc.
7. Be prepared to explain decisions on rewards and penalties to employees and provide authoritative and honest information on the administration of rewards and penalties.

INTRODUCTION TO THE
INSTRUMENTATION SECTION

In previous *Annuals* this introduction has served to explore a variety of important issues regarding the use of instruments in training and development. Perhaps the concern most commonly shared by group facilitators has to do with training effectiveness. Even group facilitators who design and conduct research studies evaluating training effects are well aware that they work in the "tainted" real world rather than in an experimentally "pure" laboratory. We can, however, say with some degree of research-based confidence that one important aid to change is *data*, especially data that are understandable (not mysterious), that reflect actual behavior, and that are discrepant from some ideal or desired self-image (see Bowers & Franklin [1974], Nadler [1977], and Peak [1955] for increasingly sophisticated discussions). Paper-and-pencil instruments are the most common and convenient approach to gathering such data. They are useful not only to examine individuals' behavior, but also to collect data in groups and organizations.

There are, by nature, disadvantages as well as advantages to using instruments in small groups. These issues are discussed at length in the introduction to the Instrumentation section of the 1973 *Annual*. Basically, efforts toward removing mysticism and allowing for adequate processing of the data generated will enable the facilitator to avoid the major pitfalls. The 1974 *Annual* introduction to Instrumentation briefly summarizes the steps in the proper use of instruments, a discussion that appears in much more detail in Pfeiffer, Heslin, and Jones (1976), while in the 1975 *Annual* this introduction consists of a tabular presentation rating the importance of each of twenty-two dimensions or concerns when choosing an instrument for one of four purposes (training, organizational assessment, personnel selection, or research). Again, a more detailed discussion is to be found in Pfeiffer, Heslin, and Jones (1976). In the 1976 and 1977 *Annuals*, important dimensions of instruments are explored: the nature of data on a subjective (soft) to objective (hard) dimension (1976) and the development of norms (1977).

There are two basic sources of instruments that are particularly useful for group facilitators. The first, noted above: Pfeiffer, Heslin, and Jones's *Instrumentation in Human Relations Training* (1976), which not only reviews ninety-two instruments but includes a basic, understandable introduction to the use of instruments, written especially for the group facilitator. The second is the categorization scheme in the second edition of Pfeiffer and Jones's *Reference Guide to Handbooks and Annuals* (1977), which presents a clear typology that includes all instruments published in the six volumes of *A Handbook of Structured Experiences for Human Relations Training* and in the 1972 through 1977 *Annuals*. For those wishing to go further in understanding specific instruments, the series of *Mental Measurements Yearbooks* edited by Buros (1972) over the past thirty-five years provides extensive evaluations of hundreds of psychological tests.

PSYCHOLOGICAL DEPTH AS A MAJOR DIMENSION

One major dimension along which instruments can be rated is the *psychological depth* or *intensity of psychological impact* the instrument may have. For example, the Embedded

Figure Test (Witkin, 1950) is a measure of internal vs. external control (see Rotter, 1966) —the extent to which an individual feels controlled by, vs. able to control, his or her environment. Much research has shown this personality measure to have important behavioral implications. People who are severely depressed often feel that they cannot control or change their environment, a feeling that reinforces the depression. Use of a test measuring internal/external control as part of a training experience could have severe and undesirable effects unless the facilitator provides individual attention to participants, is skilled at doing so, and is thoroughly familiar with the procedures of test interpretation.

At the other extreme, the Jones-Mohr Listening Test (Jones & Mohr, 1976) utilizes behavioral samples to test listening accuracy. Even though participants may rate quite poorly, the psychological impact is likely not to be very deep, since the specific behaviors involved are clear and obviously changeable. The fact that one scores poorly on a typing test, while no cause for pride, is not a serious result either; if necessary, most people can learn to type adequately, if not perfectly.

Both of the tests mentioned could be said to generate "hard," objective data. The former, however, has a much deeper psychological impact. In a general sense, this quality is *not* desirable in an instrument, for it means that skills of a high order are needed by the facilitator in order to avoid potential psychological harm. Harrison (1970), in a much-quoted article on organization development intervention, noted that the OD practitioner should intervene at the *least* depth needed for the diagnosed problem. In making this point, Harrison was adapting a basic standard for medical practice: intervene so as to cause the minimum trauma consistent with the diagnosis and needed cure. Thus, physicians typically attempt to control diabetes first by a carefully regulated diet. If this fails, oral medication is usually attempted. Only when it is clear that this treatment, too, is inadequate are insulin injections prescribed. Throughout the course of treatment the physician carefully monitors the effects of the interventions.

To complete the analogy: it is possible that listening skills, for example, could be assessed by the Minnesota Multiphasic Personality Inventory, as well as by the Jones-Mohr Listening Test. In that case, the test of choice would be the Jones-Mohr Listening Test, since the MMPI probes deeply into individuals' psychological make-up yet provides no real guidance for behavioral change.

The comparisons made so far are, admittedly, extreme. We purposely selected well-known tests that are used rather frequently and that seem to have reasonable validities. It is likely that often the group facilitator will have a choice of instruments, and it is also likely that few on the list (if any) will be well researched or validated. The facilitator then has ethical commitments to fulfill, first by selecting an instrument that does *not* impinge psychologically on participants any more deeply than is absolutely necessary. Second, the facilitator must provide adequate opportunity for the *processing* of data generated by the instruments selected.

INSTRUMENTS IN THIS *ANNUAL*

The four instruments selected for this *Annual* provide diverse content. The Organizational Norms Opinionnaire is designed to generate organization-level sensing data for organizational diagnosis. The Critical Consulting Incidents Inventory is intended for use in professional development training seminars. Individual behavioral styles are the outcome measures. The Mach V Attitude Inventory is the most recent version of a well-known research instrument designed to tap Machiavellianism, an individual personality trait with demonstrated behavioral implications. In contrast, Phases of Integrative Problem Solving is group centered and has no meaning at the individual level. It is designed for use in group-process skill training in real-world settings. In using these or any other instruments, the facilitator should take the time to evaluate his choices in light of the nature of the participants and their needs.

REFERENCES

Bowers, D. G., & Franklin, J. L. Basic concepts of survey feedback. In J. W. Pfeiffer & J. E. Jones (Eds.), *The 1974 annual handbook for group facilitators*. La Jolla, Calif.: University Associates, 1974.

Buros, O. K. (Ed.). *The seventh mental measurements yearbook*. Highland Park, N.J.: Gryphon, 1972.

Harrison, R. Choosing the depth of organizational intervention. *Journal of Applied Behavioral Science*, 1970, *6*, 181-202.

Jones, J. E., & Mohr, L. *The Jones-Mohr listening test*. La Jolla, Calif.: University Associates, 1976.

Nadler, D. A. *Feedback and organization development*. Reading, Mass.: Addison-Wesley, 1977.

Peak, H. Attitude and motivation. In M. R. Jones (Ed.), *Nebraska symposium on motivation*. Lincoln, Neb.: University of Nebraska Press, 1955.

Pfeiffer, J. W., Heslin, R., & Jones, J. E. *Instrumentation in human relations training* (2nd ed.). La Jolla, Calif.: University Associates, 1976.

Pfeiffer, J. W., & Jones, J. E. *Reference guide to handbooks and annuals* (2nd ed.). La Jolla, Calif.: University Associates, 1977.

Rotter, J. B. Generalized expectancies for internal versus external control of reinforcement. *Psychological Monographs*, 1966, *80* (1, Whole No. 609).

Witkin, H. A. Individual differences in ease of perception of embedded figures. *Journal of Personnel*, 1950, *19*, 1-15.

ORGANIZATIONAL NORMS OPINIONNAIRE

Mark Alexander

In any organization there are various norms of behavior that influence the effectiveness and job satisfaction of the employees. Norms can be positive (by supporting the organization's goals and objectives) or negative (by promoting behavior that works against organizational goals).

This opinionnaire is designed to identify these organizational norms and to divide them into the following ten categories:

1. organizational/personal pride
2. performance/excellence
3. teamwork/communication
4. leadership/supervision
5. profitability/cost effectiveness
6. colleague/associate relations
7. customer/client relations
8. innovativeness/creativity
9. training/development
10. candor/openness.

Suggested Uses

The opinionnaire can be used for several purposes: team building, management development, and organization assessment and diagnosis. For team-building purposes, group profiles can be developed through a consensus-finding process and used to identify problems. Similarly, a study of the norms and their effects on individual motivation and behavior is helpful in management development.

An especially valuable use is for organizational assessment and diagnosis. By measuring norms in each of the ten categories to see whether they are positive or negative, an organization can develop its own "normative profile." In effect, this normative profile is a statement of the strengths and weaknesses of the organization on a behavioral level. Thus, the organization can use the Organizational Norms Opinionnaire as a basis for initiating changes in work-group norms and behavior.

Although the items in the opinionnaire are phrased to be as generally useful as possible, the facilitator should feel free to adapt them to fit a particular situation.

BACKGROUND READING

Alexander, M. Organizational norms. In J. E. Jones & J. W. Pfeiffer (Eds.), *The 1977 annual handbook for group facilitators*. La Jolla, Calif.: University Associates, 1977.

Mark Alexander is the director of the Management Services Center and an assistant professor of business administration at St. Francis Xavier University in Antigonish, Nova Scotia. He is currently doing consulting involving the quality of work life and leadership development with trade union leaders and first-line supervisors. Mr. Alexander's background is in industry in the areas of management and organization development.

ORGANIZATIONAL NORMS OPINIONNAIRE
Mark Alexander

Instructions: This opinionnaire is designed to help you determine the norms that are operating in your organization. The opinionnaire asks you to assess what the reaction of most persons in your organization *would be* if another person said a particular thing or behaved in a particular manner. For example, the first item reads:

"If an employee in your organization were to criticize the organization and the people in it . . . most other employees would . . ."

To complete this statement, choose one of the following five alternatives:

A. Strongly agree with or encourage it
B. Agree with or encourage it
C. Consider it not important
D. Disagree with or discourage it
E. Strongly disagree with or discourage it

Choose the alternative that you think would be the most common response to the action or behavior stated and place the letter corresponding to that alternative in the blank space following each item. Complete all forty-two statements in the same manner, being as honest as possible.

If an employee in your organization were to . . .

Most Other Employees Would:

1. criticize the organization and the people in it . . . _____

2. try to improve things even though the operation is running smoothly . . . _____

3. listen to others and try to get their opinions . . . _____

4. think of going to a supervisor with a problem . . . _____

5. look upon himself/herself as being responsible for reducing costs . . . _____

6. take advantage of a fellow employee . . . _____

7. keep a customer or client waiting in order to look after matters of personal convenience . . . _____

8. suggest a new idea or approach for doing things . . . _____

9. actively look for ways to expand his/her knowledge in order to be able to do a better job . . . _____

10. talk freely and openly about the organization and its problems . . . _____

11. show genuine concern for the problems that face the organization and make suggestions about solving them . . . _____

12. suggest that employees should do only enough to get by . . . _____

13. go out of his/her way to help other members of the work group . . . _____

14. look upon the supervisor as a source of help and development . . . _____

15. purposely misuse equipment or privileges . . . _____

16. express concern for the well-being of other members of the organization . . . _____

17. attempt to find new and better ways to serve the customer or client . . .   _____

18. attempt to experiment in order to do things better in the work situation . . .   _____

19. show enthusiasm for going to an organization-sponsored training and development program . . .   _____

20. suggest confronting the boss about a mistake or something in the boss's style that is creating problems . . .   _____

21. look upon the job as being merely eight hours and the major reward as the month-end paycheck . . .   _____

22. say that there is no point in trying harder, as no one else does . . .   _____

23. work on his/her own rather than work with others to try to get things done . . .   _____

24. look upon the supervisor as someone to talk openly and freely to . . .   _____

25. look upon making a profit as someone else's problem . . .   _____

26. make an effort to get to know the people he/she works with . . .   _____

27. sometimes see the customer or client as a burden or obstruction to getting the job done . . .   _____

28. criticize a fellow employee who is trying to improve things in the work situation . . .   _____

29. mention that he/she was planning to attend a recently announced organization training program . . .   _____

30. talk openly about problems facing the work group, including personalities or interpersonal problems . . .   _____

31. talk about work with satisfaction . . .   _____

32. set very high personal standards of performance . . .   _____

33. try to make the work group operate more like a team when dealing with issues or problems . . .   _____

34. look upon the supervisor as the one who sets the standards of performance or goals for the work group . . .   _____

35. evaluate expenditures in terms of the benefits they will provide for the organization . . .   _____

36. always try to treat the customer or client as well as possible . . .   _____

37. think of going to the boss with an idea or suggestion . . .   _____

38. go to the boss to talk about what training he/she should get in order to do a better job . . .   _____

39. be perfectly honest in answering this questionnaire . . .   _____

40. work harder than what is considered the normal pace . . .   _____

41. look after himself/herself before the other members of the work group . . .   _____

42. do his/her job even when the supervisor is not around . . .   _____

ORGANIZATIONAL NORMS OPINIONNAIRE SCORE SHEET

Instructions. On the ten scales below, circle the value that corresponds to the response you gave for that item on the questionnaire. Total your score for each of the ten categories and follow the indicated mathematical formula for each. The result is your final percentage score.

I. Organizational/Personal Pride

Item	A	B	Response C	D	E
1	−2	−1	0	+1	+2
11	+2	+1	0	−1	−2
21	−2	−1	0	+1	+2
31	+2	+1	0	−1	−2

Total
Score _____ ÷ 8 × 100 = [   ] % **Final Score**

II. Performance/Excellence

Item	A	B	Response C	D	E
2	+2	+1	0	−1	−2
12	−2	−1	0	+1	+2
22	−2	−1	0	+1	+2
32	+2	+1	0	−1	−2
40	+2	+1	0	−1	−2

Total
Score _____ ÷ 10 × 100 = [   ] % **Final Score**

III. Teamwork/Communication

Item	A	B	Response C	D	E
3	+2	+1	0	−1	−2
13	+2	+1	0	−1	−2
23	−2	−1	0	+1	+2
33	+2	+1	0	−1	−2
41	−2	−1	0	+1	+2

Total
Score _____ ÷ 10 × 100 = [   ] % **Final Score**

IV. Leadership/Supervision

Item	Response				
	A	B	C	D	E
4	+2	+1	0	−1	−2
14	+2	+1	0	−1	−2
24	+2	+1	0	−1	−2
34	+2	+1	0	−1	−2
42	+2	+1	0	−1	−2

Total Score _____ ÷ 10 × 100 = [   ] %   **Final Score**

V. Profitability/Cost Effectiveness

Item	Response				
	A	B	C	D	E
5	+2	+1	0	−1	−2
15	−2	−1	0	+1	+2
25	−2	−1	0	+1	+2
35	+2	+1	0	−1	−2

Total Score _____ ÷ 8 × 100 = [   ] %   **Final Score**

VI. Colleague/Associate Relations

Item	Response				
	A	B	C	D	E
6	−2	−1	0	+1	+2
16	+2	+1	0	−1	−2
26	+2	+1	0	−1	−2

Total Score _____ ÷ 6 × 100 = [   ] %   **Final Score**

VII. Customer/Client Relations

Item	Response				
	A	B	C	D	E
7	−2	−1	0	+1	+2
17	+2	+1	0	−1	−2
27	−2	−1	0	+1	+2
36	+2	+1	0	−1	−2

Total Score _____ ÷ 8 × 100 = [   ] %   **Final Score**

VIII. Innovativeness/Creativity

Item			Response		
	A	B	C	D	E
8	+2	+1	0	−1	−2
18	+2	+1	0	−1	−2
28	−2	−1	0	+1	+2
37	+2	+1	0	−1	−2

Total
Score _____ ÷ 8 × 100 = [   ] % **Final Score**

IX. Training/Development

Item			Response		
	A	B	C	D	E
9	+2	+1	0	−1	−2
19	+2	+1	0	−1	−2
29	+2	+1	0	−1	−2
38	+2	+1	0	−1	−2

Total
Score _____ ÷ 8 × 100 = [   ] % **Final Score**

X. Candor/Openness

Item			Response		
	A	B	C	D	E
10	+2	+1	0	−1	−2
20	+2	+1	0	−1	−2
30	+2	+1	0	−1	−2
39	+2	+1	0	−1	−2

Total
Score _____ ÷ 8 × 100 = [   ] % **Final Score**

ORGANIZATIONAL NORMS OPINIONNAIRE PROFILE SHEET

Instructions. For each of the ten scales, enter your final percentage score from the score sheet and then plot that percentage by placing an "X" on the graph at the appropriate point. (Negative percentages are plotted to the left of the center line and positive percentages are plotted to the right.) Next, connect the "X"s you have plotted with straight lines. The result is your Organizational Norms profile.

Scale	Final Score	−100%	−50%	0%	+50%	+100%
I. Organizational/Personal Pride						
II. Performance/Excellence						
III. Teamwork/Communication						
IV. Leadership/Supervision						
V. Profitability/Cost Effectiveness						
VI. Colleague/Associate Relations						
VII. Customer/Client Relations						
VIII. Innovativeness/Creativity						
IX. Training/Development						
X. Candor/Openness						

University Associates

CRITICAL CONSULTING INCIDENTS INVENTORY (CCII)

John E. Jones and Anthony G. Banet, Jr.

Human relations consultants often intervene in situations that involve conflict, and the consulting process often is conflictive itself. This inventory is designed to (1) enable consultants to assess their own styles in response to critical incidents that sometimes occur in working with clients, (2) explore a theoretical rationale for making choices in conflict situations, and (3) provide a stimulus for individuals and groups of consultants to consider augmenting their styles.

The Critical Consulting Incidents Inventory (CCII) consists of twenty typical situations that can put pressure on consultants to take action in regard to client systems. The responses were constructed to be indicative of three major options available to consultants: (1) to provide emotional support, (2) to take charge of the situation in a directive manner, and (3) to promote problem solving. These options were extrapolated from Porter's Relationship Awareness Theory (Porter, 1976). Porter has extensively validated an instrument on this theory, entitled the Strength Deployment Inventory (SDI). It measures the gratifications that people seek in their interpersonal relationships in general. The SDI can be used in a wide array of development programs. It is reviewed in Pfeiffer, Heslin, and Jones (1976, pp. 171-172). The SDI can be used in conjunction with the CCII.

Uses of the CCII

The CCII is intended primarily as a "teaching" instrument rather than as a scientifically validated tool. Accordingly, it is best used in a consultant-training context in which individuals are guided in looking at themselves, at the theory, and at alternatives for increased effectiveness in coping with conflict situations in the consulting process.

Groups of consultants can use the CCII to study their styles, to look for possible "blind spots," and to explore ways to support each other in developing productive responses to critical situations. Co-consultants can use the inventory as a means of getting acquainted with each other. (See Pfeiffer & Jones, 1975.)

An individual consultant can use the instrument to study professional development over time by filing the responses and reconsidering them at a later date. In addition, the consultant may share scores on the CCII with key persons in client systems. Such sharing may be accompanied by a discussion of the consultant's ethical principles. (See Pfeiffer & Jones, 1977.)

SUGGESTED DESIGN FLOW

These are the steps suggested in using the CCII.

1. The CCII is introduced and the purposes of its administration are explained.
2. Participants complete the instrument independently, without discussion. They are instructed to respond according to the way they would be *most likely* to behave, rather than the way they think they should.

3. The CCII Scoring and Interpretation Sheet is distributed, and procedural questions about scoring are answered. Participants work independently and do not discuss their results with anyone at this point.
4. The facilitator provides a sample interpretation of his own CCII scores, displayed on newsprint.
5. Participants pair off and interpret each other's scores.
6. Learnings from these pairs are discussed in the total group.
7. The tallies to be recorded at the bottom of the Scoring and Interpretation Sheet are developed by a show of hands. "How many had Support as their highest score?" "As their second-highest score?" "As their lowest score?" And so on.
8. The group discusses the norms.
9. Three groups are formed according to lowest scores: Support, Direction, and Problem Solving. The groups are instructed to develop consensus on the advantages and potential disadvantages of their up-front style in conflict situations with clients.
10. The three groups briefly report and the facilitator leads a discussion of the points raised.
11. The pairs reassemble to explore implications for planning changes in their behavior in critical situations.
12. Reports of planned changes are solicited in a large-group sharing session.

REFERENCES

Pfeiffer, J. W., Heslin, R., & Jones, J. E. *Instrumentation in human relations training* (2nd ed.). La Jolla, Calif.: University Associates, 1976.

Pfeiffer, J. W., & Jones, J. E. Co-facilitating. In J. E. Jones & J. W. Pfeiffer (Eds.), *The 1975 annual handbook for group facilitators*. La Jolla, Calif.: University Associates, 1975.

Pfeiffer, J. W., & Jones, J. E. Ethical considerations in consulting. In J. E. Jones & J. W. Pfeiffer (Eds.), *The 1977 annual handbook for group facilitators*. La Jolla, Calif.: University Associates, 1977.

Porter, E. H. On the development of relationship awareness theory: A personal note. *Group & Organization Studies: The International Journal for Group Facilitators*, 1976, *1*(3), 302-309.

John E. Jones, Ph.D., *is the vice president of University Associates, La Jolla, California. He is a co-editor of* Group & Organization Studies: The International Journal for Group Facilitators *and of the Pfeiffer and Jones Series in Human Relations Training, including* A Handbook of Structured Experiences for Human Relations Training *(Vols. I-VI) and the* Annual Handbook for Group Facilitators *(1972-1978). Dr. Jones's background is in teaching and counseling, education, and organization and community-development consulting.*

Anthony G. Banet, Jr., Ph.D., *is a senior consultant for University Associates, La Jolla, California. He is an associate editor of* Group & Organization Studies: The International Journal for Group Facilitators *and the editor of* Creative Psychotherapy: A Source Book. *Dr. Banet is a clinical psychologist with experience in community mental health and has consulted with numerous public service agencies.*

CRITICAL CONSULTING INCIDENTS INVENTORY (CCII)
John E. Jones and Anthony G. Banet, Jr.

Instructions: Following are twenty critical incidents that require the consultant to respond in some way. For each incident there are three alternative actions that the consultant might consider. *Rank order the options in each item* to indicate what you would probably do in these situations. (Write "1" in front of your first choice, "2" for your second choice, and "3" for your least-preferred choice.) Do not omit any items.

1. You receive a telephone call that is a request for you to make a third-party intervention between the caller and another person. You say . . .

   _____ a. "How do you feel about the situation?"

   _____ b. That you should talk with the other person first.

   _____ c. "Could you give me some background information?"

2. During a training event a participant interrupts by criticizing your "Mickey Mouse activity." You say . . .

   _____ a. "I'm concerned that you're upset."

   _____ b. "Let me reiterate the goals of this activity."

   _____ c. "Let's check it out with others and see what they think."

3. Three hours before a training event that is expected to be difficult you meet your co-facilitator. You . . .

   _____ a. Get acquainted on a personal level.

   _____ b. Instruct the other person regarding your strategy.

   _____ c. Share data and negotiate roles.

4. After hearing your academic and experiential credentials incorrectly represented, you . . .

   _____ a. Let the incident go unnoticed to avoid embarrassment to the person(s) talking about you.

   _____ b. Set the record straight.

   _____ c. Analyze with the other person(s) later how the data about you were distorted.

5. Asked to work for a fee lower than your usual, you . . .

   _____ a. Indicate your appreciation of your client's financial problems.

   _____ b. Quote your fee schedule, justify it, and offer to make a referral.

   _____ c. Explore alternatives regarding how an acceptable remuneration can be negotiated.

6. In a sensing interview the boss discloses that a subordinate's job is in jeopardy. You . . .

   _____ a. Explore the boss's dilemma and feelings.

   _____ b. Test the boss's willingness to deal with the situation openly.

   _____ c. Explore alternative actions the boss might consider.

7. You are coaching a manager to conduct a meeting in which personnel cuts are to be announced. The manager becomes anxious and considers cancelling the meeting. You say . . .

_____ a. "I understand your reluctance to give bad news in public."

_____ b. "It is important for you to consider the possible long-term consequences for such a decision."

_____ c. "Let's look at some ways you might minimize the threat."

8. In planning your consulting activities for the coming year with your partner, you uncover a basic disagreement on priorities. You . . .

_____ a. Make certain that your partner's needs and feelings are acknowledged and carefully considered.

_____ b. Let your needs be known and propose a planning strategy.

_____ c. Approach the planning as an exercise in logical problem solving.

9. A boss calls you to ask your assessment of a subordinate who has recently attended one of your training sessions. You say . . .

_____ a. "I feel good about your taking an interest in your people."

_____ b. "You're talking to the wrong person."

_____ c. "Let's explore the implications of evaluating a person in this way."

10. Immediately prior to conducting a highly important consulting event, you experience a personally traumatic occurrence. You . . .

_____ a. Say to yourself, "The show must go on."

_____ b. Postpone the event.

_____ c. Consult with others to explore options.

11. You have spent a significant amount of effort in preparing a bid for an attractive consultation contract. Afterwards, you learn that the "winning" bidder had inside information that was not made available to you. You . . .

_____ a. Chastise yourself for your naïveté.

_____ b. Demand a full explanation.

_____ c. Reconstruct the bidding process to look for possible learnings for yourself.

12. You are discussing with a client contact person a proposed team-building session for an executive group. When pressed to specify the concrete outcomes that you can guarantee, you . . .

_____ a. Affirm the person's concern that the event be productive.

_____ b. Indicate that you can *promise* no particular results.

_____ c. Work with the person on a statement of goals and a strategy for evaluation.

13. You have conducted sensing interviews with all the members of a work team, and each has voluntarily expressed negative feelings about the behavior of a certain colleague. In a team-building session, that person solicits feedback, but the others say nothing. You . . .

_____ a. Reassure the other person in a light-hearted way that the silence could be positive.

_____ b. Confront the group with its collusion.

_____ c. Work with the person to make specific requests of individuals.

14. Between sessions of a personal growth group one of the members makes a sexual overture toward you. You . . .

_____ a. Thank the person for the compliment and politely change the subject.

_____ b. Confront the need to explore the relationship within the group sessions.

_____ c. Solicit feedback on how you may have behaved to create such an interest.

15. In planning a training event, your co-facilitator argues strongly to incorporate a "favorite" structured experience. You have serious reservations about it since the particular design involves deceiving the participants. You . . .

_____ a. Agree to go along with it in spite of your concerns.

_____ b. Insist on the necessity of undoing the possible effects of the deception.

_____ c. Explore with your partner how the design furthers the goals of the event.

16. In a team-building session, the members are "ganging up" on one person, bombarding that person with negative feedback. You say to the individual . . .

_____ a. "You must be feeling under attack."

_____ b. "You don't have to be a target right now unless you want to."

_____ c. "What would be useful for you right now?"

17. In a problem-solving meeting of a group of managers, one member, whose department is far behind schedule, begins to cry. You . . .

_____ a. Assure the person that it is understandable to be upset.

_____ b. Announce a break so that you can work with the person individually.

_____ c. Explore with the entire group what can be done to improve the situation.

18. You have become increasingly concerned that your client organization is engaging in illegal practices in hiring employees. In a meeting of the executive group, sexist and racist attitudes are expressed. You . . .

_____ a. Say nothing lest you be perceived as judgmental.

_____ b. Confront the group with your concerns about its policies.

_____ c. Suggest that the group discuss ways that the organization might ensure fairness in hiring.

19. In planning a team-building session, you become concerned that the manager's major motivation for having the event is to provide a basis for firing someone. You . . .

_____ a. Reflect the manager's feelings of frustration about the person.

_____ b. State your misgivings and explain that you are unwilling to do a "hatchet job."

_____ c. Look for other ways to resolve the conflict.

20. You have coached an organization's president on conducting an all-management meeting to announce and explore new personnel policies. During the question-and-answer period the boss "puts down" one of the managers for asking a "stupid" question. You . . .

_____ a. Attempt to salve the manager's feelings by making a joke of the situation.

_____ b. Confront the president's behavior as detrimental to open inquiry.

_____ c. Help the manager rephrase the question in order to get useful information from the president.

CCII SCORING AND INTERPRETATION SHEET

Scoring instructions: Sum the points you assigned to the alternative "a" for the twenty items, and then do the same for "b" and "c." Enter these totals in the boxes below.

a. ☐ Support

b. ☐ Direction

c. ☐ Problem Solving

Total 200

Interpretation

The major options available to the consultant in response to critical situations can be classified as follows:

- *Support:* Being sensitive to the feelings of the client contact person(s).
- *Direction:* Controlling situations through confrontation and leadership.
- *Problem Solving:* Assisting others through exploring facts, options, and strategies.

Look at your lowest score. This is your most probable, or "knee-jerk," response in difficult consulting situations. Your middle score represents your most likely back-up posture. Your highest score, of course, indicates your least-often-used strategy or posture. Although this rank ordering may be situation specific, it can give you an overall picture of your consulting style in conflict situations.

Consider the distances between your scores. These can be thought of as a crude index of the "thickness" of your "up-front" and back-up responses. A large score gap can indicate that you will persist for some time before changing to the approaches represented by higher scores.

Go back into the CCII items to study ways that you might more effectively manage your strengths in critical consulting situations. You may wish to plan new behaviors when these types of conflicts arise in the future.

Group Norms. Enter a tally of your group's results in the boxes below and compare them to your own.

	Most Probable	Second Most Probable	Least Probable
Support	☐	☐	☐
Direction	☐	☐	☐
Problem Solving	☐	☐	☐

MACH V ATTITUDE INVENTORY

Richard Christie

Since the publication of Machiavelli's *The Prince* in 1532, the name of its author has come to stand for the use of guile, deceit, and opportunism in interpersonal relations. A "Machiavellian" is traditionally thought to be someone who manipulates others for his own purposes. This inventory attempts to distinguish between the behavior of a person who agrees with Machiavelli's ideas (a "high Mach") and that of a person who disagrees with such ideas (a "low Mach"). It is an effort to measure a person's general strategy for dealing with people, especially the degree to which he feels other people can be manipulated in interpersonal situations.

It is important to guard against the conventional perjorative implications surrounding the term "Machiavellianism." None of the research evidence indicates that high Machs are more hostile, vicious, or vindictive than low Machs. It shows only that they have a cool detachment (the "cool syndrome"), making them less emotionally involved with other people and even with their own beliefs or behavior. In addition, no differences have been found between high Machs and low Machs on the basis of intelligence, social status, or social mobility. The facilitator should stress this interpretive caution clearly to participants.

Development of the Inventory

Machiavelli's *The Prince* and *The Discourses*, which present series of short essays, each augmenting a particular point the author wished to make, were scanned for statements that could be used as scale items. Some editing was necessary, and some of Machiavelli's reflections were condensed and some reversed, in order to counteract the tendency of some respondents to agree with almost any statement presented on a questionnaire. In addition to statements gathered from Machiavelli, others that were believed to tap the same syndrome were included. Mach V is the fifth version of the scale that evolved from the original items.[1]

DESCRIPTION OF THE INVENTORY

Mach V consists of twenty groups of three statements, which fall into three areas: (1) the nature of interpersonal tactics; (2) views of human nature; and (3) abstract or generalized morality. The inventory is presented in a forced-choice format in order to offset the tendency of many respondents to distort their responses on a questionnaire to reflect socially desirable traits.

In each group of statements, one statement is keyed to the variable the scale is supposed to measure; another statement refers to a different variable that has been judged

---

This introduction and inventory are adapted from Richard Christie and Florence L. Geis, *Studies in Machiavellianism*. New York: Academic Press, 1970. Used with permission.

[1]For additional detail on the construction of the scale, see Chapter II, "Scale Construction," in Christie and Geis (1970).

to be equal to the first in social desirability; a third statement is a "buffer" statement that is either much lower or much higher in social desirability than the other two (i.e., high if the two matched items were low in social desirability, low if they were high). The main function of this statement is to disguise the nature of the scale.

The respondent first chooses the statement that is *most true;* then he must decide which of the remaining two statements is *most false.* The third statement is left unmarked. The respondent's total score is determined by the number of high-Mach responses and low-Mach responses. The range is from 40 to 160, with 100 being the theoretical neutral point. Therefore, a score of 160 on Mach V means that every item keyed for Mach is most (or least) like the subject, and the item matched for social desirability is at the opposite extreme. A score key is included, with instructions on scoring the inventory.

PERSONAL CHARACTERISTICS OF HIGH AND LOW MACHS

Using the behavior of high- and low-Mach experimental subjects, it is possible to delineate their characteristics as persons. A handout sheet that summarizes these differing personal characteristics is provided at the end of the inventory.

Emotional Involvement with Others

The essential distinction between the high-Mach personality and the low-Mach individual can be identified as the difference between the "cool syndrome" and the "soft touch." High Machs are relatively unmoved by emotional involvement with others, while low Machs are more likely to do or accept what another wants simply because that person wants it.

Social Influenceability

High Machs are less susceptible to social pressure or influence than are low Machs. This finding suggests that high Machs might be more successful in bargaining, because their detachment enables them to resist social demands.

Conventional Morality

One of the characteristics of high Machs, their slight concern for conventional morality, can be seen as a consequence of their affective detachment. High Machs are less likely than low Machs to accept others' wishes or beliefs without justification.

High Machs will lie or cheat more when given "rational" justification, while low Machs will do so more when personally persuaded. Though opposed to dishonesty in principle, low Machs can be persuaded to lie or cheat if they are presented with a strong, personal inducement, especially in a face-to-face situation. In contrast, high Machs, though not opposed to dishonesty in principle, are less likely to cheat if the rational incentives are low or the costs are high.

Suspiciousness

High Machs' suspiciousness of other people can be seen as another example of their lack of susceptibility to social influence, as contrasted to low Machs' tendency to accept others' definition of a situation. However, high Machs, though suspicious of people, are not so of events, objects, or ideas.

A Cognitive vs. a Personal Orientation

In laboratory tests, it was clear that high Machs tended to ignore the potential aspects of human relations, social values, or ethical considerations in a situation and concentrate instead on the explicit, cognitive aspects. However, high Machs do not *appear* unconcerned; they may express more concern than low Machs, but they are not personally involved in those concerns.

Low Machs, on the other hand, accept implicit "shoulds": one ought to do what he believes in and believe in what he does. High Machs do not show evidence of such constraints.

High Machs concentrate on what is explicit and how to exploit it; they adapt their tactics to the specific conditions—a behavior called "opportunistic" by those who deplore it and "realistic" by those who admire it. They also adjust the amount of their manipulation and change their strategy more subtly than low Machs. High Machs are politic, not personal.

One consequence of their cool, cognitive, specific approach is that they never appear to be "obviously manipulating." The high Mach is the one who gets others to help him in such a way that they are unaware of the techniques used on them.

Although both high and low Machs are sensitive to others, they are so in quite different ways. High Machs use information *about* the other person. Low Machs take others' needs and concerns as their own, looking at the other person as a person, seeing a situation from his point of view, thinking in terms of his feelings and wishes. Low Machs attend more to the particular person confronting them. They get carried away in interactions with others, while high Machs maintain a perspective on the whole situation.

A "soft-touch" low Mach contacts others softly, does not violate the position of other people, and moves *toward* others in contacting them. In contrast, a high Mach does not move himself; instead, he attempts to move others to where he wants them to be.

Exploitation

It seems clear that, given the opportunity and incentive, high Machs will exploit whatever resources the situation provides in order to pursue their goal. However, in no instance in laboratory study were high Machs more hostile, vicious, or punitive toward others than were low Machs.

As this discussion makes clear, high Machs attend to their own cognitive analysis of a situation and view themselves as a fixed reference point in relation to others. Low Machs are influenced by private, implicit assumptions but tend to follow others more easily and view them in a personal way.

Control of Group Structure

As would be expected, high Machs tend to take over leadership in face-to-face situations. They initiate and control the group structure and thereby control both the process and the outcome. They appear to have a greater ability to organize their own and others' resources to achieve a task goal.

USES OF THE INVENTORY

Mach V can be used in several situations. In personal growth groups, the inventory can help to raise individuals' awareness of their own and others' interpersonal styles and beliefs. Leadership and management development courses and training programs would find the data from Mach V useful to the understanding of the characteristics and behavior of both supervisors and subordinates. Also an appropriate use for Mach V is team-building within a group or an organization.

REFERENCES AND READING

Christie, R., & Geis, F. L. Some consequences of taking Machiavelli seriously. In E. F. Borgalta & W. W. Lambert (Eds.), *Handbook of personality theory and research.* Chicago, Ill.: Rand McNally, 1968.

Christie, R., & Geis, F. L. *Studies in Machiavellianism.* New York: Academic Press, 1970.

Geis, F., & Christie, R. Machiavellianism and the manipulation of one's fellowman. In D. Marlowe & K. J. Gergen (Eds.), *Personality and social behavior.* Reading, Mass.: Addison-Wesley, 1969.

Guterman, S. S. *The Machiavellians: A social psychological study of moral character and organizational milieu.* Lincoln, Neb.: University of Nebraska Press, 1970.

Richard Christie, Ph.D., is a professor of social psychology at Columbia University, New York. He is currently doing research on jury selection in political trials and is a co-editor of Studies in the Scope and Method of the Authoritarian Personality *(1954) and a co-author of* Fists and Flowers: A Social Psychological Interpretation of Student Dissent *(1976). Dr. Christie's teaching and research interests are in the broad area of political behavior.*

MACH V ATTITUDE INVENTORY
Richard Christie

Instructions: You will find twenty groups of statements listed below. Each group is composed of three statements. Each statement refers to a way of thinking about people or things in general. The statements reflect opinions and not matters of fact—there are no "right" or "wrong" answers, and different people have been found to agree with different statements.

Read each of the three statements in each group. First decide which of the statements is *most true* or *the closest* to your own beliefs. Put a plus sign (+) in the space provided before that statement. Then decide which of the remaining two statements is *most false* or *the farthest* from your own beliefs. Put a minus sign (−) in the space provided before that statement. Leave the last of the three statements unmarked.

Most True = +

Most False = −

Here is an example:

_____ A. It is easy to persuade people but hard to keep them persuaded.

__+__ B. Theories that run counter to common sense are a waste of time.

__−__ C. It is only common sense to go along with what other people are doing and not be too different.

In this example, statement B would be the one you believe in *most strongly* and statements A and C would be ones that are *not* as characteristic of your opinions. Of these two, statement C would be the one you believe in *least strongly* and the one that is *least* characteristic of your beliefs.

You will find some of the choices easy to make; others will be quite difficult. Do not fail to make a choice no matter how hard it may be. Remember: mark *two* statements in each group of three—the one that is the closest to your own beliefs with a + and the one that is the farthest from your beliefs with a −. Do not mark the remaining statement. *Do not omit any group of statements.*

1. _____ A. It takes more imagination to be a successful criminal than a successful business person.

   _____ B. The phrase "the road to hell is paved with good intentions" contains a lot of truth.

   _____ C. Most people forget more easily the death of their parents than the loss of their property.

2. _____ A. People are more concerned with the car they drive than with the clothes their spouses wear.

   _____ B. It is very important that imagination and creativity in children be cultivated.

   _____ C. People suffering from incurable diseases should have the choice of being put painlessly to death.

3. _____ A. Never tell anyone the real reason you did something unless it is useful to do so.

_____ B. The well-being of the individual is the goal that should be worked for before anything else.

_____ C. Once a truly intelligent person makes up his mind about the answer to a problem he rarely continues to think about it.

4. _____ A. People are getting so lazy and self-indulgent that it is bad for our country.

_____ B. The best way to handle people is to tell them what they want to hear.

_____ C. It would be a good thing if people were kinder to others less fortunate than themselves.

5. _____ A. Most people are basically good and kind.

_____ B. The best criterion for a wife or husband is compatibility—other characteristics are nice but not essential.

_____ C. Only after you have gotten what you want from life should you concern yourself with the injustices in the world.

6. _____ A. Most people who get ahead in the world lead clean, moral lives.

_____ B. Any person worth his salt should not be blamed for putting career above family.

_____ C. People would be better off if they were concerned less with how to do things and more with what to do.

7. _____ A. A good teacher is one who points out unanswered questions rather than gives explicit answers.

_____ B. When you ask someone to do something for you, it is best to give the real reasons for wanting it rather than giving reasons that might carry more weight.

_____ C. A person's job is the best single guide to the sort of person he or she is.

8. _____ A. The construction of such monumental works as the Egyptian pyramids was worth the enslavement of the workers who built them.

_____ B. Once a way of handling problems has been worked out it is best to stick to it.

_____ C. You should take action only when you are sure that it is morally right.

9. _____ A. The world would be a much better place to live in if people would let the future take care of itself and concern themselves only with enjoying the present.

_____ B. It is wise to flatter important people.

_____ C. Once a decision has been made, it is best to keep changing it as new circumstances arise.

10. _____ A. It is a good policy to act as if you are doing the things you do because you have no other choice.

_____ B. The biggest difference between most criminals and other people is that criminals are stupid enough to get caught.

_____ C. Even the most hardened and vicious criminal has a spark of decency somewhere inside.

11. _____ A. All in all, it is better to be humble and honest than to be important and dishonest.

_____ B. People who are able and willing to work hard have a good chance of succeeding in whatever they want to do.

_____ C. If a thing does not help us in our daily lives, it is not very important.

12. _____ A. People should not be punished for breaking a law that they think is unreasonable.

_____ B. Too many criminals are not punished for their crimes.

_____ C. There is no excuse for lying to someone else.

13. _____ A. Generally speaking, people will not work hard unless they are forced to do so.

_____ B. Every person is entitled to a second chance, even after committing a serious mistake.

_____ C. People who cannot make up their minds are not worth bothering about.

14. _____ A. A person's first responsibility is to spouse, not to parents.

_____ B. Most people are brave.

_____ C. It is best to pick friends who are intellectually stimulating rather than ones who are comfortable to be around.

15. _____ A. There are very few people in the world worth concerning oneself about.

_____ B. It is hard to get ahead without cutting corners here and there.

_____ C. A capable person motivated for his or her own gain is more useful to society than a well-meaning but ineffective person.

16. _____ A. It is best to give others the impression that you can change your mind easily.

_____ B. It is a good working policy to keep on good terms with everyone.

_____ C. Honesty is the best policy in all cases.

17. _____ A. It is possible to be good in all respects.

_____ B. To help oneself is good; to help others is even better.

_____ C. War and threats of war are unchangeable facts of human life.

18. _____ A. Barnum was probably right when he said that there is at least one sucker born every minute.

_____ B. Life is pretty dull unless one deliberately stirs up some excitement.

_____ C. Most people would be better off if they controlled their emotions.

19. _____ A. Sensitivity to the feelings of others is worth more than poise in social situations.

_____ B. The ideal society is one in which all people know their place and accept it.

_____ C. It is safest to assume that all people have a vicious streak and that it will come out when the chance arises.

20. _____ A. People who talk about abstract problems usually do not know what they are talking about.

_____ B. Anyone who completely trusts anyone else is asking for trouble.

_____ C. It is essential for the functioning of a democracy that everyone vote.

MACH V ATTITUDE INVENTORY SCORE KEY

Instructions: To find your score on the Mach V Attitude Inventory, locate the combination of letters and plus or minus signs that you chose for each item (group of statements) in the inventory. For example, if for the first group of statements you marked statement B with a plus (+) and statement C with a minus (−), your score for that item would be 3.

Item	1	3	3	5	5	7	Score
1	A+	B+	A+	B+	C+	C+	
	C−	C−	B−	A−	B−	A−	3

Mark your score for each item in the appropriate place in the score column. Do this for each of the twenty items. Then sum the scores and add 20. The range is from 40 to 160, with 100 the neutral point.

Points per Item by Response Patterns

Item	1	3	3	5	5	7	Score
1	A+	B+	A+	B+	C+	C+	
	C−	C−	B−	A−	B−	A−	
2	A+	B+	A+	B+	C+	C+	
	C−	C−	B−	A−	B−	A−	
3	C+	B+	C+	B+	A+	A+	
	A−	A−	B−	C−	B−	C−	
4	A+	C+	A+	C+	B+	B+	
	B−	B−	C−	A−	C−	A−	
5	A+	C+	A+	C+	B+	B+	
	B−	B−	C−	A−	C−	A−	
6	A+	B+	A+	B+	C+	C+	
	C−	C−	B−	A−	B−	A−	
7	B+	C+	B+	C+	A+	A+	
	A−	A−	C−	B−	C−	B−	
8	C+	A+	C+	A+	B+	B+	
	B−	B−	A−	C−	A−	C−	
9	C+	A+	C+	A+	B+	B+	
	B−	B−	A−	C−	A−	C−	
10	A+	C+	A+	C+	B+	B+	
	B−	B−	C−	A−	C−	A−	
11	A+	C+	A+	C+	B+	B+	
	B−	B−	C−	A−	C−	A−	
12	C+	A+	C+	A+	B+	B+	
	B−	B−	A−	C−	A−	C−	
13	C+	B+	C+	B+	A+	A+	
	A−	A−	B−	C−	B−	C−	
14	B+	A+	B+	A+	C+	C+	
	C−	C−	A−	B−	A−	B−	

Points per Item by Response Patterns

Item	1	3	3	5	5	7	Score
15	C+ B−	A+ B−	C+ A−	A+ C−	B+ A−	B+ C−	
16	C+ B−	A+ B−	C+ A−	A+ C−	B+ A−	B+ C−	
17	A+ C−	B+ C−	A+ B−	B+ A−	C+ B−	C+ A−	
18	C+ A−	B+ A−	C+ B−	B+ C−	A+ B−	A+ C−	
19	B+ C−	A+ C−	B+ A−	A+ B−	C+ A−	C+ B−	
20	A+ B−	C+ B−	A+ C−	C+ A−	B+ C−	B+ A−	
						Total Score	

HIGH MACHS VS. LOW MACHS

This list indicates for each characteristic in the left-hand column whether that characteristic is more typical of high Machs or low Machs.

Characteristic	High Machs	Low Machs
Emotional Detachment	X	
Susceptibility to Social Pressure		X
Acceptance of Conventional Morality		X
Manipulation/Exploitation	X	
Tendency to Be Persuaded		X
Capability of Persuading Others	X	
Suspiciousness of Others	X	
Politic Attitude	X	
Personal Orientation		X
Cognitive Orientation	X	
Control over Social Structures	X	

PHASES OF INTEGRATED PROBLEM SOLVING (PIPS)

William C. Morris and Marshall Sashkin

Studying here-and-now processes in groups is one major use of instruments, although a seemingly uncommon one in practice, at least in the sense of using a carefully prepared paper-and-pencil instrument in the here-and-now process of group dynamics training. This is the use for which Phases of Integrated Problem Solving (PIPS), a group-process skill-development instrument, is designed.

The basic purpose of such a use is twofold. First, an experiential learning approach to group problem solving facilitates the development of small-group problem-solving process skills among group members. Second, such learning has greatest impact when it occurs in the context of real and relevant content issues.

Any facilitator who has tried to work on process issues during "on-line" group content work sessions knows that such a task-process combination often presents major difficulties. Sometimes group members may fear dealing directly with touchy process issues and may become enmeshed in the content, ignoring process work altogether. Alternatively, when the content is so threatening that dealing with anything else is more desirable, a group may get "hung-up" on process issues.

One common approach taken by group facilitators is to have group members develop process skills as they work on a simulated problem, thus eliminating any content threat and allowing the facilitator to devote full energies toward guiding the development of process skills. While this training approach is appropriate for many situations, its danger is that group members will not be able to transfer their skills to real life.

PIPS was developed in order to help the facilitator develop group members' process skills in the context of a real group problem, while minimizing the danger of facilitator overload and maximizing the likelihood that skills learned will be transferred.[1] By making it difficult for the group to avoid dealing with process issues or to escape from content work and by providing the group with a structure, the six-phase instrument frees the facilitator to watch for serious group-process problems and to direct more energy toward the skill development of individual members.

THE INSTRUMENT (PIPS)

PIPS provides a rather simple sequential task structure, a basic problem-solving model. Different sets of problem-solving steps have been developed (see Kepner & Tregoe, 1965; Maier, 1966), but all such approaches are similar. All start with defining the problem and gathering information about it and proceed to generating solution alternatives, determining the characteristics of good solutions (goals or objectives) based on the problem definition, evaluating the solutions generated and selecting one to try out, developing implementation plans, as well as plans for tracking and evaluating results, carrying out

---

[1]Floyd C. Mann and William C. Morris created an earlier group problem-solving process instrument. The instrument published here relies on their original training concept but is different in format, framework, and content.

implementation plans, and conducting a final evaluation. This sequence is detailed here in six phases:

Phase	Activities
I Problem Definition	Explaining the problem situation, generating information, clarifying, and defining the problem.
II Problem-Solution Generation	Brainstorming solution alternatives; reviewing, revising, elaborating, and recombining solution ideas.
III Ideas to Actions	Evaluating alternatives, examining probable effects and comparing them with desired outcomes; revising ideas; developing a list of final action alternatives and selecting one for trial.
IV Solution-Action Planning	Preparing a list of action steps, with the names of persons who will be responsible for each step; developing a coordination plan.
V Solution-Evaluation Planning	Reviewing desired outcomes and development of measures of effectiveness; creating a monitoring plan for gathering evaluation data as the solution is put into action; developing contingency plans; assigning responsibilities.
VI Evaluation of the Product and the Process	Assembling evaluation data to determine the effects of actions and the effectiveness of the group's problem-solving process.

Because of the nature of group processes and of group members' interaction process skills, however, group problem-solving discussions rarely proceed so neatly. For example, one very basic process issue is the separation of idea generation from idea evaluation. Yet many real-life groups critique and work on one idea at a time, an approach that has been proven less effective in both experimental research studies and real-life tests (Maier, 1970).

In an effort to ensure more effective group behavior, PIPS guides group members through a number of group-process issues with a series of "key questions." For each of the six problem-solving phases, five process questions and five problem-solving task activities are presented. It was found that the most important issues could be covered in five questions, and research shows that most people can comfortably attend to about five different "things" at any one time (Miller, 1967). The two sets of items are presented in a likely sequence, but it is not possible to sequence group problem-solving work perfectly. The critical point is that the group deal with all the issues—task and process—in each phase before moving to the next problem-solving phase.

Each of the six phases in PIPS is introduced with a question designed to ensure that everyone is aware of the focus of the phase. Similarly, each phase concludes with "publication" of the product—a written, shared activity ensuring that all group members agree on what was decided. This activity also provides a sense of closure to the phase and prepares group members for the next phase.

Technical Considerations

PIPS is normative (value based) to the degree that the authors' beliefs about how groups *should* work are incorporated in it. It is, however, also descriptive in that it is based on laboratory and field research. To the extent that it (1) accurately reflects valid research findings and (2) is used appropriately, it will prove a "valid" instrument. The research base was developed from the theory and training writings of Maier (1966, 1967).

The instrument is self-administering and self-scoring; all items use five-point Likert scales. The items are "transparent" in the sense that the activities being observed and measured are clearly described and more or less desirable states are self-evident. The fact that the facilitator can add to or challenge the item ratings of group members, in addition to the immediacy of the behavior being described, reduces the likelihood of "faking" or "fudging."

USING PIPS

PIPS has been used with diverse groups, including school teachers, administrators, research scientists, youth workers, and physicians. Perhaps the most important prerequisite is group members' commitment to try the instrument. This commitment will come more easily if the facilitator is able clearly to describe the nature of the instrument and its aims. A brief lecturette on group problem solving (see Maier, 1967) followed by a reading and review of the PIPS instructions is often helpful.

Due to the nature of PIPS, not all of the seven steps in using an instrument detailed by Pfeiffer, Heslin, and Jones (1976) are fully appropriate. Of those steps, *theory input, posting,* and *processing* are most important in using PIPS.

PIPS is designed to be used *during* group problem solving, rather than afterwards. It is an instrument guide, not a style test or attitude measure. One advantage is that it does not have a personal focus; thus, individual group members are not threatened in any way. A disadvantage is that group members may react negatively to it because of unfamiliarity with it or because they fear it will take too much time.

Sometimes, a group requires "proof" that working on group-process skills is needed. In that case, PIPS can be used to evaluate a recent group problem-solving discussion. Each group member "rates" the group's discussion according to the questions in Phase I; members then share and discuss their ratings. This procedure is repeated for each phase. Often this process will dramatically highlight the need for an improved problem-solving process.

While every group member should have a copy of the instrument, it is unrealistic to expect all group members to actively use it throughout a discussion. Instead, the facilitator can ask two members to take the responsibility for monitoring the group's discussion process and for ensuring that group members are made aware (1) when the group moves inappropriately from one phase to another and (2) when one of the steps in a phase is not fully accomplished. One person can watch the task items while the other keeps track of the process items. In order that everyone can share in the experience and no one is left out of the group discussion, assignments should be rotated among group members for each phase.

PIPS is designed for use with small groups—from five to fifteen people. With the smaller sized groups, the facilitator might serve as one of the observers and ask only one group member to use PIPS. In the larger sized groups, three or four group members at a time could use the instrument. With a group of ten or more, two subgroups can be formed; one can carry on the problem-solving discussion while the other uses PIPS to observe the discussion. Roles are switched with each phase, so that everyone participates in the task work and in the process-skill learning. In this application the facilitator must help the group discuss the process observations at the conclusion of a phase. It also can be helpful to use an "open chair" technique during the discussion. That is, one of the observers may move into the problem-solving half of the group by taking a chair left vacant for this purpose. The observer, by raising some particular process point or issue that seems particularly important, can learn how difficult it is to persuade a task-involved group to look, however briefly, at process issues.

The Role of the Facilitator

The facilitator plays a key role in the use of PIPS. The instrument was designed as a training aid, not as a procedural crutch that could mechanically improve a group's problem-solving work. Essentially, it is the responsibility of the facilitator to follow up on group-process issues that are brought out by PIPS and to ensure that all group members have an opportunity to practice the interaction-process skills important for effective group problem solving. The facilitator must guide the group in using PIPS, particularly in discussing process issues at the close of each phase and in evaluating the group's use of the instrument (the process part of the final phase).

After a few uses of PIPS, the problem-solving approach that it embodies, both in structure and in process, will be internalized by the group members, who have learned how an "idealistic" problem-solving approach can work if members have the needed interaction-process skills.

REFERENCES

Kepner, C. H., & Tregoe, B. B. *The rational manager*. New York: McGraw-Hill, 1965.

Maier, N. R. F. *Problem-solving discussions and conferences*. New York: McGraw-Hill, 1966.

Maier, N. R. F. Assets and liabilities in group problem solving: The need for an integrative function. *Psychological Review*, 1967, *74*, 239-249.

Maier, N. R. F. *Problem solving and creativity in individuals and groups*. Belmont, Calif.: Brooks/Cole, 1970.

Miller, G. A. *The psychology of communication*. New York: Basic Books, 1967.

Pfeiffer, J. W., Heslin, R., & Jones, J. E. *Instrumentation in human relations training* (2nd ed.). La Jolla, Calif.: University Associates, 1976.

William C. Morris, Ph.D., is an organizational consultant and adjunct professor of psychology at Northeast Missouri State University in Kirksville, Missouri. He was formerly with the Institute for Social Research at the University of Michigan. Dr. Morris is a co-author of Organization Behavior in Action *(1976). His background is in organizational change and development and in research on organizational functioning.*

Marshall Sashkin, Ph.D., is an associate professor of management at Memphis State University, Memphis, Tennessee. He is active in the organizational behavior division of the Academy of Management; is the associate editor of the newsletter of the division of industrial-organizational psychology of the American Psychological Association; is a consulting editor for University Associates, La Jolla, California; has co-authored a text, Organization Behavior in Action; *and is currently working on two books and several research papers. Dr. Sashkin's background is in group dynamics, including leadership and problem solving, and in organization development consulting with a wide variety of organizations.*

PHASES OF INTEGRATED PROBLEM SOLVING (PIPS)
William C. Morris and Marshall Sashkin

How to Use This Instrument

The following six-phase instrument is a *tool* to be used *during* a group problem-solving discussion. Unlike most questionnaires, it does not ask for ideas or opinions; each question identifies an important step that must occur for effective problem solving to come about. On the left-hand side of each page are questions that review *what* should happen (tasks). On the right, coordinated with each task question, is a process question, reviewing *how* the task should be done.

You should have your own copy of the instrument, to help guide the discussion. If at any time you feel that a step is being left out or improperly performed, interrupt whatever discussion is taking place and bring your observation to the attention of all group members. To use the instrument, each group member reads each question in turn and rates the group on that item. If anyone rates the group below "5" ("this step was *fully* accomplished"), the group as a whole reviews that step. Only when everyone agrees that the step was *fully* accomplished does the group move on to the following step.

Doing this is not as complicated as it might sound at first. You will have to look at only *one* page—thirteen questions—at any one time, and the questions are in sequence. That is, the activity described in question 2 should occur *before* the group attempts to respond to question 3.

You might also think that going through each step and taking the discussion time needed to do so will be a lengthy process. However, although the group will probably take more time than usual to solve a problem, the extra time will *not* be a great deal. And, if prior group discussions have been *extremely* poor, you might actually find that this procedure *saves* time. In any case, as the group gets better at solving problems and eventually dispenses with this tool, the time required will diminish and there will also be a clear payoff in effective, quickly implemented solutions.

Each of the six phases follows a basic problem-solving format:

Phase I: *Problem Definition.* Often we assume that we know what the problem is, but just as often we are wrong and are looking only at a symptom or, at best, only part of the problem. The questions in Phase I are designed to guide the group in fully exploring, clarifying, and defining the problem.

Phase II: *Problem-Solution Generation.* People tend to be solution minded, rather than problem oriented. Phase II is designed to prolong the idea-generating process and prevent premature decisions. Although often the solution we choose is the first or one of the first suggested, research has shown very clearly that solutions can be greatly improved by looking at as many alternatives as possible. The more ideas we consider, the more likely we are to come up with a greater number of *good* ideas.

Phase III: *Ideas to Actions. Now* the group is ready to evaluate the ideas and come up with a final solution. Even though an idea may not work alone, it may have a good "part"; time can be taken to combine these good parts of various ideas and even to classify solution ideas into "sets." Each alternative can then be carefully, critically evaluated. People will be more able to help and participate if they do not feel attacked or threatened; rather than weeding out poor alternatives (and making those who suggested them feel defensive), it is better to select the *best* ones and concentrate on those until everyone can agree on one or two solutions.

Phase IV: *Solution-Action Planning.* There is now a solution to try out, and the chances are that it will work more smoothly if the actions needed to put it into operation are carefully planned. This means looking for problems in advance, planning to involve those persons whose support will be needed, and assigning and accepting action responsibilities. Only if the group determines *who* is to do *what* and *when* can the solution have a fair test.

Phase V: *Solution-Evaluation Planning.* Unfortunately, most groups stop at Phase IV, losing the chance to *learn* from experience. Even if a solution is a tremendous success, it is useful to know *exactly* what it was about the actions taken that made the solution work so well. It can then be repeated more easily. If a solution is a total disaster, we may feel like hiding the fact that we had anything to do with it. But it is necessary to know *exactly* what went wrong so that the same things can be avoided in the future. Of course, in real life, solutions generally work moderately well—they are neither spectacular successes nor spectacular failures. Keeping track of exactly what is happening allows minor improvements or adjustments that will help significantly in solving the problem. This is best done not by guesswork or trial and error, but on the basis of hard, accurate information about the effects of actions. This phase offers the greatest potential for learning to solve problems. Again, *what* kind of evaluation information is needed, *who* will obtain it, and *when* must be specified.

Phase VI: *Evaluation of the Product and the Process.* When the "votes are all in," when there is enough information to evaluate how well and to what degree the solution worked, it is time for another group meeting, for final evaluation. At this point it is possible to see what the outcomes were and whether the problem was solved. If the problem or some part of it remains, the group can "recycle"—look at the information it has, perhaps even redefine the problem, and come up with new ideas or try out a previously chosen alternative. It will be necessary to repeat the steps in Phases III to V. If the problem *was* solved, it is important to consider what actions are necessary to keep it from reappearing. This is also the time to review and evaluate how well the group worked together.

The key to using the problem-solving procedure detailed here is to follow each step in each phase to the point at which everyone can agree that the step—and phase—is *fully* accomplished. One group member could be designated a "special observer" for the five task steps and another for the five process steps in each phase. These duties should be rotated among group members from one phase to another. Then no one will be a nonparticipant, and everyone will have the chance to develop some group-observation skills that . are important for effective group problem solving.

Before starting to work with the instrument, the group will need:

1. A copy of the instrument for each group member.
2. Paper and pencils.
3. Large sheets of paper, masking tape, and marking pens (or a large chalkboard and chalk).

Each group member must first do two things:

1. Read these instructions carefully.
2. Make a clear, verbal commitment to try out the suggestions and to put forth the effort necessary to learn to solve problems better.

Phase I. Problem Definition: Exploring, Clarifying, Defining

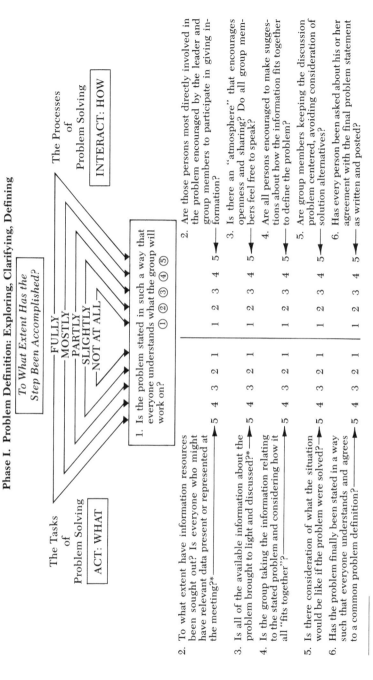

To What Extent Has the Step Been Accomplished?

The Processes of Problem Solving

INTERACT: HOW

The Tasks of Problem Solving

ACT: WHAT

FULLY
MOSTLY
PARTLY
SLIGHTLY
NOT AT ALL

1. Is the problem stated in such a way that everyone understands what the group will work on? ① ② ③ ④ ⑤

2. To what extent have information resources been sought out? Is everyone who might have relevant data present or represented at the meeting?*   5 4 3 2 1

3. Is all of the available information about the problem brought to light and discussed?*   5 4 3 2 1

4. Is the group taking the information relating to the stated problem and considering how it all "fits together"?   5 4 3 2 1

5. Is there consideration of what the situation would be like if the problem were solved?   5 4 3 2 1

6. Has the problem finally been stated in a way such that everyone understands and agrees to a common problem definition?   5 4 3 2 1

2. Are those persons most directly involved in the problem encouraged by the leader and group members to participate in giving information?   1 2 3 4 5

3. Is there an "atmosphere" that encourages openness and sharing? Do all group members feel free to speak?   1 2 3 4 5

4. Are all persons encouraged to make suggestions about how the information fits together to define the problem?   1 2 3 4 5

5. Are group members keeping the discussion problem centered, avoiding consideration of solution alternatives?   1 2 3 4 5

6. Has every person been asked about his or her agreement with the final problem statement as written and posted?   1 2 3 4 5

Record in detail the final problem statement on a separate sheet of paper.

Reproduced by permission from ORGANIZATION BEHAVIOR IN ACTION by Morris and Sashkin, copyright © 1976, West Publishing Company.

*If additional information is found to be necessary, it should be obtained before going further with the discussion.

Phase II. Problem-Solution Generation: Brainstorming, Elaborating, Creating

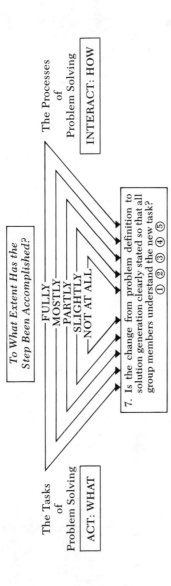

The Tasks
of
Problem Solving

ACT: WHAT

*To What Extent Has the
Step Been Accomplished?*

FULLY
MOSTLY
PARTLY
SLIGHTLY
NOT AT ALL

① ② ③ ④ ⑤

The Processes
of
Problem Solving

INTERACT: HOW

7. Is the change from problem definition to solution generation clearly stated so that all group members understand the new task?

8. Have the rules of brainstorming (all ideas accepted and posted; no criticism; repetition and "piggybacking" on other ideas OK) been reviewed and posted before beginning? —→ 5 4 3 2 1

9. Are as many ideas generated as possible, using all the resources of the group? —→ 5 4 3 2 1

10. When all ideas are out, is the list reviewed in detail, clarifying items when necessary and expanding or adding to the ideas generated? ▸ 5 4 3 2 1

11. Is the group taking time to examine the list and combine various ideas into "sets" of alternatives? —→ 5 4 3 2 1

12. Has the group developed a list of at least several clearly stated alternatives? —→ 5 4 3 2 1

8. Are the leader or other group members taking time to encourage those who might be slower at giving out ideas, pausing and asking for more ideas when necessary?
—→ 1 2 3 4 5

9. Are all ideas recognized and welcomed regardless of their content (e.g., including even ideas that seem "foolish")?
—→ 1 2 3 4 5

10. Is criticism tactfully discouraged and are evaluative comments postponed (e.g., asking for another alternative instead of criticism)?
—→ 1 2 3 4 5

11. Is the group able to prevent any one member from dominating the discussion or imposing his/her frame of reference on the group?
—→ 1 2 3 4 5

12. Have all final alternatives been posted (on chalkboard or newsprint) for everyone to see?
—→ 1 2 3 4 5

Record the list of solution alternatives on a separate sheet of paper.

Phase III. Ideas to Actions: Evaluating, Combining, Selecting

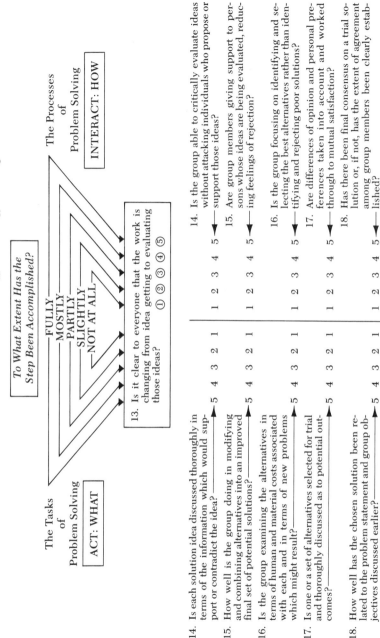

To What Extent Has the Step Been Accomplished?

FULLY — MOSTLY — PARTLY — SLIGHTLY — NOT AT ALL

① ② ③ ④ ⑤

The Tasks of Problem Solving — ACT: WHAT

The Processes of Problem Solving — INTERACT: HOW

13. Is it clear to everyone that the work is changing from idea getting to evaluating those ideas?

ACT: WHAT

14. Is each solution idea discussed thoroughly in terms of the information which would support or contradict the idea?   5 4 3 2 1

15. How well is the group doing in modifying and combining alternatives into an improved final set of potential solutions?   5 4 3 2 1

16. Is the group examining the alternatives in terms of human and material costs associated with each and in terms of new problems which might result?   5 4 3 2 1

17. Is one or a set of alternatives selected for trial and thoroughly discussed as to potential outcomes?   5 4 3 2 1

18. How well has the chosen solution been related to the problem statement and group objectives discussed earlier?   5 4 3 2 1

INTERACT: HOW

14. Is the group able to critically evaluate ideas without attacking individuals who propose or support those ideas?   1 2 3 4 5

15. Are group members giving support to persons whose ideas are being evaluated, reducing feelings of rejection?   1 2 3 4 5

16. Is the group focusing on identifying and selecting the best alternatives rather than identifying and rejecting poor solutions?   1 2 3 4 5

17. Are differences of opinion and personal preferences taken into account and worked through to mutual satisfaction?   1 2 3 4 5

18. Has there been final consensus on a trial solution or, if not, has the extent of agreement among group members been clearly established?   1 2 3 4 5

Record in detail the final trial solution on a separate sheet of paper.

Phase IV. Solution-Action Planning: Planning, Assigning, Coordinating

To What Extent Has the Step Been Accomplished?

FULLY — MOSTLY — PARTLY — SLIGHTLY — NOT AT ALL

The Tasks of Problem Solving — **ACT: WHAT**

The Processes of Problem Solving — **INTERACT: HOW**

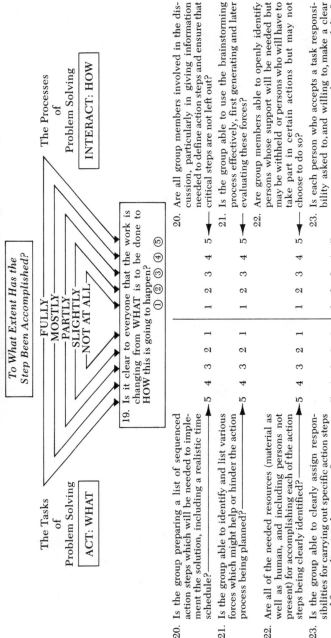

19. Is it clear to everyone that the work is changing from WHAT is to be done to HOW this is going to happen? ① ② ③ ④ ⑤

ACT: WHAT

20. Is the group preparing a list of sequenced action steps which will be needed to implement the solution, including a realistic time schedule? 5 4 3 2 1

21. Is the group able to identify and list various forces which might help or hinder the action process being planned? 5 4 3 2 1

22. Are all of the needed resources (material as well as human, and including persons not present) for accomplishing each of the action steps being clearly identified? 5 4 3 2 1

23. Is the group able to clearly assign responsibilities for carrying out specific action steps and for coordinating that process? 5 4 3 2 1

24. Have all materials (lists, etc.) been collected and responsibilities taken for recording and disseminating the work of the group? 5 4 3 2 1

INTERACT: HOW

20. Are all group members involved in the discussion, particularly in giving information needed to define action steps and ensure that critical steps are not left out? 1 2 3 4 5

21. Is the group able to use the brainstorming process effectively, first generating and later evaluating these forces? 1 2 3 4 5

22. Are group members able to openly identify persons whose support will be needed but may be withheld or persons who will have to take part in certain actions but may not choose to do so? 1 2 3 4 5

23. Is each person who accepts a task responsibility asked to, and willing to, make a clear commitment to carry out that responsibility? 1 2 3 4 5

24. Have all group members agreed to allow these materials (the specific details of the action plan) to be shared with other concerned parties? 1 2 3 4 5

Record on a separate sheet of paper the sequence of action steps agreed to, who accepted responsibility for each step, and the time schedule for actions.

Phase V. Solution-Evaluation Planning: Describing, Monitoring, Contingency Planning

The Tasks
of
Problem Solving

ACT: WHAT

The Processes
of
Problem Solving

INTERACT: HOW

*To What Extent Has the
Step Been Accomplished?*

FULLY
MOSTLY
PARTLY
SLIGHTLY
NOT AT ALL

25. Is the transition from planning for action to planning for evaluation being made clearly with the awareness and consent of all group members? ① ② ③ ④ ⑤

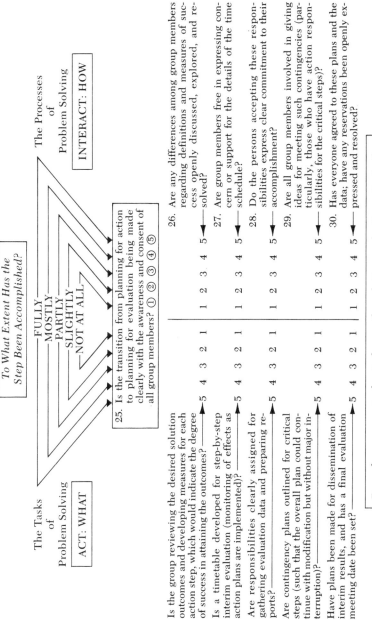

26. Is the group reviewing the desired solution outcomes and developing measures for each action step, which would indicate the degree of success in attaining the outcomes? — 5 4 3 2 1

27. Is a timetable developed for step-by-step interim evaluation (monitoring of effects as action plans are implemented)? — 5 4 3 2 1

28. Are responsibilities clearly assigned for gathering evaluation data and preparing reports? — 5 4 3 2 1

29. Are contingency plans outlined for critical steps (such that the overall plan could continue with modification but without major interruption)? — 5 4 3 2 1

30. Have plans been made for dissemination of interim results, and has a final evaluation meeting date been set? — 5 4 3 2 1

26. Are any differences among group members regarding definitions and measures of success openly discussed, explored, and resolved? — 1 2 3 4 5

27. Are group members free in expressing concern or support for the details of the time schedule? — 1 2 3 4 5

28. Do the persons accepting these responsibilities express clear commitment to their accomplishment? — 1 2 3 4 5

29. Are all group members involved in giving ideas for meeting such contingencies (particularly, those who have action responsibilities for the critical steps)? — 1 2 3 4 5

30. Has everyone agreed to these plans and the data; have any reservations been openly expressed and resolved? — 1 2 3 4 5

Record on a separate sheet of paper the solution-evaluation criteria, the specific evaluation plan (actions, timetable, and responsibilities) and the final evaluation meeting date.

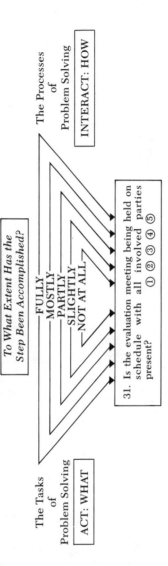

Phase VI. Evaluation of the Product and the Process

To What Extent Has the Step Been Accomplished?

FULLY
MOSTLY
PARTLY
SLIGHTLY
NOT AT ALL

The Tasks of Problem Solving

ACT: WHAT

The Processes of Problem Solving

INTERACT: HOW

31. Is the evaluation meeting being held on schedule with all involved parties present? ① ② ③ ④ ⑤

32. Has information about the effects of actions been collected as planned and made available to all group members? — 5 4 3 2 1

33. Is the group able to compare, in detail, the outcomes with the objectives set earlier? — 5 4 3 2 1

34. Can the group determine whether any new problems have been created and then set plans to deal with these new issues? — 5 4 3 2 1

35. If, based on the evaluation, the problem has not been resolved, does the group return to earlier proposed solutions and set new action plans? — 5 4 3 2 1

36. If, based on the evaluation, the problem has been successfully resolved, has the group considered what further actions, if any, will be needed to keep the problem from reappearing? — 5 4 3 2 1

32. Have all group members been involved in influencing both what the group does and how the group operates? — 1 2 3 4 5

33. To what extent have communications in the group been open, expressive of real feelings, and understood by all group members? — 1 2 3 4 5

34. Have group members been supportive of the ideas and feelings of one another throughout the problem-solving process? — 1 2 3 4 5

35. At various appropriate points throughout the session, have group members openly discussed and critiqued how the group has been working (i.e., critiquing the process)? — 1 2 3 4 5

36. To what extent has the group learned to solve problems with the process detailed in this questionnaire? Will the group be able to effectively use this problem-solving process in future work? — 1 2 3 4 5

37. Overall, how satisfied are you with the way your group solves problems?

INTRODUCTION TO THE
LECTURETTES SECTION

From the inception of the laboratory method of training, the aim has been toward the integration of affective and cognitive learning, with the two aspects reinforcing and "synergizing" one another. In the *Annuals*, we have included a focus on conceptual learning as well as the expected experiential emphasis. In past years, it seemed appropriate to offer a counterrationale to what we sometimes felt was an unjustified anti-intellectual bias (see the introductions to the Lecturettes sections of the 1974, 1975, and 1976 *Annuals*). Today, however, it seems that the vast majority of trainers are more sophisticated than ever in understanding and using the dynamics of the learning process. And there now exist clear models of the experiential learning process (for example, see Kolb & Fry, 1975) that specify the points at which cognitive inputs are needed.

The role of the facilitator in cognitive learning involves responsibility for developing concepts in a basic and clear form. The sources of concepts may be the participants themselves, as in experiential lecturettes (see the introduction to the Lecturettes section in the 1976 *Annual*), the facilitator's own thinking, or the varied professional sources of knowledge accessible to the facilitator. This section of the *Annual* can be a professional resource for the facilitator in three ways. First, the lecturettes are short enough to be quickly and cheaply reproduced as handouts. In this form, they can serve as take-home reminders, or they can be read on the spot and discussed. The facilitator can give a quick overview, allow five to ten minutes of reading time, and then conduct a full- (or small-) group discussion. This procedure, which need take no more than an hour, emphasizes participative, open conceptual learning, just as experiential activities emphasize participative affective and personally oriented learning.

A second use for lecturettes is as the basis for short verbal presentations by the facilitator. Such presentations should typically take thirty minutes or less. Delivering a good lecturette is a matter of skill, but it is a skill that most people can acquire without a great deal of difficulty. The 1975 *Annual* introduction to this section presents some useful tips, but ultimately the success of a lecturette depends on the behavioral skills of the facilitator.

Finally, the lecturettes in this *Annual* and others are intended to stimulate the thinking of the facilitator on rather specific topics. *Annual* users can follow up a subject with further reading (see the Theory and Practice section of this *Annual* and others) and develop their own unique formulations or revisions, which can then be shared with others in group training. It is certain that some users will disagree—perhaps vehemently—with one or another lecturette presentation. Such disagreement can be channelled into productive directions by using the stimulation it provides to rethink one's own position and to refine or modify that position to deal with the problems the user sees in the lecturette.

As summary handouts or group discussion tools, background for verbal presentations, and thought provokers, the lecturettes in the *Annuals* are designed to serve the group facilitator's need for sound conceptual content.

USING VISUAL AIDS

A lecturette is verbal, yet any group facilitator who has lectured and obtained feedback knows that participants want to *see* the key points of the lecturette, even if this involves no more than a summary outline written on a newsprint chart.

The great variety of such aids can be divided into three crude groups, defined by the level of technical sophistication required to use them. At the most basic level are newsprint charts and chalkboard. The mid level includes overhead projectors and handouts. The "advanced" level comprises slides, films, and videorecordings.

Most facilitators will use the technologically sophisticated aids only rarely. They are better reserved for the detailed presentation of information. Videotape can be particularly difficult; its effective use requires considerable skill, when group participants are not themselves being taped. With both videotape and film, one precaution must be kept constantly in mind: as this equipment requires technical familiarity for correct operation, as well as set-up time, everything must be prepared in advance. Slides are easier to use but have even more limited utility.

The overhead projector and handouts, at the mid level of visual-aid technology, can both be most effective for the presentation of tables of data and of complex charts and diagrams. For the most complex tables, an overhead projector is best, since the facilitator can point to the items being examined. For complex diagrams, on the other hand, handouts are better, since participants will not have to try to copy the diagram while listening to the lecturette. Little needs to be said about the technical operation as almost everyone knows how to operate an overhead projector. Handouts can also provide simple, brief summaries of the content of a presentation, which can be consulted during the lecturette, thus giving a clear structure to the talk.

Finally, on the most basic level, are the group facilitator's old standbys: newsprint charts and chalkboards. It should be obvious (yet experience says it is not) that participants should not be forced to decipher illegible handwriting. The simple way around this failing is to prepare charts in advance. (In extreme cases, a friend or an associate can do the writing.) A second major point for the facilitator to remember is to summarize and to emphasize key words; the *reason* for the written presentation is to provide emphasis or to give an outline.

Two guidelines stand out in considering *how* to use visual aids: (1) *have everything ready in advance*, and (2) *keep it simple*. When materials are ready beforehand, the facilitator can be more relaxed and let the lecturette flow more easily. And simply stated concepts can be discussed, refined, and elaborated much more easily than they can be clarified or extracted from a complex text.

When used with conceptual input, visual aids can help provide a *structure* for thought as well as a *focus* on key points. If the complexity of the structure interferes with the thought, however, or if problems with complicated technology obscure the content, the facilitator is better off avoiding such aids and concentrating on making a coherent, lively verbal presentation.

REFERENCE

Kolb, D. A., & Fry, R. Towards an applied theory of experiential learning. In C. L. Cooper (Ed.), *Theories of group processes*. New York: John Wiley, 1975.

COMMUNICATION EFFECTIVENESS: ACTIVE LISTENING AND SENDING FEELING MESSAGES

Jack N. Wismer

"I know you believe that you understand what you think I said, but I am not sure you realize that what you heard is not what I meant."

When a person communicates a message to another person, the message usually contains two elements: content and feeling. Both elements are important because both give the message meaning. However, we often do not understand other people's messages or are misunderstood by others because we forget that meanings are in people, not in words.

The Risk of Communicating Nonacceptance

The communication of mutual acceptance is vital to developing and maintaining work and personal relationships. However, various ways of responding to situations run the risk of communicating nonacceptance. To understand a person's point of view effectively, it is necessary not to communicate nonacceptance. According to Gordon (1970, pp. 41-44), author of several books on active listening, most people, in a listening situation, commonly respond in one or more of the following twelve ways:[1]

1. *Ordering, Directing:* "You have to . . ."
2. *Warning, Threatening:* "You'd better not . . ."
3. *Preaching, Moralizing:* "You ought to . . ."
4. *Advising, Giving Solutions:* "Why don't you . . ."
5. *Lecturing, Informing:* "Here are the facts . . ."
6. *Evaluating, Blaming:* "You're wrong . . ."
7. *Praising, Agreeing:* "You're right . . ."
8. *Name-calling, Shaming:* "You're stupid . . ."
9. *Interpreting, Analyzing:* "What you need . . ."
10. *Sympathizing, Supporting:* "You'll be OK . . ."
11. *Questioning, Probing:* "Why did you . . ."
12. *Withdrawing, Avoiding:* "Let's forget it . . ."

These modes of response may communicate to the sender that it is not acceptable to feel the way he or she feels. If the sender perceives one of these messages as indicating nonacceptance, there is a risk that he will become defensive about new ideas, will be resistive to changing behavior, will tend to justify certain feelings, or will turn silent because the listener is perceived as only passively interested in the sender.

---

[1]Abstracted from Thomas Gordon's *Parent Effectiveness Training*, Peter H. Wyden, New York, 1970. Used by permission.

ACTIVE LISTENING

A more effective way of responding to a listening situation is called "active listening." Gordon (1970) defines active listening as a communication skill to help people solve their own problems. In active listening, the listener is involved with the sender's need to communicate. To be effective, the listener must take an "active" responsibility to understand the content and feeling of what is being said. The listener can respond with a statement, in his own words, of what he feels the sender's message means. For example:

Sender: "The deadline for this report is not realistic!"

Listener: "You feel you're pressured to get the report done."

If the listener is to understand the sender's meaning, he will need to "put himself in the other person's place." Feeding back perceptions of intended meaning allows the listener to check the accuracy of his listening and understanding.

Benefits of Active Listening

An open communication climate for understanding is created through active listening. The listener can learn to see what a person means and how the person feels about situations and problems. Active listening is a skill that can communicate acceptance and increase interpersonal trust among people. It can also facilitate problem solving. Therefore, the appropriate use of active listening increases the communication effectiveness of people.

Pitfalls in Active Listening

Active listening is not intended to manipulate people to behave or think the way others think they should. The listener also should not "parrot" someone's message by repeating the exact words used. Empathy is a necessary ingredient—the listener should communicate warmth toward and feeling about the sender's message by putting himself in the sender's place. Timing is another pitfall; active listening is not appropriate when there is no time to deal with the situation or when someone is asking only for factual information. Also, it is important that the listener be sensitive to nonverbal messages about the right time to stop giving feedback. Avoiding these common pitfalls will make active listening a more effective communication skill.

Principle of Problem Ownership

Since active listening is most appropriate when a person expresses feelings about a problem, it is necessary to ask who owns the problem. The principle of problem ownership can be demonstrated in the following situations.

1. Person A's needs are not being satisfied by his or her own behavior, and A's behavior does not directly interfere with Person B's satisfaction of his or her own needs. Therefore, A owns the problem.
2. Person A's needs are being satisfied, but his or her behavior interferes in some way with Person B's satisfaction of his or her own needs and thus creates a problem for B. B then owns the problem.
3. Person A is satisfying his or her own needs, and his or her behavior does not directly interfere with Person B's needs. In this case, there is no problem.

Active listening is very useful, but it is not appropriate to use if another person's behavior is creating the problem.

COMMUNICATING ONE'S NEEDS

Ineffective Approaches

It is necessary for the person who owns the problem to know how to confront it and communicate his or her needs so that other people will listen. However, people frequently confront problems in a way that tends to stimulate defensiveness and resistance. The two most common approaches:

1. *Evaluating*—which communicates judgment, blame, ridicule, or shame ("Don't you know how to use that machine?"; "You're late again!"). This method has several risks: (a) it makes people defensive and resistant to further communication; (b) it implies power over the other person; and (c) it threatens and reduces the other person's self-esteem.

2. *Sending solutions*—which communicates what the other person should do rather than what the speaker is feeling ("If you don't come in on time, I'll have to report you"; "Why don't you do it this way?"). Sending solutions carries risks: (a) people become resistive if they are told what to do, even if they agree with the solution; (b) this approach indicates that the sender's needs are more important than the receiver's; (c) it communicates a lack of trust in other people's capacities to solve their own problems; and (d) it reduces the responsibility to define the problem clearly and explore feasible alternatives to a problem.

A More Effective Approach

Problems can be confronted and one's needs can be made known without making other people feel defensive. An effective communication message involves three components: (1) owning feelings, (2) sending feelings, and (3) describing behavior.

Ownership of feelings focuses on "who owns the problem." The sender of a message needs to accept responsibility for his or her own feelings. Messages that own the sender's feelings usually begin with or contain "I."

Sometimes, communicating feelings is viewed as a weakness, but the value of sending feelings is communicating honesty and openness by focusing on the problem and not evaluating the person.

Describing behavior concentrates on what one person sees and hears and feels about another person's behavior as it affects the observer's feelings and behavior. The focus is on specific situations that relate to specific times and places.

It is useful to distinguish between descriptions and evaluations of behavior. The italicized parts of the next statements illustrate *evaluations* of behavior:

"I can't finish this report *if you are so inconsiderate as to interrupt me.*"

"*You're a loudmouth.*"

The italicized parts of the following statements are *descriptions* of behavior:

"I can't finish this report *if you constantly interrupt me.*"

"I feel that *you talked considerably during the meetings.*"

A design for sending feeling messages can be portrayed as follows.

Ownership + Feeling Word + Description of Behavior = Feeling Message

Example:

"I (ownership) am concerned (feeling word) about finishing this report on time" (description of behavior).

The effectiveness of feeling messages can be attributed to several factors:

- "I" messages are more effective because they place responsibility with the sender of the message.
- "I" messages reduce the other person's defensiveness and resistance to further communication.
- Behavioral descriptions provide feedback about the other person's behavior but do not evaluate it.
- Although "I" messages require some courage, they honestly express the speaker's feelings.
- Feeling messages promote open communication in work and personal relationships.

SUMMARY

Sending feeling messages and listening actively are skills that can be applied to work, family, and personal relationships.

No one is wrong. At most someone is uninformed. If I think a man is wrong, either I am unaware of something, or he is. So unless I want to play a superiority game I had best find out what he is looking at.

"You're wrong" means "I don't understand you"—I'm not seeing what you're seeing. But there is nothing wrong with you, you are simply not me and that's not wrong. (Prather, 1970, unpaged)[2]

REFERENCES AND READINGS

Gibb, J. R. Defensive communication. *Journal of Communication*, 1961, *11*, 141-148.

Gordon, T. *Parent effectiveness training*. New York: Peter H. Wyden, 1970.

Prather, H. *Notes to myself*. Lafayette, Calif.: Real People Press, 1970.

Rogers, C. Communication: Its blocking and facilitating. *Northwestern University Information*, 1952, *20*, 9-15.

Stewart, J. (Ed.). *Bridges not walls: A book about interpersonal communication*. Reading, Mass.: Addison-Wesley, 1973.

Jack N. Wismer, Ph.D., is an employee development specialist with the Bureau of Land Management, Denver, Colorado. He is currently involved in organization development consulting and conducts public and in-house workshops on management by objectives and communication effectiveness. Dr. Wismer's background is in teaching interpersonal and organization communication, adult education, counseling, and program-evaluation research.

[2]From *Notes to Myself* by Hugh Prather. Copyright © 1970 by Real People Press. Used with permission.

COMMUNICATING COMMUNICATION

J. Ryck Luthi

> Effectiveness of management personnel of all grades is very dependent upon the ability *to communicate* orally not only the policy of the company but suggestions as to how work should be done, criticism of poor work, and the application of discipline, and of course the general field of human relationships. (Lull, 1955, p. 17)

> It seems safe to conclude from research studies that by and large, the better supervisors (better in terms of getting the work done) are those who are more sensitive to their communication responsibilities. They tend to be those, for example, who give clear instructions, who *listen empathically*, who are accessible for questions or suggestions, and who keep their subordinates properly informed. (Redding & Sanborn, 1964, p. 60)

Research leads to the conclusion that there is a positive correlation between effective communication and each of the following factors: employee productivity, personal satisfaction, rewarding relationships, and effective problem solving. Two major components of effective communication are sending and receiving messages. Techniques of listening and verbalizing help in both these dimensions.

FACTORS AFFECTING THE SENDER

Self-Feelings

In the context of each communicating situation, the sender's feelings about self will affect how the message is encoded. The following questions are conscious and subconscious tradewinds that affect the effectiveness of the message: "Do I feel worthwhile in this situation?"; "Am I safe in offering suggestions?"; "Is this the right time (place)?"; "Am I the subordinate or the boss in this situation?" Or in everyday jargon, "Am I O.K.?"; "Do I count?" Usually, the more comfortable or positive the self-concept, the more effective the sender is in communicating.

Belief in Assertive Rights

Linked to self-concept is the belief that one has some rights, such as the right to change one's mind, the right to say, "I do not understand" or "I do not know," the right to follow a "gut feeling" without justifying reasons for it, the right to make mistakes and be responsible for them, and the right to say, "I am not sure now, but let me work on it." Believing in such rights can help strengthen the sender's self-concept and avoid the defensive maneuvering that hinders communication in exchanging information. It would be wise to remember that assertive rights are not complete without responsibility. For example, one has the right to say, "I do not know," but one probably also has the responsibility to find out.

The Sender's Perception of the Message

Do I feel the information I have is valuable? Is it something I want to say or do not want to say? How do I feel it will be received? Is the topic interesting or not interesting to me? Do

I understand the information correctly, at least well enough to describe it to others, and do I know the best way to say it?

The Sender's Feelings About the Receiver

The probability of effective communication is increased if the sender feels positive or respectful toward the receiver. Positive or respectful feelings usually carry a built-in commitment and/or desire to share communication. Negative or nonrespectful feelings require conscious effort to communicate effectively. For the sender it is important to know it is all right not to like everyone, or, for the optimist, to like some persons less than others. It is also important to know that we live in a world in which not everyone is going to like or respect us and that is O.K., too.

Suggestions for Effective Expression

In order to communicate messages effectively, the sender should consider the following points.

1. *Become aware of thoughts and feelings.* Do not be quick to brand them "good," "bad," "wrong," or "right." Accept them as a reflection of the present "you," and let them become best friends by giving support and feedback to your effectiveness and to your needs; consider what they are whispering or shouting to you. By increasing your awareness of your feelings, you can better decide what to do with them.

2. *Feel comfortable in expressing your feelings.* Such expression, when it is congruent with the situation and appropriate, can enhance communication.

3. *Be aware of the listener.* Try to verbalize your message in terms of the listener's understanding and indicate why you feel the message is important to him or her. Does it have a specific significance for the listener or is it just "general information?"

4. *Focus on the importance of the message* and repeat key concepts and essential aspects of the information.

5. *Use as few words as possible* to state the message.

POINTS FOR THE LISTENER

Effective listening is as important to communication as effective sending. Effective listening is an active process in which the listener interacts with the speaker. It requires mental and verbal paraphrasing and attention to nonverbal cues like tones, gestures, and facial expressions. It is a process of listening not to every word but to main thoughts and references.

Nichols (1952) listed the following as deterrents to effective listening: (1) assuming in advance that the subject is uninteresting and unimportant, (2) mentally criticizing the speaker's delivery, (3) getting overstimulated when questioning or opposing an idea, (4) listening only for facts, wanting to skip the details, (5) outlining everything, (6) pretending to be attentive, (7) permitting the speaker to be inaudible or incomplete, (8) avoiding technical messages, (9) overreacting to certain words and phrases, and (10) withdrawing attention, daydreaming.

The feelings and attitudes of the listener can affect what he or she perceives. How the listener feels about herself or himself, how the message being received is perceived, and how the listener feels about the person sending the message affects how well the receiver listens. The listener should keep in mind the following suggestions.

1. *Be fully accessible to the sender.* Being preoccupied, letting your mind wander, and trying to do more than one thing at a time lessen your chances to hear and under-

stand efficiently. In the words of Woody Allen, "It is hard to hum a tune and contemplate one's own death at the same time." Interrupting a conversation to answer the phone may enhance your perceived ego, but the interrupted speaker feels of secondary importance.

2. *Be aware of your feelings as a listener.* Emotions such as anger, dislike, defensiveness, and prejudice are natural, but they cause us not to hear what is being said and sometimes to hear things that are *not* being said.

According to Reik (1972), listening with the "third ear" requires the listener to do the following things: (1) suspend judgment for a while, (2) develop purpose and commitment to listening, (3) avoid distraction, (4) wait before responding, (5) develop paraphrasing in his or her own words and context, particularly to review the central themes of the messages, (6) continually reflect mentally on what is trying to be said, and (7) be ready to respond when the speaker is ready for comments.

Responses That Can Block Effective Communication

Evaluation Response. The phrases "You should . . .," "Your duty . . .," "You are wrong," "You should know better," "You are bad," "You are such a good person" create blocks to communication. There is a time for evaluation, but if it is given too soon, the speaker usually becomes defensive.

Advice-Giving Response. "Why don't you try . . .," "You'll feel better when . . .," "It would be best for you to . . .," "My advice is . . . " are phrases that give advice. Advice is best given at the conclusion of conversations and generally only when one is asked.

Topping Response, or My Sore Thumb. "That's nothing, you should have seen . . .," "When that happened to me, I . . .," "When I was a child . . .," "You think you have it bad . . ." are phrases of "one-upmanship." This approach shifts attention from the person who wants to be listened to and leaves him or her feeling unimportant.

Diagnosing, Psychoanalytic Response. "What you need is . . .," "The reason you feel the way you do is . . .," "You don't really mean that," "Your problem is . . ." are phrases that tell others what they feel. Telling people how they feel or why they feel the way they do can be a two-edged sword. If the diagnoser is wrong, the speaker feels pressed; if the diagnoser is right, the speaker may feel exposed or captured. Most people do not want to be told how to feel and would rather volunteer their feelings than to have them exposed.

Prying-Questioning Response. "Why," "who," "where," "when," "how," "what" are responses common to us all. But such responses tend to make the speaker feel "on the spot" and therefore resist the interrogation. At times, however, a questioning response is helpful for clarification, and in emergencies it is needed.

Warning, Admonishing, Commanding Response. "You had better," "If you don't," "You have to," "You will," "You must" are used constantly in the everyday work environment. Usually such responses produce resentment, resistence, and rebellion. There are times, of course, when this response is necessary, such as in an emergency situation when the information being given is critical to human welfare.

Logical, Lecturing Response. "Don't you realize . . .," "Here is where you are wrong . . .," "The facts are . . .," "Yes, but . . ." can be heard in any discussion with two people of differing opinions. Such responses tend to make the other person feel inferior or defensive. Of course, persuasion is part of the world we live in. In general, however, we need to trust that when people are given correct and full data they will make logical decisions for themselves.

Devaluation Response. "It's not so bad," "Don't worry," "You'll get over it," or "Oh, you don't feel that way" are familiar phrases used in responding to others' emotions. A listener should recognize the sender's feelings and should not try to take away the feelings or deny them to the owner. In our desire to alleviate emotional pain, we apply bandages too soon and possibly in the wrong place.

Whenever a listener's responses convey nonacceptance of the speaker's feelings, the desire to change the speaker, a lack of trust, or the sense that the speaker is inferior or at fault or being bad, communication blocks will occur.

AWARENESS OF ONE'S OWN FEELINGS

For both senders and listeners, awareness of feelings requires the ability to stop and check what feelings one is presently experiencing and consciously to decide how to respond to the feelings. At first it may be uncomfortable and easy to forget, but only by using it will this technique become second nature. The individual should picture three lists:

At a given time, the person stops and mentally asks, "What am I feeling?" One usually experiences a kaleidoscope of emotions simultaneously, but the person can work on focusing on one present, dominant feeling. After the feeling is identified, the second "self-question" is what perceived behaviors are causing that feeling. Is it what the other person is saying or how he or she is saying it? Is it because I do not want to be bothered?

The next step is for the person to choose how he or she wants to react to the feeling. There is much written about letting others know one's feelings to bring congruence to actions and words. One can choose, however, *not* to express a feeling because of inappropriate time, place, or circumstances. For example, I may identify a feeling of annoyance at being interrupted. To share that feeling may not be worthwhile in the situation. The main thing is that *I am aware of my annoyance* and what caused the feeling and can now *choose whether or not to let it be a block to my listening.* I may tell myself that I am annoyed but that my feeling is not going to get in the way of my listening. I can decide if my feeling is to be a listening block and I can prevent it from becoming one, if I so choose.

Another way of becoming aware of feelings is "hindsight analysis." After any given situation, the individual can recheck his or her responses and/or feelings. What happened to cause those feelings? What was I feeling during my responses? Why do I tend to avoid certain people and why do I enjoy being around others? "Why?" is very helpful in finding feelings and behaviors that cue those feelings. As a person works with this technique, identification and decision making will become better, resulting in more effective communication.

CONCLUSION

The communication process is complex but vital to effective problem solving and meaningful personal relationships. It is a process that is never really mastered; one can continually improve on it. It requires certain attitudes, knowledge, techniques, common sense, and a willingness to try. Effective communication happens when we have achieved sufficient clarity or accuracy to handle each situation adequately.

REFERENCES

Lull, P. E., Funk, F. E., & Piersol, D. T. What communications means to the corporation president. *Advanced Management*, 1955, *20*, 17-20.

Nichols, R. G. *Listening is a ten part skill*. Chicago: Enterprise Publications, 1952.

Redding, W. C., & Sanborn, G. A. (Eds.) *Business and industrial communication: A sourcebook*. New York: Harper and Row, 1964.

Reik, T. *Listening with the third ear*. New York: Pyramid, 1972.

J. Ryck Luthi is the coordinator of student programs at the University of Utah, Salt Lake City, Utah, and is currently teaching in the areas of leadership training and value clarification and doing consulting for a number of community agencies. He has authored several articles in communication and personal development. Mr. Luthi's background is in counseling and student personnel development.

TOLERANCE OF EQUIVOCALITY:
THE BRONCO, EASY RIDER, BLOCKBUSTER,
AND NOMAD

Robert C. Rodgers

An important consideration that affects the productivity of planning in work groups is the degree of equivocality in the task undertaken. The word *equivocality* comes from the Greek word *equivoque*, which means "having a double meaning." An *equivocal* task can be defined as one having two, entirely opposite, interpretations.

According to Weick (1969), the greater the equivocality of the task undertaken, the greater is the activity of information seeking, which is directed toward "making sense" out of what appears uncertain and confusing. More simply, whenever we become confused we alert ourselves to information that lends clarity to our initial confusion.

For example, on his way to work, Joe must pass through a tunnel which is normally not congested with traffic. One morning, accompanied by two co-workers, he arrives at the tunnel entrance and finds traffic stopped. He is faced with an equivocal situation. He wants to pass through the tunnel, but he does not know whether transit is blocked because of an accident, heavy traffic, or flooding in the tunnel. He begins actively to seek out information that can explain his equivocal state of affairs: He looks at his watch—8:30 a.m.; he asks one of his riders to tell him what she can see from her side of the car; he looks when the other rider points to a red flashing light in the distance. The eyes and ears of all three are alerted to seek out and to accept whatever information is available, until they learn that the problem is a stalled car inside the tunnel. Some (Green, 1966) have argued that the greater the degree of equivocality in the task assignment, the more intense, also, is the information-seeking activity.

Similar to Weick's concept of equivocality is Cyert's (1963) argument that planning is an "uncertainty-absorbing activity." Organizations strive to achieve "manageable decision situations," says Cyert, by "avoiding planning where plans depend on predictions of uncertain events and by emphasizing planning where the plans can be made self-confirming" (p. 119).

If we accept the proposition that there are large differences in the degree of equivocality (Weick) or uncertainty (Cyert) that individuals are willing to tolerate, as well as in the amount of information they consequently seek out, we can identify four personality types that commonly surface in task-oriented work groups. Those with a low level of tolerance for equivocality are commonly identified as "task-oriented" persons and those with a high level of tolerance can be called "process-oriented" persons.

The Bronco

With a low tolerance level for ambiguity, Broncos insist that the other members of their work group continually stop to evaluate what they have done or not done and where they are going. Bucking Broncos make such statements as "We've got a deadline to meet, you know"; "I don't think we've really done anything yet, everything so far has been just talk"; "Come on, everybody, enough talk, it's time to decide what to do." Continually redirecting the group's efforts, the Bronco is forever dissatisfied with the group's progress until the task has been accomplished.

The Easy Rider

Decision makers who "trust process," Easy Riders are fully confident that they will arrive at the destination intended; in any case, they always enjoy the trip. Easy Riders do not like to stop to evaluate what has been accomplished; they are easygoing and accept the "happening" of the work group for itself. Comments that are often voiced by Easy Riders include "Don't worry about what we've done so far, we'll know where we are when we get there"; "Now is what counts, friends. If we're satisfied with the 'now' of our work, the 'later' will work out by itself." Easy Riders enjoy attending group meetings and trust that everything will come out in the wash.

The Blockbuster

This type is a tidy combination of the Easy Rider and the Bronco—easygoing today and pressuring tomorrow. Willing to settle into a moderate rate of activity today, Blockbusters nonetheless are determined to do a good job when the pressure is on. They can be heard to make such statements as "The deadline is not for two months. Let's worry about details later"; "There's plenty of time for that"; "It's time to move out, let's work all weekend." Blockbusters are the people who make sure that the job gets done in the end and are instrumental in tying all the loose ends together at the last moment.

The Nomad

As the "here today, gone tomorrow" participants in the work effort, Nomads miss many work sessions, make contributions at erratic intervals, seem to be with the effort today but in fantasy land tomorrow. They say such things as "Oh, did I forget to return your call?"; "I seem to have lost that list. It must be somewhere." Other work-group members, except Easy Riders, label the Nomad as unreliable and untrustworthy.

RESOLVING INTERPERSONAL DIFFERENCES

As facilitators and leaders of group interaction recognize, there is no such thing as a hidden technique for changing an individual's basic tolerance level for equivocality, yet interpersonal differences must be resolved if the group is to be effective.

The fact that a work group has an equivocal task assignment is a motivating force in and of itself: set into motion is information-seeking activity, which is intrinsically energizing. Attempts among group leaders to "tame" Broncos or to "activate" Nomads are usually dysfunctional. Nevertheless, the reality is that Broncos still buck, Blockbusters still postpone action, Easy Riders still enjoy the trip, and Nomads still have phones that remain unanswered.

Broncos' clearly expressed needs to chart their expectations of the future with detailed planning documents, to see what will happen before it happens, are largely reflections of their past life experiences. Only by continually looking back on past events do we make sense out of our present condition. Planning for the future, then, is partly an illusion. We plan for the future based on what we know of the past, thereby processing out some of the equivocality inherent in anticipating the future. "The future is unpredictable because the freedom of man makes him unpredictable. He is continually open to change, adopting and creating at rates we should not have believed possible before this generation" (Platt, 1970, p. 158). Each time we stop to plan for the future, we are really looking back on past accomplishments or failures and attaching meanings to them. Each meaning is unique, contingent on when and how often we stop to evaluate progress or set plans.

A METHOD OF PLANNING

It is no wonder that Broncos, Easy Riders, Blockbusters, and Nomads have disparate images of what has been or has not been accomplished. Their discussions about "where we are and where we are going" are likely to become frustrating to the members involved. What is important in planning is that the group members consider the frequency and timing with which they are willing to stop and evaluate what has been or has not been accomplished.

When the work group has decided how often and when it is willing to stop for planning purposes, it might want to consider further the merits of sloppy planning (Bateson, 1972), a consideration that does not necessarily have to alienate the Bronco, as long as a sound "stopping" routine is being carried out. If there is a grain of truth in the proposition that our vision of the future is based largely on meanings attached to past experiences and that future events can introduce unexpected knowledge, we can further argue that the work team's planning may at times best be loose, fragmented, and unordered—a proposition that would surely be comforting to Nomads and Easy Riders.

"Planning cannot, must not, be sloppy," says the Bronco. "Planning reduces risk and elicits disciplined thinking; it must begin with a clear determination of the goals to be attained."

"Perhaps," says the Easy Rider. "But consider the possibility that the United States will spend one hundred billion dollars over the next decade constructing international airports, highways, mass transportation systems, and railroad networks, all meticulously planned, only to discover in 1990 that humans have learned how to teleport themselves across space by activating their wills. All the tight planning in the world goes down the drain in one big gurgle."

The group facilitator cannot insist that Broncos become more like Blockbusters or that Nomads become more like Easy Riders, but he can encourage a loose regulation of the frequency with which members evaluate where they have been and where they are going. Although group members will still continue to attach distinctively different meanings to recent past events, such differences are more responsibly resolved when everyone is stopped at the same time.

According to Cyert (1963), a plan is a goal (something that is to be accomplished at some point in the future), a schedule (when it is to be accomplished), a theory (an explanation of how the world hangs together), and a precedent (a past event that will establish a prima facie case for the decisions of tomorrow). Of these four ingredients, many work groups often neglect the importance of scheduling.

Group activity lists (or schedules) are simple but powerful management devices that facilitate the processing of equivocal information on a routine basis, a fundamental result of the planning process. Such lists consist of activities each work-group member will engage in over a specified period of time, be it one week, one day, or one year. When the time period allotted has expired, the list is retrieved and reviewed (frequency of stopping is regulated), what has been accomplished is crossed off the list (equivocality is reduced), what has not been accomplished remains on the list (a form of sloppy planning because there is no requirement that all activities must be completed by the time allotted), and new activities are added, based on what the work group has learned (planning as a function of past experience as much as a function of future speculations). Focusing on specific activities to accomplish and times to evaluate progress is a facilitating, energizing process. Forcing Nomads to be like Broncos or insisting on loose or tight planning is dysfunctional and de-energizing.

SUGGESTED ACTIVITY

The following instrument can be used to elicit a discussion on planning. Each member of a group places a check in the column that best describes that person's attitude toward each statement.

Agree	Disagree	Don't Know	
_____	_____	_____	1. Planning prepares an organization for the future.
_____	_____	_____	2. Planning may be crude, informal, or very scientific.
_____	_____	_____	3. Planning begins with a clear determination of goals and is concerned fundamentally with the means necessary for attaining these goals.
_____	_____	_____	4. Planning is an effective management tool for risk reduction.
_____	_____	_____	5. Formal, careful planning is essential for maximizing chances for success.
_____	_____	_____	6. In a competitive setting, an organization may be committing economic suicide if it relies on haphazard, informal planning.
_____	_____	_____	7. Planning saves a considerable amount of executive time and effort.
_____	_____	_____	8. Planning elicits disciplined thinking because executives must put their thoughts in writing before acting.
_____	_____	_____	9. A major reason why an organization fails is often the inability of managers to assess realistically the capabilities and probable strategies of competing organizations.
_____	_____	_____	10. Every organization should have a six-month, a one-year, and a five-year plan.
_____	_____	_____	11. Long-range, five-year planning is more important than short-range, six-month planning.
_____	_____	_____	12. Planning should be a continuing process.
_____	_____	_____	13. Planning involves a consideration of all that has transpired in the past and is an ordering of a set of action programs based on that consideration.
_____	_____	_____	14. Planning for what is to be three years hence is a futile exercise. No one can reasonably foretell the future that far in advance.
_____	_____	_____	15. A weekly updated list of activities that need to be accomplished is a most powerful tool in planning.

Scoring

Each person adds the number of checks under the "Disagree" column for items 2, 7, 8, 12, 13, and 15. The total maximum score is 6. Persons scoring 5 or more had a negative reaction to some of the ideas introduced in the lecturette. The person or persons scoring 5 or more can be asked to take fifteen minutes to prepare a "counterlecturette" to present to the group.

While this is being done, each remaining member of the group adds the number of checks under the "Agree" column for items 1, 3, 5, 6, 10, and 11. The total maximum score is, again, 6. Persons scoring 2 or less are more likely to endorse the idea of "sloppy planning" than persons scoring 5 or more. This group can divide into two subgroups, one group of persons scoring 2 or less and one group of persons scoring 5 or more. Then any persons scoring 3 or 4 points are asked to be facilitators of a discussion on the role of "sloppy planning" in accomplishing the tasks confronting their particular work group. Upon conclusion of this discussion (fifteen minutes), the "counterlecturette" is presented and discussed.

REFERENCES AND READINGS

Bateson, G. *Steps to an ecology of mind*. New York: Chandler, 1972.

Castaneda, C. *Tales of power*. New York: Simon & Schuster, 1974.

Cyert, R. M. *A behavioral theory of the firm*. Englewood Cliffs, N.J.: Prentice-Hall, 1963.

Green, P. E. Consumer use of information. In J. W. Newman (Ed.), *On knowing the consumer*. New York: Wiley, 1966.

Platt, J. *Perception and change*. Ann Arbor, Mich.: The University of Michigan Press, 1970.

Weick, K. E. *The social psychology of organizing*. Menlo Park, Calif.: Addison-Wesley, 1969.

Robert C. Rodgers is a doctoral student in the School of Labor and Industrial Relations, Michigan State University, East Lansing, Michigan. Mr. Rodgers' background is in public administration and in university teaching and research. His interests are in public-sector unionism and in the productivity and quality of work life in public organizations.

STRATEGIES FOR DESIGNING AN INTERVENTION

Glenn H. Varney

An intervention can be defined as any planned move toward behavior change in an organization. It is usually done with a work group or with key individuals, the objective being to facilitate changes in the way members of the organization work together. An intervention predictably creates organizational disruption, but the hope is that, with proper planning, change will be as effective as possible, resulting in improved functioning for the organization. The organization development (OD) consultant is the professional identified with planned interventions.

NATURE OF AN INTERVENTION STRATEGY

An intervention strategy can be characterized in at least four different ways.

1. It is a *plan* for conducting the intervention itself; that is, it lays out a set of steps and actions that the OD consultant will follow, based on knowledge of the organization at that particular point.

2. An intervention strategy is necessarily *flexible and adaptable* to the changing organizational situation. An inflexible strategy will quite likely yield no improvement. For example, if a consultant pushes for a change in procedures even though members of the organization do not see the need for the data generated by the procedures, the strategy will only increase organizational resistance and result in a lack of cooperation and poor performance.

3. In all cases the strategy designed to meet a specific situation must have *alternate approaches* built into it in order to meet any situation that may present itself. For example, if the process consultant decides to collect data concerning a certain issue or problem in the next meeting with the client and the client then takes over that discussion for another purpose, the process consultant will be required to use an alternate strategy to meet the changed situation.

4. An intervention strategy can only be designed within a *general framework* until actual contact with the client is made. That is, the process consultant usually has a general strategy in mind but no fixed idea of how to approach the client; thus there is an opportunity to get the "lay of the land" before the strategy is designed.

One way to view an OD strategy is to consider it as something used to guide an OD intervention in a general direction. Such an overall strategy might be, for example, always to encourage the client organization to offer information relative to what is happening in the client organization at that particular point. Meetings would start off with some form of data-collecting process. Another overall strategy might be always to approach an organization with the understanding that the first step of the intervention is to be personal growth labs.

STRATEGIES FOR EACH INTERVENTION STAGE

Whatever the overall strategy, the process consultant concerned with designing an intervention for a client organization recognizes that strategies will be different for each stage of an intervention:

1. Pre-entry
2. Initial contact
3. Entry and data collection
4. Intervention design
5. Intervention, including data collection, feedback, and action steps
6. Separation

The strategy used at the pre-entry stage, for example, is likely to be quite different from the strategy used during the intervention-design stage. What the consultant knows about the client and the client organization at the pre-entry point is different from what is known at the intervention-design stage. It is, therefore, important for the consultant to be aware that strategies will change from one stage to the next and that what works in one stage may not work in another.

For each intervention stage, some questions are listed that the process consultant should be asking while designing substrategies for that stage. These questions become the consultant's way of conceptualizing what exists. Answers to the questions at a particular stage become input for the intervention strategy.

1. Pre-Entry Stage

Typical questions that need answers at this stage:

- Who is the client? What are the client's products, services? Who is the primary contact person and what is that person like? How large is the organization? How was the consultant invited to work with the client?
- What are the consultant's theories about the client organization at this stage? Being aware of these theories can help the consultant assist the client to make changes.
- What are the consultant's expectations about the way the client will behave once initial contact is made?
- What will the consultant do if these expectations are inaccurate? If for some reason the consultant has completely misjudged the client organization, what will the client do?

2. Initial-Contact Stage

Typical questions that need to be raised at this stage include the following:

- What are the objectives of the intervention and what criteria will be used to measure the results?
- How will the consultant conduct the initial meeting?
- How much of the client's time should the consultant take?
- Who will set the agenda? How?
- What additional data does the consultant need about the client and the client's problems?
- What will the consultant do if there is a basic incongruity between his or her intervention style and the client's needs?

- What will the consultant do to check the relationship with the client to see if progress is being made?
- What will the consultant do to advance the client/consultant relationship to the next step?
- What are the restraining and moving forces in the organization?

3. Entry and Data Collection Stage

Often, clients will not require a formally written proposal outlining the action steps that the consultant intends to take. When such a formal proposal/contract is expected, however, it should probably include the following items:

- objectives of the intervention: what is to be accomplished;
- questions to be explored;
- the units of the organization that will be considered a part of the relationship;
- a step-by-step indication of how the process consultant will proceed in the organization in terms of data collection, feedback, and so forth;
- who will receive the feedback;
- how the results will be evaluated;
- what the cost of the engagement will be;
- what the process consultant would like to do following the engagement and recommendations for what the client should do.

4. Intervention-Design Stage

The intervention that will be used is by definition situationally determined. In general, however, all designs must answer three questions:

- What are the key variables in the relationship that will determine the success or failure of the intervention? For example, it is essential that the consultant be aware of the values of those involved in the change; they will not be likely to accept a change that is inconsistent with their values.
- What behavioral theories and concepts will the consultant use in trying to understand the organization?
- What basic elements of the organization (climate, health, etc.) and what techniques (e.g., team building, cousins groups, mirroring, fish bowling) should be used to help the organization solve its problems?

5. Intervention Stage

At this point, four primary questions need to be answered:

- If data-collection techniques will be used, how should data be gathered (questionnaires, interviews, sensing meetings, etc.)?
- What should the timing be? How long should the process consultant be engaged in the actual process of data collection, and how should this be scheduled?
- What should the various logistics be? On site or off site? How should employees be notified of this intervention? What role should the employees play in the data-collection process?
- What feedback approach will be used? Will it be a simple report made to the client organization, or a feedback session with top management, or a series of small

meetings with all the employees of the organization? Just exactly how will the information be fed back to the organization? Will action planning be done? If so, who will participate?

In the feedback and change phase of the relationship between a consultant and a client, the responsibility for change is primarily in the hands of the client. The process consultant is obligated *only* to *help* the client develop the client's own goals, strategies, and tactics. An effective consultant can help the client organization see itself and the way it is functioning, the kinds of things happening, and how results and effectiveness may be affected, but the client cannot be *forced* to change. This is an important distinction.

For example, in a recent consulting experience, the supervisor interrupted the group members as they were processing data about the organization. She asked the consultant, "Just what makes you think you can get us to change the way we are doing things around here?" She was questioning the consulting relationship and what the consultant could do to help. The consultant told the group, "You probably can solve your own problems, if you put your mind to it. You have all the resources right here and now. The only thing I can do is help you look at yourself and perhaps facilitate some of the changes that you want to make." Later the group accepted the responsibility for designing change for itself.

6. Separation Stage

Basic questions to be answered at this point in the design of an intervention strategy are:

- What expected results of the intervention were obtained? not obtained?
- What does the client organization expect of the process consultant in terms of future commitments and follow-up?
- What can the client organization tell the process consultant about the way the intervention relationship was handled? This is very important if a process consultant is to develop his or her skills effectively. It provides an opportunity for the consultant to collect data about personal behavior and his or her effect on the organization.

CRITERIA FOR MEASURING AN EFFECTIVE INTERVENTION

An intervention into an organization can be measured in terms of the following questions:

- Does the client feel that the process consultant helped? Was the client satisfied that problems were resolved?
- Does the process consultant feel the client organization was helped? Did the consultant come away with useful information about his or her own skills and what was done to help the organization?
- In the process of solving one problem, did the consultant create another? Clearly, such a result is hardly to be considered a successful intervention.
- Does the client feel that the consultant can help in other ways? Will the consultant be invited back, and will the consultant's skills be used in future problems the client may have?
- Does the client organization have a new look or a new approach or a new feeling about how it can solve future problems? Does it seem to have a better grasp of different approaches to solving its own problems?
- Does the client organization know something new about itself that was not known before? How did the client react to this information?

ESSENTIALS IN DESIGNING AN EFFECTIVE OD INTERVENTION STRATEGY

The process consultant must be aware of the *careful planning and theorizing* that is necessary to effect a successful intervention. This means the investment of a considerable amount of time in planning strategies—an investment that not enough OD consultants make.

A great deal of *flexibility* on the part of the consultant is also necessary in order to adapt a strategy to the situation at hand. If a process consultant is rigid and inflexible, the overall strategy will usually not work in the client organization.

It is recommended that the process consultant *test the validity* of the intervention strategy designed for a specific organization by trying it out on other process consultants. It is important that a consultant make sure that strategies are designed so that they will be meaningful and useful to the organization.

Process consultants should be aware of the *basic theories* they carry around in their heads about individuals, groups, and organizations. These theories often lead consultants to follow a favorite set of strategies for all situations, even though it is obvious that one or two proven approaches may not be effective in all situations. Just because a particular strategy is comfortable for the consultant does not mean it will work for the client. The truly effective process consultant is one who can use and adapt many types and forms of OD interventions to meet any situation that arises.

Glenn H. Varney, Ph.D., is the president of Management Advisory Associates, Inc., and an associate professor at Bowling Green State University, Bowling Green, Ohio. He is the author of three books on organization development (Management by Objectives, An Organization Development Approach to Management Development, and Organization Development for Managers). Dr. Varney is a graduate of the organization behavior program at Case Western Reserve University and is active in organization development groups throughout the United States and abroad.

CONTRACTING: A PROCESS AND A TOOL

Francis L. Ulschak

"Would you tell me, please, which way I ought to go from here?" "That depends a good deal on where you want to get to," said the Cat. "I don't much care where—so long as I get somewhere," Alice added as an explanation. "Oh, you're sure to do that," said the Cat, "if you only walk long enough."

Alice's Adventures in Wonderland

Contracting may be used by a facilitator (therapist, consultant, leader, etc.):

1. to clarify and define the relationship between the facilitator and the client (the person or organization seeking the facilitator's services) and/or

2. to clarify with a client where the client is presently, where he or she would like to be (goals and objectives), and alternative ways (strategies) for getting there.

In the first case, contracting is used as a *process* to explore and define the relationship between the facilitator and the client. The client's wants and needs for services are detailed along with the range of services the facilitator is willing and able to provide. This period is a time of deciding (1) what the various parties involved want from each other, (2) whether they have the ability and resources to provide what is wanted from the relationship, and (3) whether they are willing to enter into the relationship.

In the second case, contracting is a specific *tool* the facilitator can use with a client to assist the client in evaluating the present situation (A), the desired position (B), and how to get to the desired position. Holloway and Holloway's (1973, p. 36) contracting model depicts the client's present and desired positions and the decision the client needs to make in order to move from one to the other. The "decision" can be seen as the choice of a strategy (strategies) that will accomplish the movement from A to B.

The facilitator can understand contracting both as a process and as a framework that the facilitator may use (1) to establish a relationship with the client and to set mutual goals and objectives and (2) as a specific technique to involve the client actively in detailing A and B and the possible strategies for moving from A to B. This latter use encourages the client to take active responsibility for his or her present condition and future state.

Contracting as a Process

Contracting can be seen as a dynamic process along a time line, as opposed to a single event. The facilitator and client begin with a "directional" contract, part of which may include the intent to recycle the contract; e.g., "In six weeks we will review the contract and update it." Thompson (1974, p. 31) refers to "process contracting" and states that "the original 'contract' can be an agreement to work together to progressively define the relationship and to communicate desired 'changes' to one another as each party sees more clearly the development of its interests." Part of contracting as a process is defining the relationship; one vital aspect of this is keeping the other parties involved in the contract explicitly informed of any changes.

The author wishes to give a special note of thanks to Roland Weiss for his critique of an earlier draft of this paper.

Contracting as a Tool

Contracting is also a useful tool that can be used at various levels. At one level, the intrapersonal, an individual experiencing an inner conflict may use the model as an aid in deciding on strategies that will result in clarifying and eliminating the conflict.

A second level of contracting involves two or more individuals. For example, in a group setting, one individual may feel that she dominates the discussion and make a contract with other members of the group that (1) they will tell her when they experience her as dominating the discussion and that (2) she will check with them when she experiences herself as dominating the discussion. A third level of contracting may be between the facilitator and the client, group, or organization. In this case, contracting may involve specifying issues such as time commitments, finances involved, or group maintenance issues.

TWO APPROACHES TO CONTRACTING

Two general approaches to contracting can be useful as guidelines. The first approach concentrates on establishing the relationship between the client and the facilitator. The second approach attends to defining the relationship between the client and the problem. In this approach, the facilitator assists the client in moving from A to B. Although there is a great deal of overlap between these two approaches, they are presented separately. Depending on the setting, the facilitator may find one approach or the other most useful.

Negotiating the Relationship

A basic structure (Steiner, 1971, pp. 106-112) for using contracting in therapy can be used for negotiating roles, expectations, and mutual benefits in nontherapy settings as well. There are four requirements for this negotiation: (1) mutual consent, (2) valid consideration, (3) competency, and (4) lawful object. *Mutual consent* means that both parties have an adequate understanding of the agreement. What both want and expect from the relationship should be clearly detailed. The facilitator needs to provide the client with possible time involvements, financial costs, courses of action, methods that may be used, expectations, risks involved, etc. The client provides the facilitator with information concerning expectations, the nature of the problem, objectives, people to be involved, time commitments, etc. It is important that both the client and the facilitator give each other sufficient information so that both will be able to make informed decisions. The three ingredients of *valid information, commitment,* and *free choice* (Argyris, 1973, pp. 17-21) are necessary considerations.

Valid consideration involves an explicit statement of the benefits each party to the contract will confer on the other. Benefits for the facilitator might include money, additional experience, enhanced reputation, or publishable material. For the client, they might mean new information, the alleviation of the problem, or training.

Competency concerns the ability of the parties to enter into the relationship. For the facilitator, the question is whether he or she has the competencies and the background to do what the client is requesting. For the client, competency may relate to his or her authority to enter into an agreement. Does the client have the position and the sanction of the organization to enter into such an agreement?

Finally, *lawful object* requires very simply that what both parties are agreeing to is legal.

With the framework of these requirements, a check list of questions can be provided for the facilitator and the client in order to explore their relationship.

Mutual Consent

What are the time requirements?

What are the financial costs involved?

Are there any risks the client/facilitator should be aware of?

Who will be involved?

What are the expectations of the facilitator?

Are there any ethical concerns involved?

What methods might the facilitator use?

If there is research involved, how will the information be used?

Valid Considerations

What will the client pay the facilitator?

Are there other than financial rewards? If so, what?

What rewards will the facilitator provide the client?

Competency

Is the facilitator competent to do what the client is asking? What kinds of backup services are available?

Is the client in a position to enter into the contract?

Does he or she have the authority to do so?

Lawful Object

Is the agreement legal?

Clarifying Goals and Strategies

In the second approach, contracting focuses on the client and the "problem." This approach asks four questions: (1) What are the client's wants? (2) What is the client willing to do to get the wants met? (3) What are the client's criteria for success? (4) What benefits does the client gain on completing the contract?

Determining the client's wants involves a clarification of both the present situation and future goals and objectives. The more specific and behavioral the terms of the descriptions are, the easier it is to measure if they have been met. Sometimes the client may feel totally lacking in goals or objectives. In this case, the first "want" in this first step may be to "determine goals."

To find out what the client is willing to do to get his or her wants met involves strategies and action plans. There may be many ways of moving from A to B, and part of this step is weighing the various alternatives. Again, it is important that the answer to this question be expressed in the most specific, behavioral, and measurable terms possible.

Criteria for success are essential in order to evaluate results, and, in order to determine if the criteria have been satisfied, they must be specific.

The question of benefits is linked to motivation. If the client completes the contract successfully, what will that mean to him or her? Will the client think differently? act differently? feel differently? have more income? Are these outcomes pleasing?

This approach, focusing on the client and the problem, can provide the facilitator with a frame of reference. Although the questions are presented sequentially, they are interrelated, and in practice the facilitator may experience a good deal of overlap. Both the facilitator and the client also need to be aware that the contract may be recycled at any time.

ADVANTAGES TO CONTRACTING

Contracting has advantages on many levels. First, within the contracting process, the client's integrity and autonomy are respected. The first approach emphasizes the importance of the facilitator and the client "leveling" with each other. Both need to get hidden agendas out into the open. And both are held responsible for their actions.

Second, and closely related, contracting may clarify the "helpee-helper" syndrome, a relationship filled with pitfalls. The charismatic helper may leave the client floating on a magic cloud but with no understanding for self-help when the cloud disappears. The "helpless" client may seduce the facilitator into solving the problem and then discount the solution with "Yes, but . . ." (Berne, 1964, p. 116). Contracting avoids some of these pitfalls by asking the parties to level with each other and to state expectations clearly.

A third advantage to contracting is that it can function to detect and/or eliminate latent conflict at an early stage. The emphasis on clear understanding helps here, as well as the recycling points built into the process. Contracting can also be used as a specific tool for controlling or managing conflict.

PROBLEMS WITH CONTRACTING

Although the advantages of contracting are clear, problems may arise. These can be categorized as follows:

- Problems relating to condition A, i.e., the present condition. The client may not know what the difficulty is.
- Problems relating to condition B, i.e., goals and objectives. The client may have a very confused understanding of what the future will look like.
- Problems relating to the strategies involved in moving from A to B. The client may have a clear understanding of both situations but be unaware of alternative strategies for moving from one to the other.
- Problems relating to one or more of these elements.

Problems can be identified as structured or unstructured (Thompson, 1972): structured problems have only one unknown (e.g., the desired condition [B] may be unknown, but the present condition [A] and strategies are known), while unstructured problems have at least two unknowns (e.g., the present condition [A] is known, and the desired condition [B] and strategies are unknown).

The facilitator and client faced with one or more categories of problems have options. When condition A is unknown, a contract might detail a process for determining A, e.g., the use of a research instrument. When condition B is unknown, a contract may be formulated for goal setting or long-range planning. When strategies are unclear, the contract may deal with problem solving, e.g., the use of force-field analysis to examine alternative strategies. When the problem combines several elements, a contract can identify a critical starting point and then proceed with "action plans."

Problems that arise within the contracting process may become the focus of the process itself; contracting can then be used as a problem-solving tool for contracting. It is important that the facilitator be sensitive to the problems the client experiences with the contracting process. When the problems are identified, contracting may be used to resolve or control them.

CONCLUSION

The Cat's answer to Alice provides an excellent model for contracting: which way you go depends on where you want to get to. Contracting is a tool and a process that can help people find answers to where they are, where they want to go, and how to get there.

REFERENCES

Argyris, C. *Intervention theory and method*. Reading, Mass.: Addison-Wesley, 1973.

Berne, E. *Games people play*. New York: Grove Press, 1964.

Holloway, W., & Holloway, M. *The contract setting process*. Medina, Ohio: Midwest Institute for Human Understanding (4004 Huffman Road, 44256), 1973.

Steiner, C. *Games alcoholics play*. New York: Grove Press, 1971.

Thompson, C. W. N. Edited transcript on goal defining. Unpublished manuscript, 1972.

Thompson, C. W. N. Implementation: A question of hanging together or hanging separately. *Defense Department Journal*, January 1974, pp. 30-31.

Francis L. Ulschak, Ph.D., is an organization development consultant in private practice in Center, North Dakota. He is currently working with the United Methodist Church on special projects relating to organization and community development in the coal-energy-impacted areas of North Dakota. Dr. Ulschak's background is in organizational and community consulting, education, small-group problem-solving tools, and transactional analysis.

THE PENDULUM SWING: A NECESSARY EVIL IN THE GROWTH CYCLE

Beverly A. Gaw

A person involved in the growth process can be thrown off balance by feedback such as "Say, have you changed! You used to be so quiet (cooperative, sweet, etc.). Now you're loud (bitchy, hard, etc.)." The pendulum swing offers a healthy perspective to help surmount this obstacle to continued growth. By providing a developmental framework, it allows negative feedback to be more easily assimilated.

Definition of the Pendulum Swing

At its most basic level, the pendulum swing is what learning theorists might term a simple matter of overcompensation or overlearning. Although this phenomenon is readily recognized in the development of new motor and memory skills, it is less accepted in the area of personal growth.

In experimenting with and adopting new behaviors and subsequently creating new feelings about the self, a person performs a new behavior that is generally the opposite of that individual's typical pattern of behavior. For example, if the person is usually nonassertive and decides to develop assertiveness, the pendulum does not swing immediately from nonassertiveness to assertiveness. It first swings from nonassertiveness to aggressiveness (or an insistence on assertive behavior at all times, regardless of necessity and without sensitivity to the unique situational elements and interpersonal needs of a situation). Once the behavior is practiced sufficiently so that it becomes "natural," i.e., is integrated into the person's repertoire of available responses, the pendulum centers at assertiveness (or assertive behavior when it is the appropriate response to situational elements and interpersonal needs). However, because a new behavior has been integrated, the pendulum comes to rest at a higher plane; i.e., it transcends both nonassertiveness and aggressiveness. The pendulum repeats this ascending pattern whenever a new behavior is tried out, practiced, and finally synthesized (Figure 1).

The pendulum swing can also be illustrated by a curvilinear model (Figure 2). In this model, both ends of the continuum are less effective responses and share similar characteristics. The centered and integrated point, instead, shows a more effective, i.e., appropriate, response to the total situation.

DIMENSIONS OF EFFECTIVE AND INEFFECTIVE BEHAVIOR

Ineffective (polarized) behavior (both old and new) and effective (centered) behavior can be viewed from several dimensions (Figure 3).

Pattern

Both the old and the new behaviors share similar characteristics. Although the old behavior is habitual or compulsive (performed without choice) and the new response is consciously planned to occur, both behaviors exhibit rigid patterns of response.

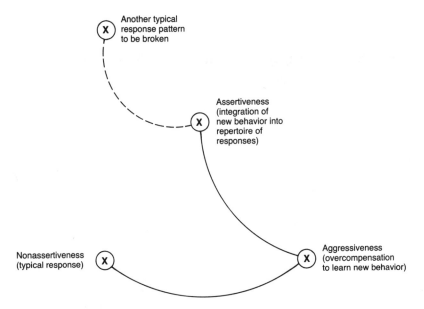

Figure 1. The Pendulum-Swing Model

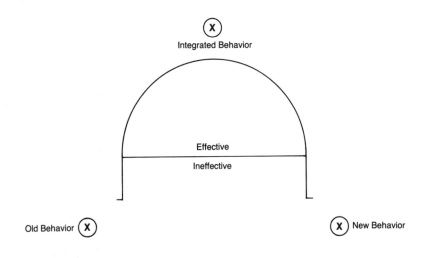

Figure 2. The Pendulum Swing as a Curvilinear Model

The effective (centered) response is neither habitual nor specifically planned. It arises spontaneously in the situation and is therefore flexible and accommodating.

Awareness

With both old behavior and new, awareness is only partial. In the old behavior (of the "interpret-act" type), past experience determines present action without utilizing data about the situation or one's feelings or intentions. The newly developed behavior is the "intend-act" type: what the person wants to do or accomplish primarily directs action.

The centered behavior, on the other hand, is executed with full awareness. Sense data, interpretation of that data, acknowledgment of feelings or emotions, recognition of one's own and others' wants are utilized as a basis for the behavior performed.

Movement

Although the old behavior actually has no movement, being static and unchanging, and the new behavior moves laterally to the extreme or opposite end of the continuum, both the old and new behaviors operate from the same baseline. In contrast, the centered behavior transcends the baseline, going beyond polarities, opposites, and the original continuum.

Level of Development

An ineffective level of overall development is exhibited by both the old and the new behaviors. The old behavior was overused, while its opposite was underdeveloped; then the new behavior is overpracticed to the point of excluding the old behavior.

Dimension	Ineffective (Polarized) Behavior		Effective (Centered) Behavior
	Old	*New*	*Integrated*
Pattern	Rigid		Flexible
	habitual	planned	spontaneous
Awareness	Partial		Total
	interpreting-acting	intending-acting	sensing-interpreting feeling-intending-acting
Movement	Lateral		Upward
	static	extreme	transcending
Level of Development	Over		Complete
	overused	overpracticed	synthesized/integrated
Focus	Partial		Full
	self-preservation	goal	self-other-situation
Response	Coping		Expressive
	reflexive	problem-solving	emerging from self-in-situation
Feelings	Negative/Dissonant		Positive/Consonant
	frustration	anxiety	harmony

Figure 3. Dimensions and Characteristics of Effective and Ineffective Behavior

In the centered behavior, however, both ends of the continuum have been integrated and synthesized; both behaviors are available for use in the person's repertoire of responses.

Focus

Both the old and the new behaviors exhibit a partial, or selective, focus. The old behavior focuses on the preservation of the person's self-image within the framework of past experience, while the new behavior focuses on the behavioral goal to be attained. Neither takes into account the unique elements of the situation.

The centered behavior exhibits a full focus. There is awareness and acknowledgment of the self and the goal and also of others and the contextual elements of the situation.

Response

In this dimension, both the old and new behaviors are characteristic of a coping response. The behavior performed in the past is utilized reflexively in the present because it renders consequences more predictable. The new behavior is a goal to be achieved, and problem-solving activity is used as a means to that goal.

The centered behavior is an expressive response. It arises naturally, without conscious planning or direction. At the centered point, it is an integral part of the person-in-the-situation.

Feelings

Negative feelings of dissonance, disharmony, or incongruence are involved in both the old and new behaviors. The old behavior is usually accompanied by vague feelings of frustration with the interaction pattern and its results. When the reason for these feelings becomes apparent, the feelings surface and the time for change has arrived. The new behavior is usually accompanied by feelings of anxiety, discomfort with the unusualness of the behavior, and concern over a less predictable outcome.

The centered behavior is accompanied by positive feelings of consonance, harmony, or congruence: the person is in harmony with self and situation.

ILLUSTRATION

The differing characteristics of the polarized behaviors as they occur before being stabilized in the centered behavior can be illustrated by the move from nonassertiveness (never upholding one's individual rights) through aggressiveness (always upholding one's rights regardless of the context) to assertiveness (upholding one's rights appropriately within the situational context).

Nonassertiveness is a habitual behavior *pattern* developed over time. For the nonassertive person, options are limited to nonassertive behavior because the person finds it difficult to respond in any other way. Nonassertive behavior is based on partial *awareness*. Because the old behavior is habitual/compulsive, past experience (interpretation) is the main information utilized in action; i.e., only one possible alternative is seen as viable—nonassertion. Likewise, because options are limited, and the need to experiment and change has not yet been felt, there is virtually no *movement*. Because only one behavior is available, nonassertiveness is at the *level of* over*development*; it has been executed so often that other behaviors have atrophied, or latent behaviors have not been exercised. The *focus* is partial because nonassertive behavior concentrates on defending

146

the self in the way it has been functionally defended in the past. Therefore, the behavior is a coping *response* because it stays with the predictable, or what has worked before. Finally, the *feelings* accompanying nonassertiveness are dissonant and involve some level of frustration. There is a feeling that something is not quite right, that in some way one is being taken advantage of. When the frustration approaches the level of awareness at which the cause (loss of one's rights) can be identified, the decision to change the pattern can be made.

Once this decision to change is put into effect, acquiring the behavior of assertiveness becomes the objective. However, before assertiveness is achieved as a centered behavior, the pendulum swing through aggressiveness is necessary. Learning a new behavior also involves a rigid *pattern*, because upholding one's rights must be consciously planned and directed to be executed. Because asserting is conscious, *awareness* is only partial, concentrating mainly on the desire to uphold one's rights as the sole basis for action. The *movement* involves a lateral swing to the extreme, in order to practice the behavior directly opposite from the norm. The behavior is consistently, frequently, and intensely asserting, always upholding one's rights regardless of whether that is the necessary behavior in the present context. Therefore, once again the behavior is at the *level of overdevelopment*—the overcompensation involved in learning. The *focus* of aggressiveness is on acquiring a new or underdeveloped behavior, and problem-solving activity characteristic of a coping *response* occurs: nonassertiveness is no longer seen to be as successful as it once was; the status quo has become undesirable and a goal (assertiveness) is chosen. Because the behavior is new and must be consciously practiced and because the outcome is not as predictable as with the former pattern, *feelings* of unnaturalness and ambiguity produce dissonance and anxiety.

After the individual has practiced the new behavior for some time, it usually becomes centered in, or a part of, the person. The *pattern* becomes less rigid and more spontaneous and flexible, as it is based on full *awareness*. The situation is sensed and interpreted with a minimum of reliance on past assumptions; emotions are acknowledged; desires and intentions of self and others are recognized and accommodated. The *movement* transcends the static and extreme polarities of never asserting and always asserting; the *level of development*, which now includes both these responses, is synthesized or integrated. At this point, the *focus* is complete and full, taking in all factors involved in self, other, and situation. With all elements being considered, the behavior is now a natural part of the person's repertoire, and the *response* is an expressive one, arising naturally from self-in-situation. The person will choose to be assertive or nonassertive, depending on what is necessary and appropriate in the here-and-now. The consequent *feelings*—which are based on total awareness, integration of dimensions, and, therefore, a full and sensitive response—are consonant. The options have been increased. The person can choose among more alternatives, and the *person*, rather than habit or a planned goal, makes the decision. At this point, the new behavior is centered.

CONCLUSION

The important point to stress with this model is that the pendulum swing appears not only to occur in growth but to be necessary to it. Because a new behavior must be desired, chosen, learned, practiced, and developed before it can be integrated, this swing needs to be supported and encouraged. It should be recognized as a natural, necessary, positive stage in the growth spiral. Far too many people become discouraged because they feel anxious when rigidly practicing a new behavior. Negative feedback from others about their new behavior only hinders the growth process; the person may see change as futile.

Instead, the growing person needs to be assured that this phase will pass: learning the latest dance or a new language is not "natural" initially either.

The pendulum swing fits into other therapeutic models, especially psychosynthesis and Gestalt, which focus specifically on owning and exercising latent potentialities or personalities. Methods of treatment used by these two psychotherapies can be utilized to accelerate centered behavior by encouraging the pendulum swing from one extreme to the other and by promoting this necessary step in growth with a minimum of conflict.

SUGGESTED READING

Blake, R. R., & Mouton, J. S. *The managerial grid*. Houston: Gulf Publishing, 1964.

Haronian, F. A psychosythetic model of personality and its implications for psychotherapy. *Journal of Humanistic Psychology*, 1975, *15* (4), 25-51.

Jourard, S. *Disclosing man to himself*. New York: Van Nostrand Reinhold, 1968.

Katz, R. *Preludes to growth*. New York: Free Press, 1973.

Kelley, C. Assertion theory. In J. W. Pfeiffer & J. E. Jones (Eds.), *The 1976 annual handbook for group facilitators*. La Jolla, Calif.: University Associates, 1976.

May, R. *Man's search for himself*. New York: Signet Books, 1967.

Miller, S., Nunnally, E. W., & Wackman, D. B. The awareness wheel. In J. W. Pfeiffer & J. E. Jones (Eds.), *The 1976 annual handbook for group facilitators*. La Jolla, Calif.: University Associates, 1976.

Perls, F. *Gestalt therapy verbatim*. New York: Bantam, 1969.

Vargiu, J. Psychosynthesis workbook. In *Synthesis*, 1974, *1*(1), WB 1-74.

Beverly A. Gaw, Ph.D., is an assistant professor in the Department of Communication at Wright State University, Dayton, Ohio. She is director of the basic interpersonal communication course, teaches courses in small-group and organizational communication, and directs workshops on communication skills. Dr. Gaw is a co-author of Personal and Interpersonal Communication.

THE ORGANIZATIONAL GESTALT

Peter Scholtes

A person's experience of another individual in his presence is formed by a system of impressions, including tone of voice, choice of words, eye contact, breathing, posture, gestures, body constrictions, use of space, physical touch, pace and tempo of transactions, shifts in focus, awareness of feelings, and manner of expressing them. The individual's total presence is that individual's Gestalt.

An organization also transmits its own system of impressions—behaviors that comprise its own total presence—its Gestalt. These behaviors are always significant. They are never accidental, although they may not be deliberate. Managers may find it revealing to look at the everyday phenomena that make up the organization's Gestalt. They should look at these elements naïvely, as would a child or a visitor from another planet, simply observing without judging and without the distortions of sophistication or the filtering of familiarity.

THE ELEMENTS OF AN ORGANIZATION'S PRESENCE

Certain behaviors and dynamics of an organization express the organization's uniqueness, distinguishing it from another organization providing the same products or services. These are the major elements of an organization's Gestalt:

- *Use of and Reaction to Authority*

  How do those in authority see themselves and how do subordinates respond to those in authority? Is the boss respected, feared, rebelled against, revered, or ignored? Is the boss a parent, partner, friend, or playmate? What makes a boss a boss? What gives a boss credibility in that role?

- *Initiative, Delegation, and the Response to Delegation*

  What is the level of tolerance for the taking of initiative or the delegating of responsibility? When, where, to whom, and by whom is responsibility taken or given?

- *Locus of Power*

  Power is where it is perceived to be. Whoever is seen as powerful and influential *is* powerful and influential. And powerful individuals lose their power when they are perceived as powerless. Who in an organization seems to have power and influence? Who bestows that power and influence? Are there nonpowerful people in positions that would ordinarily be held by someone with power (or vice versa)?

- *Locus and Levels of Energy*

  Where or when is there a high level of excitement, enthusiasm, or fun? Where or when do these levels drop? Where or when is there tiredness, listlessness, lethargy, or inertia?

- *Quality of Human Contact*

  People will have numerous transactions in an organization; there may also be some ordinary forms of exchange that are conspicuously unexpressed. An organization whose members easily make contact with each other or outsiders has a dramatically different presence from an organization in which relationships are stiff, awkward, or uncomfortable. Points of contact to observe:

o *Ordinary Civilities:* Do people engage in the ordinary hello's, thank you's, goodbye's, etc.?

o *Titles of Address:* How do people address each other—first names or nicknames, formal titles, or "Hey, you!"? What are the patterns of formality or informality?

o *Informal Conversation:* What do people talk about when they do not talk about work? Is there any "inside" topic that one must engage in to be considered a real member?

o *Physical Arrangements:* Where are people located when at work? In proximity to whom? What is their physical space—near to or far from others? Is there a connection between physical location and other elements, such as the locus of power or energy? Does the physical arrangement allow for informal conversation or visual contact?

o *Visual Contact:* Who looks at whom? Who avoids looking at whom? Is it an organization of lookers or avoiders?

o *Pace and Tempo of Contact:* How fast or slow is the pace of contact between people? Is contact terse, abrupt, driven, or leisurely and flowing? Is there time to savor experiences or is there a state of continuous crisis? Is the pace a walk, a canter, a gallop, or a stampede? What or who changes the normal pace?

o *Directness and Candor:* When or where is there secretiveness and surprise as opposed to open disclosure of information and sharing of opinion?

o *Touch:* Is physical touching an acceptable form of contact between members of the organization?

• *Conflict/Disagreement*

Is conflict engaged or avoided? Is anger O.K.? Are people aware of negative feelings? What happens to the dissident member? What form of sanction, if any, is placed on a dissenting minority?

• *Strokes and Support*

Does the organization seem to encourage the expression of positive support, compliments, optimism, or affection (as opposed to bitching, backbiting, or abandoning people in need)? Is there a pattern to the timing or location of the strokes or support, bitching or abandonment?

• *Feedback and Evaluation*

Do individuals and the organization seek and exchange reactions and evaluations regarding the quality of work? Is feedback valued, listened to, and acted upon? Or is evaluation avoided or ignored, criticism responded to with defensiveness, and blame cast for problems and mistakes?

• *Individuality Versus Uniformity*

In any organization there are indications of the extent to which members exercise conformity or choose uniqueness: the food they eat, what they do on a break, the appearance of their work space, the clothes they wear. Is uniformity among members required by the nature of the work, arbitrarily imposed by authorities, or selected by people without apparent coercion? Is there room in the organization for the nonconformist or the eccentric? How is the nonconformist treated?

- *The Physical Environment*

  Does the physical appearance of the work place—the colors and textures, the appointments and amenities, the use of space—suggest movement or stillness, stimulation or inertia? Is it tight and rigid or loose and flexible? What does the appearance of the place suggest about the people there and the work they do?

- *Turnover, Presence, and Promptness*

  What are the patterns of staff turnover and of absence or lateness at work stations, meetings, training programs, or informal gatherings of the staff?

- *Focus on Time*

  How does the organization deal with its past, present, and future? Which dominates? Which is ignored?

EXPERIENCING AND EXPLORING THE ORGANIZATIONAL GESTALT

There are many ways a manager may seek to become aware of an organization's Gestalt. He or she can explore the organization with a stranger's eyes, taking a naïve tour of the office or plant, or ask outsiders to do this. Taking a fantasy tour and experiencing the organization through the mind's eye can also help a manager to make contact with an organization's uniqueness.

What is important is to become aware of the total presence, the uniqueness . . . the Gestalt . . . and to realize that this Gestalt is not an accident. The total presence of an organization is purposeful; its characteristics can be seen as the desired results of a carefully conceived plan. Therefore, the manager and everyone else in the organization are getting exactly the kind of organization they want, tailor-made to fit their needs, wants, values, and styles.

An organization may be characterized by some behavior that is deplored by its members: "We've got to do something about the poor morale and high turnover in our clerical pool." A manager with a Gestalt approach might respond, "Assuming this situation exists because we want it to exist, let's explore two questions: How are we arranging to create and maintain low morale and high turnover in the clerical pool, and what has been the benefit for us in doing this?"

An organization will change only when it is aware of what it is, accepts what it is, recognizes how it benefits from what it is, and takes responsibility for what it is. The basis of change is a paradox: organizations change not by seeking to become what they are not, but by seeking to become, with greater clarity and responsibility, what they really are.

TWO EXAMPLES OF GESTALT INTERVENTIONS

The following examples of Gestalt organization development (OD) interventions describe real situations that have been disguised, abbreviated, and combined into composite cases.

No Strokes

Jay, a manager of a department with two hundred employees, has approximately twenty subordinates reporting directly to him. In an OD session, one of Jay's more forthright subordinates, Chris, confronted him in the following manner:

Chris: You almost never pay compliments. You almost never say something positive about my work. I can't get excited about my work when you're so stingy with strokes.

Jay:	Two weeks ago I complimented the Birmingham project.
Chris:	Yeh, you said, "This is going smoothly." You didn't say, "Chris, you did a hell of a job." You didn't compliment a person—me. You complimented an event.
Jay:	Chris, you're right. I want to pay compliments. I just don't think about it. I guess I figure that you know when you've done a good job.
Gestaltist:	Let's suppose that you two are getting exactly what you want.
Jay:	What do you mean?
Gestaltist:	Suppose, Jay, that you are doing exactly what you want to do, that there is some payoff for you in not giving strokes. What might that payoff be?
Jay:	(After much soul searching) I guess I'm surprised that my compliments are so important to people.
Gestaltist:	Try saying, "I am a person whose compliments aren't important!"
Jay:	(Repeats the sentence) Yeh, I don't see myself as being important.
Gestaltist:	Say, "I don't believe I'm important."

Jay repeats the phrase and then describes his feelings of being in his present position after having shot up through the ranks at a relatively fast rate.

Gestaltist:	What's the payoff for you in complimenting a successful event instead of the person who brought it off?
Jay:	(After more soul searching) I guess I'm awkward with the relationship that's established when you compliment the person. Complimenting the event maintains a kind of distance.
Gestaltist:	Try saying, "I'm a person who wants distance, who's awkward with relationships."

Jay repeats this and mulls it over for a while. "Yeh, that's where I am. I'm going to look at that for a while to see if that's where I want to stay."

The Gestaltist then turns to Chris.

Gestaltist:	Chris, presume for a minute that you don't get strokes because you don't want strokes. Now imagine what the payoff is for you in this no-stroke reality that you have created for yourself.
Chris:	I don't know. Maybe I don't want to acknowledge that Jay knows the difference between a good job and a bad job.
Gestaltist:	Try dropping the maybe. And make your statement directly to Jay.
Chris:	Jay, I don't want to acknowledge that you know the difference between a good job and a bad job.
Gestaltist:	Because if I acknowledge that you know the difference between a good job and a bad job . . .
Chris:	. . . then I open myself up to criticism.
Gestaltist:	Chris, say, "I'm a person who doesn't want to be criticized."

Chris repeats the statement and adds, "My fantasy is that when I'm criticized I will start going downhill. I'll give up. I'll do worse and worse."

Gestaltist:	Chris, earlier you said to Jay, "I can't get excited about my work when you're so stingy with strokes," and now you're saying, "When I'm criticized I'll give up." These are the realities you create for yourself. Try saying this: "I'm a person who controls my energy according to the compliments and criticisms of Jay."

Chris repeats the statement and agrees that this is an accurate description of where he is. He too decides to give some thought to whether that is where he wants to remain.

The Absent Supervisor

The staff of a small agency was meeting to participate in a training program conducted by a Gestalt-oriented OD consultant. The director of the agency was present, as were six employees. The supervisor of the six employees, however, a man named Ed, was absent. When one of the employees had asked Ed if he was coming to the session, Ed had responded that he had a previous commitment and would not be there.

For several minutes at the beginning of the training session, the participants—the director and the employees—complained about Ed's absence, criticizing him and accusing him of indifference toward the other staff members and claiming that by his absence Ed was diminishing the value of this one-day training program.

The Gestaltist proposed this question: "Presume that the situation that you have is exactly the situation you want. Presume that Ed isn't here because you don't want Ed to be here. Let's talk for a while about how you benefit from Ed's absence."

Subsequent discussion revealed that there was indeed relief on the part of several people when they discovered that Ed was missing. Those who had frequent contact with Ed agreed that they had never really conveyed to him how important they felt this program was. In fact, Ed was informed of the meeting well after everyone else knew that it had been scheduled. Further discussion revealed that Ed was frequently used as a scapegoat, the built-in excuse for failure.

The Gestaltist then led the group members in a discussion of other realities that they might have created for themselves, including Ed's indifference toward them and the diminishment of the value of the training program. The staff members were able to put in perspective the extent to which they were in collusion with Ed on his "shortcomings." They were able to see how they abdicated their responsibility for organizational problems by attributing them to Ed and how they let Ed do the obstructing that they in truth wanted to happen, although they were unwilling to speak up themselves. Then they criticized Ed for blocking those things that they secretly were resisting.

CONCLUSION

Taking responsibility is the recurring theme of the Gestalt approach to organization development. Managers learn to take responsibility for themselves—their opinions, preferences, feelings, needs, and styles—and for the status quo of their organization, including some of the things they complain about most. Subordinates also learn to take responsibility for themselves and for the status quo of the organization. The organization strives to become continuously aware of its presence and uniqueness—its reality—which members (individually and collectively) have created for themselves.

Peter Scholtes is coordinator of organization development for the city of Madison, Wisconsin. He conducts various kinds of open workshops (conflict resolution, assertiveness, personal growth, management styles) and system interventions for organizations under stress. Mr. Scholtes' background is in community organization, organization and management development, and adult education. He is a therapist trained by the Gestalt Institute of New England.

INTRODUCTION TO THE
THEORY AND PRACTICE SECTION

When we titled this section for the first (1972) *Annual*, we were aware that our choice of words was optimistic. Now, as then, there are few (if any) real theories in the applied behavioral sciences. But our intent has been to facilitate the development of grounded (research-based) theory. A "real" theory has *explicit assumptions*, from which are derived *hypotheses*, which are, in turn, subject to *experimental test*. In this way, specific *predictions* can be made about what will occur under specified conditions. Predictions are tested, resulting in data that either corroborate the predictions—and underlying theory—or require modifications of the theoretical assumptions.

Theory serves a variety of functions. The most important of these are (1) *codifying accumulated knowledge* within one, consistent, overall framework and in this way (2) *clarifying and simplifying* the complexity we find in the real world, while (3) *directing the further development of knowledge* through (4) *guided experimental applications*.

Good theory, then, does not ignore what is known; all information relevant to the theory is included within it. Good theory does not overcomplicate; rather, it clarifies. By describing the basic structure of relationships among data, good theory makes our world more, not less, comprehensible. Good theory leads to the development of more and deeper understanding. It does not purport to incorporate all truth, but it has clear implications for where—and how—to look for more knowledge. Good theory includes specific, practical, action implications. It enables problems to be linked to solutions, for intelligible chains of logic provide prescriptions for action. Thus, good theory is useful.

These elements of a definition come from several sources, most notably Hall and Lindzey (1970) and Lewin (1948; see also Marrow, 1969). Most *Annual* users will already have realized that the definition is *value laden*, for it makes much use of the term "good" (and, by implication, of the inverse). Good theory must be comprehensive because it should be applicable to *all* the situations related to the subject of the theory, not just some situations. Good theory must be clear and simple because it should be understandable, in its essentials, by anyone of average intelligence, not just by a few "geniuses." For example, while complex in its more intricate details and implications, the basic elements of the general theory of relativity *can* be understood by the average person and not just by ten great brains in the world (as mythology has it). Good theory must point to further research because it is desirable to understand our world (including ourselves) better, and we know that it is not possible ever to fully understand such complexity. We need guidelines and directions for the development of greater understanding. Finally, good theory must be useful because in our value system—and in many others—the final and essential test of the goodness of anything is whether it has beneficial uses and whether it can improve the quality of human life. This aim was probably Lewin's primary value, and it is one we, along with most other group facilitators, share.

Since theories are rare in the applied behavioral sciences and good theory is rarer still, we suggest that each of the papers that appear in this section not be judged in terms of "good" or "bad" theory, but that users view these contributions as informational background, ideas, and implications for practice. As more information is conceptually organized and tested through practice, we move closer to good theory.

REFERENCES

Hall, C. S., & Lindzey, G. *Theories of personality* (2nd ed.). New York: John Wiley, 1970.

Lewin, G. W. (Ed.). *Resolving social conflicts*. New York: Harper & Row, 1948.

Marrow, A. J. *The practical theorist: The life and work of Kurt Lewin*. New York: Basic Books, 1969.

UTILIZING HUMAN RESOURCES: INDIVIDUAL VERSUS GROUP APPROACHES TO PROBLEM SOLVING AND DECISION MAKING

John J. Sherwood and Florence M. Hoylman

A well-known joke belittling the effectiveness of groups says, "The camel is a horse designed by a committee." This statement reflects the attitude that groups often fail to use common sense in accomplishing their tasks. Nevertheless, from corporate boards of directors to fraternity membership committees, groups are used for problem solving and decision making by almost all organizations. Although the use of groups is frequent and the dissatisfaction with the products of group efforts is widespread, managers often lack clear and explicit criteria by which to decide when to assign a problem to a group and when to assign it to an individual. A straightforward set of criteria is needed for determining whether a group or an individual is likely to produce better results on a given task. If a task is referred to a group, some guidelines on how to manage the group for the most effective outcomes are useful.

WHEN TO CHOOSE A GROUP AND WHEN TO CHOOSE AN INDIVIDUAL

There are five factors to consider when deciding whether to assign a particular task to an individual or to a group of people for joint consideration: (1) the nature of the task itself; (2) how important the acceptance of the decision or the commitment to the solution is to the implementation of the solution; (3) the value placed on the quality of the decision; (4) the competency and investment of each person involved and the role each person plays in implementing the decision; and, finally, (5) the anticipated operating effectiveness of the group, especially its leadership.

Nature of the Task

It is the nature of the task itself that is the first and most important criterion in determining whether a problem would best be solved by a group or by an individual. Certain types of tasks, such as creative or independent tasks, are best performed by individuals; other types of tasks that involve integrative functions or goal setting are particularly appropriate for groups.

This paper was adapted from J. J. Sherwood and F. M. Hoylman, *Utilizing Human Resources: Individual Versus Group Approaches to Problem-Solving and Decision-Making*. Institute for Research in the Behavioral, Economic, and Management Sciences, Paper No. 621, Purdue University. Copyright © 1977 by John J. Sherwood and Florence M. Hoylman. It relies heavily on the original contributions of N. R. F. Maier (see especially "Assets and Liabilities in Group Problem-Solving: The Need for an Integrative Function," *Psychological Review*, 1967, 74, 239-249); L. R. Hoffman, "Group Problem Solving," in L. Berkowitz (Ed.), *Advances in Experimental Social Psychology*, Vol. 2. New York: Academic Press, 1965, 99-132; and L. Bolman (unpublished material). The authors appreciate comments by Conrad N. Jackson and Donald C. King on an earlier version of this paper.

Creative Tasks

Research reveals that individuals working separately are more creative and effective as generators of ideas and as problem solvers than individuals working together in groups (except the brainstorming group—a collection of individuals following an established procedure—which can generate more ideas than individuals working alone). When the task calls for a creative solution, that is, a new alternative or a heretofore unconsidered option, an individual is a better choice than a group. For example, individuals do better than groups at creating or constructing an original crossword puzzle, designing a technical component, or writing a computer program. When seeking a creative outcome, one would do better to find an expert in the area, rather than to assemble a number of people.

Convergent or Integrative Tasks

When the problem requires that various bits of information be brought together to produce a solution, such as developing a business strategy, evaluating a new product, or solving a crossword puzzle, groups can offer superior outcomes. The *proviso* is, of course, that the group of people is capable of working together effectively.

Independent Tasks

Sometimes an eagerness to establish more teamwork results in persons whose jobs are for the most part independent of one another being encouraged to work as a team. When interaction with others is required to get one's job done—because of the flow of the work process, the necessity to share information or skills, or other forms of task interdependency—working together frequently or occasionally as a group may be very useful. One way, however, to assure *un*satisfactory work-group meetings is to insist that people whose jobs are for the most part independent of one another work together as a team. Effective managers understand which of their subordinates need to work together to get their jobs done and which do not.

Goal Setting

The lesson of management by objectives (MBO) is that persons should be involved in determining the goals that are designed to guide their behavior and against which they are to be evaluated. When goal setting is done in relevant groupings of managers and subordinates, more commitment to individual objectives can be expected.

Importance of the Commitment to the Solution or the Acceptance of the Decision

Research has shown that when people participate in the process of reaching a decision, they have more commitment to that decision—that is, they feel more ownership over the outcome. Therefore, they are likely to have more interest in it and to make more energy available for its implementation.

On the other hand, when an individual solves a problem or makes a decision, two tasks still remain. First, others must be persuaded that the particular outcome is the best or at least is desirable. Second, others must agree to act on this decision or to carry it out. It is clear that if participation in the decision-making process increases ownership of the outcome, problems of surveillance, monitoring, and follow-up are reduced.

Not all solutions to problems are dependent on the support of other people for effective implementation. Therefore, a manager must be aware which issues require the commitment of others and convene those people who are critical to a solution's effective implementation. Clearly, all decisions do not need to be made by group action.

Importance of the Quality of the Decision

The best managers know the trade-offs involved when they choose between a decision that has greater acceptance and commitment but is of lower quality and a decision that may be more difficult to implement but is of higher quality.

If a manager is sufficiently concerned with distributing responsibility so that a solution will be carried out completely and with dispatch, he or she may accept a solution of somewhat lower quality because it has widespread acceptance, rather than insisting on a solution of somewhat higher quality that is unacceptable to those on whom the manager is dependent for its implementation. In some cases, a manager may be willing to make an unpopular decision or to assign the solving of a problem to an individual expert, knowing that these solutions require additional resources to be invested in their implementation. The manager needs to weigh the importance of the quality of the decision.

The quality of a group product, in contrast to one produced by an individual expert in the field, varies depending on the competencies of group members, the information available to them, and their effectiveness in working together as a group.

Characteristics of Individual Group Members

There are three clear guidelines to use in assembling a group of people to address an issue: (a) the expertise each individual brings to the particular problem under consideration; (b) the stake each party has in the outcome; and (c) the role each person is likely to play in implementing any decision, that is, how dependent others will be on each individual's support of the group's solution. It is obvious from these three factors that managers probably will not wish to convene the same collection of individuals to address every issue.

Operating Effectiveness of the Group

A question that deserves special consideration is how effectively the individual members of a group will be able to work together to produce a solution of merit. This question needs to be raised each time a new group is assembled. If the members will have great difficulty in working effectively as a group, it may be better to refer the decision to an individual. In considering the operating effectiveness of the group, the skills of the leader of the group are particularly important, because the leader can do more than any other person both to enhance and to block the effectiveness of group efforts.

MANAGING A GROUP EFFECTIVELY

Groups have a great deal to offer; that is, they have particular *assets*. On the other hand, groups often fail to meet expectations for performance; that is, they also have *liabilities*. To use groups effectively, one must understand both these aspects.

Assets of Groups

Greater Knowledge and Information

Even when one person (e.g., the supervisor or a technical expert) knows much more than anyone else, the limited and unique information of others can fill important gaps. There is simply more information, experience, and competencies in a group than in any one of its members. The issue, therefore, becomes how to make this expanded pool of knowledge available and how to utilize it effectively.

Greater Variety of Approaches

Each person brings a somewhat different perspective to a problem, and these different ways of viewing the world can open avenues of consideration outside the awareness of any single individual. In addition, individuals can get into ruts in their thinking or into patterned ways of defining problems and approaching issues. Assembling a number of people expands the potential ways a particular problem can be approached.

Increased Acceptance

When individuals have an active part in the decision-making process, their ownership of the outcome is increased. The responsibility people feel for making the solution work is thereby enhanced. As mentioned earlier, when an individual solves a problem, two additional problems remain—persuading others both to accept the solution and to carry it out.

Reduced Communication Problems

The implementation of a decision is likely to be smoother and require less surveillance when people know the goals and obstacles, the alternatives that were considered but rejected, and the facts, opinions, and projections associated with making the decision.

Liabilities of Groups

It is clear that a group has more firepower than an individual and an assembly of people has an expanded potential for new perspectives and integrative solutions. Yet five or ten capable persons can meet together to solve a problem or to make a decision and leave the meeting frustrated, with little progress or with outcomes that are acceptable to only a few of the principals. The following are obstacles to effective group functioning.

Social Pressures to Conform

Sometimes majorities or powerful minorities (or the boss) pressure people to go along with a lower quality decision. In their desire to be good group members or to be accepted, people sometimes keep their disagreements to themselves (or voice them only to close associates after a meeting).

Quick Convergence

In a group there is frequently a tendency to seize quickly on a solution that seems to have support. The apparent acceptance of an idea can overshadow appropriate concerns for quality or accuracy. Agreement often is erroneously assumed to signal the correct or the best solution. Ideas of higher quality that are introduced late in a discussion may have little chance of real consideration. Research has shown that when groups are required to produce two solutions to every problem, the second solution is frequently of better quality.

A Dominant Individual

Sometimes one person may prevail because of status, activity level, verbal skills, or stubborn persistence—all of which may be unrelated to competence in the particular task facing the group. Since a leader is particularly likely to dominate a discussion, his or her skills and insights into the consequences of excessive control are especially important.

Secondary Goals or Hidden Agendas

Often individuals work simultaneously on the assigned task and on their own needs (usually covertly). Their hidden agendas may include personal pride, protection of one's own position or department, desires for visibility or acceptance, or personality conflicts with others who are present. Some of these factors lead to attempts to "win the decision" rather than to find the best solution; other factors lead to moves for prominence or to deference.

Time Constraints

Available time may restrict the group's potential. It simply takes more time for a group to make a decision than it does for a single individual. It also takes a good deal of time for a group to develop the skills and procedures required for effective work—that is, to capitalize on the assets mentioned earlier and to limit the liabilities inherent in any group effort.

Problems with Disagreement

Issues are often sharpened, and therefore clarified, when there are differences or conflicts between members of a group in defining the problem, gaining preferred solutions, obtaining information, or establishing perspectives. However, disagreement affects people differently, and hard feelings between individuals may block the group's progress. Some people experience disagreement as a cue to attack; others react to conflict and controversy by freezing or withdrawing.

When disagreement is well managed, new ideas and innovative solutions are often the outcomes. When differences between people are seen as sources of new information rather than as obstacles to be overcome, solutions tend to be more creative.

Premature Discussion of Solutions

Confusion and conflict occasionally arise over proposed solutions because there is insufficient agreement or clarity concerning the problem. Unwittingly, group members offer different solutions to solve different problems. Both the quality and the acceptance of solutions increase when the seeking of solutions is delayed until both goals and potential obstacles are identified.

EFFECTIVE LEADERSHIP

Identifying and mobilizing the resources of a group and overcoming the obstacles to effective group functioning are keys to the group's success. The quality of a group's decision depends on whether the people with the best ideas or those with the worst ideas are more influential. The declaration "Let's get all the facts on the table and then make a decision" is a naïve wish, as the liabilities of groups indicate. Getting all relevant information on the table and assuring that it receives an appropriate hearing is a very difficult task. Once the decision has been made to assign a job to a group of people, the behavior of the group's leader becomes critical to its success. Again, it is important to realize that the leader can do more than anyone else to facilitate or to block effective group functioning.

In problem-solving groups, effective leadership promotes the utilization of all members as relevant resources and ensures open and accurate communication among them. It is important, therefore, to understand the *leadership dilemma:* the more power a leader has, the more positive contributions he or she can make to a group's functioning and procedures, but also the more the leader's own behavior can be a barrier to the free exchange of ideas. The best solutions come with a *strong* leader working with *strong* group members. In this situation, conflict and disagreement tend to be creative. All resources have the opportunity to be fully utilized when (1) there is two-way initiative between the leader and other group members (not simply two-way communication, but two-way initiative); and (2) responsibilities for leadership activities are shared; provided (3) that the strength of subordinates coupled with their assumption of responsibilities for leadership functions do not threaten the boss.

There are several things required from members of a problem-solving group in which leadership is conceived as a set of *functions* to be performed by anyone seeing the need, rather than as a *role* to be filled by the boss. The more that each of these requirements of effective leadership is shared and performed by all members of a problem-solving group, the more productive and creative that group is likely to be. These functions include encouraging broad participation by bringing others into the discussion and by protecting minority points of view; assuming responsibility for accurate communications between other group members; summarizing progress by pointing out where things stand at the moment; and questioning the appropriateness or the order of agenda items.

The leader can do more than anyone else to create an unintentional "camel" as the group's product and to provoke the attitude that all people who have worked in groups have experienced: "If I can only get through this meeting, then I can get some work done!" On the other hand, the leader can also do more than anyone else to provide the conditions for effective group efforts. Some guidelines for when groups are a good choice and some insights into making those groups function effectively are especially helpful in the day-to-day life of a manager.

John J. Sherwood, Ph.D., is a professor of organizational psychology and chairman of the Department of Administrative Sciences in the Krannert Graduate School of Management of Purdue University, Lafayette, Indiana. He is also an active organizational consultant interested in new methods of improving organizational effectiveness and the quality of work life. Dr. Sherwood has written extensively in the area of organization change and development and has co-edited a new book, Sociotechnical Systems, *to be published in 1978.*

Florence M. Hoylman, Ph.D., is a principal in the consulting firm of Organizational Consultants, Inc., based in West Lafayette, Indiana. She specializes in new methods for improving organizational effectiveness and the quality of work life and has developed a series of public seminars for women in management. Dr. Hoylman's background is in counseling, organization development, and consultation.

TYPES OF PROCESS INTERVENTIONS

Arthur M. Freedman

During a recent consulting experience shared by several consultants, some useful discussion surfaced concerning *how, how often,* and *when* to intervene in groups and *what kinds* of interventions to make. The consultants expressed similar uncertainties and insecurities regarding their own OD skills and knowledge. How could they be sure that they would intervene effectively at just the point when an intervention would be maximally facilitative during a process consultation? The appropriate moment for a particular intervention might easily come and go without either consultant or client realizing it.

This discussion prompted the following operational "philosophy" of making interventions, with the thought that it may be of some value to other OD practitioners.

Although all process interventions can be called merely "process interventions," they can be differentiated into three distinct and separate classes. These types might be labeled *conceptual-input, coaching,* and *process-observation interventions.* Each type could (and probably ought to) be considered in terms of (a) *what it might look or sound like* when it is made; (b) the *objective(s)* that it can facilitate; (c) *when* it can be made; and (d) the *form* or *style* it might take.

CONCEPTUAL-INPUT INTERVENTIONS

Example

Member A, a supervisor (to the client group): "I am beginning to see that you people get pretty upset when I come over to discuss the work I want you to do . . . I can see that when you get upset, the work doesn't get done as well or as fast as I think it should . . . But what I don't know is what I do that gets you all so upset? Maybe I need to hear a little of what these consultants call 'feedback.'"

Member B (after a long silence, to Member A): "Well, I guess I could give you some . . . You know, A, you can be pretty overbearing sometimes, and some of these new guys don't know how to handle you."

Member A: (Pause) "What the hell are you talking about? What's that supposed to mean?"

Consultant (to the client group): "It seems to me that we're doing a little experimenting with giving each other feedback on how our actions affect each other, but we're running into a problem. As I see it, the problem might be: 'Just what *is* feedback and how do you give it so that the person [*stating the problem*] who is getting it can use it?' Does that sound right to you?" [*double checking for agreement or disagreement*]

The client group indicates general agreement; members nod their heads and offer short affirmative statements.

Consultant (to the client group): "O.K. Maybe it would help if I laid out some ground rules for giving feedback . . ." (More nonverbal affirmation from the client group) "Dif-

I wish to express my appreciation to Drs. Irvin Roth and Franklin Weingarten for encouraging me to write this paper.

ferent consultants use the idea of feedback in different ways, but, for me, good, useful feedback has three parts to it, and if any part is left out, the value of it decreases. The three parts are, first, your description of what the other person is *saying* and *doing* that is of concern to you. Second, your description of what you *feel* when you focus your attention on the other person's actions. Third, your indication of what you would *most likely do*, yourself, if you were on the receiving end of the other person's actions—the *implications* of his behavior.

"An example of a complete piece of feedback would be something like this: 'I noticed a moment ago that you reached over and patted me on the back when I commented on Bill's idea, and when I turned around to look at you, I saw you were smiling [*description of the focal behavior*]. At the time I felt pretty good . . . as if you were telling me that you thought I was saying the right thing. I like that because I know I need some reassurance. I felt good, almost proud of myself for being able to think up something to say that led to getting a pat on the back. And I guess I did feel that I was approved of and that my ideas were actually wanted [*expression of feelings*]. Now I'm thinking that I'll probably be more of an active participant at these meetings in the future . . . I don't think I'll hold myself back so much'" [*statement of implications*].

Member B (to Member A): "Yeah . . . That helps me to organize my thoughts better. What I was trying to say to you was that when you come over to us when we're working, you seem to see yourself as trying to 'discuss' our work with us. But, from my point of view, you come across as a critic . . ."

Consultant (to Member B): "Can you say what it is that he says or does that gives you the impression he is a critic?" [*coaching*]

Member B (to Member A): "Yes . . . You never tell us that we're doing O.K. All I can remember you saying are things like how you would approach the problem in a different way from the way we'd already done it [*description of behavior*]. And when you say things like that, I just want to hide somewhere and get out of the way [*close to expression of feelings*]. So I sometimes change the subject if I can, or I 'remember' another appointment I 'have' to go to. Naturally, the work stops . . ." [*statement of implications*]

Objectives

A conceptual-input type of process intervention is intended to provide members of a client group with an "organizing principle" that has, as its payoff, the power to help them see, clearly, distinctions between typical but not optimal behavior (the things people say and do and/or the style with which the things are said and done) and less traditional but more effective behavior. Conceptual inputs also tend to be easily remembered and can, therefore, be referred to in the future. When a consultant intervenes in this way, he is providing his clients with a new vocabulary and a conceptual system that is quite *explicit* and is *shared* and *understood* by all client-group members. Confusion and misunderstandings should thus be minimized, since clients are more likely to remember, understand, and make use of the kinds of behaviors to which the new "language" refers.

Timing

A conceptual-input type of intervention can be used at any time during a process consultation—as long as the contract between the consultant and the client group legitimizes this type of consultant behavior. For maximum effectiveness and impact, the intervention should come immediately *after* a transaction between members that clearly illustrates the undesirable consequences of dysfunctional or ineffective behavior. In the preceding example, the consultant timed his intervention to "piggyback" on Member A's expressed confusion (one sort of undesirable consequence). This was the point at which the intervention was most likely to make immediate sense to the client-group members. When an intervention makes sense, people are also most likely to make use of it.

Form or Style

A conceptual input should be brief and succinct. Words and phrases that are *comprehensible* to the members of the client group should be used. It does not help to make the perfectly appropriate intervention at exactly the right time if, for example, the consultant's terms are so pedagogical that his listeners cannot understand him. Such a style could result in clients' disregarding the consultant as an irrelevant ivory-tower type.

COACHING INTERVENTIONS

A second type of process intervention aims at facilitating the acquisition of desirable, functional habits of interacting.

Example

The scene takes place after the group has received a conceptual input on giving and receiving feedback.

Member A (to Member B): "I experience you as acting in an arbitrary manner . . ." (Silence) [*A is labeling B.*]

Consultant (to Member A): "What is it about Member B's behavior that has led you to conclude she is 'arbitrary'?" [*an invitation to focus on observable behavior rather than use abstract labels*]

Member A (to Consultant): "She sometimes asks us for information to help her make decisions . . ."

Consultant (to Member A): "Talk to her . . ."

Member A (to Member B): ". . . but, after you get it, even if you say you appreciate our ideas, you don't seem to use them . . . [*description of behavior*] You act in such a way that I develop the idea that you never really wanted our ideas in the first place and that you were just going through a formality . . . as if you knew right along that you would stick to your original decision regardless of what we might say" [*conjecture*].

Consultant (to Member A): "Do you have any feelings about that that you are willing to share with Member B?" [*invitation to complete the second component of feedback, ignoring the nonproductive conjecture*]

Member A (to Member B): ". . . Yes, I do . . . I find myself a bit confused and wondering whether anything I might say to you has any meaning or significance in your eyes. It's as if I am being disregarded and held off at a distance when I really want to get close to you and work with you. I don't want to be pacified. I guess I feel pretty disappointed . . ." (Pause) "I had always hoped that I could come up with ideas that would be valuable for helping us do our work . . . Yes . . . I'm very disappointed. I feel I'm something of a failure since I don't seem to be getting the response . . . the affirmation I've been looking for [*an expression of feeling*]. Now I'm not sure if I'll even bother giving you any information about me the next time you ask for it . . . I probably won't . . . I don't see what value it would have . . . You'd probably just disregard what I say" [*a statement of implications somewhat garbled by a prediction of Member B's future behavior, which may not be accurate*].

Member B (to Member A, after a long pause): "I hear what you're saying pretty clearly. It helps me to make some sense out of what has been happening between us over the last several weeks. I recognize now that I've sort of been aware of some tension. But I guess I just let myself pretend that it didn't mean anything . . . Now, I don't know quite what to do about it all . . ." [*an acknowledgment of the feedback and of having reached an impasse. This implies the possibility that B might be ready to accept help in identifying some functional alternatives for dealing with the problem—but she is not expressing this.*]

Consultant (to Member B): "Would you be interested in spending some time now to see if there's anything we can do about this problem?" [*an inquiry to test whether B is willing to assume responsibility for searching for new alternatives*]

Member B (to Consultant, after a pause): "No . . . I guess I'm feeling a need to think about this for a while. It has a lot of implications, and I'm not yet ready to share them all with anyone else. Right now I want some quiet time alone. I'll check back with the rest of you after I've had a chance to mull it over . . ." [*owning up to and being responsible for her desire to disengage temporarily, with an option to re-open the issue at a later date*]

Objective

Such coaching interventions are intended to assist members of a client group to get into the habit of using new experimental behaviors that they have said they want to practice.

Timing

Coaching interventions are most effectively made either (a) during the early, standard-setting phases of the consultative process (to "shape" the kinds and sequence of interpersonal communications at an early point) or (b) just after a conceptual input has been made that provides a justifiable theoretical framework for the coaching efforts. In either instance, coaching interventions should be discontinued as soon as the client group's members demonstrate that they can employ the new behaviors without assistance (or when some members begin systematically to perform the coaching function for other members).

Form or Style

Coaching interventions should use up very little of the client group's "air time." They should be suggestions rather than demands or reprimands. And they should be quite precise and not at all ambiguous. No one should have to guess what the consultant is aiming at.

PROCESS-OBSERVATION INTERVENTIONS

Example A

Member A (to the client group): "A little while ago I wanted to share an observation that I thought might have been useful at the time . . . but I restrained myself. I wanted to say that you've been on this topic for twenty minutes without coming to a conclusion . . . you're wasting my time . . . you guys aren't accomplishing anything . . . you ought to move on to a different issue [*a task-related function*]. I guess I was afraid that I would alienate myself from the rest of you by doing something 'unpopular'" [*expression of feelings*].

Several members (simultaneously to Member A): ". . . Wait a minute . . . Where did this come from all of a sudden . . . ?" [*probably a defensive response*]

Consultant (to Member A): "If I am hearing it accurately [*an attempt to reach group members in a preventive move*], you seem to be saying that you were reluctant to perform a task function for the group, even though you thought it was needed, because you were

afraid you would be risking the possibility of getting hurt by the rest of the group . . .
[paraphrasing] Am I hearing you right?" *[double checking]*

Member A (to Consultant): "That's about it . . ."

Consultant (to Member A): "Well, it seems to me that an *additional* issue might be the *style* or the *manner* in which you were thinking of performing that function. By saying what you wanted to say in the way you just expressed yourself, you probably *would* have given me, at least, a basis for feeling bad about myself . . . as if I had done something wrong. And that might have led to my wanting to hurt *you* or put *you* down or cut *you* off . . . *[somewhat hypothetical personal feedback]* I wonder if you can think of a different way of saying the same thing . . . a way that is less likely to result in your feeling cut out of the group?" *[an invitation to consider and experiment with an alternative form of performing needed task or maintenance functions]*

Member A (to the client group, after a long pause): "Yeah . . . I think so . . . Let me know how this comes across" *[unilateral negotiation for focused feedback]*. (Pause) "It seems to me that we've gone over the same points several times . . . It's like we've been recycling . . . *[description of group behavior]* I'm finding myself feeling unproductive . . . like I'm not able to do anything that seems useful or helpful . . . and that leaves me pretty impatient." (Pause) "Has anyone else been experiencing anything like this? If so, what do we want to do about it?" *[Considerably more self-disclosure and ownership of the speaker's ideas and feelings are publicly expressed here; also, instead of a critical and punitive accusation being made of the other members of the client group, A is including himself as a part of the problem and is inviting the rest of the group to collaborate in dealing with it. Action, taken on the basis of the person's observations and feelings, carries the idea of implications one step forward: out of the hypothetical and into tangible reality.]*

Example B

Consultant (to the client group): "I've noticed that we've been spending a lot of time jumping from one issue to another without finishing any of them. For example, Sam raised the question about whether or not we, as a group, wanted to spend our time giving each other feedback. Then Toni pointed out that we could give feedback to one person at a time in a way that would enable the 'receiver' to decide whether he or she wanted to renegotiate some interpersonal contracts with the 'giver.' In making this point, Toni seemed to direct the group's attention away from Sam . . . a kind of topic jump . . . about which Sam did nothing. Then, before the group responded to Toni's idea, Joe stated that he thought we ought to focus on some of the things that had happened three days ago during the general session, things that he thought were getting us hung up this afternoon . . . another topic jump *[a demonstration of the tracking or summarizing task function]*. All of this seems to indicate to me that we're having trouble figuring out *how* we can make group decisions about what we're going to do with our time *[spelling out the apparent problem confronting the group]*. Now I'm finding myself rather uncertain about just what is going on and a bit impatient *[expression of feelings]* for a clear, explicit, group decision. Just what is it that we would like to do?" *[statement of expectations and a direct request to the client group's members to disclose their opinions to flesh out the statement of the apparent group-level problem]*

Objectives

A process-observation intervention may have numerous objectives, including, among others, the following.

1. It can heighten the client-group members' awareness of the distinction between the *content and process dimensions* of transactions occurring within a group. In Example B, the consultant illustrated both *what* topics or issues the group was working on (the "content") and *how* the group seemed to be operating—i.e., topic jumping and avoiding explicit, group-level decision making (the "process").

2. Another kind of process observation might be intended to heighten the group's awareness of the *implications and consequences of its members' actions*. For example, an individual's behavior may contribute to the creation or continuation of *normative standards (both functional and nonfunctional) governing group members' behavior*. In Example B, Toni's topic jump might have contributed to the creation of a group norm that, in this group, it is O.K. to jump from one topic to another and cut off another person; when Joe did the same to Toni, it was another contribution to the legitimization and continuation of that norm. A process observation can also be used to highlight implications and consequences by pointing out how the group is affected when needed task and maintenance functions are *not* being performed or what happens when different group decision-making procedures are employed.

3. A process observation also provides an *observable model of functional behaviors* that demonstrate in a tangible manner how a group's movement in the direction of its objectives can be facilitated. In Example A, the consultant modeled quite a number of functional activities, e.g., paraphrasing, double checking, personal feedback, and helping another person experiment with new ways of behaving. In Example B, the consultant modeled tracking-summarizing, stating the issue, expressing feelings and expectations, and asking for opinions and information.

Timing

A process-observation intervention is likely to be most effective during the early phase of the consultative process. When any process observation has been modeled once or twice, the consultant should refrain from making further such interventions. This gives client-group members more opportunities to experiment with and to practice performing these facilitative functions. To the extent that they do this, they acquire increased self-sufficiency. This tends to preclude their becoming dependent on the consultant, the "expert," to perform such functions. If the client-group members do *not* assume responsibility for performing these functions after they have been modeled once or twice, the consultant might keep track of the implications and consequences of this failure. Then, during a "stop action" or some other designated process session, these data could be fed back to the group along with a question: "What, if anything, do we want to do about this situation?" This explicitly invites and allows the clients to negotiate a contract among themselves (a) to insure that needed functions are used when they would be most relevant and (b) to avoid the unnecessary, undesired consequences that have been observed to follow nonperformance of the functions.

Form or Style

In style, process observations should be personalized, invitational, and not punitive. But—almost by definition—this class of interventions usually takes a bit *longer* than others. The consultant is attempting to draw a verbal portrait of dynamic, constantly shifting group processes in order to help the client-group members see what is happening "right now" and also to model behavior that the members themselves might attempt at some future time. To get this double message across adequately, sufficient care and time must be taken.

CONCLUSION

Saul Alinsky's "iron rule"—"Don't ever do anything for people that they can do for themselves"—comes to mind. If one or more client-group members have the skills and knowledge to act in a functional and objective manner, they are entitled to opportunities to use such skills and knowledge. The consultant should let them do it. If they do not possess such resources, they may require assistance in acquiring them. However, excessive "assistance" on the part of the organizational consultant—whether process, theory, structured skill-practice exercises, or simulations—leads to stultification, dependency, and indifference or apathy. In order to be as effective as possible, the consultant must learn the fine line between *not enough* help and *too much* help.

SUGGESTED READING

Banet, A. G., Jr. Therapeutic intervention and the perception of process. In J. W. Pfeiffer & J. E. Jones, *The 1974 annual handbook for group facilitators*. La Jolla, Calif.: University Associates, 1974.

Blake, R. R., & Mouton, J. S. *Consultation*. Reading, Mass.: Addison-Wesley, 1976.

Cohen, A. M., & Smith, R. D. *The critical incident in growth groups: A manual for group leaders*. La Jolla, Calif.: University Associates, 1976.

Cohen, A. M. & Smith, R. D. *The critical incident in growth groups: Theory and technique*. La Jolla, Calif.: University Associates, 1976.

Schein, E. H. *Process consultation: Its role in organization development*. Reading, Mass.: Addison-Wesley, 1969.

Arthur M. Freedman, Ph.D., is a consulting psychologist in Chicago, Illinois. He also conducts workshops, contributes to many professional organizations, and is the author of a number of journal articles and chapters in three books. Dr. Freedman's background is in business administration and clinical psychology.

PERSONAL EFFECTIVENESS

Udai Pareek

Although one precondition for personal effectiveness is better self-awareness, understanding oneself does not alone make a person effective.

The Johari Window

One simple model for self-awareness that is widely used is the Johari Window, developed by Luft and Ingham (Luft, 1973). In this model, there are two main dimensions for understanding the self: those aspects of a person's behavior and style that are known to him (Self) and those aspects of his behavior known to those with whom he interacts (Others). A combination of these two dimensions reveals four areas of knowledge about the self (Figure 1).

The upper left-hand square is the Arena or the public self—that part of an individual's behavior known both to the person and to others with whom he interacts. The Arena includes information such as name, age, physical appearance, and familial or organizational affiliation.

The Blind area contains those aspects of the person's behavior and style that others know but that the person himself does not. A person may have mannerisms of which he is not aware that are perceived by others as funny, annoying, or pleasing. For example, an individual might be surprised to hear that his method of asking questions annoys others because it is interpreted as cross-examination rather than curiosity or a request for information.

The Closed area involves that which is known to the person but not revealed to others; things in this area are secret. For example, a subordinate may be annoyed if his supervisor does not ask him to sit down during a meeting, but he will remain standing without letting the supervisor know that he is annoyed. The supervisor may think that the subordinate does not mind standing and accept his behavior as part of their hierarchical relationship. Most of us have many such feelings in our Closed areas that we are unwilling to reveal to the persons concerned.

The fourth area is the Dark area, inaccessible both to the person and to others. Some psychologists believe that this is a very large area indeed and that certain circumstances (for example, an accident), a particular life stage, or special techniques such as psychoanalysis or psychodynamics may suddenly make a person realize some hidden aspects of himself. Because the Dark area cannot be consciously controlled or changed and therefore cannot be considered in a discussion of personal effectiveness, this discussion will be limited to the Arena and the Blind and Closed areas.

THE THREE-DIMENSIONAL PERSONAL-EFFECTIVENESS CUBE

Although it might be assumed that a large Arena and small Blind and Closed areas would be desirable and would contribute to personal effectiveness, this is not necessarily so. A person with a large Arena may still be ineffective because a large Arena is not the *only* factor in effectiveness. By adding the dimension of effectiveness to the Johari Window, we produce a three-dimensional cube or grid (Figure 2) similar to those proposed by Blake and Mouton (1964) and Reddin (1970).

Effectiveness as Communication

In order to use the dimension of effectiveness, however, we must first decide what effectiveness is. Personal effectiveness may be seen in the context of communication, according to the following criteria.

1. *Fidelity of Communication*. The distortion-free quality of a message is called fidelity. An effective person gets the message across to others with a minimum of misunderstanding. If the gap between what a person wants to communicate and what the other person understands is large, the effectiveness of the person who is sending the communication is low. For example, if a supervisor intends to communicate his confidence in an employee by not oversupervising, but the employee hears the message that the supervisor is not interested in his problems, the supervisor has low effectiveness.

2. *Economy*. Economy is an important criterion of communication effectiveness. An effective person uses a minimum of energy, time, symbols, and cues to communicate a message that can be understood. A person who spends excessive time communicating is less effective.

3. *Influence*. The most important criterion of effectiveness is the influence that the communicator is able to exercise over the receiver of the communication. Influence does not mean control; it means that the communicator achieves the result he intended. If he wanted an empathetic response and he achieved that as a result of his interaction, he influenced the other person. If a supervisor sends a message of trust and confidence to his subordinate and helps the subordinate develop autonomy and the ability to take the initiative, the supervisor has succeeded in influencing the subordinate.

4. *Congruence*. An effective communication integrates both verbal and nonverbal cues. If a verbal message conflicts with the speaker's nonverbal cues, the speaker's effectiveness will be low. For example, if a supervisor tells a subordinate that he is pleased with him, but frowns while doing so, he is giving a conflicting message and is not likely to be effective.

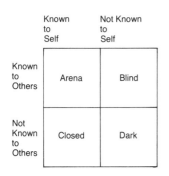

Figure 1. Johari Window

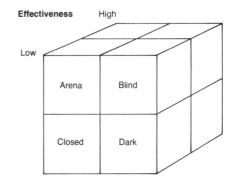

Figure 2. Personal-Effectiveness Cube (PEC)

5. *Relationship Building.* A communicator's influence is also to some extent in proportion to his ability to build a trusting relationship. Communications that contribute to the building of trust and better interpersonal relationships among individuals are more effective than those that do not.

Ranges of Effectiveness

Effectiveness may be categorized as ranging from low to high. A person who is not economical in communication, is low in fidelity, and uses conflicting cues, for example, would have very low effectiveness. The highest effectiveness would result from the most economical communication, the least distortion between what is communicated and what is understood, integrated verbal and nonverbal cues, a communication that contributes to a trusting relationship, and a communication that has maximum influence.

Possible Effectiveness Combinations

By combining high or low effectiveness with a large or small area in the Arena and the Blind and Closed areas, the three-dimensional Personal-Effectiveness Cube (PEC) shown in Figure 2 reveals twelve possible personality combinations (Table 1).

Self-Confident

A person with a large Blind area and high effectiveness (Figure 3) is likely to be self-confident. He may not be aware of his limitations, but he may also not be aware of some of his strengths. However, he is likely to rely on his strengths and be blind to his weaknesses. Although his effectiveness may see him through situations, it will certainly be limited because of his lack of awareness of some of his limitations and strengths.

Table 1. Personal-Effectiveness Cube Combinations

Arena	Blind Area	Closed Area	Effectiveness	Type of Person
	Large		High	Self-Confident
	Large		Low	Unperceptive
	Small		High	Perceptive
	Small		Low	Overly Cautious
		Large	High	Good Listener
		Large	Low	Secretive
		Small	High	Frank
		Small	Low	Egocentric
Small			High	Task-Oriented
Small			Low	Closed
Large			Low	Superficial
Large			High	Open

Unperceptive

A person with a large Blind area and low effectiveness (Figure 4) is unperceptive to the nonverbal cues that people may send about his behavior. For example, a professor who cannot see that the whole class is drowsy from a dull lecture may continue to bore the class. Unperceptive people find it difficult to understand subtle sarcasm, subdued communication of resentment and negative feelings, and body language.

Perceptive

A person with a small Blind area and with high effectiveness (Figure 5) is quite perceptive of verbal and nonverbal cues. This perceptiveness helps him to pick up such cues quickly and use them to change his strategy of interaction and hence his effectiveness. A perceptive supervisor who sees that a subordinate is preoccupied with some problem asks the subordinate about what is bothering him before pursuing task-related topics. This is likely to help the subordinate become more open and relate to the supervisor more effectively.

Overly Cautious

A person with a smaller Blind area knows more about his strengths and his limitations. However, if such a person has low effectiveness (Figure 6), he is more likely to be overly concerned with his weaknesses than he is to concentrate on his strengths. An overly cautious person finds it difficult to take the initiative and to risk because his limitations loom large to him and may immobilize him. Just having a smaller Blind area does not make a person effective.

Good Listener

A person with a large Closed area and with high effectiveness (Figure 7) is likely to be a good listener. Instead of giving his own opinions, he listens to the opinions of others and makes decisions based on his own judgment. He may not share his own point of view, even if his views are not close to the views of others.

Secretive

A person with a large Closed area and with low effectiveness (Figure 8) is likely to be secretive. Other people may wonder what criteria he uses to judge them or what he expects from them. They are also not likely to know how he feels, as he will not share his feelings with others.

Frank

A person with a small Closed area and with high effectiveness (Figure 9) is likely to be quite outspoken and frank. He gives feedback and expresses his opinions and points of view without any inhibition. He shares his personal feelings, experiences, joys, and sorrows also.

Egocentric

A person with a small Closed area but with low effectiveness (Figure 10) may tend to talk excessively about himself, his achievements, his talents, his experiences, and even his personal life. He is so egocentric he is not likely to pay attention to others and their needs.

Task-Oriented

A person with a small Arena can be quite effective in a limited way (Figure 11). One model for an effective administrator is a person with a small Arena and a high task orientation. Such a person does not relate to others on a personal or social level. He is mainly concerned with task performance and may restrict his communication and interaction with others only to the tasks involved.

Closed

A person with a small Arena and low effectiveness (Figure 12) is usually closed, neither sharing his impressions nor listening to others and using the feedback he receives. Such a person will be quite ineffective.

Superficial

A person with a large Arena but with low effectiveness (Figure 13) does not use his openness to good effect with others. He may interact with others, offer his opinions, and listen to others, but these acts are usually of a superficial nature. He does not exercise his judgment about when to be open and what to look for in the feedback he receives from others.

Open

A person with a large Arena (the open self) and high effectiveness is open (Figure 14). His opinions are given freely and are well understood, he feels free to communicate his impressions, and he gives feedback to others with a sensitivity that they appreciate. Similarly, he is eager to receive feedback from others; he solicits it and then critically examines and uses it to good effect.

DEVELOPING PERSONAL EFFECTIVENESS

Personal effectiveness must be viewed across three dimensions: openness, perceptiveness, and communication, all significant dimensions in interpersonal relationships. By becoming more open, a person reduces his Closed area; the Blind area is reduced by increasing perceptiveness; and communication can be improved in various ways discussed previously. These three dimensions, however, do not function in isolation; each interacts with the others. In order to increase effectiveness, it is necessary to work on a combination of all three.

Openness

The extent to which one shares ideas, feelings, experiences, impressions, perceptions, and various other personal data with others, openness is an important quality and contributes a great deal to a person's effectiveness. But openness can also be dysfunctional. Openness in combination with perceptiveness and communication does make a person much more effective, but openness alone is often misunderstood as sharing everything with everyone. Pfeiffer and Jones (1972) have used the term "Carolesque" openness to describe openness without accompanying sensitivity to others in a situation. The word was coined from Carol's behavior in the movie *Bob & Carol & Ted & Alice*. Carol, recently "turned on" by a weekend growth center experience, pours out her feelings in a way that embarrasses her dinner companions and confronts a waiter with feeling data. Although such behavior may indicate that the person is "in touch" with his own feelings, it also indicates that he is out of touch with the feelings of others.

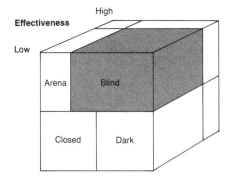

Figure 3. Self-Confident Person

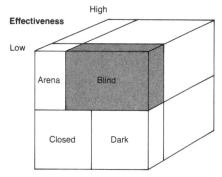

Figure 4. Unperceptive Person

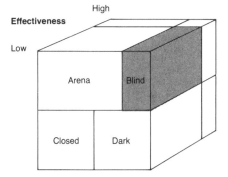

Figure 5. Perceptive Person

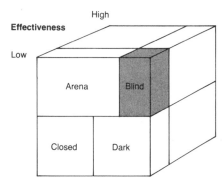

Figure 6. Overly Cautious Person

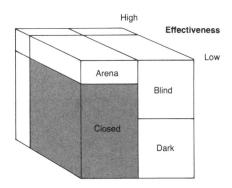

Figure 7. Good Listener

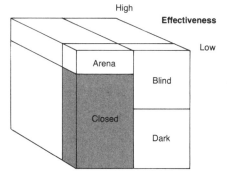

Figure 8. Secretive Person

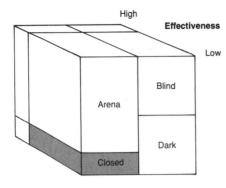

Figure 9. Frank Person

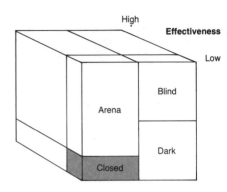

Figure 10. Egocentric Person

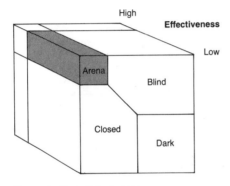

Figure 11. Task-Oriented Person

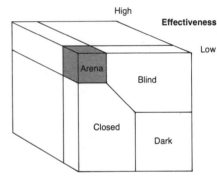

Figure 12. Closed Person

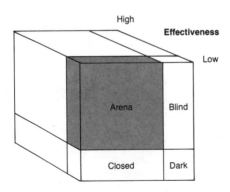

Figure 13. Superficial Person

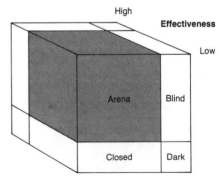

Figure 14. Open Person

176

Pfeiffer and Jones suggest that *"destructive openness* can result from an inordinate value being placed upon 'telling it like it is,' from insensitivity to the recipients of the communication, or from a desire to be punitive"* (p. 197). They suggest what they call "strategic openness" as an alternative, that is, "determining how much open data flow the system can stand and then giving it about a ten percent boost."

Openness can be characterized as effective, first, if the person sees that sharing what he wants to share is appropriate. Inappropriate sharing does not contribute to effective openness. For example, a typical task group is usually an inappropriate place for a person to share marital problems. Second, openness can be characterized as effective if the person is aware of what his openness is likely to do to others. Those who practice openness by calling others names or pouring out all their feelings are not likely to be effective. For example, a supervisor who takes out his anger on a subordinate without taking into consideration that person's ability to process and use the data generated will not be effective. The supervisor would be better advised to listen to the subordinate and share his concerns in a manner that will help the subordinate use the data he receives.

Perceptiveness

The ability to pick up verbal and nonverbal cues from others indicates perceptiveness. However, like openness, this dimension must be combined with the other two dimensions. A person who is not open himself may receive many cues and much feedback from others at first, but if a person is not open with others he may be seen as manipulating them and as generally unavailable. Perceptiveness and openness reinforce each other and, used effectively, are likely to increase personal effectiveness. Like openness, perceptiveness can be used appropriately or inappropriately. If a person is too conscious of what others might feel, he may inhibit his interactions. Similarly, a person who is overly concerned with his own limitations will tend not to take risks. Effective perceptiveness can be increased by checking with others about their reactions to what was said. If a person does not do this (in other words, if he is not open), he may become overly concerned about the cues he receives.

Conclusion

In short, personal effectiveness can be increased by moving toward appropriate perceptiveness and openness. Organizational consultants and trainers, while working on the processes leading to increased effectiveness, will find it useful to emphasize the role both of openness and of perceptiveness as contributing factors to effectiveness. However, movement in these directions is possible only through a greater emphasis on communication. People must learn to take risks in giving feedback to others and to use in an appropriate manner the feedback they receive. Only in this way can personal effectiveness truly be increased. Figure 15 demonstrates the effect on the Blind area of receiving feedback and the effect on the Closed area of giving feedback. In both instances, the Blind and Closed areas are reduced by this interaction, thus improving personal effectiveness. Using feedback this way is one of the continuing goals of human relations trainers.

REFERENCES

Blake, R. R., & Mouton, J. S. *The managerial grid*. Houston, Tex.: Gulf, 1964.

Luft, J. *Of human interaction*. Palo Alto, Calif.: National Press Books, 1961.

Pareek, U. *Interpersonal feedback*. CR Readings. New Delhi: Learning Systems, 1976.

Pfeiffer, J. W., & Jones, J. E. Openness, collusion and feedback. In J. W. Pfeiffer & J. E. Jones (Eds.), *The 1972 annual handbook for group facilitators*. La Jolla, Calif.: University Associates, 1972.

Reddin, W. J. *Managerial effectiveness*. New York: McGraw-Hill, 1970.

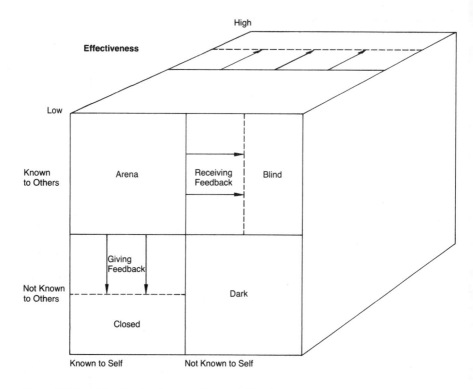

Figure 15. Use of Feedback to Increase Personal Effectiveness

Udai Pareek, Ph.D., *is Larsen & Toubro Professor of Organizational Behavior at the Indian Institute of Management, the director of Management Structure and Systems Private Limited, the chairman of Learning Systems Private Limited, and the chairman of the Policy Board of the Behavioral Sciences Center, Ahmedabad, India. He is also the editor of* Vikalpa: The Journal for Decision Makers and Survey of Research in Psychology in India, *Volume 2 (1978). Dr. Pareek's background is in organization development, organizational design, change in persons and systems, and human resources development in industry, education, and the community.*

CONFIGURATIONAL LEARNING: PRINCIPLES FOR FACILITATING CHANGE AND LEARNING FROM EXPERIENCE

Sam Farry

At the same time, different people believe things to be different, and to the same person things seem quite different than they did only a few weeks or months ago. Exactly what is different and how it is different, however, are difficult to determine. This is the nature of what is often referred to as "social change" or individual "psychological change." Configurational learning is a holistic way of understanding and consciously engaging such change.

In this article, the principles of configurational learning are outlined to help facilitators of individual, social, and organizational change to organize, "invent," and critique the activities in which they engage as "agents of change." Many times facilitators wonder "What should I do?" or "What should I do next?" This guide discusses the conditions of configurational learning, activities to stimulate such learning, and additional suggestions. Each point is considered in terms of how it relates to configurational learning, and each is illustrated with possible applications for facilitators with widely different backgrounds and from many different fields.

Concept of Change

Although the idea that everything is in a constant state of flux may seem foreign to Western thought, it is increasingly supported by the most advanced of the physical sciences—high energy particle physics. Individuals continuously participate in this ceaseless process of changing and interpret their interactions in it. The fact that confusion exists over changing and not changing is largely a function of people's lack of awareness of this changing as it occurs and a distortion in the common usage of language. Each individual, guided by tacit social agreements embedded in language patterns and previous experience, consciously or unconsciously selects what to perceive and how to interpret it and thus organizes it—i.e., he develops a *configuration*. Each configuration represents an implicit decision about what, out of a total context, is important or irrelevant and what to pay attention to or ignore. Typically this activity passes unnoticed (out of awareness), thus leaving the impression that things are static and must be made to change. Therefore, "social change" or "psychological change" usually refers to changing an only apparently static condition.

Configurational learning is the process that occurs naturally when individually determined configurations change. The process involves organization: rearranging, adding to, subtracting from, and re-evaluating previous configurations. Configurational learning may be experienced as an active process of exploration or simply as vital living. The idea of configurational learning acknowledges that people's natural interpreting and organizing activities are in fact equivalent to "changing" and encourages gaining an appreciation of and facility with this process rather than attempting to force something that occurs anyway.

Facilitation of Change

From a configurational-learning point of view, the problem of change is not how to make it happen, but how to redirect attention when a certain configuration seems unsatisfactory. The objective is to enable an individual's inherent organizing and changing process to create a new, more useful configuration. Thus, the principal functions of the facilitator are to promote clarification of existing configurations and prompt a change in those that are inadequate by sufficiently confusing their structure so as to cast them in a new light. For an individual or individuals in groups, redirecting attention is equivalent to Lewin's (1947) concept of "unfreezing." Lewin's other two stages, "moving" and "freezing," are represented respectively by configurational learning and by the emergence of a new and more satisfactory configuration.

More explanation may help in understanding this definition of facilitation and the concept of a configuration. A configuration is more than a set of ideas or an abstracted mental construct. Rather, it is a tightly integrated network of the relationships among all of one's capacities and perceptions. In fact, it could be depicted as a completely orchestrated scenario with provisions for ideas, theories, actions, images, sensations, feelings, beliefs, relationships, values, opinions, environmental props, and even consequences and predictions of the future. In terms of a person's configuration, the world is literally different for an insecure person than it is for someone who is secure. Or, when a person is hungry, the world is different for him than when he is not. Transactional analysis has popularized certain configurational arrangements as ego states, games, and scripts (Berne, 1961).

It could be said that configurations and situations are flip sides of the same coin. They evoke one another and both depend on and determine what one pays attention to. An adult's configurations typically come from a well-practiced repertoire that has become habitual; most of the configurations' properties and relationships remain unnoticed; however, everyday life involves many configurational shifts to meet individual needs and circumstances. This shifting is a less dramatic form of configurational learning that, over time, stimulates minor adjustments and gradual changes in the configurational repertoire.

Each person's configuration prepares him for organized action, but by so doing, it inhibits the formation of alternative courses of action. Paradoxically, a configuration that makes the world appear stable, and thus manageable, also precludes an appreciation of the natural propensities for changing. One configuration blocks another. This blocking phenomenon can be seen through the now classic ambiguous pictures used by Gestalt psychologists to study visual perception. In the normal course of events, when a configuration outlives its usefulness, the person becomes bored and develops a special interest in changing—in trying new ways.

Impetus for change can come about for various reasons:

1. Inhibition may not be complete; one may be confused. A person whose configuration, because of changing conditions, comes to fail often enough to effectively manage his actions eventually takes note, becomes concerned, and intentionally seeks out new possibilities. This is the most dramatic and engaging instance of the natural process of configurational learning.

2. A configuration may seem wrong or self-defeating, thus sparking an uncomfortable feeling and also bringing about change. Of course, any skilled facilitator knows that the discomfort of an unsatisfactory configuration does not always pro-

mote effective change. If a person thinks that he needs to make change happen, he is likely to push harder within the context of the existing unsatisfactory configuration rather than loosen its inhibiting effects by intentionally redirecting attention, reinterpreting, and heightening awareness. This is when the facilitator's skill effectively comes into play.

Facilitator's Role in Change

Facilitative qualities such as trust and support are very important, as is insight, the most widely accepted objective of facilitation and a sign of completed configurational learning. The most dramatic instances of configurational learning come when a person creates new configurations out of whole cloth, so to speak, a process that requires tremendous amounts of energy. The rules are by no means clear. Because there is no tried and true method to fall back on, the process can also produce discomfort, anxiety, and disorientation. Understanding, accepting, and communicating these aspects of configurational learning are important parts of the facilitator's role.

Periods of the most dramatic configurational learning are referred to as *crises*. Sudden insight into problems is the frequently experienced result of crises because the increased energy and special awareness brought to bear can contribute to unusual lucidity, perhaps even to a profound sense of wholeness and connection with the universe. More often, however, the resulting experience is one of "Aha, I've got it together," "Right on," "I feel centered," etc. Or more modest configurational rearrangements may be accompanied merely by the sense that an uncomfortable feeling has been reduced. All these experiences are evidence of completed configurational learning. Nearly everyone can remember having such experiences at some time in his life and can learn to recognize them as milestones in the life process.

CONDITIONS CONDUCIVE TO CONFIGURATIONAL LEARNING

Certain conditions are best for configurational learning; it is the facilitator's function to encourage these conditions in order that configurational learning can take place most readily.

Taking a Playful or Adventurous Attitude

A new configuration can seem as secure as an old one, but the process of forming the new configuration can cause discomfort, anxiety, and disorientation. From the perspective of a familiar existing configuration—no matter how unsatisfactory—new possibilities seem strange and foolish. A playful or adventurous attitude is helpful to set the stage for effective configurational learning. In fact, addressing a problem with either or both of these attitudes may in itself be sufficient for a new, more satisfactory configuration to emerge.

A facilitator can encourage an individual or a group to adopt such an attitude merely by being willing to appear foolish himself. Sometimes it can be useful to introduce, temporarily, a set of rules that will supplant existing rules of behavior and facilitate playfulness. For instance, the facilitator can set time limits on exploration activity or divide the total time for a group meeting into three or four subsegments by beginning and ending the meeting several times during the regularly allotted period. Other rules such as "You can be foolish only if you stand on this rug or sit in this chair" can be utilized.

Allowing Awareness

An awareness of what is happening at the moment is essential for formation of a new configuration. Because awareness is constantly shifting, however, increasing it typically requires practice. When attended to closely, awareness can be experienced to move from inside oneself (feelings and sensations) to outside, and the other way around. Frequently, it includes thoughts that have no noticeable sensory component. Few people are trained to be aware of slight shifts or to be directly aware of their several senses at once. A heightened awareness of what is happening can be threatening, and the threat can block the awareness and substitute a personal interpretation or fantasy.

The frequently heard suggestion to be "nondefensive" is an attempt to reduce any such blockage. This, however, is much easier to say than to do; openness to experience and awareness cannot be forced. But it is possible to acknowledge and appreciate the awareness that does exist until one learns that one's awareness can be trusted.

Meditation can be good practice for expanding awareness, as can answering specific questions such as "Right now what are you aware of?" Observers can contribute their observations. For group or intergroup situations, completing a narrowly defined task (such as agreeing on who talks the most or building a model) can draw attention to certain characteristics of that situation such as voice quality, interaction patterns, etc. The essential point is to allow an expanded awareness, not to try to interpret it, to solve problems, or to otherwise block it.

Redirecting Attention

Attention can be redirected to clarify the current configuration, to bring into focus how it works and what it includes and does not include, or to clarify potentially valuable dimensions previously missing or out of place.

Redirection is equivalent to disturbing a current configuration so that a new one can emerge. If ideas are most salient in the present configuration, one might try attending to feelings or actions; if one is enmeshed in emotions, being aware of concepts might prove fruitful.

Many people are not accustomed to distinguishing between what is happening to them *now* and what they think would happen under other circumstances. Calling attention to this distinction by paying attention to the here-and-now can often cause a readjustment in the current configuration.

Some people find focusing attention uncomfortable or threatening. If this is the case, practice is critical. An answer to the question "Where are you?" or "What's happening right now?" will clarify the locus of attention and what is going on (the current configuration). Making a statement as some event occurs can facilitate directing attention to that event. For example, if a tennis player is distracted and not paying attention to the ball, she can practice saying out loud "bounce" each time the ball hits the ground and "hit" each time it hits the racket (Gallway, 1974). Or a person can notice his breathing by counting each time he inhales.

In a group, someone can be appointed to call attention to the location of the discussion as it shifts—here/now/there/then. Sometimes a conceptual model of sequential stages in an activity can direct attention to the group's stage at the moment. Reports can also be used effectively to direct attention.

Owning Experience

The idea is simply to clarify whose experiences are whose by accepting responsibility for "those that are mine." If an experience or its cause has been attributed to someone else because it is not acceptable in a current configuration, merely "owning" it can spark configurational learning. Owning adds material potentially essential to a new, more satisfactory configuration. Everyone has had experiences or emotions that are considered socially or morally unacceptable, such as experiencing delight at someone else's pain or the more personal experiences of affection or anger. If some of these emotions are not acceptable in a current configuration, a person can simply own as many as he can. Perhaps he will muster the courage to own more at another time.

Owning experiences can be greatly facilitated simply by practicing statements with the correct pronoun: "I" rather than "we" or "you." Instead of "You don't like me," an owned statement might be more like "I'm uncomfortable because I believe that you don't like me." An activity to help check out owned experiences is "I believe, you believe." One person says, "I believe that you believe . . ." and the other party reciprocates. One can also try reversing pronouns to see if they fit, for instance, "I am" instead of "you are." Owning what "I want" can be a powerful antidote to feeling low and powerless.

The same condition exists for groups. Instead of "They won't let us," an owned statement might be "We're afraid." A facilitator can appoint someone to be chief nitpicker on this distinction. Owning experience also is facilitated by an individual or group assuming responsibility for a task by undertaking the completion of a tangible product such as a paper, a chart, or a model based on an immediate or recent experience. For example, a group could prepare a model showing the relationships among members of the group.

Sensitivity training groups aim for consensual validation of experience, a form of owning experience in contrast to habitual and reflexive behavior patterns such as rebelliousness, submission, or withdrawal.

Commitment, especially in the presence of others, to do something or assume responsibility for something can be an expression of having owned an experience. In this case, the experience is the involvement and perhaps anguish required merely to take the stand or make the commitment. Owning experience is equivalent to the transactional analysis notion of "I'm O.K." or the *est* notion of "I've got it." The conditions (described later) of "taking sides" and "taking a position" are also forms of owning experience.

Testing for Fit and Completion

Testing for fit and completion is one way to discover an unsatisfactory configuration or specific possibilities for a better one. Although everyone has the innate capacity to know when a configuration fits or seems right, people frequently act out of habit or at someone else's suggestions and are likely to misread evidence that a configuration is out of line with current circumstances. It is easy to deceive oneself and ignore the vague sense of discomfort that signals an unsatisfactory configuration.

Completion is the feeling that the configuration does fit and that no new exploration is necessary. Not being able to tell the distinction between "It's time to stop" and "I feel finished" can result in a backlog of unfinished material from previous situations. Although nothing is completely finished until one dies, being unaware of carryover interferes with awareness in new surroundings and serves to block spontaneous configuration-forming capacities. For example, if one is still angry with the people at work, it may be difficult to enjoy an evening with the family. Unfortunately, completion can be troublesome, and it is sometimes avoided because it involves a sense of personal loss—an accustomed configuration or longstanding problem is a reliable old friend.

To test for fit, people can take alternate positions (yes or no) on whether a particular configuration fits, in order to get a clearer sense of what is true for them. If the answer is "I don't know" or "I can't tell the difference," then clarification is necessary. One can also alternate between the following positions: it is, it is not the problem; I want it, I don't want it; I'm afraid, I'm not afraid; I will do it, I won't do it; I appreciate, I resent. If both seem to fit, then the question is *how* they both fit. Sometimes a person needs to acknowledge that feelings that commonly do not go together, such as "I love you *and* (rather than *but*) I don't want to marry you" or "I dislike the job *and* I'm willing to continue working here," can exist simultaneously. It may be difficult to discover apparent contradictions by oneself. In this case another person can be helpful to suggest lines to be tested for fit.

Sometimes a concrete action such as drawing a model can be a productive way for a group of people to test for fit, or people can act out a situation that seems unsatisfactory to pinpoint what is out of place or missing. If a number of people are available, the person whose problem it is can assign positions and characteristic actions and lines to other participants who volunteer to be actors. Trying out alternative approaches is also a good way to test for fit. Questions such as the following can be useful: "Am I finished?," "Is there more?," "When should we meet again?," or "Are you ready to sign?"

Testing for completion involves saying good-bye. To conclude a meeting systematically and effectively, it is often useful for people to express directly what they have left unsaid—residual resentments or good feelings. A clear and sharp conclusion allows the meeting to end without emotional hangover.

Testing for completion can also be a good way to start a meeting. Those attending can "leave behind" previous situations or people. Each person can complete the sentence "Right now, I am aware of . . ." to discover if he is really ready to attend to the business at hand. Often, merely checking on awareness allows the unfinished material to be put aside and attention to be focused on the meeting.

ACTIVITIES TO STIMULATE CONFIGURATIONAL LEARNING

The facilitator's function is to clarify existing but inadequate configurations in order to permit spontaneous reorganizing and changing processes to occur. Activities can be framed to show individuals how to improve their own capacity for redirecting attention and how their configurational learning is facilitated by others in individual, group, or larger social contexts.

Beginning Where the Interest Is

Configurational learning requires energy. Participant interest is a sign of energy and often is a reliable guide to what needs attention, i.e., what is unsatisfactory about a current configuration. What is wanted may be clear, but the current configuration may obscure how to get it effectively; or what is wanted may be obscure, in which case beginning with participant interest is likely to turn up valuable clues.

Approaching a problem by going over it again and again is likely to retrench a current configuration rather than produce a fresh one. Instead, a facilitator can focus on his own immediate awareness of the problem or situation, be it a person, a feeling, a condition, or an object. If interest is not clear, one can pace up and down the room or ruminate out loud about the problem in an effort to heighten awareness. Another approach is to imagine that one is "in the center of the problem," e.g., in the office or in one's retirement years.

Groups often elude configurational learning by sticking to a preset objective or agenda, but an already existing configuration can inhibit the formation of a new one. Thus, spontaneous, though apparently scattered, expressions of individual interest are likely to serve the group better. Various perceptions can be put on newsprint for a rich array of material to stimulate creative problem solving.

Doing It Differently

Doing it, as opposed to talking about it or being told about it, brings out all aspects of a configuration and is likely to uncover blockages. Doing it can take any form that feels best: writing, acting, lecturing, painting, singing, miming, etc. Intentionally doing it differently, even though "different" may not necessarily represent a more desirable configuration, mixes up the current configuration and directs attention to possibilities for a configuration previously thought to be unimportant.

To do it differently, a person who is feeling the situation can try thinking it or vice versa. Instead of going from front to back, a person can try going from back to front or turn the situation upside down or make right wrong and wrong right, etc.

Participants can be encouraged to pick a common public situation, such as walking down a street, riding on an elevator, or eating in a restaurant, and to redefine the situation and act out their new definition; e.g., groups have used elevators as a place to meet people or restaurants as a place to try out a new personality.

"Doing it" is most obvious when interpersonal problems are involved, and role playing seems natural as a kind of practice for "reality." However, even if the problem is physical or conceptual, it can be explored by "doing it." Examples of such problems would be "How could a house be invented that requires no commercial energy?" or "What is the relationship among atoms in a chloroform molecule?" Someone can play the role of a house or a molecule or a career, etc. Simulations can involve elaborately constructed props and circumstances or they can be carried out completely in one's imagination.

Taking a Position

Taking a position in this case is quite different from the way a person might typically consider a problem; i.e., "I would like to do this; but on the other hand, I want to do that; however, that would interfere with . . ." Instead, by taking a position, a person can explore these desires or considerations one at a time and can more fully experience his position without negating it by premature moderation. This approach also adds interest to the exploration.

A group as a whole can also take a position, perhaps prepare a manifesto on what is wrong with or good about another group (a typical first step in an organization development intergroup laboratory [Fordyce & Weil, 1971]).

Taking Sides, Confronting, Clarifying

Taking sides serves to contrast one aspect of a situation in relation to another, thereby clearly revealing the structure and content of a current configuration. Taking sides may seem counterproductive, but if an unsatisfactory configuration exists, trying to keep it together impedes the progress of configurational learning. The objective of taking sides is not to tear apart but to achieve clarified differentiation. By first taking one side and then the other, one can determine what the real issue is. This sets the stage for spontaneous integration of solutions.

If the issue is an interpersonal or interorganizational dispute, taking sides (contrary to many currently popular theories) can be valuable to crystallize the relative subtleties, capacities, and needs of each party. Role plays or psychodramas are useful applications; a critical point for the structuring of a role play or psychodrama, however, is the question of *who* is interested in forming a new configuration. Because each person has his own configurational learning, one person's insight may be different from the insight of others.

If advocates get locked into one side of a win-lose struggle, they are more likely to block rather than facilitate their own configurational learning. There is a higher probability that configurational learning will occur when participants alternate sides of the situation. For example, someone could write a letter to someone else and then write a response to his own letter. In an intergroup relations development laboratory, members of each group are often asked to prepare a list of what bothers them about the other group; then they are asked to prepare a list of what they think will be on the other group's list. The popular "two-chair" exercise of Gestalt therapy (Perls, 1973) is the prototype of contrasting two sides. Using this method, a person explores his own conflicts in dealing with another person by first sitting in one chair, imagining the other person in the opposite empty chair, and talking to that person. When a response is called for, he switches chairs and responds as the other person. The dialogue continues until a new configuration is reached.

Noticing and Acknowledging What Is Going On

Although one can learn to take inventory and systematically to check out what is going on in an effort to find inconsistencies or things unaccounted for in a current configuration, the process can be very difficult for an individual on his own. A facilitator can call attention to fruitful areas for exploration and inconsistencies that may be pieces of a new configuration. It is especially useful to notice movements and sensations.

Some useful activities for training one's capacity to notice specific areas include directing attention to relaxing various parts of the body, engaging one sense at a time and noting the effect of this, concentrating all senses on one object, or intentionally mixing senses, such as drawing a picture of the musical note high C. Watching body language has become a popular pastime, but rather than interpret posture, as some people are inclined to do, one might more productively study form, function, and grace and their relationship to thoughts or feelings. Listening to the qualities of voices (one's own and others), such as timbre, pitch, or rhythm, can offer extremely valuable clues to feelings, as can watching people's expressions. Paying attention to images, emotions, feelings, thoughts, and hunches perhaps takes more work, but one can heighten sensitivity to these factors by imagining oneself in situations that might provoke certain emotions, thoughts, or feelings.

Following Awareness and Interest

Determining what is significant or potentially productive in any given situation may seem to require the skills of a good theatrical director. A very useful guide for the facilitator is to follow his own interest and awareness. His own capacity for forming configurations often will enable him to call attention to what is missing, blocked, or out of place. If his interest shifts or if he is aware of something new, the facilitator can give it proper attention, savor it, and include it in the exploration activities. If the change in direction is misplaced, he can find out soon enough by testing for fit.

Despite common belief, an emotion, once experienced fully, tends to be forgotten. It is the blocked, unexperienced emotions that cause pain and attract attention. Those aspects of the situation that are currently hidden are likely to be uncovered then, if the natural flow of awareness and interest is paid attention to. Typically, much information is taken in and discarded or assimilated without notice, and immediate sensory awareness is blocked. A facilitator can redirect attention by bringing up what is most obvious and interesting to him (but perhaps not to someone else)—his own awareness.

Writing, poetry, painting, and sculpting, if conducted without concern for "correctness," can also be powerful methods for focusing attention on emotional content. To explore further, a group could act out a painting or sculpture that has been completed or engage in a dialogue between aspects of a painting.

Intensifying or Diminishing

Intensifying an action makes the underlying precepts distinct. For instance, instead of requesting we may "demand" or instead of talking we may shout. Intensifying an action encourages wholeheartedness, the engagement of all of one's faculties, and thus a deepening of the experience. Intensity can spark sensations and thoughts that are tied to an earlier experience; i.e., one may recall a moving situation from the past when he hears a certain song, etc. By experimentally intensifying an action or an emotion, a person may be able more accurately to identify its underlying characteristics and special properties.

Direct and demanding actions are taken most freely if the context is distinctly understood to be one of exploration. Phrases such as "I want" or "I demand" instead of "would you please" accentuate the transactional character of the situation and facilitate understanding, especially of relationships. "Yes" or "no" and "I will" or "I won't" are clearer than "maybe" or "I will if . . ." Sometimes lack of insight into one's immediate desires is tied to a sense of powerlessness. Experimenting with being more forceful, for instance, shouting, can often unlock awareness of these desires.

Individuals can also experiment with intensity by physically moving closer or farther away when talking with someone, to calibrate just how "close" emotionally they are at that time or to examine the effect of a certain mode of interaction on the distance. One can experiment with looking directly at or away from other people.

Intensity also can be regulated by variations such as allotted time, exacting requirements, and specifically prescribed tasks. Competition can intensify a situation and lead to the discovery of previously unnoticed abilities. However, for configurational learning to occur, the situation typically needs to be structured so that a person experiences the competition from both sides, that is, competes against himself.

If exploration seems stuck, pausing to experience the nature of "being stuck" often can intensify what is imperceptibly happening and allow a new configuration to emerge. Exaggeration can also intensify concepts: what is the worst that could occur? the best? Such expectations may provide a missing insight into what is going on and may bracket the situation and make it less threatening and easier to explore.

SUGGESTIONS FOR DIRECTING ATTENTION

Many different dimensions may be worth exploring to see what configurational learning they offer. Some may be useful in one situation, some in another. Testing for fit is one way to determine which suggestions may be useful. If a suggestion doesn't fit or capture interest, it is better dropped "for now."

Explore Gaps and Blockages

A Buddhist saying goes "The use of a cup is in its emptiness." Intentionally experiencing what is missing, what is left unsaid, or what needs to be there but is not can bring an experience into focus. Sometimes what is missing is obvious. Carl Rogers (1961) refers to "incongruent communications" in which the "lines" and their delivery do not jibe. A clenched fist accompanying an evenly modulated tone suggests that something is being held back. The speaker can be urged to say the words that the clenched fist suggests, then to select a body posture that better fits the words that were used and test for fit.

Merely calling attention to an experienced gap or deliberately acting out the gap can often suggest directions for exploration or spark insight. Paying particular attention to the color or shape of the gap typically sparks fruitful awareness. Not knowing which way to go also can be viewed as a gap to be acted out or experienced more fully, permitting productive exploration to continue.

Typically, a blockage is seen as something to be avoided, removed, overcome, or demolished. What we fail to acknowledge is that the blockage is an integral part of and essential to the situation. Without the evil dragon to slay, Sir Lancelot could not "do his thing." The blockage has something to offer—specifically, material for a new configuration, usually energy or power that has been locked into an unusable form and has sapped the situation of its vitality and potential. If avoiding or otherwise circumventing the blockage proves futile, it is often useful to confront it directly, to appreciate its essential contribution to the situation, and thus to assimilate its power and energy.

For example, it is not uncommon for an established institution to discover that in its single-minded efforts to block the progress of competitors it has itself become ineffective and needs to assimilate the vitality of this adversary in order to once again become viable. If people list their ten most valuable assets in order of priority and list separately the ten things they desire most, they often discover that their most valuable assets must be risked in order to accomplish what they desire most. The unwillingness to risk an asset represents a blockage. Continued scrutiny of one's feelings results in an awareness of blockages; when possible, the blockage can be acted out or the person can engage in an imaginary dialogue with it. Invariably the blockage is useful to explore for insight, although if a person is not ready to engage the blockage so directly, more peripheral tactics can be used.

Frequently, the gap is of a different order or a different system of logic, an apparent discontinuity. In group dynamics, if the pursuit of the subject matter seems incoherent or circular, the facilitator often directs attention to what is termed the "group process," those hidden or unacknowledged aspects of a group such as individual participant values, unexpressed desires or hidden agendas, assumed norms of group behavior, cultural imperatives, etc. A discussion of individuals' perceptions of group process, alliances, or blocking behavior redirects attention by exploring the gaps between one set of perceptions and another. A more lively approach is for the group to mimic its own process. This can be done by continuing the meeting but talking in gibberish to direct attention to the "feeling" tone of the meeting. This approach typically sparks an awareness of new avenues for progress or of process issues that must be confronted and resolved. Sometimes, merely talking in gibberish is sufficient to heighten awareness, allow unfinished business to automatically be "finished for now," and allow the meeting to proceed. For some kinds of situations, gaps can be identified by making an exhaustive listing of the variables that could be involved in a situation and their interrelationships. The list can be reviewed to determine which factors are most pertinent to the situation at hand and where gaps might occur.

Use Imagination and Fantasy

Tapping people's imaginative powers is another way to come up with a new configuration. By using metaphors one can see certain aspects of the situation in a new light and understand the relationships among the parts. Or one can act the part of an object or a process to gain insight into experience by noticing what thoughts or sensations impede progress. Dream scenes or case studies provide rich material for imaginary situations; these can be extremely valuable experiences as long as they are recognized as imaginary and not confused with the present situation. Supernatural characters are often a good vehicle to use: one can imagine gnomes or elves engaging the problem and then allow them to solve it. Imaginary journeys can also yield significant experiences. Stevens (1971) suggests journeys into a cave, an open field, a museum, or a pawn shop. In each case, it is important to experience the journey in the present tense and to notice what is happening, what is discovered, and how aspects of the journey interact. One could use active imagination to visualize what is over the hill in the picture on the wall (Jung, 1968) or imagine himself or others as an animal, a food, etc.

Because fantasy suspends ordinary rules, one has complete freedom to imagine what he will. However, a person may continue to structure the situation in his current configuration. Thus, fantasy can be extremely useful to discover how the current situation is structured and what rules are imposed. Fantasy can also be a useful source for role plays or can be used to relieve tension. At a meeting, a fantasy break (e.g., "Imagine you are in a truly delightful place") is typically more effective and less time consuming than the ordinary coffee break.

Determine Policy Functions

Policy functions are the *rules* that guide all behavior—the equivalent of the parent ego state in transactional analysis. They determine the structure of situations and a certain efficiency of behavior. Many are self-imposed and often resist transformation. They often are evident in feelings and corresponding words, such as I (you, we, etc.) should, ought, must, should not, ought not, etc. Groups can play a "Ten Commandments" game by listing the ten unspoken commandments that govern behavior in the group. Statements should begin with "thou shalt" or "thou shalt not." A group can also imagine and act out what the situation would be if certain policies were modified.

Explore Energizing Functions

Paying attention to how the energy of each person and each facet of the situation is utilized is often critical to achieving insight. Fear and desire, expressed by "I'm afraid of . . ." or "I want . . . ," are the basic indicators of energizing functions. They often represent a gap in insight. Energy trapped between "ought" and "want" or "want" and "afraid" is not available to actuate the situation. Exploring various sources of energy, whether they seem productive or not, typically contributes to a clearer picture of the whole experience.

People's interest in power generally reflects their desire to capitalize on energy functions, though the situation is often seductively deceptive. The apparently weak or helpless person is frequently thought to have little power. Yet, in order to survive, the weak and helpless have to develop inordinate skill in attracting the power and energy of the apparently more powerful. Exploring the methods whereby the apparently weak attract energy to themselves can often be instructive. This exploration can take the form of "I or we defeat you by . . ." or any of the following: "I'm interested in . . . ," "I demand . . . ," "I appreciate . . . ," "I want . . . ," "I resent . . . ," "I fear . . . ," or "I frustrate you by . . ." Testing these for fit typically offers solid clues to the nature of the energy patterns in the situation.

Explore Integrating Functions

Sometimes configurational learning is facilitated by practicing one's natural integration or configuration-forming abilities. Introducing a third character with an explicit, integrating role, such as a consultant, into an imaginary dialogue can be useful. In organizations, special task groups or more permanent integrating groups that have ties to both sides of the situation are typically used to perform integrating functions. The consumer advocate and the production planning department are examples of such groups. Or the superordinate authority, the "boss," is called in to "get it together." Individuals in a group can act the part of an all-powerful king who can arbitrarily make things happen and integrate the situation.

Explore Opposites, Complements, Subtleties

Opposites define each other. Because what is important is made so by contrast to what is unimportant, opposites can be very effective new directions for attention. If an opposite is intentionally engaged, it can help clarify a configuration. A dialogue between one aspect of the situation and its opposite often brings clarity. In many configurations, certain facets may have been confused with their opposites. As it is commonly understood, "I hate you" can also mean "I love you"; "I want it" can mean "I don't want it," etc. Sometimes the speaker confuses his own motives or feelings with those of another. Saying "you are" often means "I am." Testing the opposites for fit in these circumstances can clarify just what is intended.

Subtle distinctions often are essential to understanding a configuration. Listing simultaneously what is the problem and what is not the problem typically highlights critical distinctions in feelings, senses, intuitions, ideas, situations—all of which are useful to pursue. When something does not "fit" but it seems that it should, exploring all subtle distinctions is required. At other times, having many possibilities can lead to confusion. Simplification is in order, and one needs to decide which distinctions seem useful.

Complements also can clarify the situation by filling a gap in the structure. Discovering what goes with or what helps clarify a structure can be helpful. Although the most obvious is precisely what is required, sometimes it is overlooked or people are too embarrassed to suggest it. Another way of finding complements is through wishes, "if only's." A person can act out the situation as if he, in fact, had the special quality he desires. He can discover how it works, whether it is required, and why it is required. Perhaps he will find out that another complement is needed.

Explore Time and Space

Concepts of time and space can be extremely valuable for understanding the present. They are best engaged by seeing them as if they exist in the present. Ideas about the future or the past offer possible models for restructuring the present in such a way that insight can occur. Exploring the present as if it were in the unchangeable past or open-ended future often eases the threat of the present. On the other hand, the future could be seen as very threatening—especially if one's expectations are negative—or as impossibly good. In either case, bringing the future into the present makes it more concrete, more possible to confront. This approach uses past experience to clarify concepts.

The same approach can be taken by placing the present situation in a different space—outer space or a specially defined space, for example, one without gravity or in the mountains or at sea, at home, at work, at a party. Each context offers different dimensions to explore present configurations.

Explore Processes and Relationships

Although this concept is very broad, it is too rich in possibilities to be overlooked. Sociocultural relationships are filled with experiences, special meanings, and possible connections with the current situation: parent-child, husband-wife, child-uncle (aunt), boss-employer, master-servant, friend-friend, doctor-patient, helper-client, artist-model, to name only a few. Testing alternate relationships in the current situation can yield insight. Such relationships can also suggest metaphors for relationships in the physical world: engine to wheels, supports to a bridge, electrons to protons, light to photographs, the sky to the sea, etc.

Processes are the structures upon which relationships are built: giving birth, growing up, formulating legislation, imploding and exploding, making war, refining petroleum, splitting atoms, baking bread, paying the bills, falling in love, forming a group, etc. These processes have the special property of structuring time as relationships structure space, and they bring out other qualities such as power, affection, etc. Graphics, pictures, and models are extremely valuable in communicating processes and can be used to great advantage by groups.

When exploring processes and relationships, it is extremely important to "do" them rather than merely talk about them, for they are susceptible to infinite abstraction, discourse, and speculation and can be a way to flee from possibilities as well as a wonderful vehicle for discovering a new configuration.

REFERENCES

Berne, E. *Transactional analysis in psychotherapy*. New York: Grove, 1961.

Fordyce, J. K., & Weil, R. *Managing with people*. Reading, Mass.: Addison-Wesley, 1971.

Gallway, T. *The inner game of tennis*. New York: Random House, 1974.

Jung, C. G. *Man and his symbols*. New York: Dell, 1968.

Lewin, K. Frontiers in group dynamics. *Human Relations*, 1947, *1*, 5-41.

Perls, F. *The gestalt approach and eye witness to therapy*. Palo Alto, Calif.: Science and Behavior Books, 1973.

Rogers, C. R. *On becoming a person*. Boston: Houghton Mifflin, 1961.

Stevens, J. O. *Awareness*. Lafayette, Calif.: Real People, 1971.

Sam Farry is a consultant in management and organizational behavior in Manhattan Beach, California, a lecturer at California State College, Dominguez Hills, and a consulting associate at Social Engineering Technology, Westwood, California. He is currently conducting programs in stress management and configurational learning and consulting on projects in organization development and contextual mapping for market research and invention. Mr. Farry's background is in management, adult education, organization development, and group and Gestalt methods.

LOEVINGER'S EGO STAGES AS THE BASIS OF AN INTERVENTION MODEL

Victor Pinedo, Jr.

For decades, a basic deficiency of personal and organization development programs has been the absence of a comprehensive model of human development that is capable of encompassing the various facets of growth while at the same time permitting meaningful measurement. For the practitioner, Loevinger's model of ego development offers a major conceptual advance, an empirically derived model of maturity that is rich in detail and nuance and comprehensive enough to act as a conceptual framework for complex, personalized organizational intervention. Impacted and expanded by the Life-Cycle theory of Hersey and Blanchard (1972), McClelland's social motives (1961), and Harrison's model of cultures (1975), Loevinger's model of ego stages (1976) is a convenient basis for organizational and community intervention. In working with these theories and their interrelationships, a new model evolves that can be used to integrate three major factors: individual maturity level (from Loevinger), management style (from Hersey and Blanchard), and organizational ideology (from Harrison).[1]

LOEVINGER'S STAGES OF DEVELOPMENT

Loevinger originally developed her levels as a way to measure an individual's stage of ego development. In a sense, each of her six major stages and substages represents a point in time and space at which an individual has stopped in his developmental process. A stage represents the way a person looks at and copes with the world. Differences in people at various stages would represent differences in the following human functions: cognitive differences—how people reason and make sense of a situation (cognitive style); process differences—how people express emotions and relate to each other (character development and interrelations); system differences—how people function, cope with the world, and maintain an integrated sense of self (preoccupational needs). Figure 1 shows how each of Loevinger's six levels of ego development (impulsive, self-protective, conformist, conscientious, autonomous, integrated) is revealed in four different dimensions (impulse control/character development, interpersonal style, cognitive style, and conscious preoccupation) in an individual at that level.

Each stage or ego level is characterized by distinct emotional preoccupations, cognitive styles, and manners of behaving toward others. At different stages, people cope with the world and make sense out of it in different ways. They also have different attitudes toward their work and distinct expectations and levels of commitment.

---

[1]These theories were integrated by the author and his collaborators over the period 1970 to 1976 in a program conducted by Fundashon Humanas in Curaçao, Netherlands Antilles. The political upheavals of 1969 led to an invitation to David McClelland of Harvard to develop a training program in his methods for a group of islanders. One of the coordinators of this program was Harry Lasker, a former student of McClelland's, who, working with the author, a local management consultant and psychologist, gathered data that demonstrated an extremely strong relationship between the various patterns of motivation and levels of adult maturity or ego levels.

Ego Level	Impulse Control/ Character Development	Interpersonal Style	Cognitive Style	Conscious Preoccupation
I. *Impulsive*	Does not recognize rules Sees action as bad only if punished Impulsive Afraid of retaliation Has temper tantrums	Dependent and exploitative; dependence unconscious Treats people as sources of supply	Thinks in a dichotomous way Has simple, global ideas Conceptually confused Thinks concretely Egocentric	Sex and aggression Bodily functions
II. *Self-Protective*	Recognizes rules but obeys for immediate advantage Has expedient morality: action bad if person caught Blames others; does not see self as responsible for failure or trouble	Manipulative and exploitative Wary and distrusting of others' intentions Opportunistic Zero-sum: I win, you lose Shameless; shows little remorse	As above	Self-protection Gaining control and advantage, dominating Getting the better of others, deceiving them Fear of being dominated, controlled, or deceived by others
III. *Conformist*	Partially internalizes rules; obeys without question Feels shame for consequences Concerned with "shoulds" Morally condemns others' views Denies sexual and aggressive feelings	Wants to belong to group, to gain social acceptance Feels mutual trust within in-group, prejudice against out-groups Has pleasing social personality: superficial niceness, helpfulness Understands relationships in terms of action rather than feelings and motives	Thinks stereotypically Uses clichés Sees in terms of superlatives Has sentimental mentality Has little introspection: references to inner feelings banal and stereotyped	Appearances Social acceptance and adjustment to group norms Status symbols, material possessions, reputation, and prestige

Figure 1. Loevinger's Stages of Ego Development Across Four Dimensions *

*After Loevinger (1976).

Ego Level	Impulse Control/ Character Development	Interpersonal Style	Cognitive Style	Conscious Preoccupation
IV. *Conscientious*	Standards self-evaluated: morality internalized Self-critical tendency to be hypercritical Feels guilt for consequences	Has sense of responsibility, obligation Has mutual, intensive relationships Concerned with communication, expression of differentiated feelings	Conceptually complex Has sense of consequences, priorities Aware of contingencies, perceives alternatives Sees self in context of community, society	Achievement of long goals, as measured by inner standards Attaining ideals Motivation, reasons for behavior Self: feelings, traits
V. *Autonomous*	Add: † Behavior an expression of moral principle Tolerates multiplicity of viewpoints Concerned with conflicting duties, roles, principles	Add: † Wants autonomy in relations Sees relations as involving inevitable mutual interdependence Tolerates others' solutions of conflict Respects others' autonomy Open	Has greater conceptual complexity Tolerates ambiguity Has capacity to see paradox, contradictions Has broad scope of thought (time frame, social context) Perceives human interdependence Has greater objectivity	Individuality and self-fulfillment Conflicting inner needs Nonhostile, "existential" humor
VI. *Integrated*	Add: † Reconciles inner conflicts and conflicting external demands Renounces the unattainable Concerned with justice Spontaneous, creative	Add: † Cherishes individuality	Add: † Has sense of self as part of flow of human condition	Add: † Integrated sense of unique identity "Precious life's work" as inevitable simultaneous expression of self, principle, and one's humanity

Figure 1. (cont.)

---
†"Add" means add to the description applying to the previous level.

1. Impulsive Stage

At the first of the six stages the individual does not recognize rules and considers an action bad only if he is punished. Interpersonal relations tend to be exploitative and dependent. Other people are treated as sources of supply by the impulsive person. At level one, the central work attitude is "I'll do it only if I get rewarded," the main motivator at this level being pay. Commitment is only to oneself, to the satisfaction of one's own needs. The responsibility that can be given to a person at this level is very low.

2. Self-Protective Stage

At stage two, the opportunistic or self-protective stage, rules are recognized for the first time but are obeyed simply in order to achieve an immediate advantage. At this level, a person will manipulate rules to his or her own personal advantage. Interpersonal relations are manipulative and exploitative, and dependence on others is decreased but not eliminated. The individual can be both passively dependent and aggressively independent. However, such an aggressive independence is often betrayed by an inner sense of shame and doubt.

A person at level two has a conscious preoccupation with questions of control, advantage, and domination. He normally thinks in terms of trying to get the better of another person. This deception-oriented thinking betrays a high level of distrust. Since the individual at level two is out to exploit other people, he believes that all people are out to exploit him also. Because life is seen in competitive terms, there is no capacity at this level for the idea of cooperation. The person at this level is a lonely person because he cannot rely fully on others or trust them.

The key work attitude at this level is "I'll do only what I'm told to do" or "I'll do whatever I can get away with." Job security and working conditions are important. The individual can take some limited kinds of responsibility for small tasks but must be supervised with continuous orders and directions.

3. Conformist Stage

At level three, rules are partially internalized for the first time, but they are still obeyed simply because they are rules, with little emotional attachment to or belief in them. When the person breaks the rules, he does have a real capacity to feel shame. The conformist is deeply concerned about what other people think of him.

For the first time, the idea of reciprocity and trust emerges. But trust is extended only to the individual's in-group. For people who are outside this special group, the conformist can feel much prejudice, and he tends to think in very stereotypical terms. Therefore, he may condemn other people's views on a moral basis.

The conformist's interpersonal relations are rather superficial. He judges people by their actions rather than their feelings and motives. Someone who is superficially friendly may automatically be seen as a good person. A similar kind of superficiality exists in the conformist's preoccupation with material things—status, reputation, appearances, and adjustment. He has little introspection and self-consciousness.

Work attitudes at level three change. At the lower stages of this level, the key work attitude is "I'll do only what others do." At a higher step, the attitude becomes "I'll do only what is expected of me." The motivators at this level extend to the issues of peer relations, friendliness of supervision, competence of supervision, and company policy and administration. Generally this individual can be delegated conventional kinds of tasks that take a relatively long time to complete. The source of initiative for the level-three worker is still external, governed by company rules and what other employees do. He is very other directed and cares about what other people around him are doing and thinking. He shows the beginnings of commitment to the company and may become committed to his department or to his group of co-workers or to a department supervisor.

The work attitude of a person between levels three and four is "I'll do only what is best for my career advancement": the "yes man," the career ladder climber. He is motivated most strongly by recognition for the work he has done, possibilities of advancement, and opportunities to take responsibility.

4. Conscientious Stage

At this stage, a new pattern of thought begins to emerge. For the first time, rules and morality are fully internalized. At this level a person can feel guilt, rather than the shame of the conformist. While the person at this stage may still condemn other people's values, his inner morals begin to take precedence over group-sanctioned rules. He begins to think for himself and to be moved primarily by what he considers important—his inner principles. His conscious preoccupations are with obligations, ideals, and achievement as measured by inner standards. He has increasing awareness of his own feelings and needs. He begins to judge and appreciate others in terms of their internal feelings and traits, rather than their actions. He develops the capacity for self-criticism, which can become neurotic in its severity. This mentality is often associated with an intense desire to prevent others from making mistakes.

At level four the work attitude becomes "I'll do what is best for the company" or "I'll do what the job demands." Here, finally, is the conscious preoccupation with the quality of work being done. The key motivators for this kind of worker are opportunities to take responsibility and opportunities that permit achievement. This worker can assume great amounts of responsibility over long periods of time. He takes initiative on the basis of internal standards of excellence.

5. Autonomous Stage

At this level, the great psychological problems are coping with inner conflicts and conflicting duties. Moral issues are no longer seen as a set of absolutes, but as an attempt to resolve contradictions. There is a much-increased capacity to live with ambiguity and a greater toleration of other people and their solutions to life's conflicts. The autonomous person can accept others for what they are, fully conscious of their faults. His interpersonal relations are marked by a high level of awareness of feelings and emotions in himself and in others. He recognizes that there must inevitably be interdependence between human beings.

There is an increased recognition at this level of the need to learn from one's mistakes and to grow. The most characteristic preoccupation now is with questions of individuality, self-actualization, and self-fulfillment. The autonomous level can be a tormented one, with many unresolved inner conflicts. The person at this level tends to draw back from the rush of life and to focus on the contradictions in his own feelings and in life's needs.

6. Integrated Stage

At this stage occurs a reconciliation of the conflicting demands of life, a renunciation of the unattainable, and a tendency to cherish and appreciate differences among people. An integrated sense of identity expresses itself through the traits that Maslow (1962) calls characteristic of self-actualizing personalities: a superior perception of reality and an increased acceptance of oneself, of others, and of the way life is. In addition there is increased spontaneity, freshness of appreciation, and richness of emotional reaction. There is greater capacity to be problem centered, to give oneself completely to an idea outside oneself, as well as an increased capacity to give to other people in an open and complete way without feeling impoverished.

In addition, there is a desire for detachment and an increased desire for privacy and autonomy. But the person at the integrated level is not cut off from other people. He can experience an all-pervasive love for mankind and tends to have a democratic character structure and a genuine openness toward other people and a trust in them. The integrated personality is often highly creative.

A key aspect in the integrated personality is a higher frequency of peak experiences. Maslow (1962) has described the kinds of cognitions that are associated with peak experiences: a sense of wholeness, perfection, and completion; a greater awareness of justice; an intense sense of aliveness and richness of sensation; an appreciation of and focus on beauty and goodness; a spontaneous awareness of one's uniqueness and individuality; an awareness of honesty and a feeling of being close to truth; and an intense sensation of self-sufficiency.

McCLELLAND'S SOCIAL MOTIVES

The work of McClelland (see especially *The Achieving Society*, 1961) powerfully expresses the relationship between individual psychological patterns and social change. After years of psychological research, McClelland was able to discern three fundamental human motives: the power motive, the achievement motive, and the affiliation motive. According to an individual's motive pattern, he or she will be likely to display different kinds of behavior and have different concerns. For example, the power motive was found to be related to opportunistic defensive behavior. Persons motivated by a need for power are primarily interested in controlling others while seeking their own ends. The achievement motive characterizes persons interested in the accomplishment of tasks, professional excellence, and rational problem solving. Their behavior tends to be efficient and productive. McClelland found that the achievement motive is strongly related to socioeconomic development. More specifically, it relates to feelings of satisfaction, higher productivity, and the desire and ability of persons to organize individually and collectively for task fulfillment. McClelland developed an educational methodology that would stimulate and enhance the achievement motive in persons. The affiliation motive leads to more interpersonal behavior. This motive expresses itself in a concern for intimacy, quality of relationship, and social harmony.

The author's research with McClelland's motives found that they are, in fact, crude predictors of ego levels. Persons with high power needs tend to be at low ego levels. Persons at low ego levels will not respond to achievement motivation training because it demands more mature emotional and intellectual capacities than they have yet developed. Achievement motivation, on the other hand, is characteristic of a higher level of maturity.

THE CONCEPT OF MATURITY

According to Hersey and Blanchard's Life-Cycle theory (1972), as the level of maturity of one's followers continues to increase, appropriate leader behavior requires a change in management style. (See Figure 2.) Maturity is defined in the Life-Cycle theory by

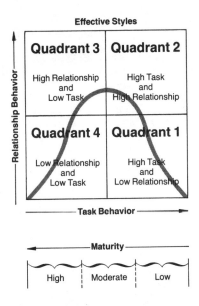

Effective Styles

Quadrant 3	Quadrant 2
High Relationship and Low Task	High Task and High Relationship
Quadrant 4	Quadrant 1
Low Relationship and Low Task	High Task and Low Relationship

Relationship Behavior

Task Behavior

Maturity

High | Moderate | Low

Figure 2. Hersey and Blanchard's Life-Cycle Leadership Theory*

*From Hersey & Blanchard (1976).

achievement motivation, the willingness and ability to take responsibility, and task relevant education and experience of an individual or a group. . . . As a person matures over time he moves from a passive state to a state of increasing activity, from dependency on others to relative independence. . . . Our concern is for psychological age, not chronological age. Beginning with structured task behavior, which is appropriate for working with immature people, Life Cycle Theory suggests that leader behavior should move through (1) high task-low relationships behavior to (2) high task-high relationships and (3) high relationships-low task behavior to (4) low task-low relationships behavior, if one's followers progress from immaturity to maturity. (pp. 134-135)

Hersey and Blanchard's definition of the integrative force of maturity, however, is simplistic and incomplete. They relate maturity to achievement motivation, but it is clear that this phenomenon is very complex, one that cannot be changed by simple behavior modification, as suggested by Hersey and Blanchard.

An individual has certain developmental needs and certain dilemmas that must be fulfilled in order for a strong sense of self to develop. The more the individual feels that he can satisfy his personal needs, the more growth energy that person is going to have to move to a higher set of needs and a more complex set of dilemmas.

Ego Stages as Unfulfilled Needs and Dilemmas

Relating Loevinger's ego stages to several developmental theories results in a much deeper way of looking at the concept of "maturity" and gives a much clearer picture of *what* type of behavior one can expect at each stage of development. (See Figure 3.) If Loevinger's ego stages are understood as unfulfilled needs and dilemmas, it is clear that a complex form of intervention is necessary, if change is the desired end. Figure 3 reveals the way an individual's various needs and dilemmas relate to each of Loevinger's ego stages. The first column indicates the predominant need, the second column the unfinished dilemma, the third column the psychological modalities that the individual must master in order to continue, the fourth column the motivation that will be predominant if stagnation occurs at a certain stage, and the fifth column the characteristics that the personality acquires by solving the dilemmas at each stage.

At the earliest stage of development, an individual is learning to satisfy his physical needs. This process gives the person self-trust and motivation to tackle the next step in the developmental process. At the second stage the person is concerned with security. His dilemmas are autonomy/shame/doubt, initiative/guilt, and industry/inferiority. Successfully completing this stage will lend the individual self-control and willpower, direction and purpose, method and competence. That person is ready to move on to the next set of dilemmas belonging to the sphere of acceptance; if these are successfully resolved, the individual moves on to those of ego and finally to those related to the need for realization. The successful satisfaction of each need seems to generate more energy and more motivation toward dealing with the next more complex set of dilemmas. With each set, the individual's impulse control, interpersonal style, cognitive style, and conscious preoccupation change nature and quality.

An interesting relationship, for example, can be seen between McClelland's three social motives (power, achievement, and affiliation) and Loevinger's ego levels. Subjects who tested at Loevinger's ego levels 1, 2, and 2/3 are high in power motive and low in achievement motive and affiliation motive. At stages 3, 3/4, and 4, there is an increase of achievement motive in both quantity and quality, a decline in power motive, and a slight increase in affiliation. At ego levels 5 and 6, achievement declines and power further declines. There is an increase in affiliation and an increase in socialized power.

Forming a Character Armor

If the individual, however, is not successful in his development, if he is unable to fulfill a need or to solve a dilemma, stagnation or the formation of a character armor occurs. This happens especially at the lower stages, which represent points in time and space where the individual has felt impotent in fulfilling his need and in solving the dilemma he faced at that stage. The individual's motivational energies are used to protect himself from feeling impotent. Power behavior, for example, becomes the defense system at these early stages of development. Behavior becomes predictive and directed toward satisfying the unsatisfied needs. The individual's whole world has stagnated into unproductive, amotivated behavior. An individual at stage two, for example, will create a self-protective world for himself. The person feels insecure but will not own his insecurity, and he projects his needs onto the world, often in polarized fashion. At stage three (conformist), all behavior seems to be directed toward being accepted.

It is possible to see how the ego-development levels provide a very important tool for managing change and for changing motivational patterns. Change from one stage of maturity to another becomes a very complex matter. It involves destructuring the character armor and facilitating the working-through of unfulfilled needs, psychological modalities, and dilemmas. Only if the individual senses his *own* power again can that individual let go of his armor.

Ego Stage	Column 1 Predominant Needs	Column 2 Unfinished Dilemmas	Column 3 Psychological Modalities	Column 4 Predominant Motivations (McClelland)	Column 5 Acquired Characteristics
1. Impulsive	physical	trust/mistrust	receiving; giving in compensation	power	drive, hope
2. Self-Protective	security	autonomy/shame/doubt	holding onto; letting go	power	self-control, willpower
2/3. Self-Protective/Conformist		initiative/guilt	doing (searching); doing as if (playing)	power	direction, purpose
		industry/inferiority	making things (completing)	deficiency affiliation	method, competence
3. Conformist	acceptance	identity/confusion	making things together	deficiency affiliation	devotion, fidelity
			being oneself (or not being)	power achievement	
3/4. Conformist/Conscientious		intimacy/isolation	sharing oneself	achievement	affiliation, love
4. Conscientious	ego	generativity/stagnation	losing oneself and finding oneself in another	growth affiliation; achievement	production, care
			creating; caring for	growth affiliation	
5. Autonomous	realization	integrity/despair	being through; having been	achievement; growth affiliation	renunciation, wisdom
6. Integrated			confronting; not me	socialized power	

Figure 3. Loevinger's Ego Stages as Related to Needs and Dilemmas

University Associates

A climate that facilitates the working-through process is necessary. A therapeutic program can facilitate the destructuring of the armor and unleash motivational growth, creating situations that will allow the person to feel potent again.

HARRISON'S ORGANIZATIONAL MODEL

Loevinger's stages are character formations at certain points of development in the individual; the individual must be touched at the core of being and must be given a map of alternatives before there can be motivation to grow. But the cultures in which people's organizational lives are structured have lives of their own and need also to be considered. Harrison's (1975) definition of four distinct competing organizational ideologies—power oriented, role oriented, task oriented, and person oriented—is useful here.

Power Orientation

An organization that is power-oriented attempts to dominate its environment and vanquish all opposition. It is unwilling to be subject to any external law or power. . . . those who are powerful strive to maintain absolute control over subordinates. . . .

Role Orientation

An organization that is role-oriented aspires to be as rational and orderly as possible. In contrast to the willful autocracy of the power-oriented organization, there is a preoccupation with legality, legitimacy, and responsibility. . . . Predictability . . . stability and respectability are often valued as much as competence. The correct response tends to be more highly valued than the effective one. Procedures for change tend to be cumbersome; therefore the system is slow to adapt to change. . . .

Task Orientation

In the organization that is task-oriented, achievement of a superordinate goal is the highest value. . . . Nothing is permitted to get in the way of accomplishing the task. . . . Emphasis is placed on rapid, flexible organization response to changed conditions. . . .

Person Orientation

The person-oriented organization exists primarily to serve the needs of its members. . . . Individuals are expected to influence each other through example, helpfulness, and caring. Consensus methods of decision making are preferred. (pp. 201-203)

INTEGRATED MODEL

Combining individual maturity levels as described by Loevinger, Hersey and Blanchard's model of management styles, and Harrison's organizational ideologies leads to the integrated model described here (Figure 4). These factors interrelate in a very interesting fashion. If individuals are at a low stage of maturity, for example, they will often form a culture at the power stage. In a company this culture would attract authoritarian managers, and the three factors would complement and perpetuate themselves. Even if the manager is taught new styles of management, the same old organizational culture will be there, and the same old character defenses will be called forth.

An understanding of Loevinger's maturity stages and the dynamics by which characters are formed will enable the facilitator to further develop these energies. Initially, a special program led by a trained leader is necessary. But by understanding individuals' unfulfilled psychological needs, psychological modalities, and dilemmas that have not been worked through, the manager can become a manager of growth. Situations can be created that will allow a successful working-through of the different management styles suggested by Hersey and Blanchard and that will further allow the manager to change his management styles as the organization and its people change.

A successful intervention, especially if the largest part of the group is at the lower ego levels, should include at least these three aspects of change. Loevinger's contribution

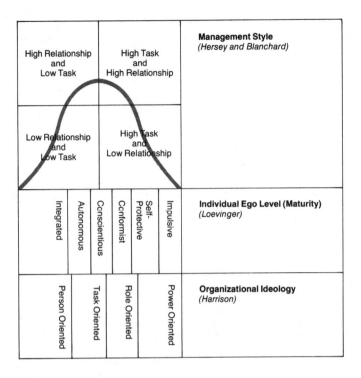

						Management Style
High Relationship and Low Task		High Task and High Relationship				*(Hersey and Blanchard)*
Low Relationship and Low Task		High Task and Low Relationship				
Integrated	Autonomous	Conscientious	Conformist	Self-Protective	Impulsive	**Individual Ego Level (Maturity)** *(Loevinger)*
Person Oriented	Task Oriented		Role Oriented		Power Oriented	**Organizational Ideology** *(Harrison)*

Figure 4. Integrated Model

becomes especially important as a point of integration for these three aspects and as a map for intervention. Her stages provide the information needed to create the necessary climate that can stimulate individual growth and also lead to organizational effectiveness. The consultant can use this information to structure an intervention that is full and encompassing, consequently stimulating more growth.

REFERENCES

Harrison, R. Understanding your organization's character. *Harvard Business Review*, May-June 1972, pp. 119-128. Also in J. E. Jones & J. W. Pfeiffer (Eds.), *The 1975 annual handbook for group facilitators*. La Jolla, Calif.: University Associates, 1975, pp. 199-209.

Hersey, P., & Blanchard, K. H. *Management of organizational behavior: Utilizing human resources* (2nd ed.). Englewood Cliffs, N.J.: Prentice-Hall, 1972.

Hersey, P., & Blanchard, K. H. Leader effectiveness and adaptability description (LEAD). In J. W. Pfeiffer & J. E. Jones (Eds.), *The 1976 annual handbook for group facilitators*. La Jolla, Calif.: University Associates, 1976.

Loevinger, J. *Ego development*. San Francisco, Calif.: Jossey-Bass, 1976.

Maslow, A. *Towards a psychology of being*. Princeton, N.J.: D. Van Nostrand, 1962.

McClelland, D. C. *The achieving society*. Princeton, N.J.: D. Van Nostrand, 1961.

Victor Pinedo, Jr., is the president of Fundashon Humanas, Curaçao, Netherland Antilles, and the director of research and development for IDO Asociados, Caracas, Venezuela. He is currently engaged in research on the relationships among human motivation, ego development, and organization development and has held various positions in community, service, and professional organizations in Curaçao. Mr. Pinedo's special areas of interest are organization development and human motivation and personnel relationships.

BEHAVIORAL CLARITY IN CONSULTATION: THE TRIADIC MODEL AS INSTRUMENT

Gerard Egan

If change is to take place in an orderly, systematic fashion, it is important that those involved in the change process get as clear a picture as possible of what is to take place. "Visualizing change" (Lippitt, 1973) through simple (but not oversimplified) models can help all involved in the change process attain this clarity.

Presented here is an adaptation and amplification of Tharp and Wetzel's (Tharp, 1975; Tharp & Wetzel, 1969) very useful "triadic" consultation model used as a simple, practical instrument to help clarify the logic of change.

According to the triadic model (Figure 1), the consultant works through a mediator (whether an individual person or a group of people) to help change the behavior of a specific target (again, an individual or a group). For instance, a school psychologist may help a teacher design a behavioral-intervention program for a student involved in self-defeating behaviors in the classroom (Figure 2).

The *target* is a single individual or a group with behavior to be modified. For example, the target might be a member of a family or the family itself, a foreman or an entire work unit, a teacher or an entire faculty, etc.

The *mediator* is an individual or a group capable of influencing the behavior of the target. Tharp and Wetzel (1969) see the mediator as an individual or a group that has control over the target's reinforcers and that can place these reinforcers on contingency. For instance, parents can tell their son that he may use the car in the evening provided that he finishes his homework and his household chores during the day. Or a foreman might allow a worker freedom to choose his or her own work hours if certain production schedules are met and maintained. The parents and the foreman control certain reinforcers and can place them on contingency.

The model presented here, however, takes a somewhat wider view of the mediator by seeing the mediator as having resources that help the target achieve desirable goals. For example, if the target wants to fix a car, a mediator can teach the target how to fix a car. The mediator in this case influences the target by training the target.

The *consultant* is a person or a group of people with the knowledge or skills or programs or vision or methodology that can help the mediator influence the target. For instance, a school psychologist might show a teacher how he or she might use behavioral contracts to influence the behavior of students. Or a consultant might train a group of people from an organization (mediators) to design a change program—from diagnosis through evaluation—for the entire organization (the target). In the triadic model, the consultant ordinarily does not deal directly with the target, though he or she might observe how the mediator interacts with the target in order to help the mediator interact more productively with the target.

The material in this article appears in a somewhat different form in the author's *Change Agent Skills*, Monterey, Calif.: Brooks/Cole, in press.

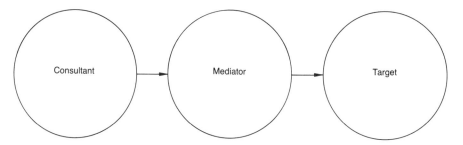

Figure 1. The Basic Triadic System

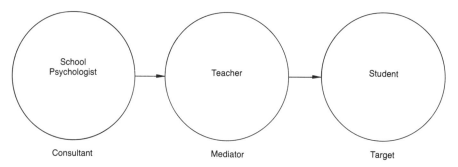

Figure 2. Example of Triadic Model

The same person, in different situations, can be target, mediator, or consultant. For example, a high school teacher might find herself successively in these roles:

Consultant	Mediator	Target
School Psychologist	Principal	*Teacher*
School Psychologist	*Teacher*	Student
Teacher	Teacher's Aide	Student

In each case the consultant shares resources with the mediator, and the mediator, enriched with these resources, influences the behavior of the target, enabling the target to engage in constructive behavioral change.

This triadic model can be expanded in both directions. (See Figure 3.) In this scheme teachers are, in different situations, targets, mediators, and consultants. The purpose of this scheme is not to establish a hierarchy or pecking order but to delineate as clearly as possible *resource relationships*. Who has the resources to influence and to help the next person or group down the line achieve desired goals?

If too much emphasis is placed on the mediators' having control over target reinforcements and on the mediators' ability to place these reinforcements on contingency, this model could appear highly controlling and even manipulative. Obviously, this need not be the case. Even though this is a social-influence model, it can be a cooperative venture. For instance, a student (the target) can cooperate in the elaboration of the behavioral contract with the teacher (the mediator), or line workers (targets) can cooperate with the foreman (mediator) in goal setting.

TARGET SPECIFICATION

One of the first tasks of the consultant is to help the mediator specify the target person or group. In many cases there might be a multiplicity of targets. The following dialogue between a consultant and the minister of a congregation illustrates this process of specification.

    C: Whom would you consider the target of your ministry?

    M: The members of the congregation.

    C: Are there subgroupings in your congregation, that is, groups that have special needs or that receive specialized forms of ministry? In a word, are there different target groups with different needs?

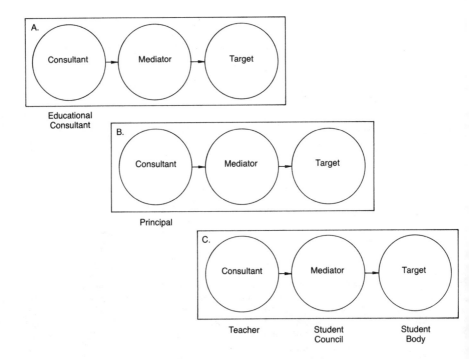

Figure 3. Expanded Triadic Model

M: Certainly. For instance, there are the members of the Ladies' Auxiliary, the elderly shut-ins, the sick or disabled (whether in the hospital or not), the youth of the parish—I could name many more.

C: Let's choose one of these target groups to use as an example of the program-development process.

M: Fine. Let's consider the youth of the parish.

C: Do you see the youth of the parish divided into subgroups?

M: Yes—those of primary school age, those of high school age, and then the young adults. I'd like to focus on the youth of high school age as the target population.

C: Do you work with these young people directly, or are others associated with you in creating and running youth programs?

M: That's the problem. I've been trying to do it myself and it's just too much. If any kind of youth programs are going to get off the ground, I think both adult volunteers and young people who are leaders in some sense will have to work with me.

C: Therefore, the model you see is something like this:

If you consider the work that I'm doing with you, then we would put me in a circle to the left of you.

M: I've never looked at myself as a ministerial consultant in the sense you're using the term, but in many ways that is what I must become if my congregation is to become one in which the members minister to one another.

In this case, specifying the ultimate target helped the minister discover the roles of mediator and ministerial consultant as dimensions of the program-development process. The minister sees that there is a multiplicity of targets needing a multiplicity of mediators and programs.

GOAL CLARITY AND THE FUNCTIONS OF CONSULTANT AND MEDIATOR

So far, the triadic model introduces a great deal of clarity and order into the relationships among people trying to help one another in a common venture. However, it is still not clear what the consultant does to help the mediator and what the mediator does to enable the target to engage in constructive behavioral change. *First* it is necessary to learn what the *target* is to do. Only then is it possible to delineate concretely what the mediator is to do to help the target. The triadic model becomes a working instrument when one attempts to discover what the target is to achieve, what target performance means, what target goals are (see Figure 4). For instance, the consultant asks the minister what things he would like to see this particular target group (youth of high school age) do.

M: I'd like to see them be better, more committed Christians.

C: What does a person of high school age who is a committed Christian do? What are some of the behaviors that such a committed Christian engages in?

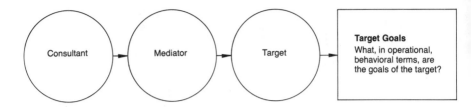

Figure 4. The Model Including Target Goals

M: Well, one example would be service to others.

C: Could you give me an example or two of what forms this service would take? Service to whom? What kind of service?

M: We have a lot of retired, elderly shut-ins in this neighborhood. Many of them could use help in household chores, shopping, help in getting to church functions and around the city. Things like that.

With respect to the target group consisting of youth of high school age, the model now looks something like Figure 5. For each target group and for each subgrouping within a particular target group, it would be necessary to get a clear picture of just what performance means. What are the goals in operational, behavioral terms? What is performance? If the target performs well, what happens?

PERFORMANCE-RELATED BEHAVIORS

If the target's goals are behaviorally clear, it is easier to determine what kinds of behaviors are related to performance, what kinds of behaviors will achieve target goals. If, for instance, a typist sings beautifully, this talent might be exciting, but it is not related to her performance as a typist. If the goal of a publishing house's typing pool is to produce neatly typed and errorless letters and manuscripts within certain time limits, then the members of the pool must engage in the behaviors that produce neatly typed and errorless manuscripts and letters. Another element has been added to the model (see Figure 6).

Unclear target goals will increase the probability that members of the target group will engage in random and unproductive behaviors, behaviors not related to performance. Drucker (1968) suggests that there is a great deal of aimless behavior in government and educational systems (as well as, we might add, ministerial and church systems) because those involved in these systems do not have clearly elaborated performance goals and criteria for success. Since government, education, and church seem to be perennial even when inefficient and ineffective, they are not forced, in the way that most businesses are, to elaborate clear-cut performance goals and to describe the behaviors that enable workers to achieve these goals. Performance-related behaviors can be seen as the means for achieving established goals. When a high school student vacuums, cleans windows, dusts furniture, and puts out the garbage for an enfeebled shut-in, that student's behaviors achieve the goal of helping the shut-in keep a clean apartment.

INFORMATION AND SKILLS

This model moves backward: the target (the last circle in the line) is the starting point; when considering the target's behavior, the goals are considered first and then the be-

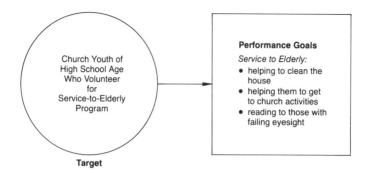

Figure 5. Target Group and Goals

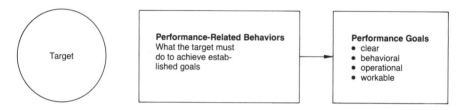

Figure 6. The Model Including Target Behaviors

haviors that achieve those goals. Following this logic, the next question is what information and what skills the target needs in order to engage in performance-related behaviors. For instance, one of the tasks of a volunteer in a hospital program is to welcome the patients after they have checked in, to show them to their rooms, and to give them the initial information and orientation they need to lessen anxiety and to make the beginning of the hospital stay less estranging. Given these goals, the volunteer needs to know how to go about doing these tasks and what information and skills are needed in order to engage in performance-related behaviors. More generally, what information and skills does the target need in order to engage in performance-related behaviors? These questions enlarge the working model (see Figure 7).

The arrow from the "Information" box points both to "Skills" and to "Performance-Related Behaviors" because information is usually needed to make skills operative. In the case of the hospital volunteer, the volunteer needs clear information about certain basic hospital procedures if he or she is going to offer any kind of meaningful orientation to the patient. The volunteer also needs certain basic interpersonal communication skills to welcome the patient in such a way as to make the entry into the hospital less estranging.

The volunteer also probably needs some information or awareness about how a patient usually feels when he or she first enters a hospital. This kind of awareness is needed to make the volunteer's interpersonal skills operative (Egan, 1976). It may be that attrition rates in volunteer programs are related, at least partially, to the fact that volunteers are asked to engage in behaviors for which they are not skilled. Very often, relatively simple skill-training programs fill this deficiency.

The information and skill elements of the model pinpoint the education (information, knowledge) and training (skills) needs of the target. A highly skilled and informed person may, for one reason or another, fail to perform, but an uninformed and unskilled person cannot perform.

ROUNDING OUT THE MODEL: OTHER RESOURCES

One more element is added to round out the model: necessary resources (see Figure 8). In many tasks the target requires more than just information and skills in order to engage in performance-related behaviors. For example, the best typist in the world cannot turn out good copy within given time limits if he or she must work with a defective typewriter. A highly skilled farmer cannot grow quality farm products by using defective seed.

THE RELATIONSHIP BETWEEN MEDIATOR AND TARGET

The function of the mediator *as mediator* (the mediator may have other functions in the organization) is to influence the target and enable him or her to engage in performance-related behavior. For instance, a principal as mediator to the faculty tries to enable the members of the faculty to teach more effectively and to carry on other education programs more creatively. The model, as it has so far been elaborated (the target system), becomes an instrument that the mediator can use to get a clear picture of the goals and needs of the target system. But this is just the beginning of the usefulness of this model. Once it is clear to the mediator what the target is to do and what the target needs to get the job done, the mediator can use *the same model* to clarify his own functions as mediator (see Figure 9).

These, then, are the basic elements of the mediator system:

1. *Performance Goals.* The mediator is successful to the degree that he influences and enables the target to achieve performance goals.

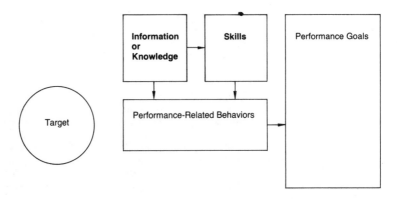

Figure 7. The Model Including Information and Skills Needed for Performance-Related Behaviors

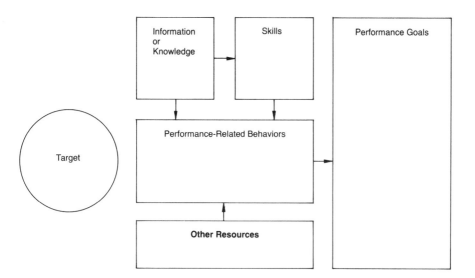

Figure 8. The Model Including Other Resources

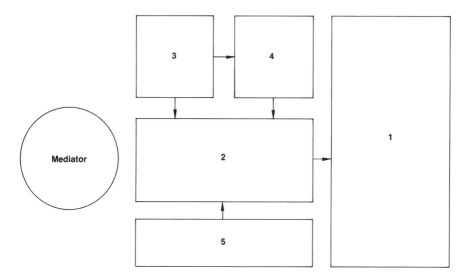

Figure 9. The Mediator System

2. *Performance-Related Behaviors.* These are the means that the mediator uses to influence and enable the target.
3. *Information or Knowledge.* This is the information the mediator needs to influence the target.
4. *Skills.* These are the social and program-influence skills, the program-development skills, the interpersonal skills needed by the mediator to be effective, to influence, to enable.
5. *Other Resources.* Different tasks will require the mediator to use a variety of resources in the influencing/enabling process.

Mediator Functions

Some common mediator functions are the following.

Goal Setting

The mediator helps the target understand the goal/performance-related-behavior system. For instance, the mediator meets with the target, the target group, or representatives of the target group and cooperatively establishes goals, objectives, and priorities for the target system. In order to do this, the mediator needs goal-development and goal-setting skills. If the goals are being set cooperatively, he or she needs interpersonal skills, bargaining skills, conflict-management skills, and so forth. The mediator certainly has to know how to spell out goals with behavioral clarity.

Program Development

With the participation of the target or target representatives, the mediator develops the means through which performance goals can be reached. If there is a variety of means, the mediator helps the target clarify which set of means might be most efficient, which set might be most reinforcing for the target, etc.

Training

Knowing the information and skill needs of the target population, the mediator either educates and trains the target population or gets competent educators/trainers to do so. For instance, a sales supervisor might work with his or her sales force directly in terms of goal setting and program development, but then have others train the sales force in the interpersonal skills and sales techniques needed for performance.

Being a Source of Reinforcement

The mediator needs a working knowledge of the laws of human behavior such as reinforcement, the effects of punishment (especially the negative side effects), the power of aversive conditioning, the usefulness of modeling, and the necessity of shaping procedures in program development and implementation. If the mediator is unaware of these principles and how they work, he or she can be incapacitated by them.

The mediator is usually a potent source of social and other kinds of reinforcement; he or she can also help targets identify and develop reinforcement systems for themselves. For example, a teacher as mediator might discover that his or her shouting at disruptive students is actually rewarding those who engage in such classroom behavior. The students like being yelled at because it is a specialized form of attention and it interrupts the tedium of ordinary classroom sessions. The teacher goes on to develop classroom programs that capture the imagination of the students, and disruptive behavior lessens.

Providing Feedback

Very often the performance of the members of a target population is directly related to the quality of the feedback they receive. The mediator is certainly one source of that feedback. The mediator can help establish feedback loops in the production system. Solid, data-based feedback (even about mistakes) is usually positive reinforcement for the target. The mediator needs confrontational skills that are neither anemic nor punishing (see Egan, 1976).

Helping

The mediator might also at times be a helper or quasi-counselor for the target. For instance, if the target is discouraged about his or her progress or is having difficulties with a fellow worker, the mediator might help him or her explore and handle the problem. To do this, however, the mediator needs a basic grasp of helping skills and procedures (see Egan, 1975).

Application

These mediator functions can be applied, using the example of a student nurse in a training hospital. The following system exists in the hospital:

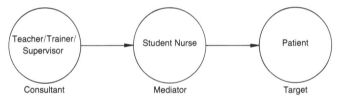

In this system the patient is considered a target because the hospital staff sees the patient as a person who cooperates in the health programs offered to him or her. The patient, then, is an agent, not just a passive target. Patient X is involved in a rehabilitation program after an automobile accident and needs certain information, skills, and other resources (for example, an exercise machine) to reach performance goals. While at times the student nurse might do things *to* the patient (for instance, administer injections), the nurse also engages in goal setting, program development, and training with the patient. In a word, he or she is a *mediator* and needs information, skills, and resources to perform mediating functions.

The model, therefore, identifies the educational and training needs not only of the target population, but also of the mediator. The mediator does not know what his or her *specific* functions should be until he or she acquires a behavioral understanding of the target system. The model now looks as it appears in Figure 10.

THE CONSULTANT

It is now clear that the interventions and the functions of the consultant are determined by the needs of both the mediator and the target systems and the interactions between these two systems. What the consultant does, *as triadic consultant*, must ultimately have an impact on the target system and on target performance. In this model the mediator influences and enables the target, and the consultant influences and enables the mediator. Therefore, the kinds of skills the consultant needs to influence the mediator effectively are similar to the skills needed by the mediator to influence the target. (See Figure 11.)

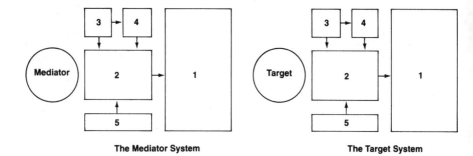

The Mediator System **The Target System**

1: Performance goals
2: Performance-related behaviors, the means to achieve the goals
3: Information or knowledge needed to engage in performance-related behaviors
4: Skills needed to engage in performance-related behaviors
5: Other resources needed to engage in performance-related behaviors

Figure 10. The Mediator System and the Target System

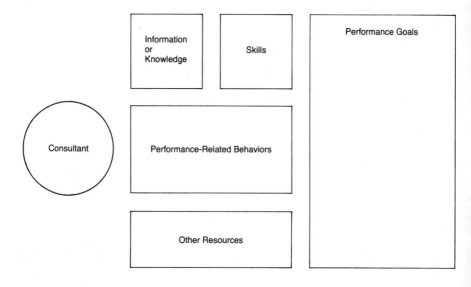

Figure 11. The Consultant System

As with the mediator, the performance goals of the consultant are relational—that is, the overall goal is to influence and enable the mediator in such a way that the latter is able to help the target more effectively achieve performance goals.

Some Common Consultant Functions

One way of looking at the functions of the consultant would be to review mediator functions to see how the consultant uses similar processes and methodologies to facilitate the work of the mediator. However, another way of visualizing some of the critical functions of the consultant is to review, briefly, how he or she would help a mediator system (and, indirectly, a target system) move through a systematic process of change, using a systematic model of change (Egan, in press). It is important to note that in all the stages of this model, the triadic consultant does not do the work of the mediator or assume the responsibilities of the mediator group. Without usurping the mediator role, the consultant can "walk" the mediator group through the model. Another way of saying this is that the consultant does not execute target-directed programs for the mediator but does whatever is necessary to increase the ability of the mediator group to fashion and execute programs.

Diagnosis

The consultant helps the mediator group discover how it goes about diagnosing and helps it discover more effective ways of going about a behavioral diagnosis of the system (target, mediator, mediator-target) and its subsystems. This includes helping the mediator assess both the readiness and the capability of an organization to change.

New Perspectives

By helping the mediator use such processes as brainstorming, scenario writing, fantasy, and similar techniques, the consultant enables the mediator to see new possibilities for the entire system—for example, new ways of manufacturing a product, new ways of ministering to a congregation through volunteer groups, new ways of relating to and interacting with the target system, and so forth. The triadic consultant does not do the brainstorming, but helps the mediator group develop brainstorming methodologies and then, perhaps, "walks" the group through some of these methodologies.

Goal Setting

The consultant shows the mediator how to go about establishing behavioral goals and setting priorities in view of the possibilities discovered during the "new perspectives" stage. The consultant may demonstrate goal-setting methodologies and train the mediator system in the skills of using them.

The Search for Means

Again, helping the mediator develop such processes as brainstorming and force-field analysis, the consultant enables the mediator to learn how to develop and consider a wide rather than a narrow range of means for accomplishing goals that have been set.

Choosing Means

The consultant helps the mediator establish ways of evaluating specific sets of means and choosing those most adapted to the human and technological needs of the organization.

Program Implementation

The mediator is helped by the consultant to become aware of the laws of behavior maintenance and change and to apply these to launching a program and maintaining momentum in it. The consultant observes how the mediator system goes about this process and gives data-based feedback. Ideally, he shows the mediator system how to get useful data-based feedback from the members of the organization.

Program Evaluation

The consultant shows the mediator group how to design program-evaluation methodologies and how to make evaluation a constructive, ongoing process within the system rather than a judgmental, end-of-the-line statement.

The consultant, then, is an educator, trainer, observer, monitor/supervisor with respect to the mediator. To the degree that the consultant takes over the functions of the mediator (for example, if the consultant does the diagnosis, if the minister runs the youth programs, if the nursing supervisor trains the rehabilitation patient), he or she ceases to be a *triadic* consultant.

A map of the full triadic system is found in Figure 12. Each section of the model (I, II, and III) becomes a work sheet (see Figure 13) for developing behavioral clarity with respect to each system's goals, means, and needs for information/skills/resources, while the full model becomes a work sheet for clarifying behavioral relationships among the individual units (I, II, and III) of the complete triadic system.

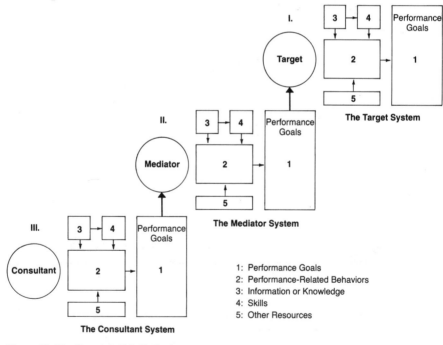

Figure 12. The Complete Triadic System

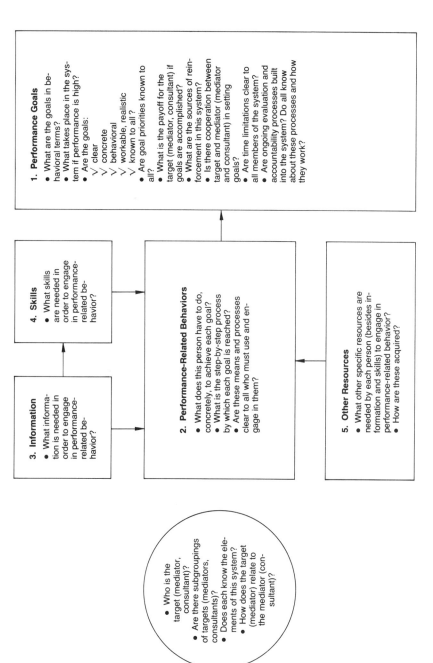

1. Performance Goals

- What are the goals in behavioral terms?
- What takes place in the system if performance is high?
- Are the goals:
  ✓ clear
  ✓ concrete
  ✓ behavioral
  ✓ workable, realistic
  ✓ known to all?
- Are goal priorities known to all?
- What is the payoff for the target (mediator, consultant) if goals are accomplished?
- What are the sources of reinforcement in this system?
- Is there cooperation between target and mediator (mediator and consultant) in setting goals?
- Are time limitations clear to all members of the system?
- Are ongoing evaluation and accountability processes built into the system? Do all know about these processes and how they work?

4. Skills

- What skills are needed in order to engage in performance-related behavior?

3. Information

- What information is needed in order to engage in performance-related behavior?

2. Performance-Related Behaviors

- What does this person have to do, concretely, to achieve each goal?
- What is the step-by-step process by which each goal is reached?
- Are these means and processes clear to all who must use and engage in them?

5. Other Resources

- What other specific resources are needed by each person (besides information and skills) to engage in performance-related behavior?
- How are these acquired?

- Who is the target (mediator, consultant)?
- Are there subgroupings of targets (mediators, consultants)?
- Does each know the elements of this system?
- How does the target (mediator) relate to the mediator (consultant)?

Figure 13. A Triadic Model Work Sheet

CONCLUSION

The purpose of this presentation is not to give an exhaustive account of the kinds of information, skills, methodologies, and other resources needed by consultants and mediators to be effective, but to describe an instrument that enables consultants, mediators, and targets to identify these needs and to see the interrelationships of these needs—and to do so with behavioral clarity. Nor is it assumed that this model as elaborated accounts for all the variables of system change and development. No model can do that and be practical. Any model must be simple enough to be practical and complex enough to be real, and this model, in many consultations, has fulfilled both conditions.

BIBLIOGRAPHY

Drucker, P. F. *The age of discontinuity: Guidelines to our changing society*. New York: Harper & Row, 1968.

Egan, G. *The skilled helper: A model for systematic helping and interpersonal relating*. Monterey, Calif.: Brooks/Cole, 1975.

Egan, G. *Interpersonal living: A skills/contract approach to human-relations training in groups*. Monterey, Calif.: Brooks/Cole, 1976.

Egan, G. *Change agent skills*. Monterey, Calif.: Brooks/Cole, in press.

Lippitt, G. L. *Visualizing change: Model building and the change process*. Fairfax, Va.: Learning Resources Corporation, 1973. (Reissued: La Jolla, Calif.: University Associates, 1976.)

Tharp, R. G. The triadic model of consultation: Current considerations. In C. A. Parker (Ed.), *Psychological consultation: Helping teachers meet special needs*. Minneapolis, Minn.: Leadership Training Institute/Special Education, University of Minnesota, 1975.

Tharp, R. G., & Wetzel, R. *Behavior modification in the natural environment*. New York: Academic Press, 1969.

Gerard Egan, Ph.D., is an associate professor of psychology at Loyola University of Chicago. He is the author of Face to Face, The Skilled Helper, Interpersonal Living, *and* You and Me *and is presently writing a book on change agent models and skills and co-authoring a book that presents a working model of human development in human systems. Dr. Egan writes, teaches, and consults in the areas of human relations training, helping skills and helper education, and organization development and consulting skills.*

OD READINESS

J. William Pfeiffer and John E. Jones

An intriguing parallel exists between the concept of organization development (OD) "readiness" and the developmental trait of "reading readiness." Once an individual child is ready to read, it is somewhat immaterial which teaching method is used. Conversely, when a child is not ready to learn to read, all strategies are relatively unsuccessful in teaching that child how to read. In an analogous way, once an organizational system has the necessary prerequisites, change is likely to take place regardless of which methodology is applied. Conversely, the most sophisticated techniques employed by the most competent and experienced consultants and managers are doomed to failure when the organization itself is unready to undertake a project of planned change.

ENTRY CONSIDERATIONS

There are four major OD entry strategies: working from the top down, intervening at "crunch" points, working with "bellwether" groups, and conducting training. Each of these approaches has both its disadvantages and its advantages; however, in the context of OD readiness, these considerations take on a significance different from that which is commonly attributed to them.

"Top-Down" Strategy

When possible, the best strategy is to begin OD efforts by conducting assessment, diagnosis, and team development activities with top management. The change agents can legitimize themselves, support for the OD effort can be garnered, and the top group can demonstrate that it is willing to subject itself to the process. It is important to recognize, however, that a top-down strategy can also create problems. Managers at lower levels often become resistant to change originated by the senior executive group. An additional, potential drawback of this strategy is that the change agents can be seen as "pawns" of the executive group.

Crisis Intervention

Intervening when the organization is experiencing some significant difficulty is often an attractive entry approach. Considerable energy can be focused on change efforts when system relief is felt to be needed within a part of the organization that is experiencing stress. This approach is a common "marketing" strategy on the part of both internal and external OD practitioners. The potential disadvantages of intervening in crisis situations include the tendency to foster a dependency on external help and the likelihood that OD will be seen as a short-term problem solution rather than long-range systemic planning for change. Return to "normal" organizational conditions can be seen as OD success, and the precipitating factors may not be confronted.

Dealing with Successful Groups

Often OD can proceed best when there is little or no stress in the organizational unit that is contemplating open-system planning. Change agents can be used to focus on problematic issues in successful parts of an organization. Here the problem-solving methods most common in OD, which are essentially cognitive in emphasis, can be utilized to good advantage. Because there is no excessive overload of emotion, persons involved in the problem situation can approach its amelioration more calmly and rationally. The disadvantage of this entry strategy is that persons in such situations are not likely to seek assistance. Sometimes managers in successful parts of the organization are reluctant to experiment with structure, communication, and participation. Since it often happens in OD efforts that things get worse before they get better, managers may resist opening up situations in which productivity is satisfactory.

Training

Management development as a pre-OD intervention is one of the best strategies. If there is any doubt that the organization is ready for large-scale problem solving, it is almost always advisable to do training first. It makes little or no sense to attempt to use OD methods on a reluctant client. It is often more advisable to concentrate efforts on training for individual managers, supervisors, and leaders, rather than on consulting services for management groups, departments, and divisions.

Training provides a foundation of skills, experience, and concepts on which OD programs can later be based. Training also legitimizes internal and external OD consultants. The consultant can find many opportunities in training to work with individual managers and supervisors on applications of their learning to the actual situations in which they find themselves.

READINESS INDICATORS

In a previous article entitled "A Current Assessment of OD: What It Is and Why It Often Fails" (Pfeiffer & Jones, 1976), we indicated some of the reasons why a particular OD intervention might be unsuccessful. These include (1) unrealistic expectations, (2) inadequate support, (3) failure to follow through, (4) ineffective use of consultants, (5) management resistance, (6) size of the organization, (7) unwillingness to model behavior, and (8) inadequate skills.

If the right questions could be asked in a brief interview or survey-feedback instrument, it would be possible to determine whether or not an organization had reached the stage of readiness to undertake an OD intervention. A number of variables seem to offer the most promise. Franklin (1976) contrasted organizations with successful and unsuccessful OD efforts along eight dimensions: (1) the organization's environment, (2) the organization itself, (3) initial contact for the OD project, (4) formal entry procedures and commitment, (5) data-gathering activities, (6) characteristics of the internal change agents, (7) characteristics of the external change agents, and (8) exit procedures. The results of the study indicated no single dimension that was essential or sufficient to distinguish between successful and unsuccessful OD interventions; however, three general areas did serve to differentiate the OD efforts:

1. *The stability of the organization.* Organizations that are more open to and involved in adjusting to change are more likely to be successful in OD efforts than those that are more stable or oriented toward the status quo.

2. *Interests and commitment to the OD effort.* More specific interests and greater commitment to the OD project, as well as strong support from top management, are associated with successful change.

3. *Characteristics of the internal change agents.* Internal change agents involved in successful interventions possess assessment-prescriptive skills and are more carefully selected and receive less change-agent training prior to the OD effort than internal change agents involved in unsuccessful OD interventions.

Stated more comprehensively, the traits identified by Franklin seem to indicate that organizations that are oriented toward and committed to planned change are more amenable to OD interventions from internal change agents who are not preconditioned toward ready-made answers. Since OD necessitates a large-scale involvement of people in identifying and solving problems in open ways, change-oriented systems are most likely to have the culture necessary for organizational experimentation and self-scrutiny. These conclusions are a helpful jumping-off point for exploring the indicators that reveal organizations ready to deal with the change implied in undertaking an OD program. The following fifteen indicators in three broad areas have been extrapolated from our experience and used as the basis of the OD Readiness Check List which appears at the end of this discussion.

General Considerations

1. Size

The size of an organization is one of the key indicators of the potential success of OD (Pfeiffer & Jones, 1976). It is worth reiterating the point: much of the technology of OD simply does not apply to large organizations. A useful question about organizational size is the following: is the organization manageable, that is, is it within the span of control of a single individual and within the realm of intervention by one or two internal change agents, with assistance by external specialists?

We contend that it is exceedingly difficult to use "traditional" OD techniques in a coordinated way to produce meaningful changes in organizations exceeding about five hundred people. Larger systems require different types of interventions and, in OD terms, can be dealt with only through subsystems. It may be that the only practical approach is OD within parts of the system. In fact, in large-scale organizations, subunit OD is, in our judgment, the most viable of the alternatives available to the consultant.

2. Growth Rate

At what rate is the organization growing? Those organizations that are declining in size, experiencing a slow rate of growth, or growing very rapidly are less likely to be ready for OD than those organizations that are growing at a moderately rapid rate. Organizations that are growing very rapidly may have little or no energy available for OD interventions; relatively static organizations may be reluctant to tamper with the status quo; organizations that are declining in growth may want quick cures rather than long-term planned change.

3. Crisis

An organization in which there is visible evidence of crisis that is perceived by a variety of people at various levels is highly likely to be ready for OD. Organizations that are experiencing significant stress tend to be receptive to intervention; however, they are also likely to become dependent on consultants rather than to develop self-renewing planning. Crisis necessitates change, and OD potentially facilitates participative solutions that can result in shared commitment to action.

4. Macroeconomics

The economic situation in which the organization functions must, of course, be considered. The Vietnam war had a great deal of impact on a number of organizations, as did the more recent oil embargo. The consultant must judge whether the macroeconomic factors are such that success in the OD intervention can be foreseen and the intervention can, in fact, be afforded.

5. OD History

Does the organization have a history of OD interventions? Experience indicates that when the history of the organization is *too* laden with OD interventions, the latest one becomes simply the "project of the year," and people tend to lose interest in the effort. Given an organizational history of several OD attempts, it is very difficult to make an intervention that will have an impact on the organization—particularly when OD efforts have been controversial, unsuccessful, or only partially successful in the past. In that case, the change agent may find himself "guilty by association." Low expectations resulting from previous OD interventions frequently limit the effectiveness of new efforts.

6. Culture

Is the culture of the organization viable, permeable, and supportive of radical change? Very frequently, the other indicators of OD readiness are positive, but commitment to the status quo in the organization may be very strong. The culture of the organization may present such a formidable block that it is virtually impossible to discuss the changes necessary for carrying out a successful OD program. Bureaucratic, heavily unionized, and ritualistic organizations are likely to be closed, nontrusting systems that do not invest heavily in efficiency and effectiveness.

Resources

7. Time Commitment

Is the time commitment of the organization or the managers of the organization adequate to allow for the development of a meaningful OD intervention? Another way to look at this point is whether the organization is committed to all the meetings necessary in OD. Since OD programs progress primarily through myriad meetings, it is important for the organization to be aware of the depth of its commitment to the process. Organizations take a long time to become the way they are, and a reasonable expectation of the time it takes to initiate and stabilize planned change is at least three years of concentrated work.

8. Money

Is the organization able to afford the cost involved in an OD effort, both indirectly in time taken away from work and directly in fees for external and internal consultants? Is the management ready to invest sufficient money in the project?

9. Access to People

Within the initial concept of the OD intervention, is access freely allowed to all people in the organization? If limitations are imposed and individuals at particular levels of an organization cannot be reached, an organization is clearly signalling its lack of readiness. OD programs are doomed to failure if particular key executives put themselves above the process. Ironically, internal OD consultants often do not have access to high-level managers, clearly reducing the impact of the OD program.

10. Labor Contract Limitations

This variable considers the limits placed on the intervention by the members of management who are responsible for negotiating labor agreements. If the limits of worker participation are too restrictive, the OD effort is severely hampered simply by the inability of the change agents to get a mandate broad enough to deal with the problems that are relatively certain to be identified.

11. Structural Flexibility

It sometimes becomes apparent during an OD project that structural changes need to be made. Does the organization have the capacity to reshuffle managers and departments and change reporting procedures, communication patterns, and reward systems?

People Variables

12. Interpersonal Skills

It is important to consider whether there are adequate interpersonal skills in the organization to deal with OD change. Very frequently, the other criteria for readiness will be apparent, but the necessary skills are absent. The methods of OD are essentially verbal, and they require communication skills. If the personnel in the organization are deficient in their ability to express themselves, to listen, and to respond creatively and productively to the ideas of others, then the discussions and meetings required in an OD program are likely to be ineffective.

13. Management Development

To what degree do managers understand and incorporate applications of behavioral science principles in their work? If managers are poorly educated and have underdeveloped interpersonal skills, OD meetings can be futile at best and at worst explosive. An ongoing management development program can provide a "floor" for organization problem solving and unfreeze individual managers for interpersonal feedback processes.

14. Flexibility at the Top

It is necessary that those people who are in positions of power in the organization be sufficiently flexible to open themselves to influence from below. Although it may not be necessary to *begin* the OD effort at the top, it clearly is critical that top executives be knowledgeable about and supportive of the program and willing to open up the system. One or two key executives who are personally and/or organizationally rigid can often preclude the success of an OD intervention.

15. Internal Change Agents

We believe that the best OD staffing consists of an interplay among managers, internal change agents, and external consultants. The major motivation of the outside consultants should be to autonomize managers so that they take responsibility for conducting the organization's ongoing developmental efforts. Without people in the organization who are familiar with experiential methods, consulting, change strategy, and training methods, the organization becomes dependent on external sources of help.

CONCLUSION

If it is determined that an organization does not have the requisite OD readiness, what strategy is open to the consultant? The most frequent answer is training as a readiness-inducing strategy within organizations. Some of the indicators previously discussed, such as size, rate of growth, and macroeconomics, are beyond the effect of training. Other important criterion variables, however, are amenable to a meaningful education program. It is possible that the conceptual skills and personal skills that are requisites of OD readiness can be taught in a variety of formal and informal organizational training programs.

If, however, the organization cannot be meaningfully affected by OD technology, the consultant should be willing to walk away. A consultant's continued history of failure in OD projects with organizations for which it is clear that OD interventions are unlikely to be successful makes it difficult for other consultants to work with clients. We consider such persistent opportunism to be unethical (Pfeiffer & Jones, 1977). The individual practitioner should examine the indicators for the given organization. If those indicators do not predict success, and if they cannot be dealt with in a training education model, the consultant should be direct and simply say that the culture is too strong to augur for the success of change, or that the sense of complacence in the organization is too high for commitment to change, or that the internal history of the organization is such that a new project will not be taken seriously. To undertake an OD effort in the face of predicted failure is unwise—both for the particular consultant and for other professionals in the field.

OD READINESS CHECK LIST

The brief instrument that follows summarizes the chief indicators of OD readiness, weighting each indicator according to its relative criticalness. The check list may be used as the basis for a subjective assessment of an organization to determine the degree to which that organism is likely to support an OD effort. This assessment can be made by a group, ideally consisting of key managers, internal change agents, and external consultants. OD practitioners can also use the instrument to analyze their own history of failures, successes, and decisions not to initiate OD interventions.

REFERENCES

Franklin, J. L. Characteristics of successful and unsuccessful organization development. *The Journal of Applied Behavioral Science*, 1976, *11*(4), 471-492.

Pfeiffer, J. W., & Jones, J. E. A current assessment of OD: What it is and why it often fails. In J. W. Pfeiffer & J. E. Jones (Eds.), *The 1976 annual handbook for group facilitators*. La Jolla, Calif.: University Associates, 1976.

Pfeiffer, J. W., & Jones, J. E. Ethical considerations in consulting. In J. E. Jones & J. W. Pfeiffer (Eds.), *The 1977 annual handbook for group facilitators*. La Jolla, Calif.: University Associates, 1977.

J. William Pfeiffer, Ph.D., is the president of University Associates, La Jolla, California. He is a co-editor of Group & Organization Studies: The International Journal for Group Facilitators *and of the Pfeiffer and Jones Series in Human Relations Training, including* A Handbook of Structured Experiences for Human Relations Training *(Vols. I-VI) and the* Annual Handbook for Group Facilitators *(1972-1978). Dr. Pfeiffer's background is in adult education, internal change agentry, Gestalt group work, and organization development.*

John E. Jones, Ph.D., is the vice president of University Associates, La Jolla, California. He is a co-editor of Group & Organization Studies: The International Journal for Group Facilitators *and of the Pfeiffer and Jones Series in Human Relations Training, including* A Handbook of Structured Experiences for Human Relations Training *(Vols. I-VI) and the* Annual Handbook for Group Facilitators *(1972-1978). Dr. Jones's background is in teaching and counseling, education, and organization and community-development consulting.*

OD READINESS CHECK LIST
J. William Pfeiffer and John E. Jones

This instrument summarizes the chief indicators of OD readiness and weights each indicator according to its relative degree of criticalness. The following interpretations of scoring can be helpful to consultants: a score of less than 50 would suggest training, small-scale projects, and crisis interventions; 50–70 would indicate management development and pre-OD activities; 70 and higher would indicate that the consultant test the willingness of the organization to commit itself to planned change.

Instructions: Using the following check list, indicate the degree to which each of the fifteen dimensions is a concern to you with regard to the organization's readiness for OD. Circle the number under the appropriate heading for each factor. Each dimension has been scaled according to its relative importance in predicting the organization's receptivity to OD interventions. Total the scores for an overall OD readiness index.

General Considerations	No Concern	Mild Concern	Moderate Concern	Significant Concern	Critical Concern
1. Size	4	3	2	1	0
2. Growth Rate	4	3	2	1	0
3. Crisis (potential positive or negative influence)	4	3	2	1	0
4. Macroeconomics	4	3	2	1	0
5. OD History	4	3	2	1	0
6. Culture	4	3	2	1	0
Resources					
7. Time Commitment	8	6	4	2	0
8. Money	8	6	4	2	0
9. Access to People	8	6	4	2	0
10. Labor Contract Limitations	8	6	4	2	0
11. Structural Flexibility	8	6	4	2	0
People Variables					
12. Interpersonal Skills	12	9	6	3	0
13. Management Development	12	9	6	3	0
14. Flexibility at the Top	12	9	6	3	0
15. Internal Change Agents	12	9	6	3	0

Total Readiness Score [ ]

INTRODUCTION TO THE
RESOURCES SECTION

Traditionally this is the eclectic section of the *Annual*; perhaps, to some, our editorial choices of materials at times seem whimsical. Our aim in the Resources section is to include useful information that just does not fit into any other section of the *Annual*. Below is a selected list of the contents of this section in previous *Annuals*.

1972   "Alphabet Soup" (list of professional associations)

"Games and Simulations: Materials, Sources and Learning Concepts" (annotated)

"Media Resources for Human Relations Training"

1973   "An Informal Glossary of Terms and Phrases in Organization Development"

"A Personalized Human Relations Training Bibliography" (annotated)

1974   "Human Relations Training in the UK and Continental Europe"

A list of book reviews, 1972-1974 (in the introduction to the section)

1975   "Applied Behavioral Science Consulting Organizations: A Directory" (by geographical regions)

"Canada's Experience with Human Relations Training"

"An Introduction to Structural Integration (Rolfing)"

"Awareness Through Movement"

"What Is Psychosynthesis?"

"A Bibliography of Small-Group Training, 1973-1974" (divided into categories)

A review of recent books on Gestalt therapy

A review of Egan's books on helping

A review of recent OD books

1976   "A Reference List for Change Agents" (resources and 591 references)

"Bioenergetic Therapy"

"Hatha Yoga"

"Humanistic Education: A Review of Books Since 1970"

"Values Clarification: A Review of Major Books"

"Transactional Analysis: A Review of the Literature"

"Encountering the World of Don Juan" (book review of Castaneda's Don Juan quartet)

1977   "A Bibliography of Nonverbal Communication"

"A Bibliography of Small-Group Training, 1974-1976"

"AHP Growth Center List"

A review of OD books

A review of books on assertion

This year, we are publishing four resources. The results of a national survey that we conducted of graduate programs in applied behavioral science are presented in directory form. Two University Associates staff members discuss considerations for selecting and contracting for training sites. A third piece provides a guide to film resources that updates our 1972 list of media resources. And an annotated guide to resources in humanistic education concludes the section.

Our readers should note that reviews of *individual* books will now appear in the University Associates quarterly journal, *Group & Organization Studies*. In future *Annuals* we will provide more updates (e.g., the directory of consulting organizations, planned for 1979) and continue to present materials that are useful as "tools of the trade." We welcome any suggestions readers may have for new resource features to be included in this section of the *Annual*.

GRADUATE PROGRAMS IN APPLIED BEHAVIORAL SCIENCE: A DIRECTORY

Susan Campbell

After attending workshops or seminars in human relations training, organization development, or some other area in the broad field of "applied behavioral science," many people find themselves asking where they can get further professional or academic training. They want to find out what graduate programs are available and what they offer, whether they are accredited, and what their theoretical or value orientation is. They want to know whom to contact for further information on specific programs. This directory is designed to provide answers to these sorts of questions.

The entries listed here are based on a survey of members of the International Association of Applied Social Scientists. They were asked to identify quality graduate programs in such areas as organization development, laboratory education, human relations training, group leadership, and community development and to rate each program according to the degree to which it was suitable for mature students. Programs so identified were then sent questionnaires requesting specific information on degrees, program goals, students' typical professional responsibilities and organizational affiliations, etc. These responses were then sorted and selected to produce the directory published here. Just before press time, each program was asked to verify the details provided in the directory and to correct or supplement them. No endorsement of any program by either University Associates or IAASS is implied by this listing.

Several nondegree programs have been included; in some cases, these can be utilized as a part of graduate study in a program that leads to a degree. It is advised, however, that students interested in attending a nondegree program for credit contact the institution and degree program in which they plan to use such study.

Although we have attempted to offer as accurate and comprehensive a directory as possible, some programs that should have been included may have been overlooked. In order to help us keep our files as current as possible, we invite our readers to send us additions, corrections, changes, and suggestions for a future, updated version of this directory.

Entries are divided into five broad geographical areas (Europe, Canada, Eastern and Southern United States, Central United States, and Western United States); within geographical areas, programs are listed alphabetically by the name of the institution. For each entry, information (as available) is given in the following order: institution sponsoring the program, name of the program, address, telephone, contact person(s); degree(s) offered; content area(s) in which study or training is offered; value orientation(s) of the program; accrediting body (if program is accredited); approximate enrollment; residency requirements; financial aid available; and additional information about the program.

EUROPE

New Experimental College
World Education Development
Skyum Bjerge 7752 Snedsted
Thy, Denmark
(07) 936234
A. R. Nielsen

Degree(s) Offered: Master of World Education, M.Ed., Ed.D.

Content Area(s): Organization development/ organizational behavior, counseling/therapy, community development/consultation, group leadership/facilitation, human relations training

Value Orientation(s): Process consultation, behavior modification, consulting-skills training, community organizing, psychodynamic approaches, existential/phenomenological approaches, general system theory and approaches; high emphasis on personal development, skills

Approximate Enrollment: Ten to twenty

Residency Requirements: None

Financial Aid Available: V.A. benefits

CANADA

University of Alberta
M.A. Program in Community Development
Edmonton, Alberta
Canada T6G 2E1
(403) 432-5630
A. S. A. Mohsen

Degree(s) Offered: M.A.

Content Area(s): Community development/ consultation

Value Orientation(s): Consulting-skill training, community organizing; high emphasis on theory/research

Approximate Enrollment: Thirty

Residency Requirements: Two semesters

Financial Aid Available: Assistantships, scholarships

EASTERN AND SOUTHERN UNITED STATES

Alfred University
School Psychology Program (M.A.)
Alfred, New York 14802
(607) 871-2212
Anthony J. Pane, Jr., Director, School Psychology Program

Degree(s) Offered: M.A.

Content Area(s): Organization development/ organizational behavior, psychological/humanistic education, individual and group counseling/therapy, school consultation, group leadership/facilitation, human relations training, individual psychological testing

Value Orientation(s): Process consultation, behavior modification, consulting-skills training, psychodynamic approaches; high emphasis on personal development, skills, theory/ research

Accreditation: New York State Permanent Certificate in School Psychology

Approximate Enrollment: Sixteen to twenty per graduating class

Residency Requirements: Two years of full-time study

Financial Aid Available: Graduate assistantships, paid internships sought for second-year students

Additional Information: Close-knit learning environment, field work and experience each semester

Antioch College—Maryland
Human Resources and Organization Development
5829 Banneker Road
Columbia, Maryland 21044
(301) 730-9175
Harts M. Brown

Degree(s) Offered: M.A.

Content Area(s): Organization development/ organizational behavior, community development/consultation, group leadership/ facilitation, human relations training, human resources development/training

Value Orientation(s): Eclectic; high emphasis on personal development, skills, theory/ research

Accreditation: North Central Association of Colleges and Secondary Schools; Maryland State Department of Education

Approximate Enrollment: Seventy-five

Residency Requirements: Forty-eight quarter hours

Financial Aid Available: Scholarships/fellowships, V.A. benefits, work-study

Antioch New England Graduate School

Department of Professional Psychology
One Elm Street
Keene, New Hampshire 03431
(603) 357-3122
David Singer, Chairperson

Degree(s) Offered: M.A.C.P. (Master of Art in Counseling Psychology), M.M.T. (Master in Dance-Movement Therapy), M.Ed.

Content Area(s): Psychological/humanistic education, individual and group counseling/therapy, community development/consultation, group leadership/facilitation, movement therapy, family therapy

Value Orientation(s): Consulting-skills training, psychodynamic approaches, existential/phenomenological approaches, general system theory and approaches; high emphasis on personal development, theory

Accreditation: North Central Association of Colleges and Secondary Schools

Approximate Enrollment: Fifty

Residency Requirements: At least one full-time term

Financial Aid Available: CWSP (College Work-Study Program), NDSL (National Direct Student Loan)

Additional Information: Flexible scheduling, active student-faculty involvement

Appalachian State University

Master of Arts in Clinical Psychology
Psychology Department
Boone, North Carolina 28608
(704) 262-2272
Richard Levin

Degree(s) Offered: M.A.

Content Area(s): Individual and group counseling/therapy, psychological assessment, community development/consultation, group leadership/facilitation, human relations training

Value Orientation(s): Process consultation, behavior modification, consulting-skills training, psychodynamic approaches, existential/phenomenological approaches, general system theory and approaches; high emphasis on skills

Approximate Enrollment: Twenty to fifty

Residency Requirements: Three semesters on campus plus six months of internship

Financial Aid Available: Scholarships/fellowships (limited)

Associates for Human Resources, Inc.

Humanistic Psychology for Graduate Students
P.O. Box 727
Concord, Massachusetts 01742
(617) 259-9624
Jack Marvin

Degree(s) Offered: Credit toward master's available through Campus-Free College or St. Mary's College

Content Area(s): Individual and group counseling/therapy (bodymind, Gestalt, T.A., fantasy work, etc.)

Value Orientation(s): Psychodynamic approaches, existential/phenomenological approaches; high emphasis on personal development, skills, theory/research

Approximate Enrollment: Ten to twenty

Residency Requirements: Two days per week for three months in workshop participation; six-month field placement

Financial Aid Available: Loans

Boston University

Graduate Program in Humanistic Education
School of Education
Department of Humanistic and Behavioral Studies
232 Bay State Road
Boston, Massachusetts 02215
(617) 353-3297
Paul Nash

Degree(s) Offered: M.Ed., C.A.G.S. (Certificate of Advanced Graduate Study), Ed.D.

Content Area(s): Organization development/organizational behavior, psychological/humanistic education, individual and group counseling/therapy, community development/consultation, group leadership/facilitation, teacher education, human relations training

Value Orientation(s): Process consultation, consulting-skills training, psychodynamic approaches, existential/phenomenological approaches; high emphasis on personal development, skills, theory

Accreditation: National Council for Accreditation of Teacher Education

Approximate Enrollment: 250

Residency Requirements: Ed.D. only: two successive semesters

Financial Aid Available: Scholarships/fellowships, V.A. benefits

Additional Information: Interdisciplinary approach; focus on theoretical foundations, practical applications

Campus-Free College
1239 G Street, N.W.
Washington, D.C. 20005
(202) 347-0721
Mark Cheren, Sue Sinnamon, Larry Lemmel

Degree(s) Offered: M.A.

Content Area(s): Curriculum designed by students to meet individual needs

Value Orientation(s): Individually determined; high emphasis on personal development, skills, theory/research

Accreditation: Middle States Association of Colleges and Secondary Schools (pending)

Approximate Enrollment: Twenty to fifty

Residency Requirements: None

Financial Aid Available: Scholarships/fellowships (from outside sources), loans, minimal work-study

Clark University
M.B.A. Degree with Specialty in
Human Resource Management and
Organization Development
Department of Management
950 Main Street
Worcester, Massachusetts 01610
(617) 793-7406
W. Warner Burke, Chairperson

Degree(s) Offered: M.B.A.

Content Area(s): Organization development/organizational behavior, group leadership/facilitation, consultation strategies and skills

Value Orientation(s): Process consultation, consulting-skills training, general system theory and approaches; high emphasis on personal development, theory/research

Approximate Enrollment: Fifty

Residency Requirements: Two years

Financial Aid Available: V.A. benefits

Columbia University Teachers College
Applied Human Development and Guidance
525 W. 120th Street
New York, New York 10027
(212) 678-3397
Jean Pierre Jordaan, Chairman

Degree(s) Offered: M.A., M.Ed., Ed.D.

Content Area(s): Organization development/organizational behavior, counseling/therapy, group leadership/facilitation, human relations training

Value Orientation(s): Process consultation, consulting-skills training, general system theory and approaches; high emphasis on personal development, skills, theory/research

Accreditation: Middle States Association of Colleges and Secondary Schools

Approximate Enrollment: 120

Residency Requirements: Doctoral: one year or one semester and one summer

Financial Aid Available: Scholarships/fellowships, V.A. benefits

Duquesne University
Graduate Psychology—A Human Science
  Approach
Psychology College Hall
Pittsburgh, Pennsylvania 15219
(412) 434-6520
David L. Smith

Degree(s) Offered: M.A., Ph.D.

Content Area(s): Counseling/therapy, phenomenologically based psychology

Value Orientation(s): Existential/phenomenological approaches; high emphasis on personal development, skills, theory/research

Approximate Enrollment: Fifty

Residency Requirements: Fulfilled in courses

Financial Aid Available: Scholarships/fellowships

Additional Information: Program integrates phenomenological approach to psychology into clinical practice

Fairleigh Dickinson University
M.A. in Human Development
Graduate Center for Human Development
223 Fairview Avenue
Rutherford, New Jersey 07070
(201) 939-1377
David Hobson, Director

Degree(s) Offered: M.A.

Content Area(s): Human development, humanistic education, group leadership/facilitation, teacher education, human relations training

Value Orientation(s): Process consultation, consulting-skills training, psychodynamic approaches, existential/phenomenological approaches; high emphasis on personal development, professional effectiveness

Accreditation: Middle States Association of Colleges and Secondary Schools

Approximate Enrollment: 500

Residency Requirements: Entire program offered throughout New Jersey

Financial Aid Available: Fellowships, V.A. benefits

George Washington University
Behavioral Science in Organization Development
Department of Management Science
815 21st Street, N.W.
Washington, D.C. 20037
(202) 676-6471
Gordon Lippitt

Degree(s) Offered: M.S., M.B.A., D.B.A., D.P.A. (Doctor of Public Administration)

Content Area(s): Core courses related to administrative theory and practice, plus organization development/organizational behavior, group leadership/facilitation, change theory and practice, consultation skills

Value Orientation(s): Process consultation, consulting-skills training, general system theory and approaches; high emphasis on skills, theory/research

Accreditation: Middle States Association of Colleges and Secondary Schools

Approximate Enrollment: Master's: 140; doctoral: thirty-eight

Residency Requirements: Contact program for further information

Financial Aid Available: V.A. benefits

George Washington University
Human Resource Development
School of Education
Washington, D.C. 20052
(202) 676-7116
Leonard Nadler

Degree(s) Offered: M.A., Ed.D.

Content Area(s): Human resource development, organization development, community development/consultation, group leadership/facilitation, training directors

Value Orientation(s): Process consultation, consulting-skills training

Accreditation: Middle States Association of Colleges and Secondary Schools

Approximate Enrollment: 100

Residency Requirements: Negotiable

Financial Aid Available: V.A. benefits

Georgia State University
Department of Psychology
Clinical and Nonclinical Programs
University Plaza
Atlanta, Georgia 30303
(404) 658-2456
Walter F. Daves, Graduate Program Director

Degree(s) Offered: M.A., Ph.D.

Content Area(s): Personality, social, developmental/comparatives, physiological, cognitive and symbolic, community/organizational

Value Orientation(s): Process consultation, behavior modification, consulting-skills training, existential/phenomenological approaches; high emphasis on personal development, skills

Accreditation: American Psychological Association (clinical only)

Approximate Enrollment: 160

Residency Requirements: Six quarters

Financial Aid Available: Scholarships/fellowships

Goddard College
Human Studies Center
Plainfield, Vermont 05667
(802) 454-8311, ext. 348
Robert Belenky

Degree(s) Offered: M.A.

Content Area(s): Organization development/organizational behavior, individual and group counseling/therapy, community development/consultation, group leadership/facilitation, teacher education, human relations training, administration, independent study and student-designed study plans

Value Orientation(s): Depends on student's needs; high emphasis on personal development, theory/research

Accreditation: New England Association of Schools and Colleges

Approximate Enrollment: Thirty-five

Residency Requirements: Five two-day overnight meetings per year

Financial Aid Available: Scholarships/fellowships, V.A. benefits

Additional Information: Average student age in the 30's; warm and informal but intensely serious atmosphere

Harvard University
Organizational Behavior and Intervention
Graduate School of Education
6 Appian Way
Cambridge, Massachusetts 02138
(617) 495-3571, 3573
Lee Bolman, Chris Argyris

Degree(s) Offered: M.Ed., Ed.D.

Content Area(s): Organization development/organizational behavior

Value Orientation(s): Process consultation, consulting-skills training; high emphasis on personal development, skills, theory/research

Approximate Enrollment: Ten

Residency Requirements: One year

Financial Aid Available: Scholarships/fellowships

Kean College of New Jersey
M.A. Program in Organizational Development
Morris Avenue
Union, New Jersey 07083
(201) 527-2000
Robert F. Allen

Degree(s) Offered: M.A.

Content Area(s): Organization development/organizational behavior, community development/consultation, group leadership/facilitation, human relations training

Value Orientation(s): Normative system theory and applications, processes of democratic change, process consultation, consulting-skills training, general system theory and approaches

Approximate Enrollment: Fifty

Residency Requirements: None

Financial Aid Available: Limited

Additional Information: Emphasis placed on building a learning community within the program

National Humanistic Education Center
Master in Humanistic Education—
  Campus Free College
110 Spring Street
Saratoga Springs, New York 12866
(518) 587-8770
Joel Goodman

Degree(s) Offered: M.A.

Content Area(s): Psychological/humanistic education, group leadership/facilitation, teacher education, human relations training

Value Orientation(s): Process consultation, consulting-skills training, humanistic curriculum development, group facilitation skills, applications of humanistic education to social issues, creativity development, value clarification, enhancing self-esteem

Accreditation: Middle States Association of Colleges and Secondary Schools (pending)

Approximate Enrollment: Fifty

Residency Requirements: None

Financial Aid Available: V.A. benefits

Additional Information: Emphasis on self-directed learning (with ongoing assistance and support from program adviser and peer support group); availability of resources of National Humanistic Education Center (staff, workshops, bookstore)

NTL Institute
Program for Specialists in Organization
  Development
P.O. Box 9155, Rosslyn Station
Arlington, Virginia 22209
(703) 527-1500
Cornelia Eschborn

Degree(s) Offered: Nondegree program

Content Area(s): Organization development/organizational behavior

Value Orientation(s): Process consultation, general system theory and approaches, personal theories of practice, use of self as a change agent; high emphasis on personal development, skills

Approximate Enrollment: Fifty

Residency Requirements: A two-week residential program conducted in various parts of the country

Financial Aid Available: Scholarships/fellowships (limited)

Saint Lawrence University
Counselor Education Program
Education Department
Canton, New York 13617
(315) 379-5863
T. F. Renick

Degree(s) Offered: M. Ed.

Content Area(s): Psychological/humanistic education, individual and group counseling/therapy, group leadership/facilitation, human relations training

Value Orientation(s): Consulting-skills training, existential/phenomenological approaches; high emphasis on personal development, skills

Accreditation: Middle States Association of Colleges and Secondary Schools

Approximate Enrollment: Twenty to fifty

Residency Requirements: None

Financial Aid Available: V.A. benefits

Additional Information: Humanistic approach; sense of community; rural setting

School for International Training

International Career Training
Kipling Road
Brattleboro, Vermont 05301
(802) 257-7751
Walter B. Johnson, Director

Degree(s) Offered: M.I.A. (Master of International Administration)

Content Area(s): Organization development/organizational behavior, humanistic education, experiential learning, community development/consultation, group leadership/facilitation, human relations training, administration, intercultural awareness and global perspectives

Value Orientation(s): Group processing, consulting-skills training, community organizing, general system theory and approaches; interpersonal, intrapersonal, cross-cultural, experiential; high emphasis on personal development, self-evaluation skills

Accreditation: New England Association of Schools and Colleges

Approximate Enrollment: Twenty-five each program (two programs annually)

Residency Requirements: Five and one-half months

Financial Aid Available: Scholarships/fellowships, V.A. benefits

Additional Information: Foreign-student services; six-to-eighteen-month internship (domestic or international); independent study

State University of New York at Buffalo

Social Psychology
Department of Psychology
4230 Ridge Lea Road
Buffalo, New York 14226
(716) 831-1386
Barbara Benedict Bunker, Director; Dean G. Pruitt

Degree(s) Offered: Ph.D

Content Area(s): Theory and research in social psychology, organization development/organizational behavior, group leadership/facilitation, human relations training

Value Orientation(s): Consulting-skills training, process consultation, general system theory and approaches; high emphasis on skills, theory/research

Accreditation: Middle States Association of Colleges and Secondary Schools

Approximate Enrollment: Twenty to thirty-five

Residency Requirements: Two years

Financial Aid Available: Scholarships/fellowships

Additional Information: Basically an academic social psychology program

Stevens Institute of Technology

Castle Point Station
Hoboken, New Jersey 07030
(201) 792-2544
J. Myron Johnson, Arthur Shapiro

Degree(s) Offered: M.S., Ph.D.

Content Area(s): Organization development/organizational behavior, individual and group counseling, group leadership/facilitation, human relations training, administration

Value Orientation(s): Process consultation, behavior modification, consulting-skills training; high emphasis on skills, theory/research

Accreditation: State of New Jersey

Approximate Enrollment: 150

Residency Requirements: Two full-time semesters

Financial Aid Available: Scholarships/fellowships, V.A. benefits

Syracuse University

Educational Administration—Organizational Behavior and Change
150 Marshall Street, Suite 499-C
Syracuse, New York 13210
(315) 423-2754
Arthur Blumberg

Degree(s) Offered: Ed.D., Ph.D.

Content Area(s): Organization development/organizational behavior, human relations training, administration

Value Orientation(s): Process consultation, consulting-skills training; high emphasis on skills, theory/research

Accreditation: New York State Department of Education

Approximate Enrollment: Ten to twenty

Residency Requirements: One year

Financial Aid Available: Scholarships/fellowships

Syracuse University

Rehabilitation Counselor Education Program
805 South Crouse Avenue
Syracuse, New York 13210
(315) 423-4126
Kenneth W. Reagles

Degree(s) Offered: M.S., Ph.D.

Content Area(s): Psychological/humanistic education, individual and group counseling/therapy, community development/consultation, rehabilitation

Value Orientation(s): Behavior modification, psychodynamic approaches, existential/phenomenological approaches; high emphasis on personal development, skills, theory/research

Accreditation: Council on Rehabilitation Education

Approximate Enrollment: Fifty

Residency Requirements: One year

Financial Aid Available: Scholarships/fellowships

Temple University

The Humanistic Education Group (HEG)
469 Ritter Hall
Philadelphia, Pennsylvania 19122
(215) 787-6154
Leland Howe

Degree(s) Offered: M.Ed., Ed.D.

Content Area(s): Psychological/humanistic education, community development/consultation, group leadership/facilitation, teacher education, human relations training

Value Orientation(s): Consulting-skills training, existential/phenomenological approaches; high emphasis on personal development, skills

Accreditation: Middle States Association of Colleges and Secondary Schools

Approximate Enrollment: Twenty to fifty

Residency Requirements: Two consecutive full-time semesters

Financial Aid Available: Limited

Trinity College

Trinity Master in Business Administration Program
Michigan Avenue and Franklin Street
Washington, D.C. 20017
(202) 269-2354
Percy L. Jones, Director

Degree(s) Offered: M.B.A.

Content Area(s): Organization development/organizational behavior, administration

Value Orientation(s): Process consultation, consulting-skills training, general system theory and approaches; high emphasis on personal development, skills; competency based, practitioner oriented

Accreditation: American Assembly of Collegiate Schools of Business (pending)

Approximate Enrollment: Twenty to fifty

Residency Requirements: A minimum of thirty hours

Financial Aid Available: Work-study

University of Georgia

College of Business Administration
Athens, Georgia 30602
(404) 542-5672
C. David Billings, Director of Graduate Studies

Degree(s) Offered: M.A., M.B.A., Ph.D.

Content Area(s): Organization development/organizational behavior, community development/consultation, group leadership/facilitation, human relations training, administration

Value Orientation(s): General system theory and approaches; high emphasis on skills, theory/research

Accreditation: American Assembly of Collegiate Schools of Business

Approximate Enrollment: Fifty

Residency Requirements: Forty-five quarter hours

Financial Aid Available: Scholarships/fellowships

University of Maryland
Human Development Education
Institute for Child Study
College of Education
College Park, Maryland 20742
(301) 454-2034
Hugh V. Perkins

Degree(s) Offered: M.A., M. Ed., Ed.D., Ph.D., A.G.S. (Advanced Graduate Specialist)

Content Area(s): Psychological/humanistic education, community development/consultation, group leadership/facilitation, teacher education

Value Orientation(s): Consulting-skills training, psychodynamic approaches, existential/phenomenological approaches; high emphasis on personal development

Accreditation: National Council for Accreditation of Teacher Education; Middle States Association of Colleges and Secondary Schools

Approximate Enrollment: 300

Residency Requirements: Doctoral: two full-time semesters

Financial Aid Available: Scholarships/fellowships, assistantships

University of Massachusetts
Human Services and Applied Behavioral
   Sciences
School of Education
356 Hills House
Amherst, Massachusetts 01002
(413) 545-3610
Donald Carew, Doug Forsyth

Degree(s) Offered: M.Ed., Ed.D.

Content Area(s): Organization development/organizational behavior, psychological/humanistic education, individual and group counseling/therapy, group leadership/facilitation, human relations training

Value Orientation(s): Process consultation, consulting-skills training, existential/phenomenological approaches, human services; high emphasis on personal development, skills, theory/research

Accreditation: National Council for Accreditation of Teacher Education

Approximate Enrollment: Fifty

Residency Requirements: Doctoral: two consecutive full-time semesters

Financial Aid Available: Scholarships/fellowships

Additional Information: All courses integrate theory and practice; separate programs in division—humanistic education, counseling, juvenile justice, human development, early childhood education, special education

University of New Hampshire
M.B.A. Program (Concentration in Organizational
   Behavior and Organizational Development)
Whittemore School of Business and Economics
McConnell Hall
Durham, New Hampshire 03824
(603) 862-2771
Allan Cohen, M.B.A. Program Director

Degree(s) Offered: M.B.A.; Ph.D. (pending)

Content Area(s): Organization development/organizational behavior, administration

Value Orientation(s): Process consultation, consulting-skills training, general system theory and approaches; high emphasis on skills

Approximate Enrollment: Forty-five each year

Residency Requirements: Two years (off-campus internship possible for one-half year)

Financial Aid Available: Assistantships/fellowships

Additional Information: First year of M.B.A. is all required subjects, second year all elective plus course in business policy; opportunities for field work in organizations

University of North Carolina at Chapel Hill
Graduate Programs in Higher and Adult
   Education
School of Education
Division of Organizational Development
Chapel Hill, North Carolina 27514
(919) 933-3083
E. R. Watson, J. Morrison

Degree(s) Offered: M.A., M.Ed., Ph.D.

Content Area(s): Organization development/organizational behavior, psychological/humanistic education, group leadership/facilitation, human relations training, administration

Value Orientation(s): Process consultation, consulting-skills training, psychodynamic approaches, general system theory and approaches; high emphasis on personal development, skills, theory/research

Accreditation: Southern Association of Colleges and Schools

Approximate Enrollment: Fifty

Residency Requirements: Master's: one year; doctoral: two years

Financial Aid Available: Assistantships

University of Rochester
Center for the Study of Helping Services
College of Education
Rochester, New York 14627
(716) 275-3937
Harold L. Munson

Degree(s) Offered: M.S., Ed.D., Ph.D.

Content Area(s): Psychological/humanistic education, individual and group counseling, community development/consultation, group leadership/facilitation

Value Orientation(s): Process consultation, consulting-skills training, adult development, career education, existential/phenomenological approaches; high emphasis on theory/research; secondary emphasis on skills

Accreditation: National Council for Accreditation of Teacher Education

Approximate Enrollment: Twenty to fifty

Residency Requirements: Doctoral: one year

Financial Aid Available: Scholarships/fellowships (at doctoral level)

Additional Information: Focus on adult counseling, career development

University of West Florida
Faculty of Psychology
Pensacola, Florida 32504
(904) 476-9500, ext. 468
Frances Dunham

Degree(s) Offered: M.A.

Content Area(s): Organization development/organizational behavior, individual and group counseling/therapy, teacher education (counseling and guidance and school psychology)

Value Orientation(s): Eclectic; high emphasis on skills, theory/research

Accreditation: Southern Association of Colleges and Schools; Florida State Department of Education

Approximate Enrollment: Fifty

Residency Requirements: Approximately one year

Financial Aid Available: Scholarships/fellowships, V.A. benefits

Wake Forest University
Counselor Education
Department of Education
Box 7266, Reynolda Station
Winston-Salem, North Carolina 27109
(919) 761-5341, 5343
Thomas M. Elmore

Degree(s) Offered: M.A.Ed.

Content Area(s): Psychological/humanistic education, individual and group counseling/therapy, group leadership/facilitation

Value Orientation(s): Consulting-skills training, existential/phenomenological approaches; high emphasis on personal development, theory/research

Accreditation: National Council for Accreditation of Teacher Education (School Counseling Sequence)

Approximate Enrollment: Thirty-five to forty-five

Residency Requirements: One full year

Financial Aid Available: Scholarships/fellowships

Additional Information: Basically a master's degree in counseling psychology with a developmental emphasis; particularly for persons interested in work in schools, colleges, community mental health agencies

West Georgia College
Department of Psychology
Carrollton, Georgia 30117
(404) 834-1335
Mike Arons, Chairman

Degree(s) Offered: M.A.

Content Area(s): Psychological/humanistic education, counseling/therapy, group leadership/facilitation, teacher education, human relations training; oriental, existential, and transpersonal parapsychology

Value Orientation(s): Process consultation, community organizing, psychodynamic approaches, existential/phenomenological approaches; high emphasis on personal development, skills, theory/research

Accreditation: Southern Association of Colleges and Schools

Approximate Enrollment: 100

Residency Requirements: Minimum of thirty hours

238

Financial Aid Available: Scholarships/fellowships (limited)

Additional Information: Separate program devoted to organization development

Yale School of Organization and Management
Organizational Behavior Doctoral Program
56 Hillhouse Avenue (3742 Yale Station)
New Haven, Connecticut 06520
(203) 436-1112
Clayton Alderfer, J. Richard Hackman, Victor Vroom

Degree(s) Offered: Ph.D.

Content Area(s): Organizational behavior/organization development

Value Orientation(s): Psychology and sociology of organizations, with some opportunity to learn about applications; high emphasis on theory/research

Approximate Enrollment: Ten to twenty

Residency Requirements: Three years

Financial Aid Available: Scholarships/fellowships

Additional Information: Favorable student-faculty ratio; access to social science departments of Yale University

CENTRAL UNITED STATES

Bowling Green State University
Master in Organization Development
Director of Graduate Studies
Business Administration Building
Bowling Green, Ohio 43403
(419) 372-2210
Glenn Varney, Coordinator

Degree(s) Offered: M.S., Master in Organization Development

Content Area(s): Organization development/organizational behavior

Value Orientation(s): Process consultation, consulting-skills training, general system theory and approaches; emphasis on theory/research

Accreditation: North Central Association of Colleges and Secondary Schools; American Assembly of Collegiate Schools of Business

Approximate Enrollment: Twenty to thirty

Residency Requirements: None

Financial Aid Available: V.A. benefits

Case Western Reserve University
Master's Program in Organization Development and Analysis
Department of Organizational Behavior
Sears Library Building
Cleveland, Ohio 44106
(216) 368-2056, 2121
Suresh Srivastva, Chairperson; Eric H. Neilsen, Director

Degree(s) Offered: M.S.

Content Area(s): Organization development/organizational behavior, psychological/humanistic education, community development/consultation, group leadership/facilitation, teacher education, human relations training, administration

Value Orientation(s): Process consultation, consulting-skills training, existential/phenomenological approaches, humanistic approaches, health care management, general system theory and approaches; high emphasis on personal development, skills

Accreditation: American Assembly of Collegiate Schools of Business

Approximate Enrollment: Twenty to thirty-five

Residency Requirements: Residency in city of Cleveland during program

Financial Aid Available: V.A. benefits

Cleveland State University
Program of Graduate Studies for Teachers of Emerging Adolescents
22nd and Euclid Avenue
Cleveland, Ohio 44115
(216) 687-4600
Stanley I. Alprin

Degree(s) Offered: M.Ed.

Content Area(s): Psychological/humanistic education, group leadership/facilitation, teacher education, human relations training

Value Orientation(s): Psychodynamic approaches, existential/phenomenological approaches; high emphasis on personal development, skills

Accreditation: National Council for Accreditation of Teacher Education

Approximate Enrollment: Eighty

Residency Requirements: None

Financial Aid Available: None

Fort Hays State University
Speech Communication Department
Hays, Kansas 67601
(913) 628-5365
James Costigan

Degree(s) Offered: M.S.

Content Area(s): Organization development/organizational behavior, group leadership/facilitation, teacher education

Value Orientation(s): Process consultation, consulting-skills training; high emphasis on skills

Accreditation: North Central Association of Colleges and Secondary Schools

Approximate Enrollment: Ten to twenty

Residency Requirements: None

Financial Aid Available: Scholarships/fellowships

Additional Information: Small classes, close student-teacher working relationships

George Williams College
M.S. in Administration and Organization Behavior
555 31st Street
Downers Grove, Illinois 60515
(312) 964-3100
Peter F. Sorensen, Jr., Department Chairman; Jerry Perlmutter, Coordinator, OD Curriculum

Degree(s) Offered: M.S.

Content Area(s): Organization development/organizational behavior, group leadership/facilitation, human relations training, administration

Value Orientation(s): Process consultation, consulting-skills training, existential/phenomenological approaches, general system theory and approaches; high emphasis on personal development, skills, theory/research

Accreditation: North Central Association of Colleges and Secondary Schools

Approximate Enrollment: 100

Residency Requirements: Two full-time quarters (may be fulfilled concurrently with full-time employment)

Financial Aid Available: Scholarships/fellowships (limited), V.A. benefits

Additional Information: Program offers four basic tracks: (1) management/organizational behavior; (2) institutional management (community service organizations, etc.); (3) human resource development (personnel); and (4) organization development (OD)

Indiana University
Bureau of Studies in Adult Education
School of Education, Room 319
Bloomington, Indiana 47401
(812) 337-5449 or (317) 264-8110
John McKinley

Degree(s) Offered: M.A., M.S., Ed.D., Ph.D.

Content Area(s): Organization development/organizational behavior, psychological/humanistic education, group leadership/facilitation, human relations training

Value Orientation(s): Process consultation, consulting-skills training, general system theory and approaches; high emphasis on personal development, skills

Accreditation: North Central Association of Colleges and Secondary Schools

Approximate Enrollment: 175

Residency Requirements: Master's: one twelve-hour semester or two six-hour summer sessions; doctoral: two nine-hour consecutive semesters

Financial Aid Available: Scholarships/fellowships (limited)

Indiana University at South Bend
Counselor Education
1825 Northside Boulevard
South Bend, Indiana 46615
(219) 237-4373
Bernard Nisenholz, Kent Laudeman

Degree(s) Offered: M.S.

Content Area(s): Individual and group counseling/therapy, group leadership/facilitation, human relations training, career development

Value Orientation(s): Existential/phenomenological approaches; high emphasis on skills

Accreditation: North Central Association of Colleges and Secondary Schools

Approximate Enrollment: Seventy-five

Residency Requirements: Part-time program requiring one course per semester over a two-and-one-half-year period

Financial Aid Available: V.A. benefits

Additional Information: Laboratory group in personal growth meets regularly throughout program

Michigan State University
M.L.I.R. Degree Program
School of Labor and Industrial Relations
430 S. Kedzie Hale
East Lansing, Michigan 48824
(517) 353-9040
Thomas H. Patten, Jr., Michael L. Moore

Degree(s) Offered: M.L.I.R. (Master of Labor and Industrial Relations), Ph.D.

Content Area(s): Organization development/ organizational behavior, personnel administration, labor relations

Value Orientation(s): Consulting-skills training, general system theory and approaches, work in labor relations, collective bargaining, personnel management, employee compensation and incentive plans; high emphasis on skills, theory/research

Accreditation: North Central Association of Colleges and Secondary Schools

Approximate Enrollment: Master's: 106; doctoral: ten

Residency Requirements: None; full-time status recommended for Ph.D.

Financial Aid Available: Scholarships/fellowships, graduate assistantships, V.A. benefits

Northwestern University
Program in Organization Behavior
Graduate School of Management
Evanston, Illinois 60201
(312) 492-3470
Coordinator, Department of Organization Behavior

Degree(s) Offered: M.M. (Master in Management), Ph.D.

Content Area(s): Behavioral and management sciences, psychology, political science, sociology, industrial relations, administration

Value Orientation(s): Highly interdisciplinary perspective; behavior of individuals and groups within organizational settings; behavior of organizations within their environments

Approximate Enrollment: Doctoral: twenty-eight

Residency Requirements: None

Financial Aid Available: Scholarships/fellowships, assistantships

Ohio State University
The Communication Analyst Program
Department of Communication
Columbus, Ohio 43210
(614) 422-3400
William Brown

Degree(s) Offered: M.A.

Content Area(s): Organization development/ organizational behavior

Value Orientation(s): Process consultation, consulting-skills training; high emphasis on personal development, skills, theory/research

Approximate Enrollment: Ten to twenty

Residency Requirements: None

Financial Aid Available: None

Additional Information: A new program

Purdue University
Ph.D. in Administrative Sciences
Krannert Graduate School of Management
Department of Administrative Sciences
West Lafayette, Indiana 47907
(317) 493-1882
John J. Sherwood

Degree(s) Offered: Ph.D.

Content Area(s): Research, organizational consultation, organization development/organizational behavior, experiential education, group leadership/facilitation

Value Orientation(s): Strong research perspective, consulting for organizational effectiveness, process consultation, general system theory; high emphasis on theory/research

Accreditation: American Assembly of Collegiate Schools of Business; Association of University Graduate Schools

Approximate Enrollment: Ten to twelve

Residency Requirements: Two years

Financial Aid Available: Scholarships/fellowships

Additional Information: Program admits only three new doctoral students a year; close student-faculty contact; all students receive financial support

R.E.M. Institute
Doctorate in Behavioral Science
4032 Mayfield Road
South Euclid, Ohio 44121
(216) 381-6633
Joseph H. Handlon, President

Degree(s) Offered: D.B. Sci., Psy.D.

Content Area(s): Organization development/
organizational behavior, individual and group
counseling/therapy, community develop-
ment/consultation, group leadership/
facilitation, human relations training, administration

Value Orientation(s): Process consultation,
consulting-skills training, community development, existential/phenomenological approaches, general system theory and approaches; high emphasis on personal development, skills

Accreditation: North Central Association of
Colleges and Secondary Schools

Approximate Enrollment: Twenty to fifty

Residency Requirements: Student must work
in area (some commuting from neighboring
states possible)

Financial Aid Available: None

Additional Information: Emphasis on developing and maintaining a learning community as a
learning/working laboratory

St. Louis University
Evaluative-Applied Doctoral Research Program
Department of Psychology
221 North Grand Boulevard
St. Louis, Missouri 63103
(314) 535-3300, ext. 379
David C. Munz

Degree(s) Offered: Ph.D.

Content Area(s): Organization development/
organizational behavior, consultation, group
leadership/facilitation, evaluation theory and
research

Value Orientation(s): Process consultation,
consulting-skills training, general system
theory and approaches; high emphasis on personal development, skills, theory/research

Approximate Enrollment: Twenty

Residency Requirements: Three years

Financial Aid Available: Scholarships/fellow-
ships, contracted work

Union Graduate School
106 Woodrow Street
Yellow Springs, Ohio 45387
(513) 767-7231
C. Emily Feistritzer, Director

Degree(s) Offered: Ph.D.

Content Area(s): Any of the applied behavioral
sciences or psychology

Value Orientation(s): Community development, community organizing, psychodynamic
approaches, existential/phenomenological
approaches, general system theory and approaches; high emphasis on personal development, skills, theory/research

Accreditation: North Central Association of
Colleges and Secondary Schools (pending)

Approximate Enrollment: 700

Residency Requirements: Thirty full days

Financial Aid Available: None

Additional Information: An off-campus, self-
directed, person-centered program

University of Iowa
School of Journalism
Iowa City, Iowa 52242
(319) 353-5414
Kenneth Starck

Degree(s) Offered: M.A., Ph.D.

Content Area(s): Organization development/
organizational behavior, community devel-
opment/consultation, group leadership/
facilitation, teacher education, international
communication

Value Orientation(s): Existential/phenom-
enological approaches, general system theory
and approaches, cultural theory and approaches; high emphasis on theory/research

Approximate Enrollment: Twenty to fifty

Residency Requirements: Master's: twenty-
four out of thirty hours; doctoral: two full-time
semesters or three part-time semesters

Financial Aid Available: Scholarships/fellow-
ships, V.A. benefits

University of Kansas
Speech Communication and Human
   Relations Division
Lawrence, Kansas 66044
(913) 864-3633, ext. 3511
Kim Giffin, Bobby R. Patton

Degree(s) Offered: M.A., Ph.D.

Content Area(s): Organization development/
organizational behavior, community develop-
ment/consultation, group leadership/facilita-
tion, teacher education, human relations training, intercultural communication

Value Orientation(s): Process consultation,
consulting-skills training, general system
theory and approaches; high emphasis on
theory/research, application

Accreditation: North Central Association of Colleges and Secondary Schools

Approximate Enrollment: 230

Residency Requirements: One year

Financial Aid Available: Scholarships/fellowships, V.A. benefits

Additional Information: Division is the university administrative agent for the Communication Research Center

University of Michigan
Interpersonal Processes
School of Education
Educational Psychology Department
3113 Education Building
Ann Arbor, Michigan 48109
(313) 764-8430
Allen Menlo

Degree(s) Offered: M.A., Ph.D.

Content Area(s): Organization development/organizational behavior, psychological/humanistic education, community development/consultation, group leadership/facilitation, human relations training, university teaching, research on human systems

Value Orientation(s): Process consultation, consulting-skills training, existential/phenomenological approaches, general system theory and approaches; high emphasis on personal development, skills, theory/research

Accreditation: National Council for Accreditation of Teacher Education

Approximate Enrollment: Master's: eight; doctoral: forty-five

Residency Requirements: Two terms

Financial Aid Available: Scholarships/fellowships (limited)

Additional Information: Wide range of field experiences

University of Missouri
Master of Public Administration (Organizational Behavior Concentration)
Kansas City, Missouri 64110
(816) 276-2894
W. B. Eddy

Degree(s) Offered: M.P.A.

Content Area(s): Organization development/organizational behavior, psychological/humanistic education, community development/consultation, group leadership/facilitation, human relations training, administration

Value Orientation(s): Process consultation, consulting-skills training, general system theory and approaches, urban problem solving, organization theory; high emphasis on personal development, skills, theory/research

Accreditation: The National Association of Schools of Public Affairs and Administration (self-evaluation process)

Approximate Enrollment: Fifty

Residency Requirements: None

Financial Aid Available: Scholarships/fellowships, V.A. benefits

Additional Information: Program focuses on change skills and processes for the public sector—particularly urban settings

University of Wisconsin
Communication Program
Merrill Hall
Milwaukee, Wisconsin 53201
(414) 863-4261
Charles Rossiter

Degree(s) Offered: M.A.

Content Area(s): Organization development/organizational behavior, teacher education, interpersonal communication—skills training

Value Orientation(s): Based on individual needs; high emphasis on theory/research

Accreditation: North Central Association of Colleges and Secondary Schools

Approximate Enrollment: Twenty to fifty

Residency Requirements: A maximum of nine to twelve hours may be transferred into program

Financial Aid Available: Scholarships/fellowships

Washington University
Organizational Behavior
Interdisciplinary (Department of Psychology and Graduate School of Business Administration)
St. Louis, Missouri 63130
(314) 863-0100
H. Meltzer, Chairman (Department of Psychology), Walter Nord (Graduate School of Business Administration)

Degree(s) Offered: Ph.D.

Content Area(s): Organization development/organizational behavior, human relations training, administration, organizational change

Value Orientation(s): Process consultation, consulting-skills training, psychodynamic approaches, existential/phenomenological approaches; high emphasis on personal development, skills, theory/research

Accreditation: Graduate Council of Liberal Arts and Sciences

Approximate Enrollment: Ten

Residency Requirements: Two years

Financial Aid Available: Scholarships/fellowships, tuition remission, internship in work settings

Additional Information: Course selections in psychology, business administration, sociology, economics, political science, engineering, law

Wayne State University
School of Education
Division of Organizational and Administrative Studies
Detroit, Michigan 48202
(313) 577-1675
Larry Hillman

Degree(s) Offered: M.Ed., Ed.D., Ph.D.

Content Area(s): Organization development/organizational behavior, group leadership/facilitation, administration

Value Orientation(s): Process consultation, consulting-skills training; high emphasis on personal development, skills, theory/research

Accreditation: National Council for Accreditation of Teacher Education

Approximate Enrollment: Twenty to fifty

Residency Requirements: Master's: none; doctoral: twenty-seven hours spread over four consecutive quarters

Financial Aid Available: Scholarships/fellowships (limited)

WESTERN UNITED STATES

Antioch College/West
Graduate Programs in Psychology
1161 Mission Street
San Francisco, California 94103
(415) 864-2575
B. G. Rosenberg

Antioch College/West
Master of Arts, Psychology
1067 N. Fairfax Avenue
Los Angeles, California 90046
(213) 656-8520

Degree(s) Offered: M.A.

Content Area(s): Psychological, individual and group counseling/therapy, developmental, personality, social psychology, conduct of inquiry

Value Orientation(s): Process consultation, behavior modification, psychodynamic approaches, existential/phenomenological approaches, developmental psychology, cognitive psychology: high emphasis on personal development, skills, theory/research

Accreditation: North Central Association of Colleges and Secondary Schools

Approximate Enrollment: Fifty

Residency Requirements: Five quarters

Financial Aid Available: Scholarships/fellowships, V.A. benefits

Additional Information: Core and individualized program; programs in San Francisco, Los Angeles, Monterey, Seattle

Brigham Young University
Master in Organization Behavior
302 Jesse Knight Building
Provo, Utah 84601
(801) 374-1211
Bill Dyer

Degree(s) Offered: M.S.

Content Area(s): Organization development/organizational behavior, human relations training, consultation skills, personnel management

Value Orientation(s): Process consultation, consulting-skills training, training theory and method; high emphasis on personal development, skills, theory/research

Accreditation: American Assembly of Collegiate Schools of Business

Approximate Enrollment: Twenty each year (two-year program)

Residency Requirements: Four semesters

Financial Aid Available: Scholarships/fellowships

Additional Information: Summer internship between the two years of program

California American University
Master of Science in Management
230 West Third Avenue
Escondido, California 92025
(714) 741-6595, 6596
William R. Hauser

Degree(s) Offered: M.S.M.

Content Area(s): Organization development/ organizational behavior, group leadership/ facilitation, human relations training

Value Orientation(s): Process consultation, behavior modification, consulting-skills training; high emphasis on personal development, skills

Approximate Enrollment: Fifty

Residency Requirements: One year

Financial Aid Available: None

California School of Professional Psychology
Professional Psychology
3755 Beverly Boulevard
Los Angeles, California 90004
(213) 665-4201
Carole Zuckerman, Assistant for Student Affairs

Degree(s) Offered: M.A., Ph.D.

Content Area(s): Organization development/ organizational behavior, individual and group counseling/therapy, community development/consultation, group leadership/ facilitation

Value Orientation(s): Psychodynamic approaches, existential/phenomenological approaches, general system theory and approaches; high emphasis on personal development, skills

Accreditation: Western Association of Schools and Colleges

Approximate Enrollment: 250

Residency Requirements: Master's: two years; doctoral: four years

Financial Aid Available: Scholarships/fellowships, V.A. benefits

Additional Information: Campuses also in Fresno, San Diego, San Francisco; central admissions office: 2152 Union Street, San Francisco, California 94123

California School of Professional Psychology
2450 17th Street
San Francisco, California 94110
(415) 864-3100
Edward F. Bourg, Dean for Professional Affairs

Degree(s) Offered: M.A., Ph.D.

Content Area(s): Professional psychology: specifically adult clinical psychology, community psychology, child clinical/school psychology

Value Orientation(s): Psychological theories and models, professional issues and ethics, sociocultural contexts, humanities and arts; high emphasis on personal development, skills

Accreditation: Western Association of Schools and Colleges

Approximate Enrollment: 235

Residency Requirements: Contact program directly

Financial Aid Available: Scholarships/fellowships, V.A. benefits

Additional Information: Campuses also in Fresno, Los Angeles, San Diego

California State University—Northridge
School Psychology Program
Psychology Department
Northridge, California 91330
(213) 885-2827
Joseph Morris, Director

Degree(s) Offered: M.A.

Content Area(s): Organization development, psychological/humanistic education, individual and group counseling, psycho-educational research, teacher education, human relations training, school psychological services, psycho-educational assessment

Value Orientation(s): Process consultation, behavior modification, consulting-skills training, existential/phenomenological approaches, general system theory and approaches; high emphasis on personal development, skills

Accreditation: California State Department of Education

Approximate Enrollment: Thirty

Residency Requirements: Two years of full-time academic work and concurrent field service

Financial Aid Available: Graduate assistantships, work-study, loans

Eastern Washington University
Interdisciplinary Studies in Organizational Development
Graduate Program Division
Cheney, Washington 99004
(509) 359-7037
William Barber, Don Harvey, Coordinators

Degree(s) Offered: M.S.

Content Area(s): Organization development/ organizational behavior, group leadership/facilitation

Value Orientation(s): Process consultation, psychodynamic approaches, general system theory and approaches; high emphasis on theory/research

Accreditation: Northwest Association of Secondary and Higher Schools

Approximate Enrollment: Ten

Residency Requirements: None

Financial Aid Available: Scholarships/fellowships, V.A. benefits

Gonzaga University
Guidance and Counseling
E. 502 Boone Avenue
Spokane, Washington 99202
(509) 328-4220
John E. D'Aboy, Director of Counselor Education

Degree(s) Offered: M.A., M.C.P.C. (Master of Clinical Pastoral Counseling)

Content Area(s): Psychological/humanistic education, individual and group counseling/therapy, group leadership/facilitation, human relations training, pastoral counseling

Value Orientation(s): Consulting-skills training, psychodynamic approaches, existential/phenomenological approaches, general system theory and approaches; competency based, with high emphasis on student development of personal theory and orientation, skills, theory/research

Accreditation: National Council for Accreditation of Teacher Education

Approximate Enrollment: Fifteen to twenty (full time)

Residency Requirements: Depends on individual experience and need

Financial Aid Available: Scholarships/fellowships, V.A. benefits

Additional Information: Off-campus programs in British Columbia and Alberta, Canada; strong practicum emphasis

Humanistic Psychology Institute
325 Ninth Street
San Francisco, California 94103
(415) 626-4494
Donald Polkinghorne

Degree(s) Offered: Ph.D.

Content Area(s): Humanistic sciences or psychology

Value Orientation(s): High emphasis on theory/research

Accreditation: State of California approval to grant degrees (A2 status)

Approximate Enrollment: 150

Residency Requirements: Five-day mandatory program planning seminar; two-year minimum time period to complete program

Financial Aid Available: None

The Institute for Organizational Behavior and Human Resource Development
4105 Medical Parkway, Suite 205
Austin, Texas 78756
(512) 451-3553
Oscar Mink, Barbara Washburn

Degree(s) Offered: One-year certificate of competency; Ph.D. program planned

Content Area(s): Organization development/organizational behavior, group leadership/facilitation, human resource development

Value Orientation(s): Process consultation, consulting-skills training, existential/phenomenological approaches, general system theory and approaches; competency based, with high emphasis on personal development, skills, theory/research

Approximate Enrollment: Sixty

Residency Requirements: Weekends and clusters established regionally throughout United States

Financial Aid Available: None

International College
1019 Gayley Avenue, Suite 105
Los Angeles, California 90024
(213) 477-6761
Alvin P. Ross, Associate Dean

Degree(s) Offered: M.A., Ph.D.

Content Area(s): Psychological/humanistic education, counseling/therapy, group leadership/facilitation

Value Orientation(s): Psychodynamic approaches, existential/phenomenological approaches, general system theory and approaches; high emphasis on skills

Approximate Enrollment: Seventy-five

Residency Requirements: Varied

Financial Aid Available: National Direct Student Loan

Additional Information: Individualized plans of study

246

John F. Kennedy University
Graduate School of Professional Psychology
12 Altarinda Road
Orinda, California 94563
(415) 254-0200
Lind Higgins, Vice President for Student Services
and Administration

Degree(s) Offered: M.A. (in psychology)

Content Area(s): Psychological/humanistic education, individual and group counseling/therapy, community development/consultation

Value Orientation(s): Psychodynamic approaches, existential/phenomenological approaches; high emphasis on personal development, skills, theory/research

Accreditation: Western Association of Schools and Colleges

Approximate Enrollment: 175

Residency Requirements: Final course work and master's exam or thesis must be completed in residence.

Financial Aid Available: V.A. benefits, work-study, loans

Oklahoma State University
Student Personnel and Guidance
313 N. Murray Hall
Stillwater, Oklahoma 74074
(405) 624-6036
Judith E. Dobson

Degree(s) Offered: M.S., Ed.D.; Ph.D. to be offered soon

Content Area(s): Organization development/organizational behavior, individual and group counseling/therapy, community development/consultation, group leadership/facilitation, human relations training

Value Orientation(s): Consulting-skills training, psychodynamic approaches, existential/phenomenological approaches, general system theory and approaches; high emphasis on skills, theory/research

Accreditation: North Central Association of Colleges and Secondary Schools

Approximate Enrollment: Fifty

Residency Requirements: Doctoral: one year

Financial Aid Available: Scholarships/fellowships, V.A. benefits

Pacific Oaks College
M.A. in Human Development
5 Westmoreland Place
Pasadena, California 91103
(213) 795-9161
Elizabeth Jones

Degree(s) Offered: M.A.; Ph.D. with Fielding Institute

Content Area(s): Psychological/humanistic education, individual and group counseling/therapy, group leadership/facilitation, teacher education, human relations training, administration

Value Orientation(s): Process consultation, psychodynamic approaches, existential/phenomenological approaches, learning and growth in a developmental framework; high emphasis on personal development, skills

Accreditation: Western Association of Schools and Colleges

Approximate Enrollment: 200

Residency Requirements: None

Financial Aid Available: Loans, scholarships/fellowships (limited), V.A. benefits

Additional Information: Small classes, individualized programs, diverse opportunities for field work

Pepperdine University (Los Angeles Branch)
Human Resources Management
8035 South Vermont Avenue
Los Angeles, California 90044
(213) 971-7714
Rona King

Degree(s) Offered: M.A.

Content Area(s): Organization development/organizational behavior, human relations training, administration

Value Orientation(s): Process consultation, consulting-skills training, community organizing, management, general system theory and approaches; high emphasis on skills

Accreditation: Western Association of Schools and Colleges

Approximate Enrollment: 1500 students at fifty locations (approximately thirty per location)

Residency Requirements: Twenty-eight units

Financial Aid Available: V.A. benefits

San Diego State University
Department of Counselor Education
San Diego, California 92182
(714) 286-6109
John D. Chamley, Chairperson

Degree(s) Offered: M.S.; counseling and school psychology credentials

Content Area(s): Organization development/ organizational behavior, psychological/humanistic education, individual and group counseling/therapy, community development/consultation, group leadership/ facilitation

Value Orientation(s): Eclectic; high emphasis on skills, theory/research

Accreditation: National Council for the Accreditation of Teacher Education

Approximate Enrollment: 425 (full and part time)

Residency Requirements: Thirty of thirty-six units

Financial Aid Available: V.A. benefits

Sonoma State College
M.A. in Psychology
1801 East Cotati Avenue
Rohnert Park, California 94928
(707) 664-2585

Degree(s) Offered: M.A.

Content Area(s): Psychological/humanistic education, community consultation

Value Orientation(s): Psychodynamic approaches, existential/phenomenological approaches, general system theory and approaches; high emphasis on personal development, theory/research

Accreditation: Western Association of Schools and Colleges

Approximate Enrollment: Twenty to fifty

Residency Requirements: One year

Financial Aid Available: V.A. benefits

Stanford University
Organizational Behavior
Graduate School of Business
Stanford, California 94305
(415) 493-5630
Jerry Porras

Degree(s) Offered: Ph.D.

Content Area(s): Organization behavior/organization development, group leadership/facilitation, organizational research

Value Orientation(s): General system theory and approaches, organizational sociology, organizational psychology; high emphasis on theory/research

Accreditation: American Assembly of Collegiate Schools of Business

Approximate Enrollment: Ten to fifteen

Residency Requirements: Two years

Financial Aid Available: Scholarships/fellowships, V.A. benefits

Additional Information: Opportunities for group training experience, organizational research

United States International University
School of Human Behavior
10455 Pomerado Road
San Diego, California 92131
(714) 271-4300, ext. 291
Ray W. Rucker, Dean

Degree(s) Offered: M.A., Ph.D.

Content Area(s): Organization development/ organizational behavior, psychological/humanistic education, counseling/therapy, community development/consultation, group leadership/facilitation, teacher education, human relations training, administration, collective bargaining

Value Orientation(s): Process consultation, consulting-skills training, psychodynamic approaches, existential/phenomenological approaches, general system theory and approaches, value analysis, direct decision therapy, actualization therapy; high emphasis on personal development, skills, theory/ research

Accreditation: Western Association of Schools and Colleges

Approximate Enrollment: Fifty

Residency Requirements: Master's: one quarter; doctoral: three quarters

Financial Aid Available: Scholarships/fellowships, V.A. benefits

University Associates, Inc.
LEIP (Laboratory Education Intern Program)
7596 Eads Avenue
La Jolla, California 92037
(714) 454-8821
Robin Reid

Degree(s) Offered: Certificate of completion

Content Area(s): Organization development/ organizational behavior, psychological/humanistic education, community development/consultation, group leadership/facilitation, human relations training

Value Orientation(s): Process consultation, consulting-skills training, psychodynamic approaches, existential/phenomenological approaches, general system theory and approaches; high emphasis on personal development, skills

Approximate Enrollment: Twenty to thirty

Residency Requirements: Four weeks of workshops

Financial Aid Available: None

Additional Information: Interns may receive twenty quarter hours of credit from University of California, San Diego Extension

University of California, Los Angeles
Human Systems Studies
Graduate School of Management
Los Angeles, California 90024
(213) 825-2503
Fred Massarik, Chairman, Sam Culbert, Joan Lasko

Degree(s) Offered: M.B.A., Ph.D.

Content Area(s): Organization development and design/organizational behavior, group leadership/facilitation, human relations training, sociotechnical systems, nontraditional methodology (phenomenology)

Value Orientation(s): Humanistic and experiential learning philosophies, process consultation, consulting-skills training, psychodynamic approaches, existential/phenomenological approaches, general system theory and approaches; high emphasis on personal development

Accreditation: Western Association of Schools and Colleges; American Assembly of Collegiate Schools of Business

Approximate Enrollment: P.M.P. (Professional Master's Program): 450; doctoral: twenty

Residency Requirements: Two years or more

Financial Aid Available: Scholarships/fellowships (limited), V.A. benefits

University of California, Santa Barbara
Graduate Program in Confluent Education
Department of Education
Santa Barbara, California 93106
(805) 961-2501, 2601
Stewart B. Shapiro, George I. Brown

Degree(s) Offered: M.A., M.Ed., Ph.D.

Content Area(s): Organization development/ organizational behavior, psychological/humanistic education, individual and group counseling/therapy, community development/consultation, group leadership/facilitation, teacher education, human relations training, confluent education

Value Orientation(s): Process consultation, consulting-skills training, psychodynamic approaches, existential/phenomenological approaches, general system theory and approaches, self-science education, psychosynthesis, ethnographic approach; high emphasis on personal development, skills, theory/research

Accreditation: Western Association of Schools and Colleges

Approximate Enrollment: Fifty

Residency Requirements: Master's: one year; doctoral: two years

Financial Aid Available: Scholarships/fellowships (limited), V.A. benefits

Additional Information: Sense of community; international flavor

University of Colorado
Graduate School of Public Affairs
Armory Building, Room 203
Boulder, Colorado 80309
(303) 492-7045
R. Wayne Boss

Degree(s) Offered: M.P.A. (Master of Public Administration), M.U.A. (Master of Urban Affairs), D.P.A. (Doctor of Public Administration)

Content Area(s): Organization development/ organizational behavior, psychological/humanistic education, community development/consultation, group leadership/facilitation, human relations training, administration

Value Orientation(s): Process consultation, behavior modification, consulting-skills training, general system theory and approaches; high emphasis on personal development, skills, theory/research

Accreditation: The National Association of Schools of Public Affairs and Administration

Approximate Enrollment: 100

Residency Requirements: One year in Colorado to waive out-of-state fees

Financial Aid Available: Scholarships/fellowships (limited)

University of Denver
Department of Speech Communication
University Park
Denver, Colorado 80208
(303) 753-2388
Alton Barbour

Degree(s) Offered: M.A., Ph.D.

Content Area(s): Interpersonal and small-group communication, communication theory, organization development/organizational behavior

Value Orientation(s): General system theory and approaches, laboratory learning, empirical approaches to research; high emphasis on theory/research

Accreditation: North Central Association of Colleges and Secondary Schools

Approximate Enrollment: Eighty

Residency Requirements: Three consecutive full-time quarters

Financial Aid Available: Teaching assistantships, scholarships

University of Hawaii
M.P.H. Degree in Health Education and
    Community Health Development
School of Public Health
1960 East-West Road (Biomed C-105 E)
Honolulu, Hawaii 96822
(808) 948-8000
William P. Golden, Jr., Jerome Grossman

Degree(s) Offered: M.P.H. (Master of Public Health)

Content Area(s): Organization development/organizational behavior, psychological/humanistic education, community development/consultation, group leadership/facilitation, human relations training, administration, health education in community and medical care settings

Value Orientation(s): Process consultation, consulting-skills training, community organizing, existential/phenomenological approaches, general system theory and approaches; high emphasis on personal development, skills

Accreditation: Council of Education for Public Health; Western Association of Schools and Colleges

Approximate Enrollment: Twenty-five each cycle (admission only during fall semester)

Residency Requirements: Three semesters, including twelve-week summer field placement and internship

Financial Aid Available: Scholarships/fellowships, some traineeships from U.S. Public Health Service

University of Oklahoma
Master of Arts in Human Relations
Human Relations Program, 601 Elm, Room 730
Norman, Oklahoma 73019
(405) 325-1756
George Henderson

Degree(s) Offered: M.A.

Content Area(s): Organization development/organizational behavior, psychological/humanistic education, individual and group counseling/therapy, community development/consultation, group leadership/facilitation, teacher education, human relations training, administration

Value Orientation(s): Eclectic; high emphasis on personal development, skills

Approximate Enrollment: Fifty

Residency Requirements: None

Financial Aid Available: Scholarships/fellowships, V.A. benefits

University of Oregon
Strategies of Organizational Change:
    An R&D Program
Center for Educational Policy and Management
1472 Kincaid
Eugene, Oregon 97401
(503) 686-5067
Richard A. Schmuck

Degree(s) Offered: M.A., M.Ed., Ed.D., Ph.D. (as part of programs in educational psychology and educational administration)

Content Area(s): Organization development/organizational behavior, psychological/humanistic education, group leadership/facilitation, administration

Value Orientation(s): Process consultation, consulting-skills training, general system theory and approaches; high emphasis on personal development, skills, theory/research

Accreditation: Oregon State Department of Education

Approximate Enrollment: Ten

Residency Requirements: One year

Financial Aid Available: None

University of San Francisco
Educational Program in Organization
  and Leadership
School of Education
Campion Hall
San Francisco, California 94117
(416) 666-6551
Wayne Doyle

Degree(s) Offered: Ed.D.

Content Area(s): Organization development/
organizational behavior, group leadership/
facilitation, administration

Value Orientation(s): Process consultation,
behavior modification, general system theory
and approaches; high emphasis on personal
development, skills

Accreditation: Western Association of Schools
and Colleges

Approximate Enrollment: 200

Residency Requirements: One week-long
seminar and two weekend courses per
semester

Financial Aid Available: V.A. benefits

University of Southern California
Applied Behavioral Science in Public
  Administration
University Park
Los Angeles, California 90007
(213) 741-2241
Neely Gardner, Warren Schmidt

Degree(s) Offered: M.P.A. (Master of Public
Administration), D.P.A., Ph.D.

Content Area(s): Organization development/
organizational behavior, community devel-
opment/consultation, group leadership/
facilitation, human relations training, administration

Value Orientation(s): Process consultation,
consulting-skills training; high emphasis on
personal development, action research

Accreditation: Western Association of Schools
and Colleges

Approximate Enrollment: Fifty

Residency Requirements: None

Financial Aid Available: Scholarships/fellow-
ships

Additional Information: M.P.A. program has
an intensive semester during which courses
are given in blocks of time from two four-day
periods to eight full days

University of Southern California
Counseling Psychology
Department of Counseling
School of Education
Los Angeles, California 90007
(213) 741-2380
Betty A. Walker

Degree(s) Offered: M.S., Ed.D., Ph.D.

Content Area(s): Psychological/humanistic
education, individual and group counseling/
therapy, group leadership/facilitation, human
relations training

Value Orientation(s): Existential/phenomen-
ological approaches; high emphasis on personal development, skills, theory/research

Approximate Enrollment: Twenty to thirty-
five

Residency Requirements: Twelve units

Financial Aid Available: Scholarships/fellow-
ships, teaching assistantships

Whitworth College
M.A./Applied Behavioral Sciences
Leadership Institute of Spokane
P.O. Box 8005
Spokane, Washington 99203
(509) 624-8437
Ron Short

Degree(s) Offered: M.A.

Content Area(s): An eclectic program, focusing
on organization development/organizational
behavior, psychological/humanistic education, individual and group counseling/therapy,
group leadership/facilitation, human relations
training

Value Orientation(s): Process consultation,
consulting-skills training, existential/phe-
nomenological approaches; competency
based, with high emphasis on personal development, skills

Accreditation: Northwest Association of
Schools and Colleges

Approximate Enrollment: Fifty

Residency Requirements: Summer: two six-
week sessions in two consecutive summers;
winter: eighteen months in Spokane or Seattle
or three four-week sessions during the month
of February in three successive years

Financial Aid Available: V.A. benefits

Additional Information: Students have access
to Leadership Institute workshops

Susan Campbell, Ph.D., *is on the home faculty of the Humanistic Psychology Institute, San Francisco, California. She teaches in the HPI doctoral program; consults with schools, organizations, and community groups; does private psychotherapy with individuals, couples, and families; and is currently writing a book on couples and doing research on women and success. Dr. Campbell is the author of* Expanding Your Teaching Potential: A Role Clarification Guide for Educators and Human Service Workers (1977), *which draws on her background in training teachers, group facilitators, and consultants.*

SELECTING WORKSHOP SITES

Timothy A. Boone and Robert A. Reid

The selection of an appropriate physical setting for a workshop is a critical variable in the learning process. Some basic considerations that can be helpful to trainers in selecting and using training sites include the location of the site, the type of setting, room and board arrangements, the psychological setting (including privacy, comfort, size of meeting rooms, normal usage of the site, and philosophy of the site management), and the negotiation and contract process. Although the "perfect" place does not exist, it is important that the advantages and disadvantages of a site be carefully weighed against the goals of each event to maximize the participants' learning potential.

LOCATION OF SITE

Training locales that take participants away from their place of work eliminate the distraction of daily routine and the interference of colleagues and contribute positively to the investment and involvement participants feel in the training event. When workshops last more than one day it is ideal to have people sleep and eat at the site. Informal interaction among participants is increased, contributing to their learning, much of which occurs outside of regular workshop hours.

Ease of transportation and proximity to public carriers are important considerations for a public workshop. Getting to and from the training site can become a major dissatisfier if directions are not clear, costs are too high, or travel time is too long. A useful rule of thumb is to hold public events within forty-five minutes of a major airport and near major cities. Going into the city is a desire of many participants.

TYPE OF SETTING

The basic considerations for appropriate settings are privacy, attractive grounds and buildings, a humanistic staff, moderate costs, and limited distractions. We strongly prefer "retreat" settings, if possible. Both religious and nonreligious locations where the staff is accustomed to offering service and direct support to conferences and workshops are satisfactory sites. The *Ecumenical Directory of Retreat and Conference Centers* (Deemer, 1974) is a useful source book for finding religious retreat houses. Many colleges and universities also have excellent facilities available, especially in the summer months. There are also several professionally run conference centers located in various parts of the United States, but they tend to be more expensive than nonprofit locations.

Many facilitators choose motels and hotels as training sites, but most motels and hotels do not meet the basic considerations. Although hotels often cater to conferences, because the house staff is usually not well trained to meet the unique needs of a workshop design and the meeting rooms are often either too sterile or too ornate, much of the trainer's energy may be spent coordinating the various details and problems. However, these difficulties can be minimized by careful shopping, close coordination with the contact persons, and a visit to the location in advance. The *Official Meeting Facilities*

Guide (Nonnenman, 1977) and the *OAG* (Official Airline Guide) *Travel Planner* (1977) are useful resource guides when searching for motels and hotels.

Country clubs are another type of site to consider. During their off-seasons, the rates are more moderate than those of hotels, and clubs often possess many of the physical and service advantages offered by retreat houses. Another plus is that, as for colleges and universities, there are usually excellent recreational facilities available. Physical activities during breaks in the schedule can add needed variety to a workshop. If a beautiful site with excellent recreational facilities is selected, time had best be planned to allow participants to use those facilities or the agenda of the event may become confused and disrupted.

ROOM AND BOARD ARRANGEMENTS

A variety of room and board arrangements can be negotiated with sites, but there are two basic options: (1) a daily rate for room, meals, and refreshments and (2) a sleeping rate only, allowing participants to take responsibility for their own meals wherever they choose. These two options can also be combined in various degrees.

The first option is advantageous for some participants, but it can be a problem for those with special dietary needs. The second option provides for individual preferences on the part of participants but may fail to foster a climate of community.

The choice of options should be based directly on the goals of the event. If team building is the goal, for example, the prearranged community meal arrangement is the best choice. If individual learning is the goal, allowing participants to be responsible for their own meals is an appropriate and simpler choice. The facilitator should be aware of these factors in deciding, for example, about the choice of a retreat setting where only prearranged meals are available or a hotel in a city known for good restaurants.

Meals that provide the greatest variety for the least cost are a basic concern when selecting a training site. Cafeteria or buffet service is preferable to served meals because of the time and menu flexibility it provides. Most retreat centers, colleges and universities, and conference centers offer this type of meal plan as a package with the room rate. However, it is important to check on the availability of vegetarian plates, diet drinks, etc.

Whether to include the cost of arranged meals in the workshop fee when using hotels and motels is always a question. Because of the problems of forty-eight-hour guarantees, costly menu items, and the relative inflexibility of serving time and range of choices, we often decide to have participants at our workshops eat in the coffee shop or at nearby restaurants. Such a decision does diminish the group's sense of community, but it is usually easier for participants. However, one major advantage to having the hotel serve lunches and/or dinners is that the meeting room (which often exceeds $100 a day) is usually free.

Even if meals are not included in the training package, it is a good idea to have coffee and tea available in the meeting room. The trainer can arrange for an informal set up that is checked by the house staff prior to the start of each session. There is usually an extra charge for this service, but many places include it in the room rate. Soft drinks may be fairly expensive, but they should be included when the workshop is being held in a warm climate. Refreshment costs, like many other necessary incidentals during a training event, however, can mount rapidly and become a major expense if not carefully monitored.

It is useful to arrange an after-hours social event with beer, wine, and soft drinks to help promote informal interaction and learning. (Many trainers schedule only 8 a.m. to 5 p.m. days, but we think that too many free nights detract from the importance of the workshop; during week-long events, however, a night off in the middle of the event is a good idea.) It is important to check the alcohol policies of the training site; sometimes liquor is prohibited, or there may be a requirement that the site provide a bartender, usually at considerable cost. If a hotel is used, the trainer can rent a large suite for parties and ask that participants contribute to the refreshment fund.

If participants will be paying for their room and board separate from tuition, it is convenient to negotiate a fixed daily rate that each person pays directly to the site. The "administrivia" of number of meals, single and double rooms, extra charges, etc., can be time consuming if assumed by the facilitator. If such a direct arrangement is not possible, one staff person can be designated to handle all the details with the site and to collect money and organize arrangements with the participants. The primary goal is to minimize problems and distractions from the participants' point of view.

PSYCHOLOGICAL SETTING

Outcomes for those involved in a training event can be dramatically impacted by the psychological setting of the site. If the site has rigid rules and people who disapprove strongly of any behavior that deviates from the conservative norm, such as crying or touching, the trainer should obviously not choose that site in which to conduct a personal growth lab. Trainers are strongly advised to consider the goals and content of the training event and select a site that will contribute to the achievement of those goals.

Privacy

The degree of privacy required in a training site varies with the purpose of the training. If the event has a personal growth focus, it is more important to provide a high degree of privacy for participants in the training room and in living accommodations. Participants are more likely to experiment with new behavior of a very personal nature in a setting that is safe from prying or judgmental eyes. If the event is less personal in its orientation and interaction is less intense, the requirement for privacy is lessened. However, some level of privacy that precludes strangers from wandering into meeting rooms and encourages participants to interact with each other during and between sessions is advisable in any training event. In organization development meetings, for example, much of the material discussed may be proprietary and confidential and require a degree of privacy.

A very important variable in privacy concerns the other groups using the site and the degree of probability that the groups will intermingle or share facilities and create dysfunctional competition and annoyances, draining energy away from the purpose of the event.

Comfort

The color, lighting, condition, and general aesthetic quality of meeting and living areas can have a dramatic effect on the learning that takes place. If the areas are drab or uncomfortable, a great deal of energy may be displaced into complaining and negative projections. If the site is extravagantly decorated or contains obviously religious art, the decoration may distract from the training content. A relatively neutral but pleasant environment seems to work best. It is wise to select a site with adequate light that is adjustable to the needs of the event and a color scheme such as pale green, off-white, or beige. Too many large windows can also be a distraction. In general the site should probably be of an aesthetic quality similar to that with which most participants are familiar.

Size of Meeting Rooms

No one likes to be crammed into a cubicle in which body heat alone can raise the temperature 15 degrees in an hour. Nor do most people enjoy the feeling of their ten-person group being lost in an auditorium designed to seat five hundred. Experience indicates that twenty-five square feet per person attending the event is a good "rule of thumb." The shape of the room is also crucial. It should be square rather than long and narrow. This criterion is one of the most difficult to meet at many sites; the trainer may often be forced to compromise to some degree. The larger the number of participants, of course, the bigger the problem. Ceiling height does not seem to have a great deal of effect as long as it is not less than eight feet (lower than this, and many people tend to feel smothered).

If more or fewer participants than expected appear, the trainer should look into the possibility of obtaining a different meeting room; it could mean the difference between mediocrity and creative success for the event.

Normal Usage of Site

Meeting sites are usually designed with some specific purpose in mind. Older sites have often been constructed for classroom arrangements, which may or may not prove adequate for a laboratory education event. Many new sites, however, are designed to accommodate laboratory learning. The purpose for which the site is most often used will give the trainer some indication of the psychological climate. If it is a country club or resort, it may be more conducive to recreation than learning. Heavy drinking may be a norm, detracting from the purpose of the event. If it is a religious retreat site, there may be very strong norms that (although peripheral to the operation of the site) may cause considerable consternation and goal diffusion for many participants. Such issues as "quiet hours," dress codes, normal age range, and the level of the staff's psychological ownership of the site may pose serious problems for or contribute materially to the success of the event. An "uptight" site manager may turn an otherwise successful event into a psychological disaster for trainers and participants alike. Whether it seems plausible or not, the behavior of a busperson assigned to the meeting area can have a great deal of influence on the participants' ability to maximize their learning. (The incentive of a good tip contingent on the achievement of very specific behaviors can ameliorate a problem in this area better than a complaint to the management.)

Philosophy of Site Management

It is crucial to the success of an event that the training objectives and procedures do not violate the philosophy or behavior norms of the site staff. For example, if nudity is part of the workshop design, the trainer had better have a very direct conversation with the site management *before* signing a contract. On the other hand, if the event is designed for senior executives, bishops, or senior citizens, the trainer would do well to look for a site not known for its radical ideas and norms. And a humanistic leadership lab is likely to do better at a site that is managed humanistically than at a site that is rigidly controlled through threat.

Whenever possible it is a very good idea for the trainer to visit a potential training site prior to contracting for its use in order to experience its psychological climate. Many commercial sites will provide the trainer with a complimentary stay, and it is advisable to take advantage of the offer if at all possible. It may make a great deal of difference in the final decision. If the trainer cannot visit the site, he should talk with someone who has been there. In any case, he should ask the site to provide references of other users.

NEGOTIATING AND CONTRACTING

The best advice in this category is to know exactly what the selection criteria are for a particular event and then shop around for the best match. The trainer should remember that in most cases it is a buyer's market. It is not necessary to grab the first offer unless everything, including the price, is perfect. Shrewd shopping and hard bargaining can substantially reduce costs.

Some things to consider in negotiating:

1. *Cost of refreshments.* Are they priced per gallon or per person? An arrangement that allows payment only for what is actually used is almost always best.

2. *Meeting room rates.* It is standard practice for these rates to be prorated, based on the number of sleeping rooms and/or meals scheduled. If over twenty sleeping rooms are used, the meeting room should be free.

3. *Payment terms.* Are all fees payable on departure, or are thirty-, sixty-, or ninety-day terms available?

4. *Advance deposit.* Some sites require this; for a public event, such a requirement could well be a disqualifier.

5. *Specific contact.* It is very important to be sure that one person from the site management who is going to be on site throughout the duration of the event is specified by name. If at all possible, the trainer should talk with this representative in advance to discuss the concerns and desires of the workshop. It is necessary to listen carefully and be sure that there is a clear mutual understanding of all requirements. When the newsprint supply runs out or the air conditioning goes off, this person is the one to call. Without such a contact, the division of labor at many sites among housekeeping, catering, sales, room reservations, and maintenance can be very trying to deal with.

6. *Advance reservations.* Perhaps most important is to make reservations as far in advance as possible so that the features of the site can be utilized to best advantage.

If the trainer conducts similar events frequently, it may be useful to prepare a "request for bid" document that outlines all requirements, schedules, etc., in detail, leaving blank spaces for the site management to fill in with exact prices. This will help make sure that needs and desires are met and that there are no surprises on the final bill. This document should be submitted to the site far in advance of the event and the site management should know that bids from other sites are also being requested.

Another helpful item for the use of the facilitator is a check list for site selection (see the sample at the end of this article). By checking off each item as it is completed or dealt with, the facilitator can keep track of the state of the negotiations with the site.

There is a wide variety of concerns and options relating to choosing a training site, and trade-offs in administering a particular workshop at a particular site always exist. Thoughtful choices, attention to details, and hard negotiation will help make the site a positive contribution to the success of a workshop.

REFERENCES AND OTHER SOURCES

Davis, L. N., & McCallon, E. *Planning, conducting, evaluating workshops.* Austin, Tex.: Learning Concepts, 1974.

Deemer, P. (Ed.). *Ecumenical directory of retreat and conference centers.* Boston, Mass.: Jarrow Press, 1974.

Nonnenman, V. (Ed.). *Official meeting facilities guide.* New York: Ziff-Davis, 1977.

OAG travel planner & hotel/motel guide. Oak Brook, Ill.: Reuben H. Donnelley, 1977.

Schindler-Rainman, E., & Lippitt, R., with Cole, J. *Taking your meetings out of the doldrums.* La Jolla, Calif.: University Associates, 1977.

Timothy A. Boone is the general manager of NTL/Learning Resources Corporation, La Jolla, California. He is involved in surveying books and training materials as well as arranging seminars for promotion by LRC. He also spends part of his time as a consultant and a training staff person for University Associates, La Jolla, and reviews books for the University Associates quarterly, Group & Organization Studies. Mr. Boone's background is in leadership and human resource management and internal organization development consulting.

Robert A. Reid is the coordinator of professional services and a consultant for University Associates, La Jolla, California. He manages professional services, serves as a staff person for public workshops, assists in negotiating consulting contracts, and coordinates the University Associates Laboratory Education Intern Program. Mr. Reid's background is in college counseling and student personnel, with special areas of interest in the training of trainers, management and leadership development, personal growth, and Gestalt group work.

CHECK LIST FOR SITE SELECTION

Instructions: Use one copy of this check list for each site being considered. In discussing the site with sales personnel be sure to cover each item, check it off, and make any pertinent notes. A consideration of all the items on this check list will provide a sound basis for contracting. Be sure to add any special requirements you may need.

Site Being Considered: _____

Event: _____

Goals of Training
to Be Conducted: _____

Participants: _____

Staff: _____

Points to Consider:

_____ Sleep at site

_____ Type and cost of sleeping rooms

_____ Price of food

_____ Prearranged meals or individual responsibility

_____ Cafeteria or waited tables

_____ Special dietary requirements

_____ Limited distractions

_____ Humanistic and competent staff

_____ Appropriateness of usual site use

_____ Quiet hours

_____ Dress codes

_____ Usual age group of people using the site

_____ Presence of other groups

_____ Reservation as far in advance as possible

_____ Size of meeting room

_____ Multiple room requirement

_____ Cost of meeting room(s)

_____ Complimentary sleeping rooms for staff

_____ Privacy

_____ Type of furniture in meeting rooms

_____ Attractiveness and quality of decor in meeting rooms

_____ Coffee, tea, and soft drinks available during sessions

_____ Cost of refreshments

_____ Ease of transportation and proximity to public carriers

_____ Alcohol policies

Advance deposit required? _____ by _____

Credit terms _____

Precontracting visit to site _____

Name of one person on site staff to coordinate all needs before, during, and after event

_____

HUMAN RELATIONS FILMS FOR GROUP FACILITATORS

Donna Lee Smith

Pictures often do what words cannot. The films listed on the following pages are a sampling from among the thousands available.[1] They can contribute dramatically to group learning situations by making the theoretical real and relevant, clarifying or illustrating a point, catalyzing experience and understanding, or unifying a group through laughter. Primarily, they can stimulate and enrich discussion. Each has been selected because it has something special to offer: some are classics that have never been bettered; others offer a new approach; one or two are unique in the field. Some are technically brilliant; some are decidedly not but nevertheless contain worthwhile information.

The films are listed alphabetically by title, rather than by subject category. Many films are useful for very diverse purposes and groups, depending on the needs of the group and the aims of the facilitator. Thus, it seemed inappropriate in this listing to restrict a particular film to a particular category. The facilitator will be able to evaluate the merit of each title for the needs of the group by using the film description as a guide.

Films should be ordered at least four weeks before the planned use date. The distributor's catalog numbers should be written on the order if possible, as well as alternative titles and dates. A substitute program should be planned in case the films fail to arrive; distributors do their best, but occasional disappointment is almost inevitable. Rental charges are usually cancelled if the film does not arrive on schedule, or it may be possible to keep the film until the next meeting of the group—but permission for this must be specifically requested and verified, not assumed. Unless special arrangements have been made, films must be shipped back on the day following the scheduled use date(s) to avoid overdue charges and/or disappointing the next scheduled user. Booking confirmations should be read carefully, and all instructions regarding dates and methods of return should be followed.

It is important to preview the film in order to be able to predict group reactions, plan an introduction, and lead an intelligent discussion afterward. A preview screening immediately before the group assembles also serves as a check on the proper functioning of the projection equipment, but many facilitators prefer to see the film earlier to allow maximum time for planning a presentation. When introducing a film, the facilitator should not tell the group so much that the film's impact is lessened, nor so little that the group wonders why the film was chosen. Films can be shown twice, or longer films can be shown one reel at a time.

The films listed are easy to obtain from one or several sources. Following each film description are the specific details of the film (date, length, color or black and white, rental price) and the name, address, and telephone number of the primary distributor (i.e., the sales source). However, most communities have their own film sources that are well worth exploring because these are sometimes more convenient, as well as significantly

---

[1]Readers should also see N. Felsenthal, "Media Resources for Human Relations Training," in J. W. Pfeiffer & J. E. Jones (Eds.), *The 1972 Annual Handbook for Group Facilitators*, La Jolla, Calif.: University Associates, 1972.

less expensive, than the primary distributors. Community sources include colleges, universities, community colleges, and public libraries. At the end of the film descriptions is a list of university film centers that offer large film collections for rent nationally. They, as well as many local sources, frequently offer free use of preview facilities and provide reference assistance or the use of self-service materials for selecting and obtaining films and other media.

The facilitator may request catalogs or information on films in specific areas of interest such as psychology, management, education, training, human relations, etc. Some libraries have subject-area catalogs, although most will send a general catalog— sometimes for a nominal fee which may be deductible from the first rental order. The catalogs explain rental policies and procedures and provide current fees and film descriptions. If a local source has a collection of film-center catalogs, personal copies of the most useful may be obtained. Commercial film distributors too may supply catalogs and brochures to individuals or institutions. Particularly relevant examples are included under Reference Sources at the end of this listing.

FILM DESCRIPTIONS

All Out

Using the television game show as a symbol of modern life, this biting satire probes people's psyches and shows how lack of love and dignity may allow some people to go to any length for money. Four contestants are asked to do increasingly degrading things for increasingly large sums of money. One by one, they discover that dignity is worth more to them than any amount of wealth. The audience seems menacing as it cheers each contestant on to further degradation. The film is a statement of man's inhumanity to man; it enables viewers to begin to understand and discuss the roots and manifestations of social ills.

1976; 27 min.; color; $35
The Media Guild, Box 881, Solana Beach, Calif. 92075; (714) 755-9191

Bach to Bach

Award-winning version of the famous Mike Nichols and Elaine May comedy record about how to start a "meaningful relationship." Concerns two strangers who have met in a bar. Now in bed, they discuss Bach, culture, and the complex structures of their own psyches. The comedy team provides the sound track as the camera slowly scans the interior of a bachelor apartment.

1967; 6 min.; color; $17
Films Incorporated, 1144 Wilmette Avenue, Wilmette, Ill. 60091; (312) 256-6600

Bargain Basement

A vignette about the chance encounter of a shoplifter and a store detective, both lonely, middle-aged people searching for human contact. A very well-acted, engrossing, and affecting psychological drama of character and communication.

1976; 27 min.; color; $30
National Film Board of Canada, 1251 Avenue of the Americas, 16th Floor, New York, N.Y. 10020; (212) 586-2400

Being Abraham Maslow

An autobiographical film portrait of one of the most important psychologists of our time, author of *Toward a Psychology of Being* and *Motivation and Personality*. Maslow is interviewed by Warren Bennis, psychologist and president of the University of Cincinnati, about the factors that shaped his life and ideas—material not included in his writing. Maslow discusses his early aspirations, some of his strengths and weaknesses, his professional conflicts, his marriage and children, and the prospect of his death. Interesting as biography, but most useful to those familiar with Maslow's work.

1972; 30 min.; b/w; $35
Filmakers Library, Inc., 290 West End Avenue, New York, N.Y. 10023; (212) 877-4486

Clarity

Emphasizes "imaging" (the process of intellectual conceptualizing) as creating limited perception for the observance of reality. Poses some very basic questions about identity, roles, awareness, and reality with a focus on male-female role playing and how it is influenced by imaging.
1976; 17 min.; color; $22
The Media Guild, Box 881, Solana Beach, Calif. 92075; (714) 755-9191

Communication: The Nonverbal Agenda

Insightful and exceptionally well-made exploration of the whole spectrum of nonverbal behavior: tone of voice, posture, facial expression, gestures, use of space, eye contact, and body movement. Employs excellent and sometimes humorous dramatic vignettes—mostly in organizational settings—to show how nonverbal signs reinforce or contradict verbal messages and how an understanding of nonverbal communication can enhance managerial effectiveness. For example, in separate meetings, a distasteful message is given to three individuals; the same words are spoken, but the effect varies from a severe reprimand to a friendly discussion, depending on nonverbal cues given and received.
1975; 30 min.; color; $45
CRM McGraw-Hill Films, 110 Fifteenth Street, Del Mar, Calif. 92014; (714) 453-5000

Doctor, Lawyer, Merchant, Chief: Case Studies in Leadership

Demonstration and discussion by Dr. John Morse of Harvard of the forces behind effective leadership: the psychological makeup of the leader and the followers and the needs posed by the situation. Effective combinations of these may result in one of two leadership styles—authoritarian/directive or participative/democratic.
1976; 17 min.; color; $70 for ten days
Salenger Educational Media, 1635-12th Street, Santa Monica, Calif. 90404; (213) 393-0311

DYNAMICS OF LEADERSHIP SERIES

Designed as a community training program for more effective group action, the set of five films features group drama presented by experienced adult role players, interspersed with commentary by Dr. Malcolm Knowles of Boston University. Participants answer searching questions, revealing the often-hidden reasons for their actions and leading to a constructive reappraisal of their values and goals. Emphasis is on leadership as it emerges from within the group rather than as imposed from outside.
1963; 30 min. each; b/w; $9.50 each
Indiana University Audio Visual Center, Bloomington, Ind. 47401; (812) 337-2103

Diagnosing Group Operations

Why do conflicts arise within groups? How do we know when a group is "in trouble"? The film treats one of the most difficult tasks for members of a working group—being both participants and observers—and points out signs of conflict, withdrawal, factionalism, and group indecision, along with their crippling effects on the group. Emphasizes the need for spotting problems and dealing with them early.

Sharing the Leadership

Members of the demonstration group become lost in the woods and discuss the best way to find their way home. Explores three categories of individual action and their relationship to group leadership: self-serving functions, task functions, and group-serving functions. Shows how leadership arises within a group, what is involved in the concept of leadership, and how group membership and leadership are related.

Roadblocks to Communication

Knowles examines some of the reasons for poor communication in group discussions and lecture presentations, distinguishing between genuine disagreements and those due to misunderstanding. He explores the concept of feedback as a way to improve communication and explains the use of the watchdog panel, reaction panel, and audience panel.

Anatomy of a Group

Illustrates the structure of a group, goals to be achieved during meetings, participation patterns, quality of communication, group standards, and group procedures. Knowles discusses the difference between a collection of individuals and a group and explains how a new group can get off to a good start.

Individual Motivation and Behavior

Why do people join groups; why do they participate or not; why do they try to block or dominate group action? Knowles offers comments before and after group demonstrations and discusses the motivation of each participant: one member is anxious to leave; one is disturbed by the arguments; one looks for the approval of the others; another feels threatened by the "domineering" attitudes of others.

THE EFFECTIVE EXECUTIVE SERIES

A well-produced five-film dramatized series featuring Peter F. Drucker, management consultant, teacher, and author, who appears in the films in the role of management consultant to the president of the mythical Hudson-Lansing Corporation. These classic films are independently useful and together form a short course in management.
1968; 25 min. each; color; $60 each for three days
BNA Communications Inc., 9401 Decoverly Hall Road, Rockville, Md. 20850; (301) 948-0540

Managing Time

Illustrates how executive time is wasted, much of it taken up by decisions that can be made by others. The effective executive stays out of the "time trap" by concentrating only on those problems that require his decision and does not allow his time to be wasted on routine tasks.

What Can I Contribute?

Demonstrates how the effective executive is the one who asks, "What is the creative contribution I can make now that will cause my job to have a whole new impact?" Drucker analyzes the contributions of each person to decide whether it was wise for the company to promote a bright young executive from another department over a proven fifteen-year veteran of the export department.

Focus on Tomorrow

Provides a down-to-earth analysis of why yesterday's successes often become today's losses. Points out that erstwhile business bonanzas tend to linger long beyond their productive life because they have become established as "investments in managerial ego."

Effective Decisions

Investigates in practical detail the process of managerial decision making. Notes that executive decision is at best a choice between two alternatives, neither of which can be proven right, and points out that the effective executive's job is to discover the reasons behind alternative opinions in order to utilize all pertinent facts.

Staffing for Strength

Points out that an organization does not have to be staffed with geniuses to be effective. The effective organization is one that can make common people achieve uncommon performance. The effective executive enables employees to rise to meet demands; no executive has ever suffered because his subordinates were strong and effective.

End of Conflict

Spiritual leader Krishnamurti speaks of the personal discontent we suffer because we compare what we are with an ideal of what we should be. This is because we accumulate emotions such as hatred and aggression, which limit our freedom to be aware of life. To end the conflict, we must become totally attentive to and aware of our present environment without interference from memory and past experience. A filmed lecture from the Real Revolution: Talks by Krishnamurti Series.

1968; 29 min.; b/w; $9.50
Indiana University Audio Visual Center, Bloomington, Ind. 47401; (812) 337-2103

Everybody Rides the Carousel

An illuminating, superbly animated rendering of the eight stages of life and personality development, described by noted psychologist Erik Erikson. Uses brief, universally understandable vignettes to illustrate the principal developmental challenges and crises that characterize each stage, as well as to symbolize the primary conflicting forces in the personality—trust and mistrust in the newborn, autonomy and shame/doubt in toddlers, initiative and guilt in childhood, competence and inferiority in school, search for identity and role diffusion in adolescence, intimacy and isolation in young adulthood, generativity (caring for the next generation) and stagnation in middle age, and ego integrity and acceptance of death in old age. Brilliantly conceived and executed.

1976; 72 min.; color; offered as a series of three 24-minute films for $30 each; or $75 for all three; available from other distributors as one film
Pyramid Films, Box 1048, Santa Monica, Calif. 90406; (213) 828-7577

The Fable of He and She

An animated contemporary fable about sex stereotyping for ages six to adult, set in the mythical land of Baramel, where there are two different kinds of people: Hardybars, who hunt and build and do rough things, and Mushamels, who raise children and flowers and cook. One day when everyone is doing her/his thing, on opposite sides of the island of course, the island suddenly splits apart. Each group at first finds it impossible to cope without the other, but after the initial consternation subsides into despair, two individuals save the day. He-bar shows his group that it can cook and take care of the kids; She-mel shows hers that it can hunt and build. A "reversaquake" reunites the land, and all the people, with their new-found skills, honor the two heroes.

1974; 11 min.; color; $15
Learning Corporation of America, 1350 Avenue of the Americas, New York, N.Y. 10019; (212) 397-9330

Games People Play

Part 1 (Theory)

A candid, personal interview with Dr. Eric Berne, who talks about his theory of transactional analysis, made famous by his best-selling book, Games People Play. He explains how people in social situations, motivated by a psychological payoff, begin a game complex and draw others into the action. Each game is composed of a cause, a gimmick, and a payoff, and each player assumes the role of parent, child, or adult. When all players assume the adult role, the game ends short of its payoff, and a constructive relationship is established. Berne demonstrates the relationships involved in several specific games such as "Con," "Rapo," and "PTA."

Part 2 (Practice)

Continues the interview with Berne, who further explains the dynamics behind transactional analysis and applies his theory in a group-therapy session held in his home. He points out game behavior and explains the meaning of the terms "game," "script," and "ego state." He cites the

case of a patient whose "script" is constructed in the form of a fairy tale. Human interrelationships are dealt with as interpersonal "contracts" in which all parties have definite responsibilities.
1967; 30 min. each; b/w; $9.50 each
Indiana University Audio Visual Center, Bloomington, Ind. 47401; (812) 337-2103

How Not To Succeed in Business

An animated film that demonstrates the meaning of Parkinson's Law and the fact that many hands make heavy work. Shows how activities can expand and multiply in every conceivable business situation. An excellent comic touch for any organizational program.
1976; 10 min.; color; $20
Phoenix Films, Inc., 470 Park Avenue South, New York, N.Y. 10016; (212) 684-5910

The Human Potential Movement: Journey to the Center of the Self

Described as "a business, a means of recreation, a form of theater, a philosophy of education, a guide for institutional development, a warning to corporations, an underground religion, a dangerous sub-culture," the human potential movement is a grass-roots phenomenon attracting hundreds of thousands of ordinary people. Dr. Will Schutz, co-founder of the Esalen Institute, explains the principles and possibilities of the movement as the film shows a micro-lab group development session, nude therapy, bioenergetics, meditation, and yoga. From the Towards the Year 2000 Series.
1976; 17 min.; color; $40
Document Associates, Inc., 880 Third Avenue, New York, N.Y. 10022; (212) 593-1647

Invisible Walls

Focuses on common American beliefs about personal space, showing that people encase themselves in invisible walls about eighteen inches from their bodies and that violation of these walls causes discomfort. An actor and actress trained in middle-class modes of dress and behavior are shown randomly stopping unsuspecting subjects in Los Angeles shopping centers. While ostensibly conducting a consumer survey, they continually violate each subject's personal space, moving closer and closer as a hidden camera films this interaction. Analysis reveals several patterns of subject response, which are shown to vary to some degree with the sex of the subject, to be learned rather than innate, and to be culturally derived. Shows how children learn these response patterns and ends with the observation that as population pressures continue to mount, Americans may have to learn new notions about personal space.
1969; 12 min.; b/w; $12
University of California Extension Media Center, Berkeley, Calif. 94720; (415) 642-0460

Is It Always Right To Be Right?

A parable in animation, stills, and live action, narrated by Orson Welles, focusing on divisive issues in society—war, poverty, the generation gap, race. Each opposing group states its position . . . "and they were right, of course, and they knew it." In a land in which everyone is always right, divisions become so great that no one talks to anyone else. One day someone admits he may be wrong—and shock spreads throughout the land. But as others listen to him, they realize that there are truths even in opposing views and that this knowledge can lead to understanding rather than mutual antagonism.
1970; 8 min.; color; $35
Stephen Bosustow Productions, P.O. Box 2127, Santa Monica, Calif. 90406; (213) 394-0218

I Told 'Em Exactly How To Do It!

An engrossing animated film in which Mitt Mittle succumbs to pressure from his supervisor and makes hopeless attempts at conveying instructions to production line workers. Fortunately, they pay little attention to his advice, and production soars despite him. The film stimulates analysis of communication problems, management practices, training methods, and worker initiative, as well as the pitfalls of being "the guy in the middle."

1974; 12 min.; color; $50 for five days
Stephen Bosustow Productions, P.O. Box 2127, Santa Monica, Calif. 90406; (213) 394-0218

I've Got a Woman Boss!

An entertaining and instructive animated film about Mitt Mittle's experience with his new female boss. Mittle is in an explosive mood when he hears the news, but as usual things go well in spite of him. The film shows that any organizational change is a psychological and systemic challenge and that successful transitions depend on the manner in which change is handled.

1977; 11 min.; color; $50 for five days
Stephen Bosustow Productions, P.O. Box 2127, Santa Monica, Calif. 90406; (213) 394-0218

Journey Into Self

Dramatic documentary highlights of an intensive sixteen-hour encounter group session among eight adults, all total strangers. Focuses on four group members, recording the most emotional moments of their interactions. The group is led by Drs. Carl Rogers and Richard Farson, two of the country's foremost psychologists. Academy Award-winning classic.

1968; 47 min.; b/w; $50
NTL/Learning Resources Corporation, 7594 Eads Avenue, La Jolla, Calif. 92037; (800) 854-2143. California, Alaska, and Hawaii: (714) 454-3193

Last of the Great Male Chauvinists

A film about feminism, showing the need for women to develop a sense of their own importance and for men to sustain them in this effort. Ann has led a full and happy life as the wife of a successful businessman and the mother of three boys, who are now in college. She finds herself in the throes of middle age with plenty of time on her hands and no interests beyond her front door. She feels used and develops a debilitating view of herself as a mere cook and laundress. Her husband is typically bewildered by her sudden rebellion and self-depreciation: "I'm your wife and their mother. But who the hell am I?"

1976; 27 min.; color; $35
The Media Guild, Box 881, Solana Beach, Calif. 92075; (714) 755-9191

Leadership: Style or Circumstance?

Examines the concept and role of leadership in organizations, distinguishing between the relationship-oriented and the task-oriented leader. The first tends to organize work along democratic lines, giving employees a major voice in decision making; the second tends to be more directive and forceful, relying heavily on his own judgment and expecting obedience from his staff. Uses interviews and a documentary look at the daily activities of the presidents of a major ice cream chain and a large film laboratory to show that the effectiveness of each style of leadership depends on the specific situation. Suggests ways of developing leaders and ensuring their effectiveness and longevity once on the job. From the Behavior in Business Series.

1975; 27 min.; color; $45
CRM McGraw-Hill Films, 110 Fifteenth Street, Del Mar, Calif. 92014; (714) 453-5000

LEARNING TO LIVE SERIES

An eight-film series on transactional analysis that explores the everyday frustrations we all experience and offers alternatives for more honest and open communication. In each film, TA therapist Stephen Winners introduces a topic or situation through the use of dramatic vignettes, cartoons, and diagrams. Winners and six persons representing a variety of ages and backgrounds examine the subject through informal interaction, role playing, questions, and discussion. Moments of humor and quiet seriousness prove to be equally revealing.

1974; 30 min. each; color; $25 each; $175 for the series
Mass Media, 2116 North Charles Street, Baltimore, Md. 21218; (301) 727-3270; or 1720 Chouteau Avenue, St. Louis, Mo. 63103; (314) 436-0418

Ego States (1)

Provides the conceptual foundation for TA by exploring three basic behavior patterns or ego states from which we can feel and act—the parent, the adult, and the child. Teaches the specific communication skill of identifying and monitoring ego states to better understand ourselves and others.

Transactions (2)

Illustrates various stimulus-and-response transactions that occur in two-person transactions. Shows how to analyze and diagram transactions to understand what is happening as well as what is really being said when two people communicate and shows that we can exercise conscious choice and flexibility in our responses.

Strokes (3)

Strokes—messages that tell us we're O.K.—are necessary for healthy existence; this film explores ways in which we can develop more freedom both for giving and for receiving strokes. Strokes are defined as recognition or appreciation that may be physical (a touch, a smile, a hug, a look) or verbal (praise, understanding); their contribution to self-esteem is discussed.

Time Structures (4)

Shows how time structures—the ways we use our time to get strokes—affect relationships. Illustrates time structures as withdrawal, rituals, activities, games, and intimacy—an open and direct exchange of strokes that arouses O.K. feelings of tenderness and affection and frees us to let others see our real selves and to see others as they really are.

Feelings (5)

Discusses ways to develop authentic relationships and to avoid playing games by learning to "own" and experience our feelings as they arise. Shows that our actions are based, consciously or unconsciously, on choices we have made. No one can *make* us feel angry, guilty, or ashamed.

Games (6)

In games, a recurring series of ulterior transactions results in a predictable "payoff" that reaffirms the not-O.K. life scripts of the persons involved. Steve Winners plays the role of victim and seeks help from the group; when he then refuses to accept the help they offer, the roles of victim, rescuer, and persecutor switch. Illustrates how game playing prevents us from experiencing the O.K. feelings of authentic relationships.

Acquiring Life Scripts (7)

As members of the group explore life scripts, we see how these patterns or positions begin early in life and determine our O.K. or not-O.K. images of ourselves and others, how scripts are unconsciously learned, and how, by examining our individual scripts and understanding them, we can begin to make changes instead of unconsciously acting out our scripts.

Changing Life Scripts (8)

How we can alter our life scripts and become winners instead of losers. How we can change by cultivating awareness of ourselves and others—by monitoring ego states and transactions, accepting and giving strokes, examining and rearranging our use of time, owning and expressing our feelings, giving up habitual roles that contribute to game playing, and examining and naming our life scripts. How we can change by accepting responsibility for our own lives.

Looking for Me

A film about the delights of experiencing one's body, as well as a document supporting a talented teacher's belief that movement awareness is essential for all children and that for psychotic or handicapped children body language is an important means of communication. Shows Janet Adler, a dance or movement therapist, working with normal and emotionally disturbed children and with a group of therapists and teachers. Effective and well photographed, with brief and concise narration; a remarkable example of a good film editor's ability to telescope time, make comparisons, and provide quick insights.

1970; 29 min.; b/w; $18
University of California Extension Media Center, Berkeley, Calif. 94720; (415) 642-0460

A Man

In a men's group, a young man shares the experience of his father's death and his own emotions and grief. As the other group members comfort him, the viewer can feel the difficulty men may have in expressing and handling their emotions and the effort required to overcome their sense of separation and aloneness.

1976; 21 min.; b/w; $30
Polymorph Films, 331 Newbury Street, Boston, Mass. 02115; (617) 262-5560

THE MANAGEMENT DEVELOPMENT SERIES

A continuing series of films dating from 1961 to 1977, produced by Dr. Charles K. Ferguson of UCLA, in which leading educators, research specialists, psychologists, and management consultants present research, experience, and theories of interest for all areas of management and general audiences as well. Each film is intended to be used independently and is a filmed lecture unless otherwise noted. Although the lecture format is unacceptable to some film audiences, the content is often exciting and the visual, personal presentation of the well-known authority offers an advantage over a written or aural presentation. Some of the material in this series is also available on audiotape from the primary distributor; contact the audio coordinator for information.

University of California Extension Media Center, Berkeley, Calif. 94720; (415) 642-0460

Constructive Use of the Emotions

Sherman Kingsbury reviews the classic methods parents use to isolate, inhibit, and disorient children, surveys some emotions and typical responses to these methods, and concludes that "if learning is the game, then passivity is the enemy."

1970; 22 min.; color; $21

Effective Leadership

UCLA behavioral scientist Dr. Robert Tannenbaum focuses on characteristics of effective leadership such as "social sensitivity" and "action flexibility," pointing out that the only tool an individual can use in a leadership role is himself.

1968; 32 min.; b/w; $20

Emergent Management

Psychologist Dr. Jack R. Gibb, describing his theory of "emergent management," explains that the central problem in management is developing conditions of mutual trust and concludes that when workers are given more freedom they respond with higher productivity.

1968; 29 min.; b/w; $18

Emotional Styles in Human Behavior

Psychologist Dr. Richard Wallen discusses a variety of personnel problems and proposes, through greater insight into individuals' personalities, a simplified way of understanding people. He defines personality types and predicts how each type will react to normal and stress conditions.

1962; 24 min.; b/w; $17

Grid Organizational Development

Robert R. Blake and Jane S. Mouton, pioneers of the organization development grid concept, utilize the grid approach to discuss developments in the field for the past twenty years and current thinking about the management and development of people and organizations. The film is most effective when used as a sequel to *Managerial Grid* (in this series).
1970; 35 min.; color; $28

Group Leadership: The History of the Group Process Movement

Dr. Leland P. Bradford discusses the history, basic assumptions, and principal discoveries of the group process movement, out of which came some of the most important advances in self-awareness learning and organization development theory.
1976; 28 min.; b/w; $18

Human Considerations in Management

Abraham Kaplan pinpoints the seemingly insoluble problems of morale, productivity, and turnover in a lively and spontaneous lecture, stressing the simple but often neglected fact that managers, too, are human beings.
1969; 29 min.; b/w; $18

Human Skills of Management

William J. Crockett defines the management task in terms of both relationship (human) skills and task (technical) skills and discusses the importance in one's personal as well as organizational life of creating a climate of positive emotions so that all involved retain a feeling of self-esteem and dignity.
1977; 29 min.; b/w; $18

Importance of Relationships in Organizational Life—Why People Need People

Dr. Martin C. Nalder, psychiatrist, explains how managers can help create an organizational environment that satisfies the social needs of their employees. He comments on specific interpersonal needs, suggesting ways to satisfy them and stressing the importance of considering these needs in decision making.
1976; 16 min.; color; $18

Introducing Managers to Organizational Development—Development of Teams, Individuals, and Organizations

Dr. Thomas Wickes, psychologist and management consultant, presents a wide-ranging lecture designed to introduce management personnel to the organization development problems that they will increasingly face in the future and to show them the kinds of abilities they will need to cope with these problems.
1976; 55 min.; b/w; $28

Leadership and Small Work-Group Dynamics

Dr. Verne J. Kallejian, psychologist and management consultant, explains how to integrate the needs of people within an organization and the tasks of the organization itself; he defines organizational efficiency as the optimization of need-oriented and task-oriented factors.
1976; 27 min.; color; $24

Management of Creativity

Senior engineering students at UCLA, as they approach employment in industry, manifest their doubts about management's receptiveness to new ideas and project the fear that their creativity will be stifled. Working engineers and managerial staff respond to the questions raised primarily in terms of profitability and the mechanics of production. (Not a lecture.)
1970; 36 min.; b/w; $21

Management: The New Challenges

Prominent executives and behavioral scientists outline present challenges and future requirements for administrators who wish to provide management that will remain viable and prosper in a fast-changing, complex environment. (Not a lecture.)
1970; 24 min.; b/w; $17

Managerial Grid

Robert Blake presents the managerial grid technique as a way to evaluate various approaches to management. Concern for people and concern for production are discussed in terms of the degree of commitment, creativity, and conflict that can be expected with each management approach.
1963; 35 min.; b/w; $21

Organizational Development

Sheldon Davis of TRW Inc. discusses the fresh, dynamic approaches his company has developed in the application of behavioral science principles to the complex social structures found in every large organization.
1968; 30 min.; color; $25

Problem Solving in Groups

Dr. Richard Wallen lectures on management committees and how they function, explaining the problem-solving process, how committees usually deal with problems, and how their methods can be improved.
1961; 25 min.; b/w; $17

Sociotechnical Systems

G. K. Jayaram, organizational consultant and advocate of open-systems design and planning, summarizes the history of organizational theory and explains the concepts of open and sociotechnical systems and calls for a synthesis of scientific management and sensitivity training.
1974; 33 min.; b/w; $16

Some Personal Learnings About Interpersonal Relationships

Dr. Carl R. Rogers, founder of client-centered therapy, discusses the "mysterious business of relating with other human beings," the rewards of genuine communication, the satisfaction of being real and of communicating that quality to another person, and the pleasure of fearlessly giving and receiving positive feelings.
1967; 33 min.; b/w; $20

Theory of Management Development

Dr. Charles Ferguson of UCLA gives an introductory lecture on some of the assumptions upon which management-development theory is based and on the application of theory to a management-development program.
1961; 28 min.; b/w; $18

War on Bureaucracy

Sheldon Davis of TRW Inc. takes a new look at organization development and describes methods by which large organizations may minimize the confinement and depersonalization often experienced by their members.
1974; 32 min.; b/w; $23

Ways of Dealing with Conflict in Organizations

Herbert Shepard discusses three methods of resolving organizational conflict: suppression, or all-out war; bargaining, or limited war; and problem solving, or creative resolution. A conflict's

procedures, tools, values, and assumed relationships between parties are described for each method, and each method's shortcomings are emphasized.
1962; 27 min.; b/w; $18

The Pigs vs. the Freaks

A humorous film about one of those rare times when people with conflicting life styles make contact and learn something about each other. Long-haired students at Michigan State University and members of the local town police force compete in an annual football game. Shows pregame activities and postgame reactions as well as the game itself. With each side playing to win, the players take their opponents seriously and no longer see them as nonpersons. Common ground is explored, and a certain respect for the alien side remains as the outcome.
1974; 15 min.; color; $25
Pyramid Films, Box 1048, Santa Monica, Calif. 90406; (213) 828-7577

The Power

This powerful, disturbing film about the power of man's mind to control absolutely both other men and himself is an irresistible discussion stimulus because viewers tend to be outraged by it. It is a beautifully realized and integrated documentary of an authentic hypnosis lesson titled "How To Rule over Others." Without words, it captures the hypnotist's skill through vivid images of the dark dungeon setting, the black-clothed men whose disembodied faces and hands are emphasized by lighting, and the sinister tools of instruction. The sound, too, is perfectly conceived—natural sounds, electronic music, and, at the conclusion, a chorale counterpointed with masculine sobs, devastating because of their unfamiliarity. The film seems to demonstrate that man wants to be controlled by some power and that both the desire and the capability are potentially destructive. It shows increasingly difficult, punishing demands of the hypnotist being carried out by submissive subjects.
1973; 34 min.; color; $35
Phoenix Films, Inc., 470 Park Avenue South, New York, N.Y. 10016; (212) 684-5910

Primal Therapy: In Search of the Real You

Interviews with psychiatrist Arthur Janov and filmed portions of therapy sessions describe and illustrate Janov's theory, proven through his experience with patients, that neurotic tensions come from unresolved situations that caused intense pain and that remembering and reliving the original (primal) event, with its pain, is often curative.
1976; 20 min.; color; $40
Document Associates, Inc., 880 Third Avenue, New York, N.Y. 10022; (212) 593-1647

Productivity and the Self-Fulfilling Prophecy: The Pygmalion Effect

Employs interviews with authorities, animated sequences, and live-action vignettes in organizational settings to present the theory and practical applications of the Pygmalion effect—the influence that one's expectations alone, negative or positive, have on others' behavior. Demonstrates that an understanding of the power of this effect is vital to modern management, citing recent studies showing that the fulfillment of expectations can be a crucial factor in improving performance, productivity, and profitability. Very well produced, entertaining, and appealing for diverse groups. From the Behavior in Business Series.
1975; 31 min.; color; $45
CRM McGraw-Hill Films, 110 Fifteenth Street, Del Mar, Calif. (714) 453-5000

Replay

Satirical cinematic collage showing that today's generation is not so different from older ones and that contemporary history is often a replay of past events. "Shots of contemporary young people, personal comments from their elders, and sequences depicting the youth of the older generations are juxtaposed and combined in a visually slick and provocative comment on the generation gap. Employing negative images, slow motion, and color filters, the film compares the rather disdainful views toward current rock dancing, unconventional fashions, women's liberation, sex in the movies, and fun with flashbacks of exhausting dance marathons, flapper fashions, early suffragettes, sultry silent screen stars and the good clean fun of a tug-of-war in a mud puddle. In the charming conclusion a little old lady delightedly chats with a hippie, admiring his clothes and handmade neck beads, as a lyrical song comments upon the fact that we're not so far apart . . . life is just a replay."—BOOKLIST.

1971; 8 min.; color; $15
Contemporary/McGraw-Hill Films, 1221 Avenue of the Americas, New York, N.Y. 10020; (609) 448-1700

Situational Leadership

Provides a simple, clear, visual presentation of the Hersey-Blanchard situational leadership model—a successful approach that focuses on situational differences and types of leadership behaviors appropriate in particular situations. Paul Hersey presents the theory to two trainers in simple, easy-to-understand terms. An introduction to the concepts for all levels, from first-line managers to executives.

1977; 16 min.; color; $75 for five days
NTL/Learning Resources Corporation, 7594 Eads Avenue, La Jolla, Calif. 92037; (800) 854-2143. California, Alaska, and Hawaii: (714) 454-3193

Sociobiology: Doing What Comes Naturally

Surveys research on the biological origins of human behavior. Several biologists and anthropologists—citing their work with monkeys, rats, fish, insects, etc.—explain their theories about male competitiveness and aggression, female "sexual reticence" (whether social or biological), the origins of warfare, and reasons for the current rebellion by young people. A controversial and stimulating film. From the Towards the Year 2000 Series.

1972; 22 min.; color; $40
Document Associates, Inc., 880 Third Avenue, New York, N.Y. 10022; (212) 593-1647

Theory X and Theory Y

Part 1: Description of the Theory

Three colleagues of the influential behavioral scientist Douglas McGregor discuss and illustrate his theories on management assumptions concerning employees. Part 1 compares and exemplifies both theories. Theory X assumes that human capabilities are potentially static, unimprovable, and not very impressive and that management must compensate for these deficiencies. Theory Y stresses potential for opportunity, achievement, and human development and a belief that humans respond to the challenge of a responsible, satisfying job.

Part 2: Application of the Theory

Continues previous discussion, showing why a manager using Theory-Y assumptions is likely to elicit greater productivity from his employees.

1969; 25 min. each; color; $60 each for three days
BNA Communications Inc., 9401 Decoverly Hall Road, Rockville, Md. 20850; (301) 948-0540

To Live and Move According to Your Nature Is Called Love

Shows Jefferson Community Mental Health Center, an experimental black community-organizing project in Philadelphia founded on the belief that mental illness is often caused or aggravated by social problems for which solutions must be found before major improvements in mental health can begin. By being encouraged to organize and influence their futures, the participants can be helped to solve the problems they face.

1971; 29 min.; b/w; $9.50
Indiana University Audio Visual Center, Bloomington, Ind. 47401; (812) 337-2103

What Do You Mean, What Do I Mean?:
Case Studies in Communication

The influence that opinion has on perception and the resulting misunderstandings and communication breakdowns are covered. Major problems taken from two case histories—one illustrating how preconceived ideas (assumptions) affect perceptions and one illustrating the interplay of assumption-perceptions and feelings—are analyzed by Dr. John J. Morse of the Harvard Business School.

1976; 18 min.; color; $70 for ten days
Salenger Educational Media, 1635-12th Street, Santa Monica, Calif. 90404; (213) 393-0311

The Women's Prejudice Film: Myths and Realities

This semidocumentary approach to contemporary lifestyles of women explores myths and clichés and presents alternative viewpoints that stimulate the viewer to reappraise his or her attitudes concerning the equality of roles among women and men. Shows the significance of women in the work force and in jobs traditionally assigned to men. Encourages women to explore the working world more fully, as those who have not identified their full capabilities and potential may well be victims of their own acceptance of the outdated and outmoded myths and clichés that continue to surround them.

1974; 18 min.; color; $30 for five days
Sandler Institutional Films Inc., 1001 North Poinsettia Place, Hollywood, Calif. 90046; (213) 876-2021

The Work Prejudice Film: People, Jobs & Stereotypes

Investigates the working world as it relates to stereotypes, attitudes, and job opportunities. Explores and explodes some preconceived misconceptions about the existence of relationships between identifiable segments of society and the kinds of jobs they perform. Uses documentation, humor, and statistics to indicate that women are succeeding in business; that a variety of ethnic groups are achieving in a broad assortment of jobs, crafts, and professions; and that opportunities exist for people who prepare for them, regardless of gender, cultural heritage, and socioeconomic status.

1974; 13 min.; color; $20 for five days
Sandler Institutional Films Inc., 1001 North Poinsettia Place, Hollywood, Calif. 90046; (213) 876-2021

SOME MAJOR UNIVERSITY FILM COLLECTIONS

East

Boston University
Krasker Memorial Film Library
765 Commonwealth Avenue
Boston, Mass. 02215
(617) 353-3272

New York University Film Library
41 Press Annex
Washington Square
New York, N.Y. 10003
(212) 598-2250

Pennsylvania State University
Audio Visual Services
Psychological Cinema Register
Willard Building
State College, Pa. 16802
(814) 865-6315

Midwest

Indiana University
Audio Visual Center
Bloomington, Ind. 47401
(812) 337-2853

Kent State University
Instructional Resources Center
215 Education
Kent, Ohio 44242
(216) 672-2454

Southern Illinois University
Learning Resources Services
Film Rental Library
Carbondale, Ill. 62901
(618) 453-2258

University of Illinois
Visual Aids Service
1325 South Oak
Champaign, Ill. 61820
(217) 333-1360

University of Iowa
Audio Visual Center
C-5 East Hall
Iowa City, Iowa 52242
(319) 353-3724

University of Kansas
Film Services
746 Massachusetts
Lawrence, Kans. 66044
(913) 864-3352

University of Michigan
Audio Visual Education Center
416 Fourth Street
Ann Arbor, Mich. 48103
(313) 764-5360

University of Minnesota
Audio Visual Library Service
3300 University Avenue S.E.
Minneapolis, Minn. 55415
(612) 373-3764

University of Missouri—Columbia
Academic Support Center
505 East Stewart Road
Columbia, Mo. 65201
(314) 882-3601

University of Nebraska—Lincoln
Instructional Media Center
Nebraska Hall 421
Lincoln, Neb. 68508
(402) 472-1911

Wayne State University
Systems Distribution and Utilization
4841 Cass
Detroit, Mich. 48202
(313) 577-1980

Southwest

Oklahoma State University
Audiovisual Center
Stillwater, Okla. 74074
(405) 624-7214

University of Arizona
Bureau of Audio Visual Services
Tucson, Ariz. 85721
(602) 884-2560

University of Texas—Austin
Visual Instruction Bureau
Drawer W. University Station
Austin, Tex. 78712
(512) 471-3573

West

University of California
Extension Media Center
2223 Fulton Street
Berkeley, Calif. 94720
(415) 642-0460

University of Colorado
Educational Media Center
320 Stadium Building
Boulder, Colo. 80302
(303) 492-7341

VIDEOTAPE

The 16mm film medium has been emphasized because it is still the most readily obtainable and usable for most groups. But many other media are available (frequently for purchase only) from a vast array of sources. If videotape is preferred, the facilitator can inquire of 16mm film sources about the availability of tape versions of films and of material offered only on tape. Many distributors offer tapes for sale; a few rent tapes; some will license the user to produce a tape copy of a film for a specified limited use. One major source of tapes is Great Plains National Instructional TV Library, Box 80669, Lincoln, Neb. 68501; (402) 467-2502.

Two useful resource books: *Video and Cable: A Bibliography and Source List*, published by the Educational Film Library Association (EFLA), 43 West 61st Street, New York, N.Y. 10023; (212) 246-4533; and *The Video Bluebook*, Knowledge Industry Publications, Inc., 2 Corporate Park Drive, White Plains, N.Y. 10604.

AUDIOTAPE

Audiorecordings present an extremely viable medium for subject areas that are of an abstract nature not amenable to or in need of visual amplification. They have the additional advantage of being significantly cheaper and easier to use and transport than either film or videotape. Five major sources for purchase of audiorecordings, which generally are not offered for rental or audition, are listed below. A growing number of public libraries circulate audiotapes; their number will increase with demand.

Audiorecordings
University of California
Extension Media Center
Berkeley, Calif. 94720

National Center for Audio Tapes
University of Colorado
348 Stadium Building
Boulder, Colo. 80302

Center for Cassette Studies
8110 Webb Avenue
North Hollywood, Calif. 91605

Pacifica Tape Library
2217 Shattuck Avenue
Berkeley, Calif. 94704

The Center for the Study of
  Democratic Institutions
P.O. Box 4446
Santa Barbara, Calif. 93103

REFERENCE SOURCES

BNA Communications Inc. Film Catalog. 9401 Decoverly Hall Road, Rockville, Md. 20850; (301) 948-0540. Also 5615 Fishers Lane, Rockville, Md. 20852; (301) 881-2090. More than ninety titles especially for management and human relations, including some of the best series available: Effective Communication, Effective Executive, Effective Organization, Management by Objectives, Management Practice, Managing Discontinuity, Motivation and Productivity, Organization Renewal, and Tough-Minded Management. Video and audiotapes as well as films. Free previews by reservation at screening locations in Atlanta, Chicago, Los Angeles, New York, Phoenix, and Rockville.

CRM Films Psychology Catalog. CRM McGraw-Hill Films, 110 Fifteenth Street, Del Mar, Calif. 92014; (714) 453-5000. Forty-nine films "produced to reflect the depth and breadth of the discipline of psychology," featuring some excellent business and management films. See also their *Visions '77* catalog.

The Educational Film Library Association (EFLA), 43 West 61st Street, New York, N.Y. 10023; (212) 246-4533. A clearing house for information about film. Publishes film evaluations and other materials; provides assistance in locating films.

Educational Film Locator. Of the Consortium of University Film Centers and R. R. Bowker, 1977. R. R. Bowker, P.O. Box 992, Ann Arbor, Mich. 48106. A catalog listing and describing all the films held by the fifty member institutions of the Consortium. Includes a user's guide, rental instructions for each participating university library, a subject index with audience level, and descriptions of 45,000 films in title sequence.

Educators Guide to Free Films. Wisconsin: Educators Progress Service, 1976. Compiled and edited by Mary Foley Horkheimer and John C. Diffor.

Feature Films on 8mm and 16mm (4th ed.). R. R. Bowker, P.O. Box 992, Ann Arbor, Mich. 48106. A 1974 directory of feature films available for rental, sale, and lease in the United States, compiled and edited by James L. Limbacher. Lists more than 15,000 movies with their stars, directors, and distributors. Many films we remember from our youth or from recent years can be rented and shared with a group. Rental rates are complicated and must be discussed with distributors.

Mental Health Materials Center, 419 Park Avenue, New York, N.Y. 10016. Publishers of "The MHMC Guide to Recent Mental Health Films," "IRC Recommends," the IRC Newsletter. Excellent, no-nonsense reviews of films in the broadest mental health category.

Motivational Media Film Catalog. 8271 Melrose Avenue, Los Angeles, Calif. 90046. Contains a study guide as well as a description of each film.

Olympic Media Information, 71 West 23rd Street, New York, N.Y. 10010; (212) 675-4500. Publishes "Training Film Profiles," excellent evaluations of films useful to group facilitators.

PCR: Films in the Behavioral Sciences. Psychological Cinema Register, The Pennsylvania State University, Audio-Visual Services, University Park, Pa. 16802; (814) 865-6315. Edited by Lori A. Baldwin, this catalog offers a comprehensive collection of films in the areas of psychology, psychiatry, and related behavioral sciences.

Selected Mental Health Audiovisuals. National Institute of Mental Health, 5600 Fishers Lane, Rockville, Md. 20852. A catalog of films, filmstrips, audiotapes, and videotapes.

> *Donna Lee Smith is the film sales manager of the University of California Extension Media Center in Berkeley, California. She selects and distributes 16mm films and is active in the Educational Film Library Association (for which she serves as an American Film Festival jury chairperson and a filmography consultant and writer), the Consortium of University Film Centers, and the Association for Humanistic Psychology. Ms. Smith's background is in film festival management and film evaluation and programming.*

HUMANISTIC AND TRANSPERSONAL EDUCATION: A GUIDE TO RESOURCES

Jack Canfield

For the past ten years increasing numbers of educators have been turning their attention to the education of the *whole* student: body, mind, emotions, and spirit. This rapidly growing movement has been variously referred to as humanistic education, affective education, confluent education, transpersonal education, and, most recently, holistic education. Working with psychologists on the frontiers of the human potential movement, educators are beginning to introduce into the schools new courses, activities, and learning designs that address themselves primarily to the psychological growth of students.

In response to this growing interest, such a vast number of books, pamphlets, journals, newsletters, and curricula and learning kits have appeared that it has become difficult to select intelligently among them. This guide is an attempt to provide some assistance in this area for teachers, teacher trainers, administrators, and consultants. It offers up-to-date information in six categories: Books (subdivided into A Basic Library, General Books, Classroom Activities, and Transpersonal Education), Curricula and Student Materials, and Journals and Newsletters.

No guide of this sort can ever be complete. At best it is a working bibliography-in-progress. Every day new books are written, new curricula published, new courses offered, and new projects begun. While this may make compilers of bibliographies anxious, it is nevertheless reassuring to those who are struggling to make schools more human places for students and teachers.[1]

BOOKS

In the past seven years there has been an increasing flood of books published in this field. This list is based on those books that the reviewer has found most useful in his own work, that colleagues have lauded, and that beginning teachers in this area have found most helpful.

The first section, A Basic Library, is intended for newcomers to the field and for school libraries to use in making initial purchases. The second section, General Books, might be called a "secondary library." It contains books related to humanistic education that the reviewer considers nonessential but highly recommended. In a sense, it is a catchall for the many worthwhile books that did not fit into the other sections or categories. The third section, Classroom Activities, lists books containing activities that teachers can use to enhance self-concept, increase self-awareness, clarify values, develop

---

[1]For a comprehensive, complete listing of resources see *A Guide to Resources in Humanistic and Transpersonal Education* by Jack Canfield. Available from Institute for Humanistic and Transpersonal Education, Box 575, Amherst, Mass. 01002, $5.50.

communication skills, etc. To the practitioner it is probably the most useful section in this category. The fourth section, Transpersonal Education, concerns itself with those titles that especially concentrate on this aspect of humanistic and transpersonal education.

A Basic Library

Anger and the Rocking Chair: Gestalt Awareness with Children by Janet Lederman, with photographs by Lillian R. Cutler. New York: McGraw-Hill, 1969; paperback, Viking Compass, 1976. This book is a dramatic, visual account of Gestalt methods with so-called "difficult" or "disturbed" children in elementary school. Rather than suppressing students' rebellion and anger, Lederman helps her pupils transform these powerful impulses into constructive attitudes and behavior.

Fantasy and Feeling in Education by Richard M. Jones. New York: New York University Press, 1968. One of the few books in humanistic education written from the viewpoint of a Freudian-oriented psychoanalyst. Jones begins with a perceptive critique of the Educational Development Corporation's curriculum "Man: A Course of Study" and goes on to point out the limitations of Jerome Bruner's work and the importance of fantasy and creative thinking in education. He explores the implications of Erick Erikson's theories and makes specific recommendations for new approaches to affective education. Tough to read at times, but worth the effort.

Human Teaching for Human Learning: An Introduction to Confluent Education by George Brown. New York: The Viking Press, 1971; paperback, Viking Compass, 1972. George Brown has been working with both the University of California at Santa Barbara and the Esalen Institute as part of a Ford Foundation project in affective education. This book contains a statement of the purposes of the project, extensive examples of affective techniques and their classroom applications, and personal commentaries by teachers involved in the project.

Humanistic Education: An Interpretation by Elizabeth Leonie Simpson, with an annotated bibliography by Mary Anne Gray. Cambridge, Mass.: Ballinger, 1976. Contains sixty-seven pages of description of different approaches to implementing humanistic education and 261 pages of annotated bibliography and resource guides. A useful resource book.

Humanistic Education Sourcebook by Don Read and Sidney B. Simon. Englewood Cliffs, N.J.: Prentice-Hall, 1975. The best single "first book" in humanistic education for a teacher. It contains fifty-five articles by the leaders of the movement (Carl Rogers, George Brown, Gerald Weinstein, Sidney Jourard, Sid Simon) of both a philosophical/theoretical nature and a practical, how-to-do-it nature. No aspect of the humanistic education movement is left uncovered.

Learning to Be Free by Clark Moustakas and Cereta Perry. Englewood Cliffs, N.J.: Prentice-Hall, 1973. This is a lovely and beautifully written book by two people who love children and who know how to translate that love into practical action. Highly recommended.

Learning to Feel—Feeling to Learn by Harold C. Lyon, Jr. Columbus, Ohio: Charles E. Merrill, 1971. This is an early survey of the people, places, and ideas in the field of affective education. The sections "Humanistic Education Techniques" and "Applying Humanistic Education to Classroom Situations" are particularly valuable.

Left-Handed Teaching: Lessons in Affective Education by Gloria Castillo. New York: Praeger, 1974. This book is a real treasure of affective exercises. It contains 146 activities in such areas as awareness of here-and-now, sensory awareness, imagination, polarities, communication, building trust, aggression, nature, space, art, blindfolds, and sheets.

The Live Classroom: Innovations Through Confluent Education and Gestalt edited by George I. Brown, with Thomas Yeomans and Liles Grizzard. New York: The Viking Press, 1975. This book contains twenty-eight articles by psychologists and teachers involved in applying confluent practices, Gestalt, and psychosynthesis to the classroom. The range is from first grade to high school, and it covers such subjects as the sciences, social studies, English, art, and foreign languages.

The Other Side of the Report Card: A How-to-do-it Program for Affective Education by Larry Chase. Pacific Palisades, Calif.: Goodyear, 1975. For one book, this contains more affective exercises than could ever be used in two years, even at the rate of two a day. A real treasure trove of excellent activities.

Personalizing Education: Values Clarification and Beyond by Leland and Mary Martha Howe. New York: Hart, 1975. This immense volume contains over one hundred strategies for classroom use in a wide variety of humanistic education areas: values clarification, self-concept, goal setting, trust development, communication skills, self-directed learning, etc. A valuable resource guide.

Toward Humanistic Education edited by Gerald Weinstein and Mario Fantini. New York: Praeger, 1970. The outgrowth of the Elementary School Teaching Project of the Ford Foundation, this book outlines a model for curriculum and instruction based on pupils' concerns and feelings rather than on purely cognitive goals. The book contains many new ideas that can be immediately applied by classroom teachers.

Values Clarification: A Handbook of Practical Strategies for Teachers and Students by Sidney B. Simon, Leland W. Howe, and Howard Kirschenbaum. New York: Hart, 1972. This extremely practical and valuable book contains seventy-nine classroom exercises designed to help students clarify their values. Each exercise is clearly written and contains many examples of ways in which it can be used. This book promises to become a classic in humanistic education.

Values and Teaching: Working with Values in the Classroom by Louis E. Raths, Merrill Harmin, and Sidney B. Simon. Columbus, Ohio: Charles E. Merrill, 1966. This book outlines a theory of values and a classroom methodology for the clarification of values. It contains many practical classroom activities.

Will the Real Teacher Please Stand Up?: A Primer in Humanistic Education by Mary Greer and Bonnie Rubenstein. Pacific Palisades, Calif.: Goodyear, 1972. Charles Weingartner writes: "It's about kids and how fragile and vulnerable they are—like seedlings. (Kids are seedlings.) And it's about how they need to be nurtured to help them in the process of growing and becoming so that they can develop and flower rather than be broken and get stunted and withered. And, in a wistful way, it's about the little kid somewhere inside each of us. And it's about how sad it is when little kids (inside or outside of us) are squashed or denied. . . . It is full of smart stuff by smart people who think and feel deeply about educating kids. It's full of stuff that makes you think about yourself, and stuff that makes you wistful, and stuff that makes you smile."

General Books

Advanced Value Clarification by Howard Kirschenbaum. La Jolla, Calif.: University Associates, 1977. This volume is the fruit of a ten-year involvement with value clarification by one of the most probing and prolific authors in the field. The text explores theory and current research, develops designs for workshops and classes, describes how value clarification can be built into school curricula, and surveys past and present developments in the field and forecasts the future. The author responds directly to the theoretical issues raised by both the critics and the proponents of value clarification. A comprehensive, annotated bibliography, 1965-1975, lists 185 sources that are directly related to value-clarification theory, process, and practice.

Building Positive Self-Concepts by Donald W. Felker. Minneapolis, Minn.: Burgess, 1974. This book contains one of the most cogent statements that exists of what self-concept is and how to develop it in the classroom. I use the ideas a great deal in my own work.

Discovering Your Teaching Self: Humanistic Approaches to Effective Teaching by Richard L. Curwin and Barbara Schneider Fuhrmann. Englewood Cliffs, N.J.: Prentice-Hall, 1975. This is a do-it-yourself guide to self-knowledge as a teacher. It contains numerous activities that can be done alone, in a group, and in the classroom to develop self-awareness and awareness of the classroom climate. It also shows how to apply this self-awareness in relating to students of all ages.

Discussing Death: A Guide to Death Education by Gretchen C. Mills, Raymond Reisler, Jr., Alice E. Robinson, and Gretchen Vermilye. Homewood, Ill.: ETC Publications (Dept. M, 18512 Pierce Terrace, 60430), 1976. The importance of dealing with the subject of death has now become widely acknowledged. This book is a curriculum guide that will help teachers and students to approach this subject. Written for grades K-12, it includes numerous activities; stimuli for open, informed, and sensitive discussion; field trips; resources; and references.

Educational Change: A Humanistic Approach edited by Ray Eiben and Al Milliren. La Jolla, Calif.: University Associates, 1976. Humanistic education and planned change are the main emphasis in this book, designed for pre-service and in-service teachers, educational consultants, school administrators, and others in the field of education. Forty-seven readings, focusing on the affective and experiential components of the educational process, are divided into five sections. Part one deals with group techniques; part two details the background and applications of psychodrama and role playing; part three, Change Strategies, focuses on goal setting, force-field analysis, and planning; part four focuses on the open classroom and other structural interventions. The last section, In-Service Programs, includes a confluent education model, workshops in learning theory and consultation, and techniques for analyzing nonverbal communication and conducting meetings.

Encouraging Creativity in the Classroom by E. Paul Torrance; *Expanding the Self: Personal Growth for Teachers* by Angelo Boy and Gerald Pine; and *Group Processes in the Classroom* by Richard and Patricia Schmuck. Dubuque, Iowa: William C. Brown, 1971. These three books in a series entitled "Issues and Innovations in Education" provide excellent introductions to the specific subjects and are likely to be particularly useful for teachers who are beginning to introduce humanistic education into their classrooms and for administrators who want to introduce humanistic processes to their staffs.

Games Students Play (and What to Do About Them) by Ken Ernst. Millbrae, Calif.: Celestial Arts (231 Adrian Road, 94030), 1972. Explains the manipulative games students play in the classroom and how to stop them without getting hooked. Very useful little book.

Getting It All Together: Confluent Education by George I. Brown, Mark Phillips, and Stewart Shapiro. Bloomington, Ind.: Phi Delta Kappa (Box 789, 47401; 50¢), 1976. A very useful brief introduction to "confluent" education, which means "the flowing together of the affective and cognitive domains in education."

Glad to Be Me: Building Self-Esteem in Yourself and Others by Dov Peretz Elkins. Englewood, N.J.: Prentice-Hall, 1976. A delightful, inspiring, exciting, lovable collection of readings, poems, and photographs about raising self-esteem in yourself, your family, your students, your employees, your clients, and anyone else whom you care about. It is beautifully illustrated with moving photographs. Includes writings of Carl Rogers, Abraham Maslow, Virginia Satir, Erich Fromm, Paul Tillich, and many others.

Human Interaction in Education by Gene Stanford and Albert E. Roark. Boston: Allyn & Bacon, 1974. The focus is on interactive processes of teacher and students; includes many useful activities.

Human Values in the Classroom: Teaching for Personal and Social Growth by Robert C. Hawley. Amherst, Mass.: Educational Research Associates (Box 767, 01002), 1973. An exposition of a sequence of teaching concerns and related material to help teachers move toward the teaching of human values.

Liberating Our Children, Ourselves by Suzanne Howard. Washington, D.C.: American Association of University Women, 1975. This is a handbook of course material in women's studies for teacher educators and classroom teachers. There are nearly three hundred articles, books, papers, organizations, and other resources listed. An important resource for anyone interested in eliminating sexism in the schools.

Magic Circle: An Overview of the Human Development Program by Geraldine Ball and Uvaldo Palomares. La Mesa, Calif.: Human Development Training Institute (7574 University Avenue,

92041), 1976. Contains a theoretical overview of the program as well as sample units from the extensive HDP curriculum materials. A good introduction to a very solid program.

Moral Education in Theory and Practice by Robert T. Hall and John U. Davis. Buffalo, N.Y.: Prometheus, 1975. This book suggests ways the theories of moral education and values clarification can be translated into practical classroom activities and shows the use of case studies and simulation games.

Opening: A Primer for Self-Actualization by Bob Samples and Bob Wohlford. Reading, Mass.: Addison-Wesley, 1973. A beautifully designed book, each page like a poster, it opens the reader up to a new dimension in the process of growth. The book is both inspirational and practical. Highly recommended.

Organization Development in Schools edited by Richard A. Schmuck and Matthew B. Miles. La Jolla, Calif.: University Associates, 1970. Written with the intention of stimulating and strengthening interest in continuing scholarly research on OD theories and techniques as related to the educational process. Following an introductory chapter dealing with background information on improving schools through OD, the editors present nine studies that are based on theory, are explicit about training techniques, and include evaluative research data on OD in schools.

A Practical Guide to Value Clarification by Maury Smith. La Jolla, Calif.: University Associates, 1977. Provides anyone interested in the field of value clarification with a complete range of essential material. The opening two sections describe the basic theory behind value clarification and describe twenty-nine value-clarification strategies and exercises. A third part examines the considerations that are crucial to designing value-clarification programs. A fourth part consists of readings in various aspects of value clarification by a dozen well-known authors in the field. The final section offers a selected, annotated bibliography in value clarification.

Readings in Values Clarification edited by Sidney B. Simon and Howard Kirschenbaum. Minneapolis, Minn.: Winston Press, 1973. In addition to sixteen theoretical articles on various aspects of values clarification and moral development, there are sixteen articles on teaching school subjects through values clarification, including four dealing with religious education. English, history, science, environmental education, math, home economics, foreign languages, health education, and sex education are all included.

Real Learning: A Sourcebook for Teachers by Melvin L. Silberman, Jerome S. Allender, and Jay M. Yanoff. Boston, Mass.: Little, Brown, 1976. A collection of very useful articles on humanistic/affective education.

TA for Tots, TA for Kids, and *TA for Teens* by Alvyn M. Freed. Sacramento, Calif.: Jalmar Press, 1974-76. Three books created for kids to give them an understanding of their intrinsic OK-ness as postulated by transactional analysis. All are very good.

Taxonomy of Educational Objectives: The Classification of Educational Goals, Handbook II: The Affective Domain by David R. Kratwohl, Benjamin S. Bloom, and Bertram B. Masia. New York: David McKay, 1964. In an age in which "accountability" seemingly rules the land, the statement of objectives has become a vital survival strategy. This book should be used as a starting point for affective curriculum development and for survival. Its objectives are limited in scope and its categories and hierarchy are arbitrary, but until somebody revises it or improves upon it, it will remain the standard source book on the subject.

Teachers and Learners: The Interactive Process in Education by Alfred H. Gorman. Boston, Mass.: Allyn & Bacon, 1969. This is one of the best books for classroom teachers in the field of human communication in the classroom. It contains a minimum of theory with emphasis on application to the classroom.

Teaching Is . . . by Merrill Harmin and Tom Gregory. Chicago: Science Research Associates, 1974. Contains experiences and readings that help a teacher explore his or her own teaching style.

Teaching Significant Social Studies in the Elementary School by Elliot Seif. Chicago: Rand McNally, 1977. A practical guide to developing an elementary social studies program, including such topics as relevance, value clarification, self-awareness, self-concept development, group dynamics, environmental education, etc. A useful resource for the elementary teacher.

Values Education Sourcebook: Conceptual Approaches, Materials Analyses, and an Annotated Bibliography by Douglas P. Superka, Christine Ahrens, Luther Ford, Judith Hedstrom, and Patricia Johnson. Boulder, Colo.: Social Science Education Consortium (855 Broadway, 80302; publication #176), 1976. Designed as a resource guide for teachers, curriculum coordinators, and other educators, the *Sourcebook* focuses on five major approaches to values education: inculcation, moral development, analysis, clarification, and action learning. For each approach, there is a detailed explanation of the rationale and purpose; a description of teaching methods and an instructional model; and an illustrative activity, followed by several analyses of student and teacher materials. Each of the eighty-four analyses includes data on availability and grade level, a statement of rationale and objectives of the particular material, a summary of content and teaching procedures, and information on student evaluation as well as materials evaluation, when available.

WA-JA-GET? The Grading Game in American Education by Howard A. Kirschenbaum, Sidney Simon, and Rodney W. Napier. New York: Hart, 1971. If schools are to emphasize the psychological development of children and are to place a major emphasis on feelings, creativity, communication, etc., the issue of grades becomes a vital one. The authors of this book present their case against grades in the form of a fictional account of one teacher and one class who decide to challenge the system. The book's appendices, a compilation of alternative grading systems and an annotated bibliography of research on grading, are, by themselves, worth the price of the book.

Yearbook in Humanistic Education—1976 edited by Jim Ballard and Tim Timmerman. Amherst, Mass.: Mandala (Box 796, 01002; $12). Contains position papers, reprints, original articles, and lists of new strategies from the best in the field. The first of a yearly series. Recommended.

Classroom Activities

Affective Education Guidebook: Classroom Activities in the Realm of Feeling by Bob Eberle and Rosie Emery Hall. Buffalo, N.Y.: D.O.K. Publishers (771 East Delevan Avenue, 14215; $7.50), 1975. This highly useful collection of affective activities contains exercises to improve self-concept, enhance interpersonal relationships, increase social awareness, develop trust, and improve mental health. The book is stimulating, creative, and practical. Highly recommended.

Affective Education: Innovations for Learning edited by Lou Thayer and Kent D. Beeler. Available from SIG: Affective Education, Eastern Michigan University, Ypsilanti, Mich. 48197. Contains thirty-five structured experiences to develop affective awareness in the classroom. Includes self-awareness, group dynamics, confluent exercises, creativity, guided fantasy, value clarification, and self trust.

Affective Education: Strategies for Experiential Learning edited by Louis Thayer, with Kent D. Beeler. La Jolla, Calif.: University Associates, 1976. Designed to be applicable in a wide range of educational-learning settings and subject matter areas, the fifty structured experiences in this handbook seek to strengthen the affective components of learning—the learners' self-awareness, learning climates, interpersonal relationships in learning, recognition of learner needs and perceptions, and competencies needed for facilitating learning approaches. Topical areas include teachers, teaching, and helping processes; group processes; feedback techniques; creativity; trust; values exploration; simulations on school and higher education; image recall; and assessment practices. Each activity has a standard format that includes the goals, group size, time required, physical setting, materials, step-by-step process, variations, and notes.

Awareness by John O. Stevens. Moab, Utah: Real People Press (Box F, 84532), 1971; paperback, New York: Bantam, 1973. This is an excellent book combining theory and over one hundred exercises drawn from Gestalt awareness training, almost all of which can be used in the classroom. The exercises include personal awareness; communication with others; fantasy journeys;

exercises for couples and groups; exercises utilizing art, movement, and sound; and a special section entitled "To the Group Leader or Teacher." Highly recommended.

Awareness Experiences for School Use by Bette Hamlen. Dayton, Ohio: Pflaum Publishing, 1975. Activities of a Gestalt nature for helping youth become more responsible and self-accepting.

Born to Win: Transactional Analysis with Gestalt Experiments by Muriel James and Dorothy Jongeward. Reading, Mass.: Addison-Wesley, 1971. This book is valuable in many ways. It contains a clear-cut statement of the theory of transactional analysis and its applications to everyday life, as well as Gestalt-oriented experiments to help people discover the many parts of their personality, integrate them, and develop an inner core of self-confidence.

Caring, Feeling, Touching by Sidney B. Simon. Niles, Ill.: Argus Communications, 1976. A collection of exercises for teaching the expression of physical caring. Methods for overcoming "skin hunger."

Circlebook by Jim Ballard. Amherst, Mass.: Mandala (Box 796, 01002), 1976. The teacher's handbook for conducting circletime, a curriculum of affective growth. Contains the basic theory of circletime, as well as a detailed methodology for conducting the program. Three hundred tasks are included, as well as hints on alternate ways to implement the circle topics. Graded for use by teachers of preschool to adult.

Clarifying Values Through Subject Matter: Applications for the Classroom by Merrill Harmin, Howard Kirschenbaum, and Sidney B. Simon. Minneapolis, Minn.: Winston Press, 1973. This book draws together and simplifies all the work of the authors in the values approach to teaching subject matter. There are references to all areas of the school curriculum.

Classroom Ideas for Encouraging Thinking and Feelings by Frank Williams. Buffalo, N.Y.: D.O.K. Publishers (771 East Delevan Avenue, 14215), 1975. Contains four hundred activities cross-referenced in skills and subject areas.

Communication Games by Karen R. Krupar. New York: The Free Press, 1973. Contains exercises to help develop awareness of communication skills. Based on NTL-type activities.

Composition for Personal Growth: Values Clarification Through Writing by Sidney B. Simon, Robert C. Hawley, and David D. Britton. Amherst, Mass.: Education Research Associates (Box 767, 01002; $7). This useful manual contains a variety of self-awareness exercises that lead to creative writing and greater self-identity. A large part of the work is based on the value-clarification exercises developed by Sid Simon.

Consulting: Facilitating Human Potential and Change Processes by Don Dinkmeyer and J. Carlson. Columbus, Ohio: Charles E. Merrill, 1972. This approach offers a concrete model for training teachers in humanistic approaches through group process. It is labeled C-Group because so many of its components begin with the letter *c*—collaboration, consultation, clarification, confidential, confrontation, communication, concern, and commitment.

Designs in Affective Education by Elizabeth W. Flynn and John F. LaFaso. New York: Paulist Press, 1974. Contains 126 teaching strategies on themes of communication, freedom, happiness, life, peace, and love. Each strategy is categorized by traditional high school courses, is flexible as to time and content, and may be used in a variety of settings.

Education of the Self by Jerry Weinstein, Joy Harden, and Matt Weinstein. Amherst, Mass.: Mandala, 1976. This popular University of Massachusetts course is now offered as a guide to developing courses in self-knowledge. Using the "Trumpet" model, the book outlines in detail a group approach to moving beyond self-awareness to action, discovering and analyzing one's personal behavior patterns, and expanding one's responses to this self-knowledge. Appropriate for high school and college level.

Growing Up Alive by Tim Timmerman. Amherst, Mass.: Mandala, 1975. Humanistic education at the middle school. Utilizing the eight-stage developmental theory of Erik Erikson, the book provides an educational rationale for an entire year's curriculum at the preteen level (grades 5-8). Also included are chapters on group process, listening skills, and problem-solving/decision-making skills.

A Handbook of Personal Growth Activities for Classroom Use by Robert C. Hawley and Isabel L. Hawley. Amherst, Mass.: Education Research Associates (Box 767, 01002; $5). Contains a wealth of activities in such areas as achievement motivation, effective communication, creativity, decision making, brainstorming, value clarification, fantasy work, and enhancing positive self-concepts.

A Handbook of Structured Experiences for Human Relations Training, Volumes I, II, III, IV, V, and VI, edited by J. William Pfeiffer and John E. Jones. La Jolla, Calif.: University Associates, 1969-1977. These handbooks are compilations of techniques, ideas, and forms useful in a variety of human relations training designs. They range from exercises requiring little or no training in human relations work to ones used by facilitators with extensive behavioral science background. These are incredibly useful books and should be included in any basic library.

Health Education: The Search for Values by Donald A. Read, Sidney B. Simon, and Joel B. Goodman. Englewood Cliffs, N.J.: Prentice-Hall, 1977. Contains hundreds of value-clarification exercises to be used in health education classes.

The IALAC (I Am Loveable and Capable) Story by Sidney B. Simon. Niles, Ill.: Argus Communications, 1973. This booklet demonstrates that personal affirmations are the beginning point for shaping creative learning environments and that put-downs damage the human spirit. Colorfully illustrated; can be used by students as well as read to them by the teacher. Contains suggestions for use.

Improvisation for the Theater by Viola Spolin. Evanston, Ill.: Northwestern University Press, 1963. This is the most popular text on theater games and is written primarily for the teacher. It contains more than two hundred games and exercises in manual form, almost all of which are designed to help develop spontaneity and release creativity. The book has served as a primary reference for almost all of the educators who are developing and implementing humanistic classroom approaches.

Learning Discussion Skills Through Games by Gene Stanford and Barbara Dobbs Stanford. New York: Citation Press, 1969. Drawing ideas from the encounter-group movement, group dynamics, and their own experiences in the classroom, the authors suggest a sequence of activities to help students get acquainted, organize their group for effective action, overcome reluctance to participate, listen in depth to other members, draw others out rather than argue, and arrive at a consensus.

Learning Handbooks. A series of books written by leaders in the field in conjunction with the editors of *Learning* magazine (530 University Avenue, Palo Alto, Calif. 94301). The series includes:

Building Independent Learning Skills by Beth S. Atwood, with the editors of *Learning* magazine, © 1974. Content includes: activities for developing specific learning skills, discussion questions to provoke in-depth analysis, suggested topics for individual investigation, common pitfalls for students becoming independent learners and how to avoid them, and more than one hundred activities and projects to help the student learn to define problems, plan investigations, find information, record and report findings, and evaluate results.

Developing Individual Values in the Classroom by Richard L. Curwin and Geri Curwin, with the editors of *Learning* magazine. © 1974. This down-to-earth little book contains many practical activities, teaching strategies, and procedures to help teachers develop each child's own values.

Motivating Today's Students by Walter F. Drew, Anita R. Olds, and Henry F. Olds, Jr., with the editors of *Learning* magazine. © 1974. This handbook deals with specific motivational problems and describes successful strategies to help students become motivated achievers. Topics covered include games and activities that help students understand their need to achieve, one-to-one motivational techniques, involving parents, open-space classrooms, and how to motivate by developing self-esteem and close, personal relationships.

Resolving Classroom Conflict by Craig Pearson, with the editors of *Learning* magazine. © 1974. This handbook is loaded with practical suggestions for early classroom conflict among students and between teacher and students. It will help the teacher create a classroom where cooperation, communication, self-discovery, and awareness will grow.

Loving and Beyond: Science Teaching for the Humanistic Classroom by Joe Abruscato and Jack Hassard. Pacific Palisades, Calif.: Goodyear, 1976. A delightful book full of useful ideas and warm, sensitive illustrations for the elementary and junior high science teacher. Integrates human potential exercises and processes with science curriculum. Highly recommended.

Meeting Yourself Halfway by Sidney B. Simon. Niles, Ill.: Argus Communications, 1974; $4.95. Designed for use with adults and high school students, this book gives teachers and students strategies for looking at and assessing their lives. There are thirty-one activities for personal or group use. Also available as a kit with thirty spirit masters paced for individualized learning throughout the entire year ($18.50).

The New Games Book by the New Games Foundation. Garden City, N.J.: Doubleday, 1976. A collection of new-age games for classroom and outdoor use. An incredibly valuable resource.

Not Just Schoolwork: New Directions in Written Expression by Amy Maid and Roger Wallace. Amherst, Mass.: Mandala, 1976. Includes 160 suggestions and outlines for involving students in dynamic written expression. Helps students examine the stimuli that affect them, as well as their feelings about those stimuli, and then transmit those thoughts and feelings to others through creative forms of expression.

100 Ways to Enhance Self-Concept in the Classroom by Jack Canfield and Harold C. Wells. Englewood Cliffs, N.J.: Prentice-Hall, 1976. (Also available for $6.95 from the Institute for Humanistic and Transpersonal Education, Box 575, Amherst, Mass. 01002.) An annotation by Sidney Simon: "This book is an absolute delight . . . Jack Canfield and Harold Wells have compiled some of the sweetest, most gentle, most instantly useful and gripping exercises, strategies and techniques ever put between the covers of a book. . . . The average teacher will find the concise clarity of the descriptions of each strategy almost magical."

Personalized Learning: Confluent Processes in the Classroom by Jack Canfield. Amherst, Mass.: Institute for Humanistic and Transpersonal Education (Box 575, 01002; $7). This is a rough-draft manuscript that presents forty affective processes that can be applied to the teaching of traditional subjects such as history, reading, English, health, biology, etc. The processes include guided fantasy, human machines, role playing, brainstorming circles, collages, games, "I learned" statements, metaphor, sensitivity modules, and internal wisdom. Includes extensive bibliography of resources in confluent education.

Poster Ideas for Personalized Learning by Betsy Caprio. Niles, Ill.: Argus Communications, 1974. This creative little book contains over one hundred classroom activities of an affective nature that utilize posters published by Argus. The reproductions of the posters alone make the book worth its price ($1.00), and the author's activities make it a real treasure. Highly recommended.

Reaching Out: Interpersonal Effectiveness and Self-Actualization by David W. Johnson. Englewood Cliffs, N.J.: Prentice-Hall, 1972. Seeks to provide the theory and experiences necessary to develop effective interpersonal skills. It is more than a book of exercises; the theory presented places the exercises within a context that will give meaning to the reader's experiences in participating in the exercises. Contains sections on interpersonal skills, self-disclosure, development of trust, expression of feelings, listening and responding, accepting self and others, constructive confrontation, and solving problems and conflicts. An excellent resource.

SCAMPER: Games for Imagination Development by Robert F. Eberle. Buffalo, N.Y.: D.O.K. Publishers (771 East Delevan Avenue, 14215), 1971. Excellent fantasy and creative games for K-4 or even older.

Strategies in Humanistic Education, Volume I, by Tim Timmerman and Jim Ballard. Amherst, Mass.: Mandala, 1975. The first of a series, this humanistic education cookbook contains over two hundred recipes for structured classroom experiences geared to the social-emotional needs of the students. Experiences are grouped under twelve themes, including imagination, anger, joy, death, prejudice, and acceptance.

Strategies in Humanistic Education, Volume II, by Tim Timmerman and Jim Ballard. Amherst, Mass.: Mandala, 1976. This book contains over two hundred new activities on the themes of privacy, misery, brothers and sisters, the future, feeling safe, careers, giving and taking, being crazy, mysteries, wanting, and money.

Teacher Effectiveness Training by Tom Gordon. New York: Peter H. Wyden, 1974. A detailed description of how principles of Parent Effectiveness Training can be used in all classrooms, from kindergarten to senior high school. Specifically teaches classroom teachers (1) non-evaluative skills for helping students solve their own problems, (2) a method for involving a teacher and a student in the process of resolving their own conflicts, (3) a method for getting a class to work out with the teacher a contract that defines rules of classroom behavior, and (4) methods for conducting effective group counseling with troubled or underachieving students.

Teaching Achievement Motivation by Alfred Alschuler, Diane Tabor, and James McIntyre. Middletown, Conn.: Educational Ventures, 1970. Alschuler's work has been directed toward providing opportunities for students to achieve goals they set for themselves. This book outlines the theory behind achievement motivation and provides the basic framework for using the approach with both teachers and students.

Teaching Human Beings: 101 Subversive Activities for the Classroom by Jeffrey Schrank. Boston, Mass.: Beacon Press, 1972. Contains a wealth of material and activities utilizing encounter techniques, self-awareness exercises, simulation games, and the use of books and films that rarely appear in traditional classrooms.

Teaching People to Love Themselves: A Leader's Handbook of Theory and Technique for Self-Esteem and Affirmation Training by Dov Peretz Elkins, with preface by Jack Canfield. Rochester, N.Y.: Growth Associates (P.O. Box 8429, 14618; $16), 1977. The most valuable aspect of this handbook is its collection of activities, techniques, and group methods that enhance self-esteem. I have seen them used over and over in groups and in classrooms with astounding success. To help the less experienced teacher, Elkins has also provided two different designs for short- and long-term units. These designs are the result of much experience in the field and are a useful resource.

Threads. Glencoe, Ill.: Open Door Books (205 West 16th Street, 55336; $6.50). Contains five hundred relations activities relevant for all grades K-12.

Toward Self-Understanding: Group Techniques in Self-Confrontation by Daniel Malamud and S. Machover. Springfield, Ill.: Charles C Thomas, 1965. This very useful book provides the rationale and exercises for a course in self-understanding that the authors conducted at New York University.

TRIBES: A Human Development Process for Educational Systems by Jeanne Gibbs and Andre Allen. Oakland, Calif.: TRIBES (166 Capricorn Avenue, 94611; $16). It is a practical guide to creating on-going classroom support groups (Tribes) for affective development. Includes group-formation, trust-building, self-concept, value-clarification, and communication skills. While many of the activities are familiar, the warm and practical approach of the book is special.

Value Clarification in the Classroom: A Primer by J. Doyle Casteel and Robert J. Stahl. Pacific Palisades, Calif.: Goodyear, 1975. A comprehensive study of values in the secondary classroom that encourages the development of values education as an integral part of academic study. A really great book! Contains units on friendship, fear, sensory awareness, trust, attention, self-control, tolerance, goal setting, self-disclosure, personal strengths, promises, successes, etc. Thirty-nine specific lessons are included.

Values in Sexuality: A New Approach to Sex Education by Eleanor S. Morrison and Mila Underhill Price. New York: Hart, 1974. The activities and exercises in this book are designed to involve high school and college students directly in the examination and evaluation of their personal feelings and beliefs in an effort to help them attain a mature sexuality.

Transpersonal Education

Transpersonal education refers to education that deals with the part of the person that transcends the personality level. This includes education of the right hemisphere of the brain, spiritual education, education of the higher qualities of love, joy, wisdom, peace, and harmony—what one transpersonal educator calls "the education of essence." The methods and tools utilized in transpersonal education include meditation, biofeedback, relaxation, centering, yoga, guided fantasy, visualization, development of the intuition, affirmation, and altered states of consciousness. While the field of transpersonal psychology has grown rapidly in the past ten years, transpersonal education has just begun to develop. Listed below are the basic resources currently available in the field. For the most comprehensive bibliography in the field see *The Second Centering Book* by Gay Hendricks and Thomas B. Roberts, Englewood Cliffs, N.J.: Prentice-Hall, 1977.

The Centering Book: Awareness Activities for Parents and Teachers by Gay Hendricks and Russel Wills. Englewood Cliffs, N.J.: Prentice-Hall, 1975. This is the first book of classroom activities for transpersonal development that has been published. It includes such areas as meditation, yoga, relaxation, Senoi dream analysis, guided imagery, and much more.

Everybody's a Winner: A Kid's Guide to New Sports and Fitness by Tom Schneider. Boston, Mass.: Little, Brown, 1976. A guide to all-new, noncompetitive sports and games that do not need special equipment and that anyone can play. Includes such games as New Frisbee, Infinity Volleyball, Pruie, Dho-Dho-Dho, and information on fitness, yoga, breathing, relaxation, t'ai • chi ch'uan, and aikido.

Experiences in Visual Thinking by Robert H. McKim. Belmont, Calif.: Wadsworth, 1972. This book is filled to the brim with specific exercises to explore the concept of visual thinking. Its step-by-step process from seeing to imaging to idea sketching is fascinating—a must for everyone doing in-depth work in creativity and/or imaging.

The Flowering of Childhood. Special fall 1976 issue of *The American Theosophist* (P.O. Box 270, Wheaton, Ill., 60187). Articles include "Moral Development: Some Psychological Issues," "Aspects of Child Rearing and Education from the Edgar Cayce Readings," "Children Evolving," "The Child Within," "The Flowering of Childhood Theory of Meditation," and "Opening Our Capacities."

Four Psychologies Applied to Education: Freudian, Behavioral, Humanistic, Transpersonal by Thomas B. Roberts. Somerset, N.J.: John Wiley, 1975. Explores the dynamic relationship between modern psychology and educational theory. Each of the four sections is a well-organized collection of articles by psychologists and educators such as Anna Freud, C. G. Jung, Erik Erikson, A. S. Neill, Aldous Huxley, Martha Crampton, Frances Clark, Carl Rogers, Abraham Maslow, Arthur Combs, Richard Jones, Stanley Krippner, and Jack Canfield. Contains sixty-two selections.

Handbook for Educating in the New Age (based on the Edgar Cayce Readings) by Walene Janes. Virginia Beach, Va.: A.R.E. Press, 1977. This is the best introduction to the *essense* of transpersonal education. In addition to being full of useful information and suggestions, the book is a moving experience. Highly recommended.

Meditating with Children: The Art of Concentration and Centering by Deborah Rozman. Boulder Creek, Calif.: University of the Trees Press (P.O. Box 655, 95006), 1975. A step-by-step guide to meditation and awareness expansion for children, this is the best introduction to meditation and centering activities that the reviewer has discovered. Through opening up new avenues of self-discovery for parents, teachers, and children, this book answers a crying need for alternative education while showing a new direction. This illustrated handbook is currently used in numerous public school programs in California. The reviewer has used it in several projects, and the response has been overwhelmingly enthusiastic.

Meditation for Children by Deborah Rozman. Millbrae, Calif.: Celestial Arts, 1976. This book is an excellent source to explain the basic concepts of using meditation both in the classroom and •

as a family affair. It contains specific meditations for kids of all age levels, yoga exercises, various concentration exercises, and delightful photographs.

The Metaphoric Mind by Bob Samples. Reading, Mass.: Addison-Wesley, 1976. This book is a celebration of the right half of the brain, the dwelling place of our intuition and creativity. The book is filled with inspirational sources of metaphor ranging from Hopi Indians to the writings of Piaget and Maslow and has an excellent description of our metaphoric modes of thinkings—a valuable source for teachers and any persons interested in their creative consciousness.

Psychosynthesis and Education by Jack Canfield. Amherst, Mass.: Institute for Humanistic and Transpersonal Education (Box 575, 01002; $2.50). Outlines the theory and application of psychosynthesis principles and methods to education and includes an extensive bibliography of psychosynthesis resources.

Put Your Mother on the Ceiling by Richard DeMille. New York: Penguin, 1976. A collection of classroom activities designed to develop students' ability to visualize and to use their imaginal capacity. A classic in the field of guided fantasy in education.

Seeing with the Mind's Eye: The History, Techniques and Uses of Visualization by Mike Samuels and Nancy Samuels. New York: Random House, 1975. This is the most comprehensive guide to the use of visualization and guided imagery that the reviewer is familiar with. It includes self-awareness, healing, religious experiences, etc. Anyone using guided imagery should have this book.

Suggestive, Accelerative Learning and Teaching: A Manual of Classroom Procedures Based on the Lozanov Method by Donald H. Schuster, Ray Benitez-Bordon, and Charles A. Gritton. Des Moines, Iowa: SALT (2740 Richmond Avenue, 50317; $7). The SALT method utilizes aspects of suggestion and unusual styles of presenting material to accelerate classroom learning. The essence of the technique is an unusual combination of physical relaxation exercises, mental concentration, and suggestive principles to strengthen a person's ego and expand his memory capabilities, plus relaxing music and mental imagery while material to be learned is presented dynamically.

Transpersonal Education: A Curriculum for Feeling and Being by Gay Hendricks and Jim Fadiman. Englewood Cliffs, N.J.: Prentice-Hall, 1976. This is the first book of readings to appear on transpersonal education. It contains twenty-five articles covering a wide range of subjects including dream sharing, fantasy, psychic development, meditation, centering, "the new sports," and the application of Buddhism, Taoism, and Sufism to education. Relevant from K to graduate school. Contributors include George Leonard, Will Schutz, Thomas Roberts, Frances Clark, Aldous Huxley, J. Krishnamurti, Robert Frager, Reshad Feild, and Idries Shah.

Transpersonal Psychology in Education by Thomas B. Roberts and Frances V. Clark. Bloomington, Ind.: Phi Delta Kappa (Box 789, 47401; 50¢), 1975. This thirty-seven-page booklet provides a brief introduction to the various aspects of transpersonal education: relaxation, guided fantasy, creativity, dreams, meditation and centering, biofeedback, parapsychology, spirituality, altered states of consciousness, and undeveloped human potential. It is the best brief introduction in print.

CURRICULA AND STUDENT MATERIALS

About Life. The Center for Learning, Box 910, Villa Maria, Pa. 16155. A sixteen-unit values program for junior and senior high school students currently being developed. Nine-week units are now available: Try to Remember, The Personality Puzzle, Awakening of a Social Conscience, The Spirit of Man and His Future. The units are heavily influenced by the values clarification work of Sid Simon.

About Me: A Curriculum for a Developing Self by Harold Wells and Jack Canfield. Encyclopedia Britannica Educational Corporation, 425 North Michigan Avenue, Chicago, Ill. 60611. This inex-

288   *University Associates*

pensive curriculum is designed to help children in grades 4-6 develop positive self-concepts. Lessons include I Know Who I Am, I Know My Strengths, I Can Set and Achieve Goals, I Try to Be Myself, and I Am in Charge of Becoming Myself.

Achievement Competence Training (ACT!) by Russell A. Hill and the staff of the Humanizing Learning Program of Research for Better Schools, Inc. Research for Better Schools, Suite 1700, 1700 Market Street, Philadelphia, Pa. 19103. ACT is a comprehensive learning package designed to teach students a variety of strategies for setting and reaching their goals. Hill and his colleagues have developed a solid program to enhance students' self-motivation, self-confidence, and self-actualization. The program is a bit expensive but well worth checking into.

Achievement Motivation Materials by Alfred Alschuler, Diane Tabor, and James McIntyre. Education Ventures, Inc., 209 Court Street, Middletown, Conn. 06457. The materials were adapted for ninth-grade use from those developed by the Achievement Motivation Development Project at Harvard University. Brief teacher's guides accompany these materials and suggest variations of their use. Includes *Who Am I: An Approach to Self-Understanding, Ten Thoughts: A Program for Learning Achievement Thinking, The Origami Game, The Ring Toss Game, The Darts-Dice Game, Aiming: A Handbook for Reaching Real Goals, The N-Ach Match Game,* and *Achieving: Case Studies.*

Choose Life: Value Education for the Young Adult by Patricia Kennedy Arlin. Niles, Ill.: Argus Communications. This is an amazing curriculum, to say the least. Not only are the booklets, tapes, and filmstrips useful in promoting self-awareness, they are a model of communication in graphics. The package includes resource and training materials for teachers.

Come to Your Senses by David Sohn. Scholastic Book Services, 904 Sylvan Avenue, Englewood Cliffs, N.J. 07632. A series of four filmstrips and a teaching guide that are designed to increase students' awareness of themselves, others, and the world around them. This is primarily designed to direct students toward writing more sensitively and effectively.

The Coping with Books by Gilbert Wreen and Shirley Schwarzock. American Guidance Service, Publishers' Building, Circle Pines, Minn. 55014. A really exciting series of books for teenagers, dealing with their problems, interests, and concerns. Some of the seventeen titles in this series are: *Coping with Cliques, Living with Loneliness, To Like and Be Liked, Easing the Scene, Can You Talk With Someone Else?,* and *Some Common Crutches.*

Developing Understanding of Self and Others by Don Dinkmeyer. American Guidance Service, Inc., Dept. EL-4, Publishers' Building, Circle Pines, Minn. 55014. A program designed to help elementary children understand themselves and those around them. The DUSO kits provide a wide variety of experiences designed to reach children with unique learning styles through varied media and modes.

Dimensions of Personality Series by Walter J. Limbacher. George A. Pflaum, Publisher, 38 West Fifth Street, Dayton, Ohio 45402. This series is based on the belief that the classroom teacher can be an enormously successful partner in helping youngsters live useful and happy lives. The program is experiential and discussion centered, built around a book of very good readings for each grade level. The books are *Here I Am* (grade 4), *I'm Not Alone* (grade 5), and *Becoming Myself* (grade 6).

Effective Communication by Jeffrey Schrank. Niles, Ill.: Argus Communications. A four-tape series with spirit masters for student materials. The tapes cover listening, reflective listening, identifying and expressing feelings, brainstorming, nonverbal communication, and feedback mechanisms.

Experiences in Being edited by Bernice Marshall. Monterey, Calif.: Brooks/Cole, 1970. A book of readings applicable to any high school or college course in English, social studies, psychology, or human relations. The book provides a good overview of humanistic psychology.

Focus on Self Development by Judith L. Anderson, Carole J. Lang, and Virginia R. Scott. Science Research Associates, 259 East Erie Street, Chicago, Ill. 60611. This is a developmental affective educational program for grades one through three. The overall objectives are to lead the child toward an understanding of self, an understanding of others, and an understanding of the environment and its effects. The program includes filmstrips, records, photoboards, pupil activity books, and a teacher's guide.

Hello People by Judith O'Connell and Janet Cosmos. Niles, Ill.: Argus Communications. A multimedia, multiethnic social studies program for six- to nine-year-olds, which focuses directly on the growth of the child's self-concept and teaches the child to relate to others in a humane way. The program's emphasis on social integration meets an important need of the child in coping with today's complex society.

The Human Development Program by Uvaldo Palomares and Harold Bessell. Human Development Training Institute, 4455 Twain Avenue, Suite H, San Diego, Calif. 92120. This program is designed to facilitate learning in the affective domain, thereby improving motivation and achievement in all areas of education. The strategy is to employ cumulative, sequential activities on a daily basis as outlined in the lesson guides. One of the best programs available.

Social Science Laboratory Units by Ronald Lippitt, Robert Fox, and Lucille Schible. Science Research Associates, 259 East Erie Street, Chicago, Ill. 60611. An intermediate-grade social studies curriculum providing a modified laboratory approach to learning. The classroom becomes a laboratory for guided inquiries into the causes and effects of human behavior.

A Teaching Program in Human Behavior and Mental Health by Alice S. Hawkins and Ralph H. Ojemann. Educational Research Council of America, Rockefeller Building, Cleveland, Ohio 44113. A pioneer program in human behavior for classroom use K-8, its principal methodology is teacher-read stories with appropriate questioning.

Value Formation and Change by Brian Hall. Niles, Ill.: Argus Communications. This is an in-service teacher kit to develop humanistic skills for good teacher-student rapport and a high school classroom program for direct student-teacher exploration of change and values.

JOURNALS AND NEWSLETTERS

The Affective Educator. Harold Stonehouse, Department of Geology, Michigan State University, East Lansing, Mich. 48824. $5 per year; $25 for institutions. The newsletter of the Michigan Affective Education Association.

AHP Newsletter (free to members) and *Journal of Humanistic Psychology* ($10 per year). Association for Humanistic Psychology, 325 Ninth Street, San Francisco, Calif. 94108. Both publications contain mountains of useful information for those trying to humanize education.

Confluent Education Journal. P.O. Box 30128, Santa Barbara, Calif. 93105. $8 per year. Contains articles on various aspects of confluent education—integrating affective and cognitive teaching—including research, curricula, lesson plans, and book reviews. Very useful for the classroom teacher.

Confluent Education Newsletter. Confluent Education Program, Box 219, Minnedosa, Manitoba, Canada. Published periodically by the Confluent Education Project in Manitoba. The project also runs workshops on confluent education and has several demonstration schools set up.

Dawnpoint. Association for Humanistic Psychology, 325 Ninth Street, San Francisco, Calif. 94103. Two years for $8 or one year for $5. A new magazine, published semi-annually, it contains sixty-four pages of beautiful images and a language of graphics and words vividly conveying the complete message and spirit of humanistic psychology.

Essentia. P.O. Box 129, Tiburon, Calif. 94920. Free. The new newsletter published by Bob Samples and Associates. The last issue contained articles on "The Metaphoric Mind," "Visions in Motion," "Aikido," and "Solstice 77."

Group and Organization Studies: The International Journal for Group Facilitators. University Associates, 7596 Eads Avenue, La Jolla, Calif. 92037. $18 (one year); $32 (two years); $45 (three years). A new quarterly journal designed to bridge the gap between research and practice for group facilitators, educators, and consultants, it is practical and nontechnical in orientation. The first issue contained an excellent article entitled "The Application of Gestalt Principles in Classroom Teaching" by Mark Phillips. Back issues are available at $5 per copy.

Humanistic Educators Network. National Humanistic Education Center, Upper Jay, N.Y. 12987. $10 per year. A good compilation of new techniques, new materials, book reviews, articles, interviews, and listings of upcoming events in the area of humanistic education. Totally devoted to the discussion of the affective development of students.

Interface Journal: Alternatives in Higher Education. P.O. Box 970, Utica, N.Y. 13505. $6 per year. Dedicated to alternative approaches to higher education, the first two issues have contained articles on affective approaches to college teaching.

Journal of Creative Behavior. Creative Education Foundation, State University College, 1300 Elmwood Avenue, Buffalo, N.Y. 14222. $9 per year. Articles, research, reports, and book reviews on creativity and education.

Journal of Humanistic Education. West Georgia College, Carrollton, Ga. 30017. Published annually; individual subscription rate, $2.50 per copy, $5 for institutions. One can also receive the journal—and a newsletter—by joining the Association for Humanistic Education at the same address. The first issue—January/February, 1977—included articles by Carl Rogers, Daniel Fader, Myron Arons, and Dorothy Nolte.

Journal of Mental Imagery. Brandon House, P.O. Box 240, Bronx, N.Y. 10471. $15 per year; $20 for institutions; $12 for students. A new journal. Issue number one contains, among other articles, "Eidetics: An Overview," "Guided Affective Imagery: An Account of Its Development," "Imagination and Make-Believe Play in Early Childhood: Some Educational Implications," and "Imagery and Verbal Behavior."

Journal of Transpersonal Psychology. P.O. Box 4437, Stanford, Calif. 94305. $15 per year. Concerned with the publication of "articles and studies in metaneeds, ultimate values, unitive consciousness, peak experiences, ecstasy, mystical experience, B values, essence, bliss, awe, wonder, self-actualization, ultimate meaning, transcendence of the self, spirit . . . oneness, cosmic awareness, cosmic play, individual and species-wide synergy, maximal interpersonal encounter, transcendental phenomena, maximal sensory awareness, responsiveness and expression, and related concepts, experiences, and activities." The journal does what it promises and does it in issues that elicit cover-to-cover reading.

Learning Magazine. 1255 Portland Place, Boulder, Colo. 80302. $8 per year. Consistently the best major magazine in education. It is full of useful articles on new approaches to teaching, new materials available, and new ways of conceptualizing the teaching-learning process. In a recent publicity piece the magazine described itself as one that "simply gives you a good feeling—about yourself, your kids, and the job you're trying so hard to do for them." It states what it does very well. Well worth it.

The LINK: Social Science Education Consortium Newsletter. Social Science Education Consortium, 855 Broadway, Boulder, Colo. 80302. $5 per year. Covers the broad range of the social sciences in the classroom, including areas such as mental health, values clarification, etc.

Media and Methods. 134 N. 13th Street, Philadelphia, Pa. 19107. $6 per year. It always contains its fair share of articles about humanizing the learning process. *M&M* is of special interest to teachers of English and teachers using film and movies in their teaching.

Media Mix. Box 5139, Chicago, Ill. 60680. $6 per year. A newsletter containing a great deal of valuable information regarding innovative educational media, simulation games, affective teaching techniques, reviews, and resource guides. Past issues have included guides on ecology, sexism, the psychology of prejudice, and creative classroom experiments.

Moral Education Forum. 221 East 72nd Street, New York, N.Y. 10021. $5 per year (five issues). A newsletter containing conference news, reviews of relevant books, articles, and papers. It also features selected bibliographies and descriptions of new research, as well as information about experimental programs and curricula that have a strong value dimension.

New Directions in Teaching. Department of Education, Bowling Green State University, Bowling Green, Ohio 43402. $5 per year. Calling itself a "Non-Journal Committed to the Improvement of Undergraduate Teaching," *NDIT* is one of the best periodicals in education. Each issue has five or six articles with practical suggestions about how to humanize undergraduate teaching and learning. Contributors have included Abraham Maslow, Jeanette Veatch, and Robert Primack. Highly recommended.

New Schools Exchange Newsletter. Pettigrew, Ark. 72752. $12 per year; $15 for institutions. The major central resource and clearing house for people involved in alternatives in education.

Synthesis. 830 Woodside Road, Redwood City, Calif. 94061. $8 per year. A journal presenting articles on psychology and education based on and aligned with psychosynthesis. This is a very valuable journal.

Value Education Newsletter. P.O. Box 947, Campbell, Calif. 95008. $11 per year (nine issues). Contains information on new trends, programs, products, and ideas in value education.

Wholistic Education: The Journal of Humanistic and Transpersonal Education. Box 575, Amherst, Mass. 01002. $12 per year; $15 for institutions and foreign memberships; $8 for students. Contains "articles, classroom activities, lesson plans, a guide to new resources, book reviews, and whatever else will expand your vision, heighten your consciousness, and increase your skills in the areas of humanistic and transpersonal education." A special feature is "The Teacher's Workshop," which includes a course in one aspect of humanistic/transpersonal education such as guided fantasy, meditation, value clarification, or death education. Has included articles by Jack Canfield, Sid Simon, Gerry Weinstein, Jean Houston, and Thomas B. Roberts.

> *Jack Canfield is the founder and a co-director of the New England Center and the director of the Institute for Humanistic and Transpersonal Education, Amherst, Massachusetts. He is president-elect of the Association for Humanistic Education, editor of* Wholistic Education: The Journal of Humanistic and Transpersonal Education, *a member of the field faculty of the Humanistic Psychology Institute, and a consultant to numerous boards of education and universities, as well as a trainer in Gestalt therapy, transpersonal psychology, and humanistic education. Mr. Canfield is the author of many works in the field, including* About Me, 100 Ways to Enhance Self-Concept in the Classroom, A Guide to Humanistic Education, A Guide to Resources in Humanistic and Transpersonal Education, *and* The Transpersonal Education Network.

CONTRIBUTORS

Mark Alexander
Assistant Professor of Business Administration
St. Francis Xavier University
Antigonish, Nova Scotia
Canada
(902) 867-2217

Anthony G. Banet, Jr., Ph.D.
Senior Consultant
University Associates
7596 Eads Avenue
La Jolla, California 92037
(714) 454-8821

Timothy A. Boone
General Manager
NTL/Learning Resources Corporation
7594 Eads Avenue
La Jolla, California 92037
(714) 454-3193

Richard W. Budd, Ph.D.
Chairman, Department of Human
  Communication
Van Dyck Hall
Rutgers University
New Brunswick, New Jersey 08903
(201) 932-7354

Richard L. Bunning, Ph.D.
Director of Organization Development
Samaritan Health Service
P.O. Box 2989
Phoenix, Arizona 85062
(602) 257-4466

Susan Campbell, Ph.D.
1423 Arch Street
Berkeley, California 94707
(415) 848-1444

Jack Canfield
Director
Institute for Humanistic and Transpersonal
  Education
Box 575
Amherst, Massachusetts 01002
(413) 367-2385

Richard Christie, Ph.D.
Professor of Social Psychology
Department of Psychology
Columbia University
New York, New York 10027
(212) 280-3959

Gerard Egan, Ph.D.
Associate Professor of Psychology
Loyola University of Chicago
6525 North Sheridan Road
Chicago, Illinois 60626
(312) 274-3000

John Elliott-Kemp
Principal Lecturer in Education Management
Sheffield City Polytechnic
Pond Street
Sheffield S1 1WB
England
Sheffield 738621

Sam Farry
Consultant in Management and
  Organizational Behavior
620 35th Street
Manhattan Beach, California 90266
(213) 545-1548

John C. Ferrie, Ed.D.
Senior Consultant
Integrative Systems
P.O. Box 17061
West Hartford, Connecticut 06117
(203) 232-9185

Arthur M. Freedman, Ph.D.
Consulting Psychologist
700 W. Aldine Avenue
Chicago, Illinois 60657
(312) 525-8283

Beverly A. Gaw, Ph.D.
Assistant Professor
Department of Communication
Wright State University
201 Chatham Drive
Dayton, Ohio 45429
(513) 298-8213

William J. Heisler, Ph.D.
Associate Professor of Management
Babcock Graduate School of Management
Wake Forest University
7659 Reynolda Station
Winston-Salem, North Carolina 27109
(919) 761-5416

Florence M. Hoylman, Ph.D.
Organizational Consultants, Inc.
Box 3111
West Lafayette, Indiana 47906
(317) 463-2793

John E. Jones, Ph.D.
Vice President
University Associates
7596 Eads Avenue
La Jolla, California 92037
(714) 454-8821

J. Ryck Luthi
Coordinator of Student Programs
A. Ray Olpin University Union
University of Utah
Salt Lake City, Utah 84112
(801) 581-5318

William C. Morris, Ph.D.
Organizational Consultant
Dalton, Missouri 65246
(816) 544-2191

William R. Mulford, Ph.D.
Senior Lecturer in Education Administration
School of Teacher Education
Canberra College of Advanced Education
P.O. Box 381
Canberra City A.C.T. 2601
Australia
52 2111, 2453, 2386

David D. Palmer, Ph.D.
Assistant Professor
Department of Management and
 Administrative Sciences
School of Business Administration
University of Connecticut
Box U41 MAS
Storrs, Connecticut 06268
(203) 486-3461

Udai Pareek, Ph.D.
Larson & Toubro Professor of Organizational
 Behavior
Indian Institute of Management
Vastrapur, Ahmedabad 380015
India
 83-411/2/3/4/6/8

Lucian Parshall, Ed.D.
Human Relations Consultant
19949 Great Oaks Circle North
Mount Clemens, Michigan 48043
 (313) 293-2400, ext. 224, 203
 (313) 468-7253

Thomas H. Patten, Jr., Ph.D.
Professor of Organizational Behavior and
 Personnel Management
School of Labor and Industrial Relations
South Kedzie Hall
Michigan State University
East Lansing, Michigan 48824
 (517) 353-9040

J. William Pfeiffer, Ph.D.
President
University Associates
7596 Eads Avenue
La Jolla, California 92037
 (714) 454-8821

Victor Pinedo, Jr.
President
Fundashon Humanas
Curaçao, Netherland Antilles
 and
Director of Research and Development
IDO Asociados
Caracas, Venezuela
 35800 (office) or 36775 (home)—Curaçao
 781-2589, 9290—Caracas

W. Alan Randolph, Ph.D.
Assistant Professor of Organization Behavior
College of Business Administration
University of South Carolina
Columbia, South Carolina 29208
 (803) 777-7285

Robert A. Reid
Coordinator of Professional Services
University Associates
7596 Eads Avenue
La Jolla, California 92037
 (714) 454-8821

Robert C. Rodgers
School of Labor and Industrial Relations
225 South Kedzie Hall
Michigan State University
East Lansing, Michigan 48824
(517) 355-3284

Brent D. Ruben, Ph.D.
Assistant Chairman, Department of Human
  Communication, and
Director, Institute for Communication Studies
Van Dyck Hall
Rutgers University
New Brunswick, New Jersey 08903
(201) 932-7450

Marshall Sashkin, Ph.D.
Associate Professor of Management
College of Business Administration
Memphis State University
Memphis, Tennessee 38152
(901) 454-2437 (office)
(901) 452-8917 (home)

Peter Scholtes
Coordinator of Organization Development,
  City of Madison
Room 405 City/County Building
210 Monona Avenue
Madison, Wisconsin 53709
(608) 266-4220

John J. Sherwood, Ph.D.
Professor of Organizational Psychology and
Chairman, Department of Administrative
  Sciences
Krannert Graduate School of Management
Purdue University
Lafayette, Indiana 47907
(317) 493-1882

Donna Lee Smith
Film Sales Manager
University of California
  Extension Media Center
Berkeley, California 94720
(415) 642-0678

Francis L. Ulschak, Ph.D.
Organizational and Community Consultant
Box 346
Center, North Dakota 58530
(701) 794-3568

Glenn H. Varney, Ph.D.
Associate Professor
College of Business Administration
Bowling Green State University
Bowling Green, Ohio 43403
(419) 352-7782

Paul S. Weikert
Consultant
Human Relations Consultants, Inc.
535 Haslett Road
Williamston, Michigan 48895
(517) 655-2060

Graham Williams
Senior Lecturer in Social Psychology
Sheffield City Polytechnic
Pond Street
Sheffield S1 1WB
England
Sheffield 738621

Jack N. Wismer, Ph.D.
7925 W. Layton
620 Bedford
Littleton, Colorado 80123
(303) 234-2169

Julia T. Wood, Ph.D.
Assistant Professor
Department of Speech Communication
University of North Carolina at
  Chapel Hill
Chapel Hill, North Carolina 27514
(919) 933-5096

Joel Zimmerman, Ph.D.
Associate Professor of Management
College of Business Administration
Creighton University
2500 California Street
Omaha, Nebraska 68178
(402) 449-2616